BASIC ADVERTISING

BASIC ADVERTISING

Donald W. Jugenheimer
Chair
Department of Communications and Speech
Fairleigh Dickinson University

Gordon E. White
Department of Advertising
University of Illinois at Urbana-Champaign

COLLEGE DIVISION South-Western Publishing Co.

CINCINNATI DALLAS LIVERMORE

S09

Library of Congress Cataloging-in-Publication Data

Jugenheimer, Donald W.
Basic advertising / Donald W. Jugenheimer, Gordon E. White.
p. cm.
Includes bibliographies and index.
ISBN 0-538-19090-6
1. Advertising. 2. White, Gordon E. I. Title.
HF5821. J83 1991
659. 1–dc20 89-34290
CIP

1 2 3 4 5 6 MT 6 5 4 3 2 1

Printed in the United States of America

Contents

Section 2
Creative

Section 3
Channels

Section 4
Campaigns

Section 5
Your Life With Advertising

Preface

Basic Advertising is a study of advertising stripped to its fundamentals. It is lean and tight. No padding. No extraneous material. No technical mumbo-jumbo. It is designed to make perfect sense to advertisers on Main Street as well as on Madison Avenue.

Basic Advertising was conceived, organized, and written strictly with the student in mind. You might think that all textbooks are written for students, but the fact is that some textbooks are written as much for the course instructor as for the student. But in this text, the student comes first. There are many teaching/learning aids built into this book, and they will certainly be of assistance to any instructor; but these aids are designed primarily to help students learn. There is an Instructor's Manual available for professors using *Basic Advertising*.

LEARNING AIDS

These built-in teaching/learning aids are divided into three different types of materials: first, those that help students in classroom situations; second, those that help students in their individual reading of the book; and third, a set of activities that help students understand, remember, and use what they read in this book.

Logical Organization

Basic Advertising is logically organized. The arrangement of topics, headings, and chapters matches the way actual advertising is planned and practiced today. The organization of the text uses a special set of key words to help you remember the advertising process. We'll talk more about these words in a moment.

Easy-to-Read Style

The writing style of the book is basic, too—an easy-to-read style. Word specialists have read and edited the manuscript to make it easy and fun to read. Therefore, you can concentrate on what you are reading *about*, instead of worrying about the reading itself.

Numerous Illustrations

There are numerous illustrations in the book. They help break up the text, true, making it easier and faster to read, but that's not why they are there.

Instead, these illustrations have been carefully chosen to help explain a particular concept or show how a certain approach may actually be used in advertising. The illustrations are an important part of the book. Look at them carefully and read their captions thoroughly. They should help you learn more and understand better.

Term Definitions in the Margins

To help you note important points and remember them easily, key words and phrases from the main text are highlighted in the margin of almost every page with a crisp definition of each. Key words and phrases are also highlighted in bold type in the text itself.

End-of-Chapter Questions

At the end of each chapter, you will find a series of questions. One set is called "Things to Think About." These questions are for your own use. Go through them to test yourself on how well you understand the chapter you have just read. If you have difficulty, go back through the chapter again until you can answer these questions.

Another list of questions, called "Things to Talk About," should be used *in* your class. Your instructor may want to use these questions as the basis for class discussions. If a certain question is not discussed, you may want to raise the point in class or in a conversation with your instructor. These questions are not as easy to answer as "Things to Think About" because they are intended to provoke discussion. There may be two or more sides to these questions, with arguments for and against each viewpoint.

The third set of questions involve "Things To Do. " Here you will have an opportunity to use what you have been reading and talking about. Some of these "Things To Do " may bring you into direct contact with advertising practitioners. You may be asked to apply your knowledge to a realistic advertising situation. The purpose here is for you to become involved with advertising.

Complete Advertising Campaigns

Basic Advertising also has an extensive section dealing with advertising campaigns. This is where you see all the things you've learned put together in real-world campaigns. It does little good to know where to get advertising information, which advertising media to use, and how to write an advertisement unless you know how to combine all these skills into a long-term advertising campaign. This section tells you how three actual advertising campaigns worked. If you read carefully, you will understand how the general principles of advertising were applied in real campaigns. This should make your study of advertising more meaningful and realistic.

Glossary

Following the main text, you will find a Glossary of important terms. The Glossary offers a quick but accurate review of the entire course.

Activities in Advertising Section

At the end of the main text is a section on advertising activities that covers, chapter by chapter, every key principle you have studied in the book. You will find the activities challenging and helpful. If you complete all or most of the activities assignments, you will end up as a highly knowledgeable advertising person. You will be able to make a genuine contribution toward solving any given advertising problem.

TEXT ORGANIZATION

As we suggested earlier, the organization of *Basic Advertising* uses several key words to help you remember the advertising process. Let's look at the process first, then the key words.

The Advertising Process

The first concern of advertising is **consumers**, and the basic aim of advertising is **communication** to consumers about goods, services, or ideas. An advertiser must also operate within certain **constraints**, such as governmental regulations and laws that limit what can be said or may specify that certain kinds of information must be included in an advertisement. So the advertiser must be constantly aware of what consumers want and need, while communicating with them within the constraints imposed by government and society.

Then, the **creative** effort prepares the advertisements, planned and written for the right kinds of prospective consumers for a particular product or service. The proper **channels** must also be selected, to be certain that the correct prospective customers receive the creative message. This whole process, taking place over a period of time, is called an advertising **campaign**.

The Six Cs of Advertising

No doubt you have noticed that all these important terms start with the letter *c*. That is not just coincidence. Instead, it was done on purpose to help you remember the advertising process, as reflected in the organization of this book:

1. Consumers
2. Communication
3. Constraints
4. Creativity
5. Channels
6. Campaigns

You may find it convenient to remember the advertising process by calling it the six *C*s of advertising—a helpful memory aid.

Now that you understand this format, let it help you. First, you will need to learn something about what advertising is and how it functions before you can study how advertising fits into the six *C*s process. But after the first chapter, you'll be ready to move into the first two parts of the six *C*s—**consumers** and **communication**. Then we'll go on to **constraints**.

The second section of the book deals with the next *C*: **creativity**. Following that is an examination of **channels**. And the last of the six *C*s discussed in this book is advertising **campaigns**.

Advertising in Daily Life

As you learn about the various aspects of advertising, you may also want to learn about possible career opportunities in advertising. But even if you don't want to work in advertising, you will still be exposed to it every day of your life. Your knowledge of advertising can help you become a wise shopper and an informed consumer. The final two chapters of this book will tell you about these applied uses of advertising. They are not part of the six *C*s, but they are still important and interesting.

As we have mentioned, the Activities in Advertising section closes out the book with challenging assignments keyed to each chapter. Combine what you learn from these activities assignments and from study of the book itself, and the fascinating world of advertising will hold no mysteries for you.

Now that you understand what *Basic Advertising* is all about and what it is trying to do, let's get started. Let's learn about advertising.

ACKNOWLEDGMENTS

We are grateful to all the people who have helped in creating *Basic Advertising*. We are especially grateful to the following individuals who reviewed our manuscript at various stages of its development:

Robert J. Bouck
Lansing Community College

Myrtle R. Cooper
Midlands Technical College

James W. Halloran
Clayton State College

Charlene Bomrad-Held
Onondaga Community College

Randi Ellis
North Harris County College

George S. Gramlich
Fullerton College

Thomas Paczkowski
Cayuga Community College

Victor Saier
Kalamazoo Valley Community College

Janice Kelly
Tarrant County Jr. College-Northwest

William Motz
Lansing Community College

Marcia K. Shallcross
Palomar College

Larry Zigler
Highland Community College

Donald W. Jugenheimer
Fairleigh Dickinson University

Gordon E. White
University of Illinois at Urbana-Champaign

BASIC ADVERTISING

SECTION 1

Consumers, Communication, and Constraints

To begin our study of the exciting and dynamic field of advertising, we cannot look at the advertisements themselves. First, it is necessary for us to look at and understand the background of advertising.

We must understand what advertising is, what it does, and what it cannot do—either because it is not able to accomplish some things, or because it is forbidden in some instances. We must do all of this before we look at advertisements.

While you read this first section of the book, keep in mind that advertising cannot work alone. It must work in harmony with the entire marketing effort, with other forms of promotion besides advertising, and with the total sales program. Even the planning of products and services to be made and advertised and sold must be done together with the advertising effort, not separate from it.

Advertising also has a big impact on your life. It is something you see and hear every day, something that you are already very familiar with, but there is still much more to learn about it. Advertising is with you much of your life, which is exactly where we will begin our study of this fascinating topic.

CHAPTERS

1 You and Advertising

?
hart
WITHOUT ADVERTISING EVEN THE BEST IDEAS TAKE AGES TO CATCH ON.
Every now and then, a new product becomes popular by word of mouth alone. But that process usually takes many months. Sometimes years. By then, the company that makes the new product may be in serious trouble—if they're around at all.
Advertising is the surest way to get an idea to the public. By advertising a new product or service, more people are able to try it more quickly than if it were allowed to "catch on" by itself.
Good ideas become popular right away and bad ideas...well, who needs a square wheel, anyway?
ADVERTISING.
ANOTHER WORD FOR FREEDOM OF CHOICE.
American Association of Advertising Agencies

Courtesy of Michall Belk & Company

CHAPTER OUTLINE

The Size of the Advertising Industry
Why Study Advertising?
A Brief History of Advertising
- Printing Brought Changes to Advertising
- Some Advertising Was Dishonest
- Advertising Regulation Begins

What Is Advertising?
- Advertising Must Have Four Components
- What Advertising Is
- What Advertising Is Not

Organization of the Advertising Industry
- How an Advertising Agency Works
- A Look at Local Advertising
- Sales Representatives Help Buyers and Sellers

The Six *C*s

By the time you finish this chapter, you should understand:

1. **The size of the advertising industry in the United States today.**
2. **Why it is useful to study advertising.**
3. **How advertising has developed and progressed.**
4. **What advertising is and what it is not.**
5. **How advertisers, advertising agencies, and mass media work together.**
6. **How national and local retail advertising differ.**

What do you do hundreds of times every day? You breathe, of course, and blink your eyes, and your heart beats. Most of those functions are fairly automatic. You do something else, probably more than three hundred times each day, that is not automatic, that you may not even be aware of: You see or read or hear advertisements.

That's right: Experts believe that the average American sees or hears at least three hundred advertisements every day. Some think the number may be as high as fifteen hundred. In fact, some authorities have recently estimated that Americans are exposed to an unbelievable five thousand advertisements a day!

So, as a typical American, you already know a lot about advertising. On the other hand, you have probably studied it less than most of the other things to which you are often exposed. And that is too bad, because you can learn from advertising; you can use advertising to help you; you can learn to examine advertising critically; you can learn to understand advertising better.

What's more, advertising is an intriguing subject. It holds a natural interest for most of us. Because we are in touch with advertising so much and so often, because we have grown up with advertising in our everyday lives, we find it interesting. And advertising is *supposed* to be interesting because the companies that pay for advertisements are using them to *make* you interested.

THE SIZE OF THE ADVERTISING INDUSTRY

How large is the advertising industry, and just how much impact does it have on our lives? Let's put it in terms of dollars per person. How would you like to have $400? Or, more accurately, how would you like to have someone else spend a little bit more than $400 for you each year?

That's exactly what advertisers do: They spend more than $100 billion in the United States each year on advertising. And that amounts to more than $400 for every man, woman, and child each year, or $1.20 per person per day. So that's why you see and hear hundreds of advertisements every day.

WHY STUDY ADVERTISING?

Like any other subject, advertising has many facets and can be complicated. However, as you learn more about it, it becomes logical, sensible, and even helpful. In fact, once you understand advertising, you can make it work for you.

Learning about advertising can lead to an exciting and interesting career, but, on an everyday basis, it can also make you a more knowledgeable consumer who gets more for every dollar you spend. Your knowledge can save you time and money by guiding you through advertisements, helping you judge their claims, and providing insights into the rationale behind them.

A BRIEF HISTORY OF ADVERTISING

Advertising is really a very natural process. Suppose you are walking around your school or campus and discover that you have lost your wallet with all your spending money in it. What are you going to do? Well, you might put up a notice on the bulletin board that says, "Lost: Wallet. Reward," along with your name, address, and telephone number. Or you might buy a classified advertisement in the Lost and Found section of your local or school newspaper. People of long ago were not much different from you. Archaeologists have found the forerunners of lost-and-found notices in the ruins of ancient Egypt: papyrus posters offering rewards for the return of runaway slaves. They've also found political advertisements—a lot like the kind you see today—painted on walls along the streets of the ancient Roman city of Pompeii. These advertisements said, roughly, "Vote for Marcellus. He's the friend of the people!"

In later years, the villages of Europe had town criers who went around calling out the latest news and reassuring residents that their community was safe. It would not have been too unlikely for a tavern owner to offer the town crier something to eat or drink between his rounds if only he would include a word or two in his report about the fine hospitality to be found at that establishment. Today's radio and television news programs have advertising messages that are not very different from this.

Printing Brought Changes to Advertising

Early printers often found that they had extra pages in their books. Rather than leave them blank, they got the idea of using them to list the other books they had published, an early form of printed advertising. And then came another kind of announcement on those blank pages, not for other books, but for coffee—described as a rare new beverage from Arabia that would help those who drank it!

With the development of newspapers came much more advertising. Early on, merchants began placing advertising notices for new shipments of goods but told little about the products for sale or their price. Because merchandise was in short supply, simply telling people that an item was available might bring them into the stores. As strange as such advertisements may seem to us now, the merchants who advertised in this way were doing the same thing that today's store advertisements try to do: They were telling more people about their merchandise than they could reach in person, or by the town crier, or with a sign in front of the store.

Some Advertising Was Dishonest

During the latter half of the 1800s and into the early 1900s, much advertising was less than honest. As the example in Figure 1–1 shows, advertisers often made exaggerated claims and promises they did not intend to keep. Practices were not standardized, so newspaper owners might claim to be reaching thousands of readers, when they had actually reached only a few hundred. So both the advertisers and the newspapers themselves often misled their customers.

The only limits on advertising were what writers could think up and what customers might believe. Many products that we use today, such as coffee, were advertised as having vast and miraculous medical powers that could cure all sorts of ailments. Because there was no regulation of advertising, its claims could not be trusted.

Advertising Regulation Begins

In 1912, a group of newspaper publishers founded the **Audit Bureau of Circulations (A.B.C.)** to check on publishers' claims of the number of newspapers circulated. This would ensure that newspaper publishers were telling the truth when merchants wanted to know how many customers their advertisements might reach in a certain newspaper. The founding of the A.B.C. was therefore the first major step in the regulation of advertising.

Audit Bureau of Circulations (A.B.C.) A group of newspaper publishers founded this bureau to check on publishers' claims of newspapers circulated.

WHAT IS ADVERTISING?

Fairfax Cone, a famous advertiser, has said that "advertising is something you do when you can't go see somebody." And he is right: It would probably be more effective to make a personal sales call on each customer. But that is not practical, because most companies have too many customers in too large an area. Instead, such companies rely on advertising to take the information to their customers.

Even though it costs more than $400 each year to reach every American with advertising, that is far less than it would cost to reach those same people in person or in any other way. So advertising is a way of gaining sales effectiveness while keeping selling expenses low.

FIGURE 1–1
In the early days of print advertising, the claims made by advertisers were often exaggerated and untrue.

Do You Make These Mistakes in English?

Sherwin Cody's remarkable invention has enabled more than 100,000 people to correct their mistakes in English. Only 15 minutes a day required to improve your speech and writing.

SHERWIN CODY

FREE — Book on English

"Look at All THREE!

BUT DON'T BUY ANY LOW-PRICED CAR UNTIL YOU'VE DRIVEN THE NEW PLYMOUTH WITH FLOATING POWER"

A STATEMENT BY WALTER P. CHRYSLER

THOUSANDS of people have been waiting expectantly until today before buying a new car. I hope that you are one of them.

Now that the new low-priced cars are here (including the new Plymouth which will be shown on Saturday) I urge you to carefully *compare* values.

This is the time for you to "shop" and buy wisely. Don't make a deposit on any automobile until you've actually had a demonstration.

It is my opinion that the automobile industry as a whole has never offered such values to the public.

In the new Plymouth we have achieved more than I had ever dared to hope for. If you had told me two years ago that such a big, powerful, beautiful automobile could be sold at the astonishing prices we will announce on Saturday, I'd have said it was absolutely impossible.

I have spent my life building fine cars. But no achievement in my career has given me the deep-down satisfaction that I derive from the value you get in this 1932 Plymouth.

To me, its outstanding feature is Floating Power. We already know how the public feels about this. Last summer it was news, but today it is an established engineering achievement.

It is my opinion, and I think that of leading engineering authorities, that any new car without Floating Power is obsolete. Drive a Plymouth with Patented Floating Power, and note its utter lack of vibration . . . then drive a car with old fashioned engine mountings and you will understand what I mean. *There's absolutely no comparison.*

We have made the Plymouth a much larger automobile. It is a BIG car. We have increased its power, lengthened the wheelbase and greatly improved its beauty.

In my opinion you will find the new Plymouth the easiest riding car you have ever driven. Yet with all these improvements we have been able to lower prices.

Again let me urge you, go and see the new Plymouth with Floating Power on Saturday. Be sure to look at all THREE low-priced cars and don't buy any until you do. That is the way to get the most for your money.

FIRST SHOWING NEXT SATURDAY, APRIL 2nd, AT DESOTO, DODGE AND CHRYSLER DEALERS

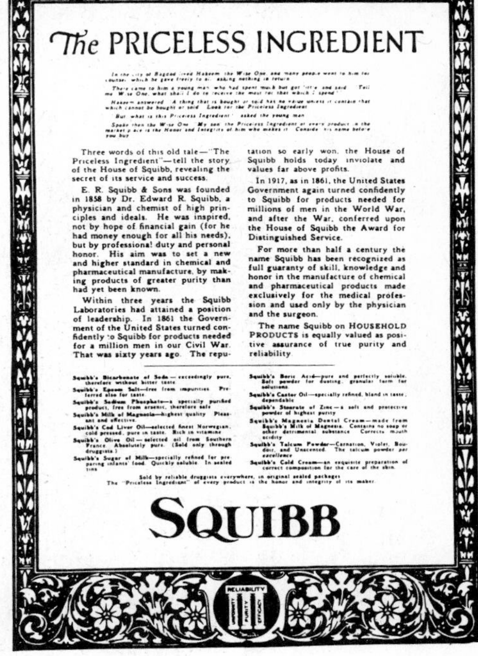

FIGURE 1–2
These early advertisements look quite different from the kinds you are accustomed to seeing today.

Advertising Must Have Four Components

advertising Any paid form of nonpersonal presentation and promotion of ideas, goods, or services through the mass media by an identified sponsor.

mass media Channels of communication designed to reach the general public.

sponsor The individual or organization that pays for the advertisement.

The American Marketing Association has defined **advertising** as "any paid form of nonpersonal presentation and promotion of ideas, goods, or services by an identified sponsor."[1] Advertising, then, has four basic features:

1. It is a *paid* presentation.
2. It is a *nonpersonal* presentation.
3. It *promotes* specific ideas, goods, or services through the **mass media,** channels of communication designed to reach the general public. These may include television, newspapers, magazines, radio, billboards, and the like.
4. It must *identify* its **sponsor,** the individual or organization that pays for the advertisement.

Here's how it works in practice: Businesses can benefit from advertisements only if they, their stores, and their products are identified to the general public. For this reason, they use mass media, which they must pay for the space or time used for their advertisements. In return for this kind of investment, a business can reach more people than it could if it relied on personal sales calls.

Of course, there's more to advertising than just products. Look back at the definition. In addition to goods, organizations also advertise services such as automobile repair, house cleaning, clothes alterations, and even college classes. They also advertise ideas: Political parties may sponsor television commercials to reach voters, and citizens may advertise to attract others who feel as they do to sign a petition or to attend the local school board meeting. But whatever is being advertised, the *definition* of advertising remains the same.

What Advertising Is

Our definition of advertising can help you decide whether promotional messages are advertising or something else. In each case, ask yourself these questions:

Is it paid for?
Is it nonpersonal?
Does it use the mass media?
Is there an identified sponsor?

If a local insurance agent sends you a calendar at the beginning of the year, is that advertising? Yes, because (1) we usually think of mail used for promotional messages as a mass medium, (2) the insurance agent had to pay

[1] Ralph S. Alexander and the Committee on Definitions of the American Marketing Association, *Marketing Definitions* 4 (1963), 9.

for the calendar and postage, (3) the agent is identified on the calendar, and (4) the message was not delivered in person.

If you attend a professional football game and an airplane tows a large banner over the stadium telling about a nearby pizza parlor that will be open after the game, is that advertising? Yes, because (1) the large crowd at the game makes this banner a mass medium, (2) it had to be paid for, (3) the pizza parlor is identified, and (4) you are not being called on in person. For similar reasons, advertising can appear in the form of a pencil with the name of a local clothing store on it, a paid announcement in the Yellow Pages, a sign on the side of a bus or in a subway station, a large electronic time-and-temperature display in front of a bank, or a paid message in the margin of a road map.

What Advertising Is Not

But what about a special display or sign that is in the aisle of a grocery store and promotes a new soft drink? Is that advertising? Maybe and maybe not. Certainly that display comes from an identified sponsor, and it is not personal. But is the sign a mass medium when it's placed in a store aisle? And did the sponsor pay the store to put the sign there? If the aisle display is a mass medium, and if the space in the aisle was paid for, then the soft drink display is advertising.

We can also use the four questions listed in the previous section to identify promotional messages that are definitely *not* advertising. A story in the newspaper announcing a grand opening of a new store is not advertising because the store didn't pay for it: The newspaper ran the story as a service to its readers. A sales booth at a local automobile show is not advertising because it is not a mass medium and the information is presented in person.

If a politician declares opposition to a particular bill at the luncheon meeting of a service club, this is not advertising, because it is personal and does not use a mass medium. If the same politician pays for a newspaper announcement that opposes this same bill, but without giving his or her name, this would not be advertising because the announcement would not have an identifiable sponsor. Most political messages are required to include the sponsor's name so the public will know who is trying to use such influence.

ORGANIZATION OF THE ADVERTISING INDUSTRY

In the early-to-mid 1800s, most newspapers in the United States were on the east coast. Settlers were beginning to move into what was then known as "the West"—what we now call western Pennsylvania, Ohio, Kentucky, and surrounding states. These settlers still had to rely on stores that were farther east in cities such as New York, Philadelphia, Boston, and Charleston. Merchants in these cities wanted to sell to the settlers, and some of the new mining and manufacturing operations wanted to advertise their products in the Eastern newspapers.

To serve these Western producers, the newspapers hired salespeople (or agents) who traveled around selling newspaper advertising. In return for each advertising order, the agent would get a **commission**, a share or percentage of the dollar amount of the order. Eventually, these sales agents were asked by the manufacturers to write the advertising too. This made sense because the sales agents worked with advertisements regularly and the manufacturers did not. So these advertising agents began to work for the advertisers even though they were still paid by the newspapers. From such humble beginnings sprang advertising agencies, which now handle billions of advertising dollars.

commission The salesperson's share or percentage of the dollar amount of an order.

How an Advertising Agency Works

The modern advertising agencies that have evolved from the old traveling agents basically work this way: Let's say that a large manufacturing firm has hired an agency to handle its advertising program. The firm, which we'll call the advertiser, indicates the purposes and goals of its program and the amount of money it is able to spend. The advertising agency then prepares the advertisements, selects the mass media to carry them, and orders the necessary time or space. All these arrangements must be approved by the advertiser.

But even in modern agencies, some old traditions remain. This is especially true in the way agencies are paid. Like the traveling agents of long ago, today's advertising agencies are still paid mainly by the media although they are hired by and work for the advertisers. Newspapers, magazines, radio and television stations and networks, and other advertising media still grant a commission to the agencies for recommending them to the advertiser. This commission is now usually 15 percent of the cost of the advertising time (in broadcast media) or space (in print media).

Suppose a certain advertisement in a magazine will cost $100. After the advertisement is printed, the magazine sends a bill for $100 to the advertising agency, which then forwards the bill to the advertiser. The advertiser pays $100 to the advertising agency. But the agency sends only $85 to the magazine and keeps 15 percent ($15 in this case) as a commission. So the agency does most of its work for the advertiser, but it is paid by the medium. Figure 1–3 shows how the payment process works.

Sometimes, however, a medium cannot grant a commission. For example, if an agency prepares a brochure for mailing to customers, it obviously gets no commission on the postage. Instead, the agency operates on a **cost plus** basis—which means that the advertiser pays the cost of the brochure and the postage, plus some additional money to the agency for its time and effort. Usually this is approximately the same amount as the agency would earn on a commission.

cost plus The advertiser pays the actual costs plus additional money for time and effort.

Other kinds of work for which an agency cannot earn a commission include designing and setting up a trade show exhibit, preparing a price list of merchandise for sale, or conducting research on a product in the design stage.

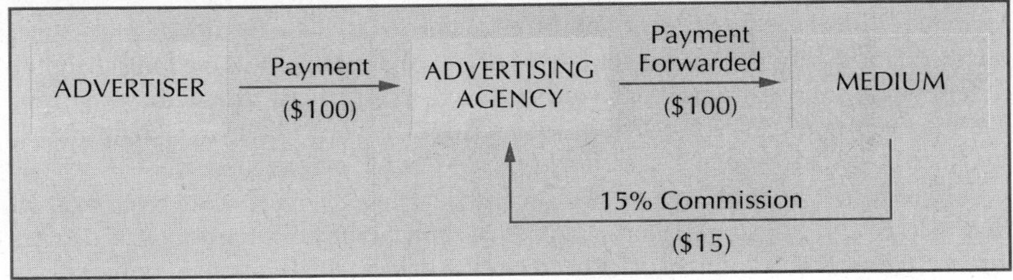

FIGURE 1–3
This diagram shows how the advertising agency works between the advertiser and the media. The advertiser hires and pays the advertising agency. This payment is forwarded to the medium. The agency is usually granted a 15 percent commission.

In most of these situations, the advertiser either pays the agency for its time and effort on a cost plus basis, or guarantees the agency a certain amount of money, called a **fee**.

fee A guaranteed payment.

A Look at Local Advertising

So far, we have been talking primarily about national advertising. Local advertising is somewhat different. Chrysler Corporation, for example, uses national advertising because it sells to people nationwide, but local Chrysler dealerships use local advertising because their customers are mostly nearby.

Local advertisers such as department stores or car dealerships may not use advertising agencies for two main reasons. The first reason is that most mass media do not let agencies take commissions on local advertising. The second reason is that local retailers need to take advantage of local events and therefore have little time to plan their advertising programs. Having an agency prepare their advertising slows down the process.

Instead, many retail stores have employees who can help prepare advertising, and larger stores may even have their own advertising departments. Local advertising media, such as newspapers, radio stations, and television stations, will help retail stores prepare their advertisements. One reason the media are unwilling to let an agency take a commission for local advertising, then, is that they are already doing part of an agency's job.

Local stores can also get prepared advertising materials such as pictures of merchandise and suggested selling ideas from the manufacturers who make the goods and the wholesalers who sell them directly to the stores. These aids help make an agency less necessary in much local advertising.

Sales Representatives Help Buyers and Sellers

But local and national advertising are not completely unrelated: There are some important connections between them. National advertising media such as magazines or television networks may have sales representatives, or "reps," who try to sell media space (in print media) and media time (in broadcast media) to local advertisers in major cities around the country. These reps are paid a sales commission on the amount of advertising they sell. Nearby contacts like these help local advertisers and local advertising agencies form close relationships with representatives of national firms and save long-distance telephone or travel money. Of course, the reps also help the media they represent by bringing in advertising orders from different cities and maintaining sales contacts with potential advertisers, no matter where they are.

There are other ties between local and national advertising, too, as we shall learn in detail later on. Local advertising shows what local stores and dealers are offering, yet it often works together with large-scale national promotions and campaigns. Local stores or local outlets of large store chains such as Sears or J.C. Penney may be interested in regional or perhaps even national advertising. National magazines may print and circulate some advertisements in limited local areas. Local newspapers encourage local retail advertising but also rely on national manufacturers and other large-scale advertisers for much of the advertising they carry. These kinds of advertising efforts require much cooperation and contact.

THE SIX Cs

Any topic is easier to understand when you know how it is organized. To help you understand how advertising is organized, we are going to base the following discussions on an outline that uses six key words. We call them the "six *C*s":

consumers
communication
constraints
creativity
channels
campaigns

Together, these six words cover the entire topic of advertising. What's more, they show how work flows in the preparation of advertisements. As advertisers, we must know who our *consumers* are likely to be, develop effective *communication* with those consumers, be aware of the *constraints* that affect our communication, use *creativity* to prepare the message we want to communicate, send it through the proper *channels,* and finally combine all these steps into an advertising *campaign*. Using the six *C*s will help you understand and remember the process of advertising preparation.

Now, with this background understanding of the practice of advertising, and with your own everyday exposure to advertisements, you are ready to learn how advertising uses communication techniques to reach the right consumers with the advertising message.

SUMMARY

So now you know what advertising is and a little about how it works. You need to remember that advertising can help promote ideas and services as well as products. You should also keep in mind how an advertising agency operates and what a "rep" does. The size and scope of the advertising business are growing day by day, but understanding the development of advertising may also help you comprehend how advertising grew into such an important part of our commercial economy.

TERMS TO KNOW

Now that you have finished this chapter, you should understand the following terms:

Audit Bureau of Circulations (A.B.C.)
Advertising
Mass media
Commission
Cost plus
Fee
Sponsor

If you are not certain of the meaning of any of these terms, go back through the chapter and review them.

THINGS TO THINK ABOUT

1. Why did advertising need controls like those of the Audit Bureau of Circulations?
2. What are three methods of paying advertising agencies for their work?
3. Why do mass media (such as newspapers, television stations, etc.) pay advertising agencies when the agencies actually do most of their work for the advertisers?
4. What are the various advertising functions of the advertiser, the advertising agency, and the mass media?
5. Why is so much money spent for advertising in this country?

THINGS TO TALK ABOUT

1. What recent developments in technology and communication may have helped advertising develop?
2. Why is it so important for advertising to be paid for, to use the mass media, to be nonpersonal, and to have an identified sponsor?
3. What are the advantages and disadvantages of commissions for advertising agencies? Consider the agency, advertiser, and media.
4. What are the differences between national and local advertising?
5. What takes the place of an advertising agency in much advertising done by a local retailer? Why do most retailers not use an advertising agency?

THINGS TO DO

1. Try to find advertisements from fifty or more years ago and compare them with modern advertisements.
2. Visit a nearby advertising agency or the advertising department of a large local retail store and find out who prepares the advertisements.
3. Figure out the agency commission on a network television advertisement that costs $78,000. Do the same with other advertising prices. Draw a diagram, like the one in Figure 1–3, to show where the money goes.

2 Consumers and Communication

The art of communication.
From the beginning, we've been committed to achieving excellence in communications. It's only natural for us to support excellence in the arts that communicate.

Courtesy of AT&T

CHAPTER OUTLINE

- Marketing
  - The Marketing Concept Focuses on the Consumer
  - The Advertising Concept Works in a Similar Way
- Consumer Protection
- Consumer Behavior
  - Motivation Is an Unknown Quantity
  - Understanding Uncertainty
  - Some Individual Characteristics Affect Consumer Behavior
  - Groups Can Also Affect Behavior
  - How Powerful Is Advertising?
- Consumer Segments
  - Age
  - Income
  - Sex
  - Education
  - Occupation
  - Many Factors Are Related
  - Some Factors Apply to Households
- Target Groups and Target Markets
- Communication
  - How Mass Communication Works
  - Know Your Audience

By the time you finish this chapter, you should understand:

1. **How advertising and marketing are related.**
2. **How the marketing concept and the advertising concept work.**
3. **How the need for consumer protection affects advertising.**
4. **How advertisers use consumer behavior.**
5. **What consumer segments are and how they help make advertising more efficient.**
6. **What advertisers mean by target groups and target markets.**
7. **How communication works in advertising.**

Our first two *C*s are consumers and communication. Although these are two separate topics, they fit together very well because advertising must communicate with consumers. Advertising communication comes under the general heading of marketing, so let's first take a look at the broader marketing process before we focus in on the specifics of advertising.

MARKETING

Many people who work in marketing feel that advertising is too narrow a term for the many aspects of communication involved in marketing. Instead, they think in terms of **marketing communication,** a form of communication that includes all contacts with customers. For example, marketing communication may involve promotional activities that do not use paid media time or space, such as telephoning, so it is not strictly advertising. But these promotional efforts involve the same kinds of considerations as advertising efforts. Of course, we are mainly concerned with advertising, but to understand advertising fully, we must also understand how advertising fits into the marketing process.

marketing communication A form of communication that includes all contacts with consumers.

Marketing is involved in all stages of a product's life. The manufacturer makes the product and sells it directly to the wholesaler. The wholesaler keeps large inventories of the product and makes it available to many retailers. The retailers, in turn, sell the product to the final consumer. The marketing channel most products follow therefore looks like this:

Manufacturer → Wholesaler → Retailer → Consumer

At each stage of this process, some new alteration is made and some value is added. The manufacturer turns raw materials into a finished product; the wholesaler sends the merchandise to widespread locations and makes large amounts available in smaller, more salable, quantities; the retailer makes sure the product suits the consumer's needs, helps service the product, offers credit, demonstrates the product, and makes it available directly to the consumer. To stay in operation and make a reasonable profit, therefore, the manufacturer, wholesaler, and retailer must price the product slightly higher than they paid for it.

The Marketing Concept Focuses on the Consumer

marketing concept An approach that places the consumer at the center of all marketing decisions.

In times past, when manufacturing was young and goods were in short supply, consumers took whatever product was available with no questions asked. But in our wealthier times, marketers and advertisers have begun using the **marketing concept,**[1] which places the consumer at the center of all marketing decisions. Now marketers ask what consumers want and need and then develop the kinds of products and services that will meet their requirements. The focus is on the consumer, and the entire marketing effort is aimed at meeting the consumer's needs and wants, rather than simply developing products and then trying to sell them.

Because marketers now consider the consumer before manufacturing begins—in fact, before a product or service is thought up or designed—we actually need to expand our picture of the marketing channel to include the premanufacturing stages:

Consumer → Product Development → Manufacturer →
Wholesaler → Retailer → Consumer

Consumers aren't the only ones who benefit from the marketing concept. Manufacturing companies also benefit because products designed specifically around the consumer's desires are easier to sell. And when a company sells more products, it has a better chance of increasing its profits.

The Advertising Concept Works in a Similar Way

In the past, manufacturers, wholesalers, and retailers all aimed their advertising messages at the consumer, something like this:

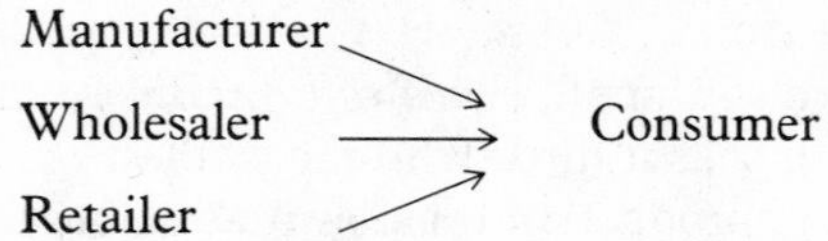

They were telling consumers what they wanted them to know about the product—not necessarily what the *consumers* wanted to know. But what if advertising were to begin using the marketing concept, basing advertisements on the wants and needs of consumers? Wouldn't consumers benefit from

[1] E. Jerome McCarthy and William D. Perreault, Jr., *Basic Marketing*, 10th ed. (Homewood, Illinois: Richard D. Irwin, Inc., 1990).

having more informative and usable advertising? And wouldn't the knowledge of consumer expectations make advertising more efficient and effective?

That is exactly what happens in modern advertising. The manufacturer asks consumers about their wants and needs before developing the product and then uses this knowledge to prepare effective advertising. The manufacturer or its advertising agency may also go to consumers to find the best ways to present information in the advertisement: for instance, what product features to stress and which media to use. It may also ask the consumers how effective a completed advertising effort was. Even wholesalers who do not advertise directly to consumers may use consumer information before advertising to retailers. And retailers want to know what products and services their consumers want so they can feature them in store advertisements.

The idea of asking consumers before developing advertising is similar to the marketing concept, so we shall call it the **advertising concept,** an approach that places the consumer at the center of all advertising decisions. Now our advertising process looks like this:

advertising concept An approach that places the consumer at the center of all advertising decisions.

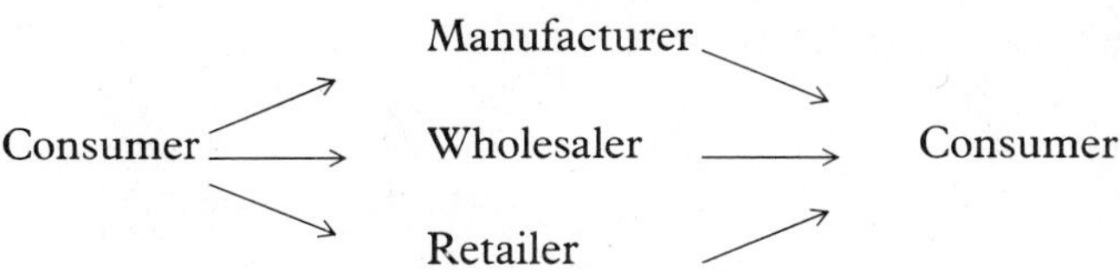

Even though manufacturers, wholesalers, or retailers usually pay for advertising, consumers can benefit from it as well. Knowing more about consumers has helped marketers, advertisers, and agencies improve their advertising efforts. This helps their businesses make money, but it also helps consumers improve their shopping and purchasing skills. Some ways advertising can help you become a smarter shopper and buyer are outlined in Chapter 19.

CONSUMER PROTECTION

In the United States, there is a popular **consumer movement** dedicated to protecting consumers from being cheated or misled by the sellers of all kinds of goods and services. It has been so successful that consumers often take it for granted that the advertising information they see or hear will be a reliable guide to help them with their purchase decisions. And it is, in fact, unfair—and sometimes illegal—to misrepresent merchandise that is for sale, whether in an outright lie or simply through the omission of some important information.

consumer movement A movement dedicated to protecting consumers from being cheated or misled by sellers.

Few modern-day advertisers really want to lie to consumers or mislead them in any way. But advertisers must be aware that they *can* mislead consumers unintentionally. For example, some people may not understand technical language in the advertising for certain kinds of specialized industrial equipment. The advertiser can protect such people by using language that they can understand. But some portion of the public may misunderstand even the simplest advertisement just as it may misunderstand a newspaper editorial or a television news broadcast. Advertisers may try to be as clear as possible, but still not everyone will understand.

We must decide how far to go in protecting the average consumer without limiting the rights of advertisers. It is one thing to insist that advertisments supply enough information to help consumers judge and choose from competing products; it is another thing to assume that the advertisement is illegal if it misleads even a single member of the audience.

It is possible to make much of our advertising more direct and informative without harming advertisers, though for instance, supplying price information and warranty and care instructions with an advertisement featuring a sale on lawn mowers would not restrict the retailer's ability to tell consumers about the store and the product. It would, however, let consumers do a better job of shopping and buying.

The development of the marketing and advertising concepts has given the consumer a more important position in the marketing and promotion channel than ever before. This increased importance means that consumers must be as fully informed as possible about the products, services, and ideas that are being offered. Advertising that protects the interests of the consumer can play an important part in keeping consumers informed—and this in turn benefits the businesses that rely on consumer input in developing their products.

CONSUMER BEHAVIOR

consumer behavior A study that uses findings in the behavioral sciences to explain the actions of consumers in marketing and advertising.

Another popular development in the field of advertising is the study of **consumer behavior,** which uses findings in the behavioral sciences (such as psychology, sociology, and anthropology) to explain the actions of consumers in marketing and advertising. Understanding how consumers behave or intend to behave and how advertising may influence that behavior is vital to successful advertising.

Motivation Is an Unknown Quantity

motivation Why people act the way they do.

Advertisers are interested in many aspects of consumer behavior, but what they would most like to know about is **motivation,** why people act the way they do. Do consumers buy things because of advertising? Do advertisements make them consider certain products and services and avoid others? Does advertising only make people curious about an item, or can it lead to the final sale? Obviously, these are questions that most advertisers would like to answer.

But there is a problem here: Consumers cannot determine why they make purchases because even they do not know. How then can advertisers discover hidden motivations that the consumers themselves cannot recognize? Motivation is a vital issue in advertising, but it presents a lot of unanswerable questions because of the many unknowns involved.

Understanding Uncertainty

We have a better understanding of consumers' problems both before and after making purchase decisions. We know, for instance, that consumers feel a certain degree of risk when deciding whether to buy a product and which product to buy. This feeling, called **perceived risk,** exists when consumers are uncertain whether the product in which they might invest their money will help them meet certain objectives and avoid potentially bad results. Advertisers can respond to consumers' desire to reduce this uncertainty by providing advertising that offers information and assurance.[2]

perceived risk The sense of risk a consumer feels when deciding whether to buy something.

Consumers feel a similar uncertainty after they make their purchase decisions. They are not sure that they have made the right choice. This postdecision anxiety is called **cognitive dissonance**. Consumers often search for reassurance in advertising. For example, buyers of automobiles purposely look for advertisements about the make of car that they bought and avoid advertisements for other kinds of cars.[3] Advertisers can help reduce cognitive dissonance by reassuring buyers that they made the correct choice. Figure 2–1 shows an advertisement that is intended to relieve cognitive dissonance by comparing a product favorably against similar products.

cognitive dissonance The sense of anxiety a customer feels after buying something.

Advertising can also *increase* cognitive dissonance by telling purchasers of a competing brand that they could have made a better choice. This kind of advertising is trying to make consumers think about the advertised product the next time they buy.

Some Individual Characteristics Affect Consumer Behavior

To a certain extent, the individual behavioral traits that we call **personality** help determine how much cognitive dissonance and perceived risk will affect people. For instance, self-assured, innovative people may not have as much anxiety before and after a purchase decision as dependent, conventional people. Various personality traits can also account for the way people receive an advertising message, how well they remember it, and whether it influences their decisions.

personality The collection of individual behavior traits that make up a person's character.

People with different kinds of personalities also have different ways of selecting what they want to see or hear. This characteristic, called **selectivity,** can either limit or extend people's exposure to advertisements. Consumers are also selective in their perception and memory of advertisements and in their decisions to buy a particular product.

selectivity The extent to which people choose what they want to see or hear.

---

[2] John S. Hadley, "The Interaction of Personality, Products and Strategic Communications as Viewed through a Framework of Perceived Risk" (Ph.D. diss., University of Illinois, 1970).

[3] Danuta Ehrlick, Isaiah Guttman, Peter Schonbach, and Judson Mills, "Postdecision Exposure to Relevant Information," *Journal of Abnormal and Social Psychology* 64 (January 1967):96–102.

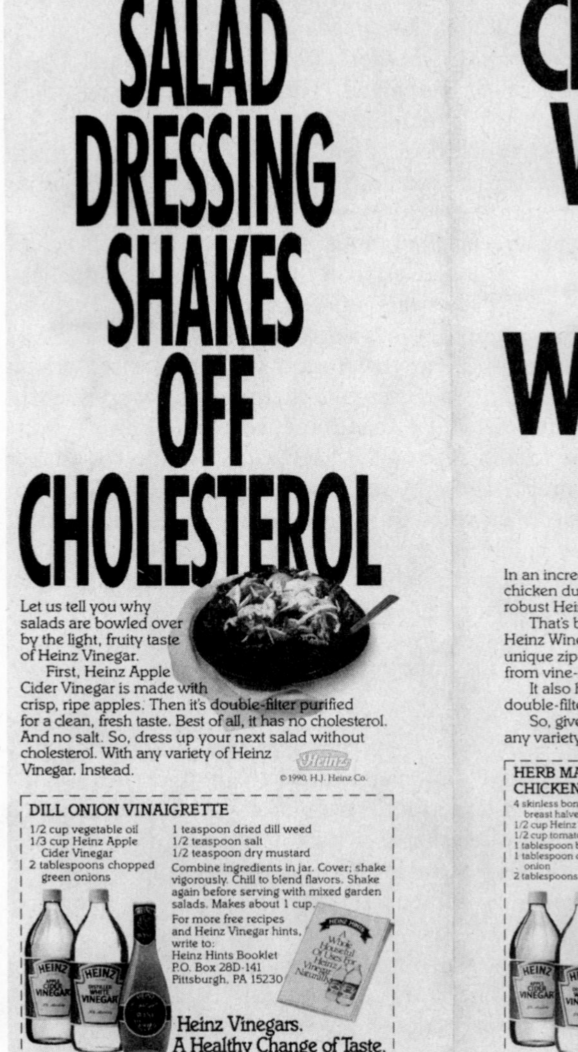

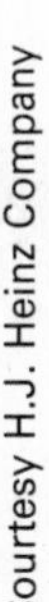

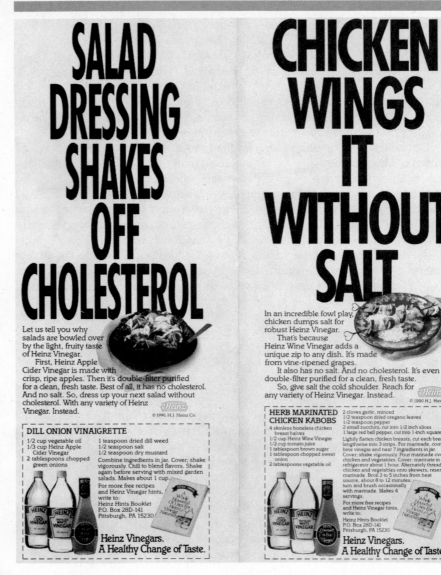

FIGURE 2–1
This advertisement reassures purchasers who use this brand of vinegar, while it also creates anxiety among those who use other brands. Perhaps they will purchase this brand the next time they buy vinegar.

Individuals also vary in their ability and even their willingness to learn about a product. Advertisers who want to inform consumers about an idea, service, or product rely on the willingness to learn and also make use of a learning process similar to the one that you go through in your classes. (See Figure 2–2.)

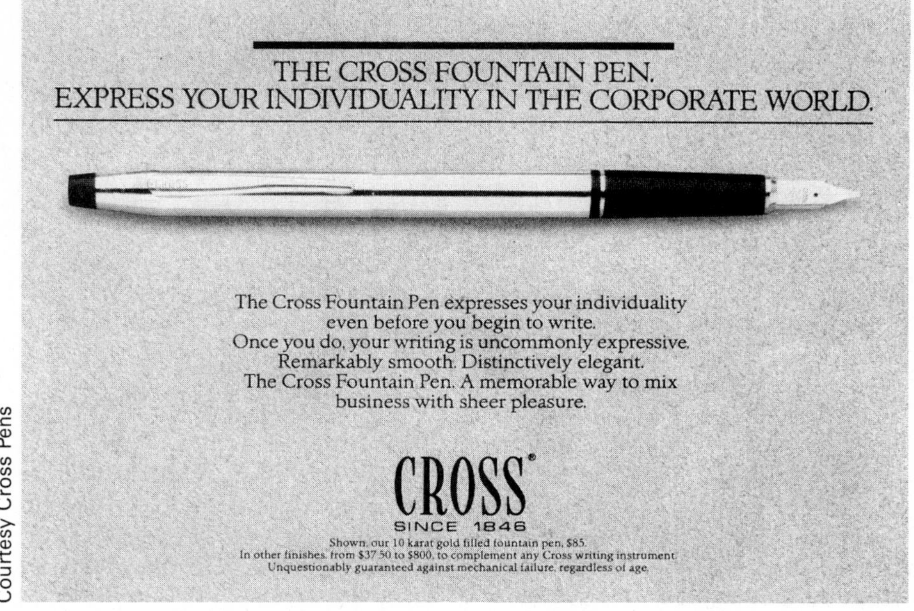

THE CROSS FOUNTAIN PEN.
EXPRESS YOUR INDIVIDUALITY IN THE CORPORATE WORLD.
The Cross Fountain Pen expresses your individuality even before you begin to write.
Once you do, your writing is uncommonly expressive.
Remarkably smooth. Distinctively elegant.
The Cross Fountain Pen. A memorable way to mix business with sheer pleasure.
CROSS®
SINCE 1846
Shown, our 10 karat gold filled fountain pen, $85.
In other finishes, from $37.50 to $800, to complement any Cross writing instrument.
Unquestionably guaranteed against mechanical failure, regardless of age.

Courtesy Cross Pens

FIGURE 2–2
Notice how the prestige of the pen is tied to the consumer's self-worth and self-esteem. This advertisement does a good job of communicating prestige of the product and relating to the customer's need for expression.

Groups Can Also Affect Behavior

Many of our decisions to purchase a product are influenced by our relationships with other people. We may want to be like people we admire, so we buy products that will make us look and act like them. Or we may simply buy products they recommend because we respect their opinions.

We also like to have other people admire us, so an advertisement may appeal to our need for status or to our individuality. But advertisements can also appeal to our sense of responsibility to our friends or family by urging us to buy a product that is beneficial to ourselves or to others.

Some people are more influenced by the people around them than others. They want to be sure that new products have been thoroughly tested by other consumers before they buy. Sometimes advertising appeals to this "join-the-group" mentality, but often advertisers look for more individualistic people who like to try new products. These people are called **innovators**. Advertisers may try to reach these people with a "be-the-first" approach: "Be the first one in your neighborhood" to drive a new kind of car or drink a new kind of soft drink.

innovators People who like to try new products.

How Powerful Is Advertising?

Human behavior can be very complex, but understanding it is important to advertising. Advertisers therefore try to use certain concepts of consumer behavior to help make their messages more effective. But we should realize that experts know relatively little about how to predict the actions of consumers and their purchase decisions. Not everyone acts the same way under the same conditions. Because of these uncertainties, we do not know exactly how effective advertising can be in the variety of promotional situations in which it is used. Therefore it is almost impossible for advertising to use the power of suggestion, unconscious manipulation, or appeals to consumer behavior characteristics to make people buy what they do not want.

CONSUMER SEGMENTS

consumer segments Groups of potential buyers with similar buying characteristics.

segmentation The process of defining consumer segments.

Because people who have things in common tend to act in similar ways, advertisers like to break down the population into **consumer segments,** groups of potential buyers with similar characteristics. This process of **segmentation** allows advertisers to design their messages specifically for the people who are most likely to buy their product.

As an example, we know that young people in the age group of 13 to 17 are more likely to buy records and tapes than are people 65 and older—and we can even predict the kind of music that will be most popular with each age group. We also know that men in the age group of 50 to 65 are more likely to use electric shavers than men ages 35 to 49, who are more likely to shave with razor blades.[4] These consumer segments are based on age, but there are many other ways of dividing the population.

demographic characteristics Population facts such as age, sex, and income.

The most common consumer segments use population facts such as age, income, sex, and the like. We call these **demographic characteristics.** (See Figure 2–3). In the rest of this section, we'll look at some of the demographic consumer segments advertisers often use.

Age

As people grow older, their tastes, preferences, and needs change, and peer pressure affects them differently—that is, their friends may have more influence on their purchases at one age than at another. At one time, people in their 30s and 40s or older established clothing styles; now younger people more often set styles of dress, and older people copy them. Age can also affect other demographic factors. Up to a point, we tend to earn higher incomes, have more education, and have more children as we grow older. After a certain point, we tend to have fewer opportunities to go to school, and after we reach retirement age, our incomes are often reduced.

Income

The amount of money people have to spend has a great deal of impact on their shopping patterns. People in lower income categories may not spend less money

[4] Simmons Market Research Bureau, "1990 Study of Media and Markets."

Household Characteristics

County size:	____	"A"size county (one of the largest 26 cities' areas)
	____	"B" size county (population more than 120,000)
	____	"C" size county (32,000 to 120,000 population)
	____	"D" size county (less than 32,000 population)
Geographic area:	____	In metropolitan area
	____	Outside metropolitan area
	____	Urban
	____	Rural
	____	Farm
	____	Nonfarm
Geographic region:	____	New England
	____	Metropolitan New York
	____	Mid-Atlantic
	____	East Central
	____	Metropolitan Chicago
	____	West Central
	____	South East
	____	South West
	____	Pacific
Ages of children:	____	No child under 18
	____	Youngest child 6-17
	____	Youngest child under 6
Family size:	____	1 or 2 members
	____	3 or 4 members
	____	5 or more members
Family income:	____	Under $10,000
	____	$10,000 to $19,999
	____	$20,000 to $29,999
	____	$30,000 to $39,999
	____	$40,000 to $74,999
	____	$75,000 and more
Home ownership:	____	Own home
	____	Rent home
Dwelling characteristic:	____	Single-family dwelling
	____	Multiple-family dwelling

FIGURE 2–3
These are the categories often used for demographic descriptions. Where do *you* fit into each category?

on groceries than people who make more money, but they generally have less left over to spend on housing, clothing, recreation, health, automobiles, and other items. And once people reach a certain income level, they may not keep spending more and more. Instead, they might want to reduce their working time and increase their leisure time as long as they make enough to keep up their standard of living.

Sex

Men and women do not buy the same kinds of items. Cosmetics, toiletries, clothing, home furnishings, hobby and craft items, and even automobiles may appeal more to one sex than the other. At the same time, changes in our way of living have reduced the differences between the sexes, offering more equal opportunities and interests to both women and men. This change is important to some marketers of work clothing, toys, grooming aids, restaurants and groceries, and many other products and services.

Education

Education is a difficult classification for advertisers to use. As people become more educated, they may learn about more things they would like to get out of life as well as more things they would like to own. But they can also learn that material goods are not vital to happiness and that satisfaction is not necessarily related to possessions. So there is a problem: Education may lead to either more or less desire for goods and services. In any case, however, additional education makes consumers more receptive to new ideas.

Occupation

If you are a farmer, you need certain farm implements and tools. If you are a carpenter, again you need certain implements and tools. But your occupation may also lead to purchases that are more indirectly related to your job. A regional sales representative may need to buy automobiles more regularly than other people; a national sales representative may need to buy more airline tickets.

Many Factors Are Related

Demographic factors tend to be related to one another. For example, hobbies are directly related to occupation. A person who enjoys woodworking may want to own the same kinds of tools as a carpenter, and a person who enjoys boating may want the same kinds of accessories as a person who runs a fishing boat for a living. Changes in one demographic factor often cause changes in other factors as well. In the years immediately following marriage, for instance, family size tends to increase. As the number of children increases, the likelihood of owning a home increases. So changes in marital status are closely related to changes in family size and lifestyle.

Some Factors Apply to Households

Not all the factors we use to define consumer segments apply to individuals; sometimes we find it easier to describe the household, the group in which people live. This is because factors such as family size and home ownership may relate more directly to the household than to the individual. Also, some individual factors are really more useful when we combine them according to household than when we view them separately. Information on income from one individual may not be as useful as information on the total income for all the working people in the household, for example, because the earnings may be pooled and used together to buy products and services for the group.

Try using household and individual factors to describe your own characteristics and compare them with those of other people you know. Your own characteristics and consumer segments are related to the products, services, and ideas that you are in the market for, and an advertiser might make use of these groupings to reach you through the mass media, attract your attention, and explain how the advertised item fulfills your needs or wants.

TARGET GROUPS AND TARGET MARKETS

The consumer segments that advertisers consider the best prospects for their product or service are called **target groups,** groups of potential buyers to whom advertising should be directed. Advertisers often rank target groups in their order of importance: the best prospects are called *primary* target groups, the next are called *secondary* target groups, and the third—if they exist—are called *tertiary* target groups.

target groups Groups of potential buyers to whom the advertising should be directed.

The geographic areas or regions where target groups can be found are called **target markets.** As with target groups, there may be primary, secondary, and tertiary target markets. To avoid confusion, remember that target groups identify consumer segments while target markets identify geographic areas.

target markets Geographic areas in which target groups are found.

Many times, a target market will include a city along with all the built up residential areas in the city and in the suburban areas nearby. A city with a population of 50,000 or more, along with the area around it, is called a **metropolitan area**. The federal government will designate this area and the surrounding county or counties as a **standard metropolitan statistical area (SMSA).** Since such a metropolitan area includes the city and the socially and economically related territory around the city, it might include one county or several. In some major population centers such as New York and Chicago—and even in smaller cities such as Baton Rouge and Sacramento—two or more counties may be included in a single metropolitan area.

metropolitan area The area in and around a city with a population of 50,000 or more

standard metropolitan statistical area (SMSA) A federal designation that combines a city of 50,000 or more with its surrounding county or counties for statistical purposes.

COMMUNICATION

In advertising, one person or organization, the advertiser, sends a message to a large audience, the consumers, through the mass media. We call the advertiser the *sender* of the message and the audience the *receiver*. Between sender and receiver, there are other stages in the total mass communication process as well. Let's see how the system works.

How Mass Communication Works

It is not enough simply to create an advertising message. To get the message across, the sender must first put it into a format that can be sent to the

FIGURE 2–4
A simple model of the communication process.

encoding Putting an advertising message into a format that can be sent to the audience.

channel The medium through which the advertising message travels.

decoding Changing an advertising message from a signal into words and from words into thoughts in the minds of the audience.

audience. For example, the sender might have to change thoughts into words and speech into radio signals or letters on a printed page. This process is called **encoding**. The message must then travel through a **channel,** the mass medium through which advertising reaches its audience. Before the receivers can understand the signal, however, it must be changed from a signal into words and from words into meaningful thoughts in the minds of the audience members. This is called **decoding**[5]. You can see how this process works in television advertising in Figure 2–4.

Know Your Audience

Members of an audience read, hear, or watch advertisements because they expect to gain something from them—usually information about either products for sale or the stores that sell them. If audience members do not feel that

[5] C. Wilbur Schramm, "How Communication Works," in *The Process and Effects of Mass Communication* (Urbana, Illinois: University of Illinois Press, 1964), 3–26.

they are gaining useful information, they will not bother to spend time on an advertisement.

An advertisement that attracts the attention of the audience and offers information or some other kind of payoff in return for the audience's time can succeed only if it meets the following criteria:

1. It uses language that the audience can understand.
2. It does not conflict too much with the beliefs or values of audience members.
3. It shows what the product or service will do for the consumer and how the consumer's family and friends will feel about it.

These conditions are necessary for the success of any advertisement, but they create a problem for advertisers. How are they to know what their audience will understand, what its beliefs and values are, what its needs and wants are? Yet these are just the things advertisers *must* know to develop effective advertisements.

One of the basic rules of effective advertising, then, is: "Know your audience." But to do so, you must know where and how to gather the necessary information. We shall examine this problem in two different but related activities: research (Chapter 3) and copywriting (Chapters 6–8).

SUMMARY

So now we understand the first two Cs—*consumers* and *communication*—of the six Cs outlined in Chapter 1. The purpose of advertising is to communicate a message to consumers. This communication can help not only the advertiser, by selling a product or service, but the consumer as well, by providing needed information. But before we can communicate effectively, we need to find out more information about consumers who might buy what we have for sale—and how best to get our message across to them. That's where research comes in, as we shall see in the next chapter. Then, in Chapter 4, we'll learn about the limits on advertising and what it can communicate.

TERMS TO KNOW

Now that you have finished this chapter, you should understand the following terms:

- marketing communication
- marketing concept
- advertising concept
- consumer movement
- consumer behavior
- motivation
- perceived risk
- cognitive dissonance
- personality
- selectivity
- innovators
- consumer segments
- segmentation
- demographic characteristics
- target groups
- target markets
- metropolitan area
- standard metropolitan statistical area (SMSA)
- encoding
- channel
- decoding

If you are not certain of the meanings of any of these terms, go back through the chapter and review them.

THINGS TO THINK ABOUT

1. What is the role of the consumer in the marketing concept?
2. Why are the behavioral sciences (such as psychology, sociology, and anthropology) important to advertising's use of consumer behavior concepts? How are the behavioral sciences used in consumer research?
3. What consumer segments are you in? How might they affect your purchases and your way of life?
4. How do target groups differ from target markets?

THINGS TO TALK ABOUT

1. How do marketing and advertising work together? How do they differ?
2. How are the marketing concept and the advertising concept alike? How are they different?
3. How can the advertising industry best use the current consumer movement?
4. Why are target groups and target markets important in advertising and marketing?
5. The actual communication signal is left out of the discussion and illustration of the communication process in this chapter. Where do you think the signal fits in?
6. How do consumers use advertising communication? How does advertising communication use information about consumers?

THINGS TO DO

1. Draw out the complete marketing channel for a product that you use.
2. Outline the various types of personalities that might be attracted to three or four different models of automobiles. Then do the same using other categories of consumer segments.
3. Visit a communications organization such as a local newspaper or radio station?

3 Research

CHAPTER OUTLINE

Basic and Applied Research
Secondary Research
- How to Find Secondary Research Information
- Secondary Market Research
- Secondary Advertising Research

Primary Research
- Research before the Campaign Begins
- Research during Advertising Preparation
- Research after the Advertising Is Ready
- Problems in Conducting Research

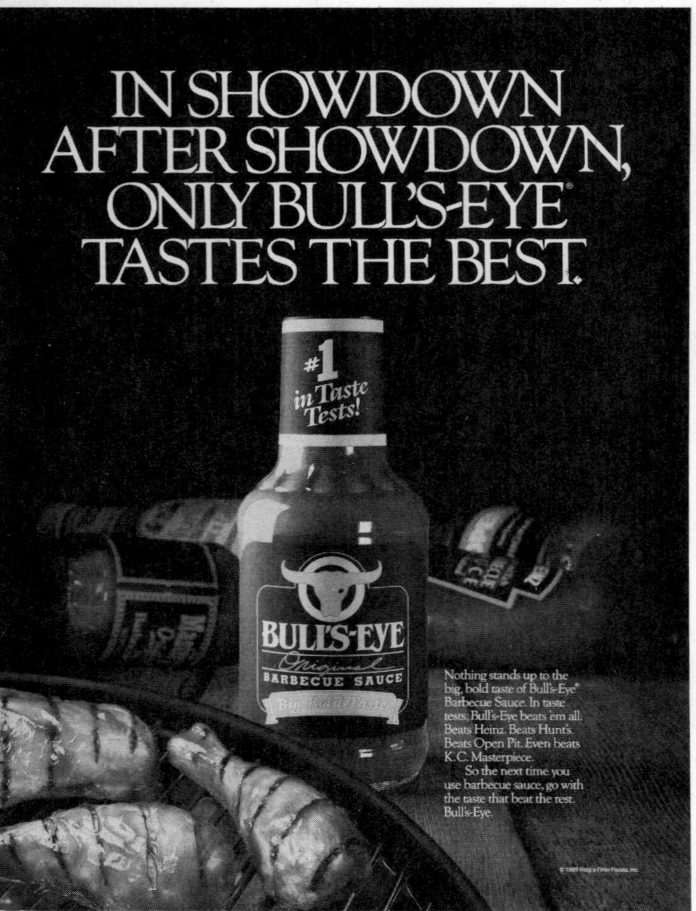

Courtesy of Kraft General Foods, Inc.

By the time you finish this chapter, you should understand:

1. **The role of basic and applied research in advertising.**
2. **Where you can find secondary research information and what kinds are available.**
3. **What primary research is and why it may be needed.**
4. **What kinds of primary research can be done during the development of an advertising campaign.**
5. **Some of the problems involved in research.**

How can we as advertisers find out about our audience before we even write our advertisements? How can we learn about the consumers of our products or services, their needs and wants, the consumer segments to which they belong, and other basic facts about them?

The answer lies in **research,** which is the thorough search for and investigation of information. Through research, you can find out things that you do not already know. Sometimes this will involve complicated experiments or long studies; sometimes you may be able to get the information you need from a book you find in the library. And of course there are many stages in between.

research The thorough search for and investigation of information.

You are not going to learn everything you need to know about research in advertising by reading this chapter. In fact, you are going to learn only the basic facts about how advertisers use research in advertising and where they can find advertising research information. You will *not* learn how to do research. That is a complicated topic, and it requires a lot of study and experience before you can be really good at it. What this chapter *will* do is give you the foundation you need to build effective research skills.

BASIC AND APPLIED RESEARCH

Advertising research is a fairly new field. Its practitioners have had to borrow many research techniques from other disciplines. And, because advertising research is in its beginning stages, its theories are not highly refined.

Advertising research can be either general or specific. **Basic research,** sometimes called *theoretical research,* is a general form of research that explores ideas about advertising as a whole. The broad scope of basic research makes it useful in explaining how advertising works. It also helps to explain how all the parts of an advertising campaign relate to consumers' decisions and marketing practices.

basic research General research that explores ideas about advertising as a whole.

The findings of basic research studies appear in such scholarly and professional publications as the *Journal of Advertising* and the *Journal of Marketing Research.* Groups of researchers or scholars also meet to discuss their work, and these meetings can be good sources of current research findings. Other fields that have ties to advertising, such as psychology, sociology, marketing, retailing, and communication, also provide useful basic findings.

applied research Research that focuses on specific aspects or problems of advertising.

Applied research, also called *pragmatic research,* is more specific than basic research. It is more likely to focus on certain areas of advertising, such as copywriting, media selection, management, and production, or on particular problems that arise.

Applied research findings appear in advertising research journals and advertising trade publications. Some professional advertising meetings feature such findings, as do many academic and scholarly organizations.

SECONDARY RESEARCH

primary research Original research that you do yourself or hire someone to do specifically for you.

secondary research Research based on facts and figures that are already available.

Original research that you do yourself or hire someone to do specifically for you is called **primary research.** We'll discuss this later in the chapter. Research based on facts and figures that are already available is called **secondary research.** It is probably the most common, easiest, and least costly way to get the information you need.

How to Find Secondary Research Information

Experts in the advertising field—and in related fields like psychology, sociology, and communication—are doing research all the time. And they usually publish their results. Even the federal government does research that can be useful to advertisers. For example, the U.S. Bureau of the Census provides much valuable information about the American population—not just how many people there are. All you need to know is where to look for the information you want and how to apply it to your particular situation.

Although it can be very useful to check through professional journals and government statistics, advertisers get most of the secondary research information they need by buying it from research firms. These firms conduct their own research, often on a variety of products and services, and sell the results. Many advertisers subscribe to a research firm in the same way you might subscribe to a magazine. They pay a subscription fee and receive research findings every month or so. Research conducted for a number of firms that pay a fee for the results is called **syndicated research.**

syndicated research Research conducted for a number of firms that pay a fee for the results.

Advertisers have many reasons for relying on syndicated research instead of gathering information themselves. The firms that perform syndicated research are experts. They often specialize in certain kinds of research or in various research methods and are therefore able to do the job quickly and efficiently. Also, accurate research requires expertise in statistics, research study design, report writing, and presentation. Someone who is not skilled in these areas may do a poor job—wasting money and time in the process. And, finally, researchers must remain objective. Advertisers and their agencies sometimes have biased points of view that can affect their studies. Independent researchers are better able to conduct honest studies that yield reliable results.

Secondary Market Research

If you have a product or service to sell, one of the first things you want to know about is your market. As you learned in Chapter 2, a market is the region or city in which something is sold. In fact, you might have many different markets, and it will be important to know as much as possible about all of them.

You can gather market data yourself, but research firms also provide a great deal of syndicated market information. As we said in the last section, syndicated research is often more efficient and less costly than the do-it-yourself kind. Syndicated research firms provide information on the number of people in different areas, their ages, the amount of money they have to spend, and the kinds of products and services they buy. They can also tell you about the main industries in your target markets, the kinds of transportation available, and even the number of automobiles registered.

Suppose you are a manufacturer of laundry detergent, and you want to change the formula of your product to match the water in various areas around the country. Syndicated research could tell you how hard the water is in each area, how many people own washing machines, and how many own water softeners. Let's take a look at some of the most popular sources of syndicated market research information.

Simmons Market Research Bureau. One widely used firm that conducts syndicated market research is Simmons Market Research Bureau (called SMRB or Simmons in the advertising business). Simmons conducts very complicated research, but the findings it publishes are easy to read and simple to use, as Figure 3–1 shows.

Simmons provides very detailed and specific information about target groups and their media and purchase habits. Gathering such information is naturally very expensive. Simmons researchers ask more than 25,000 people throughout the United States about their use of products and brands; their use of television, radio, magazines, and newspapers; their traits and characteristics; and other information. Clearly, interviewing so many people would be impossible for any single advertiser or agency. But because Simmons can sell the results to a large number of interested firms, it can afford to perform this costly and complicated research.

Every six months, Simmons publishes its results in about sixty volumes of printed information. These include forty books of information about products and services and twenty volumes about consumers: their use of media and the kinds of demographic characteristics we discussed in Chapter 2. Subscribers can also receive the information on computer diskettes or tapes or through media information services such as Telmar or IMS. These services store information in on-line computer systems.

Other firms provide some of the same kinds of information as Simmons. One example is Mediamark Research, Inc. (known as MRI). Advertisers like the accuracy and completeness of the information Simmons and firms like MRI provide. They find that they can apply it to general marketing problems as well

0172
P-13

SNEAKERS: BOUGHT AND NUMBER IN LAST 12 MONTHS
(MALES)

0172
P-13

	TOTAL U.S.	BOUGHT IN LAST 12 MONTHS				1 ITEM				2 ITEMS				3 OR MORE ITEMS			
		A	B	C	D	A	B	C	D	A	B	C	D	A	B	C	D
			% ACROSS				% ACROSS				% ACROSS				% ACROSS		
	'000	'000	DOWN	%	INDX	'000	DOWN	%	INDX	'000	DOWN	%	INDX	'000	DOWN	%	INDX
TOTAL MALES	80052	16287	100.0	20.3	100	9118	100.0	11.4	100	4307	100.0	5.4	100	2862	100.0	3.6	100
HOUSEHOLD HEADS	65885	12307	75.6	18.7	92	6927	76.0	10.5	92	3437	79.8	5.2	97	1943	67.9	2.9	82
18 - 24	14056	4428	27.2	31.5	155	2277	25.0	16.2	142	1128	26.2	8.0	149	1024	35.8	7.3	204
25 - 34	19681	5402	33.2	27.4	135	2942	32.3	14.9	131	1711	39.7	8.7	162	749	26.2	3.8	106
35 - 44	14659	3118	19.1	21.3	105	1945	21.3	13.3	116	684	15.9	4.7	87	490	17.1	3.3	93
45 - 54	10805	1663	10.2	15.4	76	1011	11.1	9.4	82	296	6.9	2.7	51	356	12.4	3.3	92
55 - 64	10181	1105	6.8	10.9	53	610	6.7	6.0	53	295	6.8	2.9	54	200	7.0	2.0	55
65 OR OLDER	10670	571	3.5	5.4	26	333	3.7	3.1	27	195	4.5	1.8	34	43	1.5	0.4	11
18 - 34	33737	9830	60.4	29.1	143	5219	57.2	15.5	136	2839	65.9	8.4	156	1773	61.9	5.3	147
18 - 49	54025	13931	85.5	25.8	127	7757	85.1	14.4	126	3688	85.6	6.8	127	2486	86.9	4.6	129
25 - 54	45145	10183	62.5	22.6	111	5898	64.7	13.1	115	2690	62.5	6.0	111	1595	55.7	3.5	99
35 - 49	20288	4101	25.2	20.2	99	2539	27.8	12.5	110	849	19.7	4.2	78	713	24.9	3.5	98
50 OR OLDER	26027	2356	14.5	9.1	44	1361	14.9	5.2	46	620	14.4	2.4	44	376	13.1	1.4	40
GRADUATED COLLEGE	16071	3644	22.4	22.7	111	2012	22.1	12.5	110	1123	26.1	7.0	130	510	17.8	3.2	89
ATTENDED COLLEGE	14142	3759	23.1	26.6	131	2126	23.3	15.0	132	1013	23.5	7.2	133	621	21.7	4.4	123
GRADUATED HIGH SCHOOL	29230	5940	36.5	20.3	100	3251	35.7	11.1	98	1647	38.2	5.6	105	1043	36.4	3.6	100
DID NOT GRADUATE HIGH SCHOOL	20609	2944	18.1	14.3	70	1730	19.0	8.4	74	525	12.2	2.5	47	689	24.1	3.3	94
EMPLOYED FULL-TIME	53010	12366	75.9	23.3	115	6847	75.1	12.9	113	3464	80.4	6.5	121	2056	71.8	3.9	108
EMPLOYED PART-TIME	3754	989	6.1	26.3	129	608	6.7	16.2	142	183	4.2	4.9	91	198	6.9	5.3	148
NOT EMPLOYED	23288	2932	18.0	12.6	62	1663	18.2	7.1	63	661	15.3	2.8	53	609	21.3	2.6	73
PROFESSIONAL/MANAGER	15165	3441	21.1	22.7	112	1943	21.3	12.8	112	865	20.1	5.7	106	632	22.1	4.2	117
TECH/CLERICAL/SALES	11265	3048	18.7	27.1	133	1657	18.2	14.7	129	1036	24.1	9.2	171	355	12.4	3.2	88
PRECISION/CRAFT	11802	2862	17.6	24.3	119	1692	18.6	14.3	126	618	14.3	5.2	97	552	19.3	4.7	131
OTHER EMPLOYED	18531	4004	24.6	21.6	106	2163	23.7	11.7	102	1127	26.2	6.1	113	714	24.9	3.9	108
SINGLE	20270	5895	36.2	29.1	143	2901	31.8	14.3	126	1797	41.7	8.9	165	1197	41.8	5.9	165
MARRIED	51466	8705	53.4	16.9	83	5137	56.3	10.0	88	2152	50.0	4.2	78	1416	49.5	2.8	77
DIVORCED/SEPARATED/WIDOWED	8316	1688	10.4	20.3	100	1080	11.8	13.0	114	358	8.3	4.3	80	249	8.7	3.0	84
PARENTS	25528	5483	33.7	21.5	106	3210	35.2	12.6	110	1306	30.3	5.1	95	968	33.8	3.8	106
WHITE	70147	14272	87.6	20.3	100	8135	89.2	11.6	102	3786	87.9	5.4	100	2350	82.1	3.4	94
BLACK	8168	1744	10.7	21.4	105	821	9.0	10.1	88	454	10.5	5.6	103	469	16.4	5.7	161
OTHER	1737	271	1.7	15.6	77	162	1.8	9.3	82	67	1.6	3.9	72	43	1.5	2.5	69
NORTHEAST-CENSUS	17421	4269	26.2	24.5	120	2423	26.6	13.9	122	1009	23.4	5.8	108	838	29.3	4.8	135
NORTH CENTRAL	20153	3760	23.1	18.7	92	2338	25.6	11.6	102	954	22.1	4.7	88	468	16.4	2.3	65
SOUTH	27146	4891	30.0	18.0	89	2701	29.6	9.9	87	1269	29.5	4.7	87	921	32.2	3.4	95
WEST	15332	3367	20.7	22.0	108	1656	18.2	10.8	95	1075	25.0	7.0	130	635	22.2	4.1	116
NORTHEAST-MKTG.	18167	4184	25.7	23.0	113	2267	24.9	12.5	110	1057	24.5	5.8	108	860	30.0	4.7	132
EAST CENTRAL	11589	2291	14.1	19.8	97	1423	15.6	12.3	108	610	14.2	5.3	98	258	9.0	2.2	62
WEST CENTRAL	13425	2596	15.9	19.3	95	1615	17.7	12.0	106	658	15.3	4.9	91	323	11.3	2.4	67
SOUTH	23366	4245	26.1	18.2	89	2355	25.8	10.1	88	1060	24.6	4.5	84	830	29.0	3.6	99
PACIFIC	13505	2972	18.2	22.0	108	1459	16.0	10.8	95	923	21.4	6.8	127	590	20.6	4.4	122
COUNTY SIZE A	33290	7157	43.9	21.5	106	3996	43.8	12.0	105	2102	48.8	6.3	117	1059	37.0	3.2	89
COUNTY SIZE B	23935	4887	30.0	20.4	100	2718	29.8	11.4	100	1166	27.1	4.9	91	1003	35.0	4.2	117
COUNTY SIZE C	12125	2486	15.3	20.5	101	1322	14.5	10.9	96	667	15.5	5.5	102	497	17.4	4.1	115
COUNTY SIZE D	10702	1758	10.8	16.4	81	1082	11.9	10.1	89	373	8.7	3.5	65	303	10.6	2.8	79
METRO CENTRAL CITY	23602	5022	30.8	21.3	105	2819	30.9	11.9	105	1323	30.7	5.6	104	880	30.7	3.7	104
METRO SUBURBAN	37277	7804	47.9	20.9	103	4360	47.8	11.7	103	2082	48.3	5.6	104	1361	47.6	3.7	102
NON METRO	19173	3462	21.3	18.1	89	1939	21.3	10.1	89	902	20.9	4.7	87	621	21.7	3.2	91
TOP 5 ADI'S	17318	4268	26.2	24.6	121	2309	25.3	13.3	117	1208	28.0	7.0	130	751	26.2	4.3	121
TOP 10 ADI'S	24023	5364	32.9	22.3	110	2928	32.1	12.2	107	1556	36.1	6.5	120	879	30.7	3.7	102
TOP 20 ADI'S	34232	7289	44.8	21.3	105	4037	44.3	11.8	104	2164	50.2	6.3	117	1088	38.0	3.2	89
HSHLD INC. $50,000 OR MORE	11606	2949	18.1	25.4	125	1603	17.6	13.8	121	929	21.6	8.0	149	417	14.6	3.6	100
$40,000 OR MORE	20897	4823	29.6	23.1	113	2573	28.2	12.3	108	1469	34.1	7.0	131	781	27.3	3.7	105
$30,000 OR MORE	34400	7766	47.7	22.6	111	4216	46.2	12.3	108	2287	53.1	6.6	124	1263	44.1	3.7	103
$25,000 OR MORE	42807	9936	61.0	23.2	114	5462	59.9	12.8	112	2810	65.2	6.6	122	1665	58.2	3.9	109
$20,000 - $24,999	8606	1657	10.2	19.3	95	973	10.7	11.3	99	363	8.4	4.2	78	321	11.2	3.7	104
$15,000 - $19,999	7347	1342	8.2	18.3	90	874	9.6	11.9	104	256	5.9	3.5	65	213	7.4	2.9	81
$10,000 - $14,999	11021	1789	11.0	16.2	80	973	10.7	8.8	78	528	12.[illegible]	4.8	89	288	10.1	2.6	73
UNDER $10,000	10272	1563	9.6	15.2	75	836	9.2	8.1	71	351	8.1	3.4	64	376	13.1	3.7	102
HOUSEHOLD OF 1 PERSON	7531	1647	10.1	21.9	107	876	9.6	11.6	102	538	12.5	7.1	133	232	8.1	3.1	86
2 PEOPLE	25145	4035	24.8	16.0	79	2417	26.5	9.6	84	985	22.9	3.9	73	634	22.2	2.5	71
3 OR 4 PEOPLE	33306	7676	47.1	23.0	113	4346	47.7	13.0	115	2027	47.1	6.1	113	1302	45.5	3.9	109
5 OR MORE PEOPLE	14070	2930	18.0	20.8	102	1480	16.2	10.5	92	757	17.6	5.4	100	693	24.2	4.9	138
NO CHILD IN HSHLD	47711	8942	54.9	18.7	92	4952	54.3	10.4	91	2673	62.1	5.6	104	1317	46.0	2.8	77
CHILD(REN) UNDER 2 YRS	4809	1227	7.5	25.5	125	816	8.9	17.0	149	156	3.6	3.2	60	255	8.9	5.3	148
2 - 5 YEARS	11316	2647	16.3	23.4	115	1388	15.2	12.3	108	647	15.0	5.7	106	612	21.4	5.4	151
6 - 11 YEARS	14421	3094	19.0	21.5	105	1686	18.5	11.7	103	860	20.0	6.0	111	549	19.2	3.8	106
12 - 17 YEARS	16384	3611	22.2	22.0	108	1952	21.4	11.9	105	801	18.6	4.9	91	859	30.0	5.2	147
RESIDENCE OWNED	56689	10266	63.0	18.1	89	5837	64.0	10.3	90	2769	64.3	4.9	91	1661	58.0	2.9	82
VALUE: $60,000 OR MORE	29882	5679	34.9	19.0	93	3179	34.9	10.6	93	1656	38.4	5.5	103	844	29.5	2.8	79
VALUE: UNDER $60,000	26807	4587	28.2	17.1	84	2658	29.2	9.9	87	1112	25.8	4.1	77	816	28.5	3.0	85

FIGURE 3–1
A sample of the detailed research information available from Simmons Market Research Bureau (SMRB).

as to specific advertising situations. As a result, these sources have become very popular in the past few years.

Other Syndicated Market Researchers. Many other firms also provide syndicated market research information. For example, the annual *Survey of Buying Power* published by *Sales & Marketing Management* magazine helps companies prepare their budgets for various regions and cities. Another trade publication, *Editor & Publisher,* provides an annual *E&P Market Guide* with detailed information about every market where a daily newspaper is published.

Marketers can use this information to learn more about the cities where they want to sell their products or services.

You probably know the name A.C. Nielsen because of the television ratings service. But the A.C. Nielsen Company also provides data on how much a product and its competitors have actually sold in various markets. Selling Areas-Marketing, Inc. (SAMI) also provides this kind of data. Such information can help marketers decide how successful an item is and identify the parts of the country where it may need more advertising support.

Many other syndicated research services offer even more specific information to advertisers. We'll discuss them in later sections of this chapter. Much of this syndicated research helps advertisers keep track of advertising activities and spending of the competition.

Secondary Advertising Research

Learning about the competition is one of the most important steps in advertising research. Suppose you are planning an advertising campaign. Wouldn't you like to know the kinds of advertising that your competitors are using? Wouldn't you like to know when and where those advertisements appear and how much they cost?

You could try to find all your competitors' advertising yourself by searching through newspapers and magazines, watching lots of television, and listening to all the radio stations. You could drive around looking at billboards—watching and waiting for an advertisement from one of your competitors. But you would waste a lot of time and money and probably still miss some advertisements. You couldn't keep up with all the media at once, and you wouldn't have time for anything else.

Luckily, syndicated research firms provide a lot of information about the competition. You can subscribe to a research firm that will give you information on the newspaper, magazine, outdoor, television, and radio advertising that competitive firms are using. The materials you get will tell you about the cities where the advertisements are running, the number of times they are displayed, the media that carry them, and their estimated cost.

Research firms can keep track of your competitors because they watch, read, and listen to all the media for all advertisers—not just for one advertiser or even for the advertisers in one industry. They learn when advertisements appear, who the sponsor is, and how long or how large they are. Then they publish their findings for their subscribers to use. Probably the best-known advertising research firm is Leading National Advertisers (LNA), which tracks the competition in several advertising media (see Figure 3–2).

Many other sources offer syndicated advertising research information. They may provide information about cities and markets, consumers, or competitors. Some give the costs and technical information necessary to select an advertising medium and to place an advertisement. So syndicated research is a valuable advertising tool. It saves money and time and provides information that you probably would not be able to find in any other ways.

BAR/LNA MULTI-MEDIA SERVICE

CLASS/BRAND $

January - September 1988

CLASS/COMPANY/BRAND		CLASS CODE	QUARTERLY AND YEAR-TO-DATE ADVERTISING DOLLARS (000)									
			9-MEDIA TOTAL	LNA MAGAZINES	LNA NEWSPAPER SUPPLEMENTS	MEDIA RECORDS NEWSPAPERS	LNA OUTDOOR	BAR NETWORK TELEVISION	BAR SPOT TELEVISION	BAR SYNDICATED TELEVISION	BAR CABLE TV NETWORKS	BAR NETWORK RADIO
T111 PASSENGER CARS, DOMESTIC - - - CONTINUED												
GENERAL MOTORS CORP												
CADILLAC FLEETWOOD (CONTINUED)												
	88 YTD		**1,019.9**	**1,019.9**	- -	- -	- -	- -	- -	- -	- -	- -
	87 YTD		142.3	47.9	- -	- -	- -	- -	94.4	- -	- -	- -
CADILLAC PASSENGER CARS		T111										
	Q1		4,196.0	387.5	- -	72.1	16.4	2,556.1	1,158.9	- -	5.0	- -
	Q2		6,903.2	78.1	- -	38.3	- -	4,741.1	1,979.4	- -	66.3	- -
	Q3		1,296.0	- -	- -	611.7	16.4	155.0	462.5	- -	50.4	- -
	88 YTD		**12,395.2**	**465.6**	- -	**722.1**	**32.8**	**7,452.2**	**3,600.8**	- -	**121.7**	- -
	87 YTD		2,042.2	- -	- -	1,220.1	0.3	632.5	84.4	- -	104.9	- -
CADILLAC SEDAN DE VILLE		T111										
	Q1		20.9	- -	- -	- -	- -	- -	20.9	- -	- -	- -
	Q2		44.5	- -	- -	- -	- -	- -	44.5	- -	- -	- -
	Q3		386.0	- -	- -	- -	- -	- -	386.0	- -	- -	- -
	88 YTD		**451.4**	- -	- -	- -	- -	- -	**451.4**	- -	- -	- -
	87 YTD		2,348.4	67.5	- -	- -	- -	1,974.2	136.1	- -	170.6	- -
CADILLAC SEVILLE		T111										
	Q1		97.7	97.7	- -	- -	- -	- -	- -	- -	- -	- -
	Q2		932.6	929.9	- -	- -	- -	- -	0.6	- -	2.1	- -
	Q3		486.3	- -	- -	- -	- -	465.0	20.8	- -	0.5	- -
	88 YTD		**1,516.6**	**1,027.6**	- -	- -	- -	**465.0**	**21.4**	- -	**2.6**	- -
	87 YTD		2,985.2	486.0	- -	- -	- -	2,305.7	4.2	- -	189.3	- -
CADILLAC SEVILLE & SEDAN DE VILLE		T111										
	Q1		73.4	73.4	- -	- -	- -	- -	- -	- -	- -	- -
	88 YTD		**73.4**	**73.4**	- -	- -	- -	- -	- -	- -	- -	- -
	87 YTD		117.2	117.2	- -	- -	- -	- -	- -	- -	- -	- -
CHEVROLET BERETTA		T111										
	Q1		3,068.6	648.6	- -	178.2	0.2	670.9	1,524.4	- -	46.3	- -
	Q2		6,313.4	815.7	756.6	205.4	2.6	2,488.6	1,841.2	63.3	140.0	- -
	Q3		4,238.9	568.2	132.5	78.5	6.5	2,293.5	1,036.5	100.4	22.8	- -
	88 YTD		**13,620.9**	**2,032.5**	**889.1**	**462.1**	**9.3**	**5,453.0**	**4,402.1**	**163.7**	**209.1**	- -
	87 YTD		23,929.1	8,965.0	- -	633.3	617.2	11,745.9	1,299.7	161.8	506.2	- -
CHEVROLET BERETTA & CORSICA		T111										
	Q1		754.0	241.1	- -	- -	- -	335.5	149.9	- -	27.5	- -
	Q2		159.0	150.1	- -	- -	- -	- -	8.9	- -	- -	- -
	Q3		117.7	- -	- -	- -	- -	- -	117.7	- -	- -	- -
	88 YTD		**1,030.7**	**391.2**	- -	- -	- -	**335.5**	**276.5**	- -	**27.5**	- -
	87 YTD		1,017.7	72.3	- -	944.7	0.6	- -	0.1	- -	- -	- -
CHEVROLET CAMARO		T111										
	Q1		703.7	283.8	- -	- -	1.3	73.3	321.0	- -	24.3	- -
	Q2		1,320.7	396.0	- -	246.5	1.1	431.5	205.5	- -	40.1	- -
	Q3		1,946.0	- -	- -	- -	0.4	1,175.8	768.7	- -	1.1	- -
	88 YTD		**3,970.4**	**679.8**	- -	**246.5**	**2.8**	**1,680.6**	**1,295.2**	- -	**65.5**	- -
	87 YTD		2,165.0	407.1	- -	21.5	25.1	613.7	1,058.4	- -	39.2	- -
CHEVROLET CAPRICE		T111										
	Q1		515.5	294.0	- -	51.9	- -	77.5	78.4	- -	13.7	- -
	Q2		1,410.9	547.1	- -	113.6	- -	615.2	135.0	- -	- -	- -
	Q3		260.9	85.2	- -	16.8	- -	115.1	43.8	- -	- -	- -
	88 YTD		**2,187.3**	**926.3**	- -	**182.3**	- -	**807.8**	**257.2**	- -	**13.7**	- -
	87 YTD		931.6	797.7	- -	132.0	1.2	- -	0.7	- -	- -	- -
CHEVROLET CAPRICE & CELEBRITY		T111										
	Q1		2.0	- -	- -	- -	- -	- -	2.0	- -	- -	- -
	Q3		5.4	- -	- -	- -	- -	- -	5.4	- -	- -	- -
	88 YTD		**7.4**	- -	- -	- -	- -	- -	**7.4**	- -	- -	- -
CHEVROLET CAVALIER		T111										
	Q1		10,487.1	2,584.4	- -	79.1	159.7	6,382.3	1,143.2	53.6	84.8	- -
	Q2		9,535.3	2,636.2	- -	148.6	326.3	4,888.0	1,363.5	82.4	90.3	- -
	Q3		4,318.9	607.9	- -	- -	60.2	2,388.9	1,245.9	- -	16.0	- -
	88 YTD		**24,341.3**	**5,828.5**	- -	**227.7**	**546.2**	**13,659.2**	**3,752.6**	**136.0**	**191.1**	- -
	87 YTD		8,342.5	2,582.1	90.5	619.5	16.9	1,702.1	3,315.7	- -	15.7	- -
CHEVROLET CAVALIER & CELEBRITY		T111										
	Q1		768.8	- -	- -	- -	- -	477.4	255.9	- -	35.5	- -
---- CONTINUED ----												

FOOTNOTE: 1987 YTD EXPENDITURES INCLUDE ONLY THOSE BRANDS ACTIVE IN 1988.

FIGURE 3–2
This kind of syndicated research provides information about competitors' spending on advertising. Courtesy BAR/LNA Multi-Media Service as compiled and published by Leading National Advertisers, Inc.

PRIMARY RESEARCH

Many times the information you need will not be available from books, journals, or syndicated research. Then you will need to conduct your own research or hire someone to do it for you. Primary research that you hire a research firm to do specifically for you is called **nonsyndicated research.**

nonsyndicated research Primary research that you hire someone to do specifically for you.

But either way, primary research can be expensive and time-consuming. In secondary research, the results are already there—you just have to find or buy them. In primary research, you or the agency you hire will have to conduct a study and *get* the results.

However, the information you gain from primary research can be vital to the success of your advertising campaign. For example, if you're developing new or improved products, there may not *be* any useful facts available from secondary sources. In a case like this, the extra time and money spent on primary research can be well worth it.

But should you do it yourself or hire someone else to do it? In the real world, even very experienced advertisers and agencies usually hire outside experts to conduct their research. The reason is that these experts are skilled *and* objective. Non-syndicated research may cost money, but it can be money well spent if it saves a company from making costly mistakes in conducting its own research. Most Yellow Pages directories list lots of research agencies to help in this critical work.

In the rest of this section, we'll talk about research *you* do, but remember that agencies often do it *for* you.

Primary research is usually needed at any of three times during an advertising campaign:

1. Before the advertising campaign begins.
2. During the preparation of the advertising.
3. After the advertising is ready.

Research before the Campaign Begins

Any research you do before an advertising campaign begins usually involves the product or service itself, the people who are likely to buy it, or the markets where you want to sell it. You do this research before you prepare your advertising to get the background information you need. For example, you could ask consumers how they would use a new personal computer. This information could give you ideas for promotions to add to your advertisements.

product or service research Research to find out if consumers have needs and wants that items already on the market do not satisfy or if consumers who already use a product would like a newly developed version.

Product or Service Research. The purpose of **product or service research** is to find out if consumers have needs or wants that items already on the market do not satisfy or if customers who already use a product would like a newly developed version. The problem with the first kind of research is that consumers don't usually know they want a new product before it is available.

Few people ever thought they wanted instant coffee, for example, until it was sold in stores. What was wrong with regular coffee, people wondered, and why would we ever need instant? Then they listened to people who had tried it and heard about its taste, convenience, and economical price. And suddenly people realized that they had wanted instant coffee all along, but just didn't know it.

You can imagine how hard it is to get consumers to guess what their needs and wants will be in the future. Try to do it yourself. Think of some item that is not now available or of an improvement in some current item. Or try to write down what you would like in a new automobile if you buy one ten years from now. Do you suppose that people who were brought up to want big luxury cars would have said, back in the early 1970s, that they would someday want smaller and more economical cars?

It is also hard to find out if people who already use a product would like a newly developed version. In this case, the new development must already exist so that consumers can test it—so this kind of research cannot really help us come up with the ideas for new products and services and for improvements in current items.

Once we find out what features of a new product consumers like best, we can highlight them in our advertisements. Suppose you think the best feature of a new powdered soft-drink mix you are selling is its price. But product research shows that the good flavor is the selling point.

positioning Portraying a product or service in the consumers' minds.

This kind of information can help you portray or "position" your product or service in the consumers' minds. This is called **positioning.** For example, Seven-Up is positioned as a caffeine-free beverage that competes with but is different from colas.

consumer research Research that tries to find out what people are going to buy and why; it also finds out what consumers think about a product they already use.

Consumer Research. **Consumer research** tries to find out what people are going to buy and why. It can also tell us what consumers think about our products and services. We may then want to design our advertising to change their views. This kind of research is very complex because people often do not know why they buy a product or use a service. In fact, consumers often fool themselves. They may not want to admit that they are buying a new car to keep up with their neighbors or to look sporty when they drive down the street, so they tell themselves that they need a car that is more economical and efficient instead.

mall intercepts Interviews with consumers in shopping malls.

One way to collect consumer research information is through **mall intercepts,** in which an interviewer asks questions of customers in shopping malls. This information is quick and easy to collect. But these shoppers may not represent the population as a whole.

focus group interview An interview with a small group of consumers familiar with the product.

Another type of consumer research is the **focus group interview.** In it, an interviewer asks a small group of consumers who are familiar with the product questions designed to start a discussion. The aim is to learn opinions that may help prepare advertising that will take into account the views of past and present customers.

Some consumer research involves **projective techniques.** These research methods, borrowed from psychology and sociology, are supposed to find out how a consumer who is answering research questions would act in some situation. For instance, one projective technique would try to learn how a consumer would act in a store where two competing products are for sale. Figures 3–3 and 3–4 are examples of projective techniques used in advertising.

projective techniques Research techniques designed to see how a consumer would act in a specific situation.

Market Research. The other major kind of research advertisers do before the campaign is **market research.** We've already discussed secondary market research. Here we're talking about *primary* or original market research. But it has the same purpose: finding out about the kinds of people who live in certain cities or regions and the kinds of jobs, industries, and salaries available there. Information like this tells us how well our products and services are likely to sell in each market. Because it involves so much traveling and dealing with so many items of information, advertisers usually rely on syndicated research.

market research Investigation into the product, distribution, price or promotion for a proposed marketing or advertising effort.

Research during Advertising Preparation

It is hard to conduct research during an advertising campaign because we need to pay attention to so many other constantly changing factors. However, a few research tests used during preparation can help us learn whether we are on the right track.

Some tests work only when we have already prepared a trial advertisement. Until the trial advertisements are actually prepared, they cannot be tested. And we may not be able to wait until the entire campaign is finished, because that may be too late: Tests performed at this point can find problems or mistakes that we can correct before the entire campaign is finished. This makes our advertisements as effective as possible.

Ranking Tests. In a **ranking test,** we ask consumers to put several advertisements in order from best liked to least liked. We can ask them to rank several possible versions of a single advertisement, several possible advertisements for a single campaign, or several different advertisements for a variety of products or services, including the one under study.

ranking test A test in which consumers rank advertisements from best liked to least liked.

A ranking test tells us how much consumers like an advertisement. But that may not be as important as finding out if the advertisement will bring people into stores or make sales. Most of the time the goal of an advertisement is not just to please readers or listeners, but to communicate and sell as well. So a ranking test may not show how effective an advertisement will be. Only the actual use of an advertisement can prove that it works.

Paired Comparison Tests. People usually find it hard to rank several items at once. To make the task easier, we sometimes change the ranking test technique slightly by having consumers look at only two advertisements at a time. We still use the same overall number, but we match up every advertisement

FIGURE 3–3
This is an example of a projective technique used in advertising research. Try projecting yourself into the role of one of the persons in the drawing.

FIGURE 3–4
This is another example of a projective technique. Tell what *you* think is happening here.

with every other advertisement one at a time. This is called **paired comparison.** It often takes more time than a ranking test, but it more accurately shows how consumers really feel.

paired comparison A test in which consumers rank pairs of advertisements.

Cloze Procedure. Another useful test for advertising that is being prepared involves the principle of "closure," borrowed from psychology. According to this principle, the way people "close" a sentence with missing words tells us how effective the message is. The test based on the closure principle is called a **cloze procedure.** In it we show consumers an advertising message with some words left out and ask them to fill in what they think the missing words are. If people can fill in the missing words accurately, the advertisement is supposed to convey its message well. (See Figure 3–5.)

cloze procedure A test in which consumers fill in the missing words of an advertisement.

A. Fill in the missing words in this advertisement.

"These distinctive works of art will add ________ to your home. You'll be ________ to display them and every time you ________ them you'll ________."

B Supply the brand name that is related to each of these advertising slogans:

"Where America Shops."

"____ adds life."

"The un-cola."

"Wouldn't you really rather have a ____?"

"We put a little blue jean in everything we make."

C What brand name do you associate with each of these shapes?

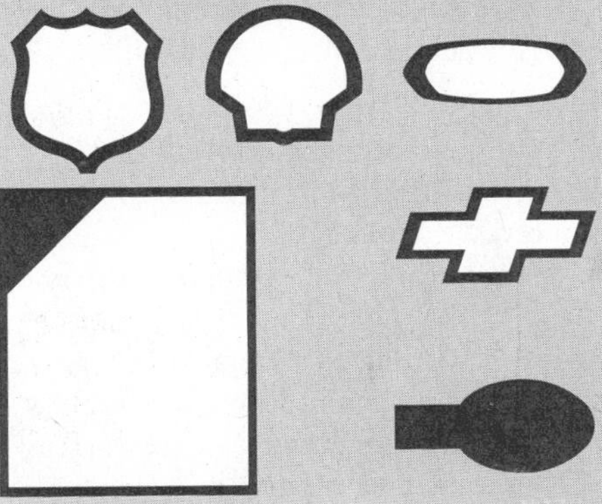

FIGURE 3–5
This cloze procedure is used in advertising to find out how well various parts of ideas communicate. The consumer is asked to provide the missing parts of the message. (Some of the items portrayed are portions of registered trademarks.)

There is a problem with this procedure, however. If consumers can fill in the missing words without much difficulty, the advertisement may just be trite. Perhaps it was so easy because it communicated no new information.

copy test A test that checks readability and comprehension in the words of an advertisement.

theater test A test that shows a TV commercial in preparation to a sample audience.

Copy and Theater Tests. The final types of research advertisers do during the development of the advertising are copy tests or theater tests. In a **copy test,** words the advertiser wants to use in the advertisement are checked for readability or comprehension. (The words in an advertisement are called the "copy.") This shows how easy or hard it is to read and understand the message.

Some copy tests use a sample audience. Readers or listeners are asked what impressions they got from the advertising copy. If any problems arise, the advertiser can change the copy to make it clearer or easier to understand.

Advertisers preparing television commercials use sample audiences, too. They show people an advertisement and see how they react. This is called a **theater test.** The commercial doesn't work exactly the way it would in real life, but it can provide useful insights into audience reactions.

Research after the Advertising Is Ready

pretest A test conducted before a completed advertisement is made public.

posttest A test conducted after an advertisement has been made public.

Much of our research is done after the advertising has been prepared, when it is ready to be run in the media as well as after it appears. Many of these studies are before-and-after tests, with a **pretest** to determine the situation before the advertising begins and a **posttest** to find out what changes occurred during the advertising campaign. In pretests, we are trying to find out how effective the advertising campaign may turn out to be. Will it meet its objectives? Will it bring more customers into the store? Will it help sell the product, service, or idea? Will it change consumers' opinions about the items? In posttests, we want to learn how effective the advertisement really *was*. How many persons saw or read the advertisement? How much of the advertisement did they pay attention to? How should the advertising effort be adjusted or changed?

No single research test can answer all these questions. You will need a specific goal for each test, as well as a specific research method, to answer these questions. We have a variety of techniques that we can use.

recognition test A test to find out if consumers have seen an advertisement before.

Recognition Tests. In a **recognition test** advertisers show an advertisement in a publication to consumers and ask if they remember seeing it before. Problems may arise here. We do not know for certain *where* consumers may have seen an advertisement before. Also consumers may confuse one advertisement with another. As a result, their answers may not be completely accurate.

The oldest and most widely used recognition test is conducted by Daniel Starch and Staff. These Starch tests, a sample of which is shown in Figure 3–6, are recognition studies of magazine advertisements. They give information on what percentage of the audience saw parts of a print advertisement. You will learn more about how to use them later in this book.

Courtesy of Revlon Inc., and of Daniel Starch and Staff.

FIGURE 3–6
This research shows what percentage of the readers remember paying attention to each part of this advertisement. It is an example of the Starch recognition test.

recall test A test in which the researcher names the place where an advertisement appeared and the consumer must describe the advertisements he or she remembers seeing there.

Recall Tests. A **recall test** may be more accurate than a recognition test because it makes consumers prove that they really saw an advertisement. In it, the tester names the place where the advertisement appeared and has the consumer describe any advertisement that he or she remembers seeing there.

For instance, the research may show the consumer the front cover of a magazine and ask what advertisements he or she remembers from that publication. This test can be used with broadcast media as well. The researcher names a television program and asks consumers to describe the advertisements they saw during that program. The Burke Day-After Recall test is widely used for this purpose.

If the consumer cannot remember very many advertisements, the researcher may help by mentioning certain product categories and letting the consumer name the particular item advertised and describe the advertisement. If prompting occurs, it is called an **aided recall test**. If no help is given, it is called an **unaided recall test.**

aided recall test A recall test where the respondent may be helped by the interviewer, usually by prompting responses.

unaided recall test A recall test where the respondent receives no help from the interviewer.

Both the recognition and the recall tests can be used to find out how many people have seen either print or broadcast advertisements, how many people read or watched the advertisement, and what portion of the advertisement each person read or watched. A recall test can also show if our advertising is promising more than our product can deliver, misleading the consumer, or missing the main selling points. To do this, we merely ask people what the advertisement led them to believe the product would do for them and see if this is what we were trying to say in the advertisement.

A well-known recall test conducted by Gallup and Robinson estimates the percentage of the audience that remembers an advertisement. The findings this company publishes include actual comments made by the respondents, which can provide additional insights into an advertisment's effectiveness.

awareness test A test to see if people know a product or service is for sale.

Awareness Tests. If we want to find out how many people in the audience know that a product or service is for sale, we can use an **awareness test.** This is especially useful for new products and services and for items that have been greatly changed or improved. It would probably help to find out how many people know about the item before the advertising begins and then compare that with the percentage who are aware of it after the advertising campaign has been run. It is possible to use only follow-up awareness tests, too, just to find out if the target groups know that the product is for sale.

top-of-head recognition An awareness test that asks what brand name comes to mind when a certain product or service category is mentioned.

The most common awareness test is the **top-of-head recognition.** For example, the researcher asks what brand name comes to mind when a certain product or service category is mentioned. Consumers are most aware of the brand names that are mentioned most.

knowledge test A test to find out how much consumers know about a product or service.

Knowledge Tests. You may want to go further than an awareness test by finding out how much consumers know about a product or service. To do this, you would use a **knowledge test.**

This kind of test has questions designed to find out how much consumers know about certain features of a product or about stores where the item is for sale. For example, if a consumer has seen an advertisement for a certain product, the researcher may ask what product features the consumer is aware of and what these features mean for the user of the product.

Association Tests. To find out if consumers have mentally connected the advertising and the item for sale, you can use an **association test.** This may be the most important test of all. Knowing that you saw an advertisement for shampoo is not enough; the advertiser wants you to connect the advertising with the features and with the brand names.

association test A test to find out if consumers connect the advertising with the item for sale.

For example, the researcher might ask, "Which local store has a free parking lot located only twenty feet from its back entrance?" A consumer who can supply the name of the store has associated the message with the selling points and store name.

Tracking Studies. To measure changes over a period of time, we can use a **tracking study.** We may try to track changes in attitudes or opinions, increases in knowledge, or the amount of advertising seen before purchase. This type of test is used because it takes time for advertising to have an effect and for consumers to absorb the information in advertisements.

tracking study A study that shows changes over a period of time.

Problems in Conducting Research

This chapter should give you a good idea of the kinds of primary research that advertisers often use. But researchers must be very careful. Conducting good, accurate, useful research is both an art and a science, and it requires a lot of practice and effort.

You will need to use a statistical formula to decide on the number of people to interview. And you will also need to consider a variety of other factors. Where and how you ask questions can change the answers people give. The wording of questions can lead people to answer a certain way, letting bias enter the research process. The pattern of questions, the order of topics covered, and the stated purpose of the research all can affect the responses. Even your tone of voice can change the way people answer a question.

Doing research is not easy. You can make plenty of mistakes. And, worse, if you do not know that you have made a mistake, you may have to rely on inaccurate and misleading findings.

And, finally, whether you conduct your own research or use research findings from some other source, be careful how you interpret the results. It is hard to measure how effective your advertising has been; nobody really knows if consumers bought the item because they read about it in an advertisement, heard about it from a friend, or were convinced by a good salesperson. And maybe the salesperson did a better job because the advertising inspired confidence in the product.

Just exactly what contributes to the total selling effort is a problem that has not yet been resolved. Keep that in mind when you use research in advertising. You will learn more about how these research methods are applied to various advertising situations and problems when you read later chapters.

SUMMARY

Remember that basic research is essential to understand the general way in which things work and happen but that advertising more often uses applied research, which relates to a particular emphasis or application. If secondary research is available, it can save time, money, and effort; but primary research is also used in advertising.

Syndicated research information can provide answers more quickly to advertising research questions. Of course, other advertisers may also be using the same syndicated sources of information, so conducting your own nonsyndicated research may provide information that only you have or information that applies to your particular problem or situation.

Advertising research goes on throughout the advertising process: before the advertising is prepared, during the preparation of the advertising, after the advertising is prepared but before it is shown to the general public, and then after the entire advertising campaign has run its course. There are particular problems that can occur during each of these stages in the advertising research process.

TERMS TO KNOW

Now that you have finished this chapter, you should understand the following terms:

research
basic research
applied research
primary research
secondary research
syndicated research
product or service research
positioning
consumer research
mall intercepts
focus group interview
projective techniques
ranking test
paired comparison
cloze procedure
copy test
theater test
pretest
posttest
recognition test
recall test
aided recall test
unaided recall test
awareness test
top-of-head recognition
knowledge test
association test
tracking study

If you are not certain of the meaning of any of these terms, go back through the chapter and review them.

THINGS TO THINK ABOUT

1. What differences can you see between the kinds of information that you can gather with research *before* the advertising begins, *during* the advertising, and *after* the advertising effort?
2. Why is it easier to use syndicated research than to do your own research?
3. Why is it important to find out what the competition may be doing in its advertising?
4. How does market research differ from consumer research? How do both of them differ from product research?

THINGS TO TALK ABOUT

1. What advertising information sources could you use for different advertising purposes? How might someone who writes advertisements use consumer information differently from someone who selects media for the advertisements?
2. Why is it hard to find out how successful an advertisement has been?
3. What are the shortcomings of recognition and recall types of tests?
4. Why do you suppose many advertisers and advertising agencies do little of their own research?

THINGS TO DO

1. Check in your school library and find out what advertising and marketing information sources are available. Make a list of those that you can find, and let the entire class consult it.
2. Visit a local advertising agency (or an advertising department of a large company) and find out what advertising information sources are used there.

4 Constraints

Ludicrous Laws.

Put a smile on your face when you pass through Pocatello, Idaho. Because it's against the law to frown or look gloomy.

In Raton, New Mexico, it's against the law for a woman to ride horseback down the street while wearing a kimono.

Believe it or not, it's against the law for any team to beat the Arizona Wildcats on their home ground in Tucson, Arizona.*

The Outdated Laws That Regulate Banking Aren't So Funny.

A lot of these old-time laws are really good for a laugh, and no one gets hurt. But there are others that can cause serious consequences.

For instance, look at the archaic laws that prevent banks from really competing to serve the needs of today's customers. These laws have long outlived their reasons for being. Some go back more than 50 years.

Recently, you have begun to notice many changes in the financial services marketplace. Everyone seems to be getting into banking. Insurance companies, brokers, even retailers are aggressively selling what used to be banking products. But banks are prohibited from fighting back.

Unless banks are soon permitted to offer a fully competitive range of financial services, their capabilities could be undermined to the point where they can no longer effectively serve their home communities.

From the smallest towns to the largest cities, it has always been the home-town banks that have financed most of the growth.

Agriculture, trade, transportation, manufacturing, construction, municipal projects, and even the various levels of government have always turned to their local banks for economic participation and leadership. Unfortunately, most of the new competitors have no similar commitments to, or even interest in, this aspect of banking.

Besides that, you as a consumer will be denied the benefits that could come with increased competition.

*Some of these inane laws may have been changed.

1120 Connecticut Avenue, N.W.
Washington, D.C. 20036

American Bankers Association

CHAPTER OUTLINE

By the time you finish this chapter, you should understand:

1. That advertisers cannot do just anything they want.
2. The role of economics in advertising.
3. The influence of advertising on competition, costs, prices, and profits.
4. Advertising's role in politics, society, and the mass media.
5. The special problems of advertising to children.
6. The problems of ethics and truth in advertising.
7. Governmental regulation of advertising.
8. Internal regulation of advertising.

Our third *C* stands for **constraints,** the factors that limit and regulate the practice of advertising. Like any other public activity, advertising affects society and is in turn affected by it in many ways. Each of these relationships forms constraints that keep advertisers from doing just anything they want. In this chapter, we shall discuss four kinds of constraints: economic, social, ethical, and regulatory.

ECONOMIC CONSTRAINTS

Economic constraints define and limit the role of advertising in our country. The first and most important economic constraint is **competition,** the contest between rival companies for the consumer's business. The economic system of the United States is based on competition to develop new products and services and to sell, price, and promote the products and services that are in the market. A few industries, such as electric power and local telephone, do not compete; they are regulated by the government. Most companies, however, compete with the other companies within their industries. General Motors competes with Ford, Chrysler, and other automobile manufacturers; Safeway competes with A&P, Kroger, and many smaller grocery operations.

Does Advertising Help Create Monopolies?

The opposite of competition is **monopoly,** which occurs when one company has the only product on the market or when only one company serves a certain area with some kind of product or service. For example, a firm that markets a new product has a temporary monopoly until other firms develop competing products and offer them for sale.

Some critics have said that advertising creates monopolies. They charge that advertising makes consumers prefer a certain brand or item over all competing items by showing how it is better than its competitors. And, they say, if people prefer an item exclusively, the firm that produces it has a monopoly. These same critics believe that the use of a brand name leads to a form of monopoly because no competing firm can use that same brand name.

But *does* advertising create monopolies? Probably not. Advertising appears to work just as hard to fight monopolies as it does to create them. Advertisers with leading brands may try to get everyone to use their products, but advertisers with competing brands will try at the same time to show that their products are just as good. In other words, advertising lets all marketers—competitors as well as market leaders—promote products and communicate information to consumers.[1] As a result, efforts for and against monopoly tend to balance out.

product differentiation Offering a variety of products that differ from those of the competition.

A competitive economy can work only if consumers have a lot of information about the products, services, and ideas offered in the marketplace. And advertising is one of the best ways to deliver this information. So advertising strongly supports the competitive economic system used in the United States. If you decide you want to start a new shoe store and there is already one in town that has all the local business, how would you compete? You would advertise, of course! And you might offer a variety of brands that differ from your competition—what we call **product differentiation.**

Does Competition Mean Wastefulness?

The critics of advertising also say that advertising is wasteful and the resources given to it should be used for other purposes—especially because advertising spends so much time and effort telling the same people the same messages over and over. But, in fact, people tend to forget what they have heard, new customers enter the marketplace, people move into a town who do not know about the stores there, and new services and products are introduced. So not all the repetition in advertising is wasted.[2]

Sometimes advertisements may cost too much or be used too many times. But keep in mind that advertisers can also make mistakes in exactly the opposite way: Some firms may not spend enough on advertising to achieve their goals, and some advertisements may not appear often enough.

The critics of wastefulness in advertising are really attacking the basic competitive process itself. Any competition may involve some waste and duplication, but it may also provide more choices to the consumers. The inefficiencies in advertising are very easy to see, but there is a lot of wastefulness in our economy that does not involve advertising: too much inventory in a warehouse; three or four gas stations at one major intersection; the ability to manufacture more steel than we can consume or more electric power than we need to survive.[3] Advertising does not cause this kind of waste.

[1] Jules Backman, *Advertising and Competition* (New York: New York University Press, 1967), 52–59.
[2] Backman, *Advertising and Competition*, 28–34.
[3] Neil H. Borden, *The Economic Effects of Advertising* (Chicago: Richard D. Irwin, Inc., 1942), 484–88.

Should society try to control waste in advertising? If so, who should have the power to make these decisions for us? In America, we have decided that consumers should decide which products and services should succeed and which should fail. They do this by either buying or not buying an item offered for sale. If we allow some regulatory agency to make these decisions, we are taking away a basic right of consumers. Why? Because it's advertising that

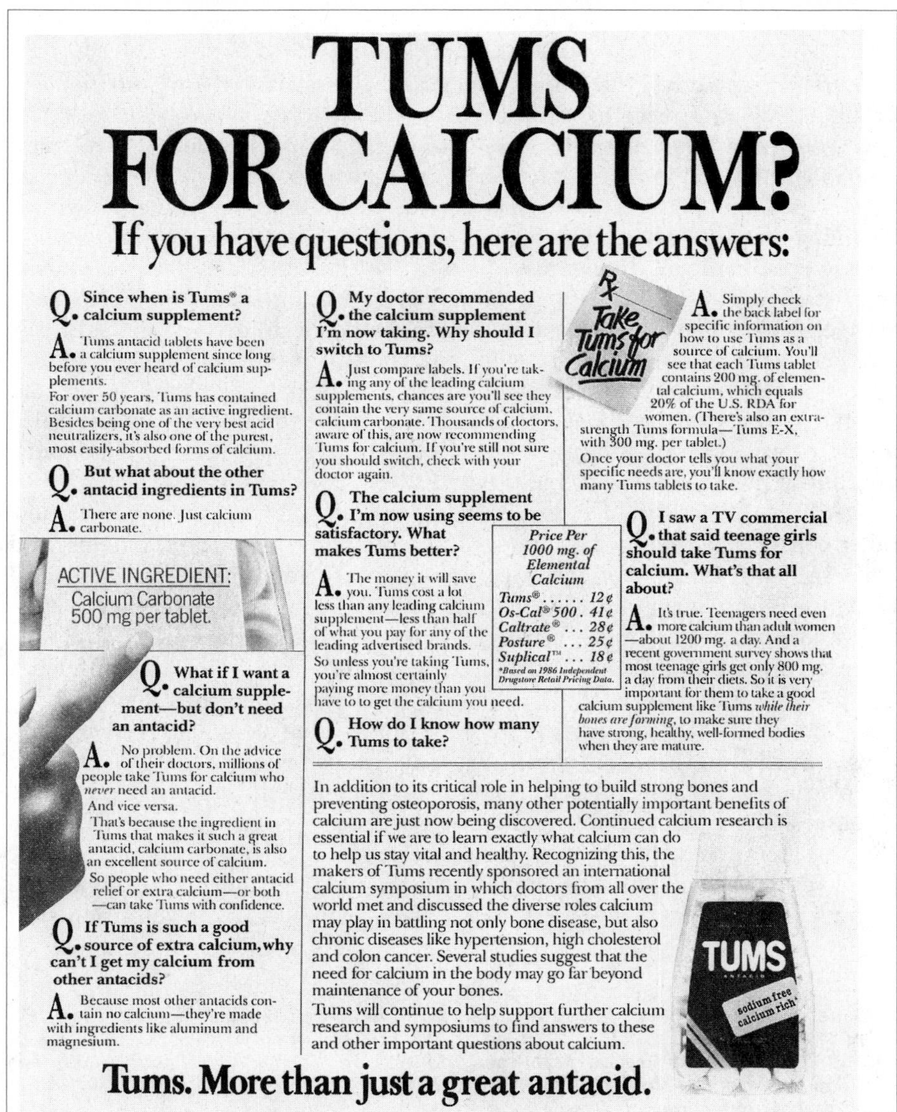

FIGURE 4–1
From this advertisement, the reader can learn a great deal about the product. Because it teaches new ways to use the product, it adds value.

lets people know what products and services are for sale and how each one is unique.

Also, if we limit advertising, we may limit the number of new items on the market because advertising plays a vital role in the introduction of new and improved services and goods. It took several years of promoting instant coffee before many consumers started to use it; the same was true of frozen foods.[4] In fact, before most new products enter the marketplace, consumers have rarely known that they wanted them.

Does Advertising Add Value and Utility?

added value The worth added to an item by a particular process.

added utility Value added to an item in the form of new uses.

consumer's gain More value and utility than existed with the product's basic uses.

Manufacturing adds value to raw materials by turning them into finished products. When a piece of wood becomes a chair or iron ore becomes steel, it is worth more than it was before. This is called **added value.** Advertising also adds value to products and services by showing more ways to use a product or gain the most value from a service (see Figure 4–1). Faced with a declining market for home baking supplies, researchers at the Arm & Hammer baking soda company found new ways to use their product. Advertisements then showed consumers how an open box of baking soda could help keep refrigerators and kitchen drains smelling fresh and clean, deodorize pets' areas, and help condition the water in swimming pools. These advertisements helped add value to the baking soda by showing consumers more ways to use the product. Value that has been added to an item in the form of new uses is called **added utility.**[5] Added utility can bring **consumer's gain,** that is, more value and utility than existed with the product's basic uses.

Advertising may add value in other ways, too. By showing people how other consumers feel about an item, how it compares to competing items, and what special features it offers, advertising can provide valuable psychological benefits. People may gain a feeling of security in knowing that they have a well-known brand of smoke alarm in their homes, for example, or that they drive a respected make of automobile. This additional feeling of confidence can be more useful to consumers than any other sort of added value.[6]

Consumers may, of course, lose some of the value of an item if advertising causes them to throw away something that still has good use left just to buy a replacement.[7] If a useful item is completely discarded, there is a real loss of resources. But often the old item is not discarded; instead, it is traded in on the new item, sold, or given to someone who can still make good use of it. People do not usually discard an old car when they buy a new one; they trade it in and the dealer resells it. The same thing may occur with television sets,

[4] "General Foods Is Five Billion Particulars," *Fortune* (March 1964), 117.

[5] Paul A. Samuelson, *Economics*, 12th ed. (New York: McGraw-Hill, 1985), 108.

[6] C. H. Sandage and Vernon Fryburger, *Advertising Theory and Practice*, 9th ed. (Homewood, Ill.: Richard D. Irwin, 1975), 39.

[7] Backman, *Advertising and Competition,* 143.

typewriters, sewing machines, and similar items that are still useful enough to be valuable to someone else.

Does Advertising Raise Costs?

Critics also charge that advertising increases the cost of producing services and products. If companies advertise a lot, they reason, they must pass along their advertising costs to consumers. But advertising does not necessarily increase costs. Sometimes it even lowers them.

One way to reduce costs is by making—and selling—large numbers of the same kind of product. That way you can spread production and selling costs across more items. When each unit has to bear fewer of the costs involved, you can sell it for less and still get back the money you spent to make and sell it. This is called an **economy of scale**—the ability to lower the cost of an item by increasing the number of items produced and sold. This is true even though increased production may *raise* overall costs, because the profits from sales will always rise faster than the costs of production.

economy of scale The ability to lower the cost of an item by increasing the number of items produced and sold.

And what method do companies use to increase their sales so that they can increase production and benefit from an economy of scale? Most of them use advertising, because it is the best way to reach large groups of potential customers. By bringing in more sales and helping to increase productivity, then, advertising can actually reduce costs.[8]

You should also remember that advertising is just *one* way of promoting a product. If a company decides not to advertise, it will promote its product in another way. So the money saved by not advertising will go toward another means of promotion.[9] In fact, other promotional methods usually cost more than advertising does. Therefore, since advertising generally does not raise costs as much as its alternatives would, it really helps to keep costs low.

Do We Pay Higher Prices Because of Advertising?

Many people argue that advertising causes the prices we pay for goods and services to be higher than they would be without advertising. We have already seen how advertising helps to reduce the costs of production in most cases, but even if advertising *does* sometimes raise the cost of producing an item, it may not raise the price people actually pay. Let's look at the factors that a company must consider when it sets a price for its services or products:

1. The value consumers will place on the item is the most important consideration.
2. The prices charged by the competition for similar replacement items are next in importance.

---

[8] Backman, *Advertising and Competition*, 120.
[9] Backman, *Advertising and Competition*, 120.

3. Public demand for the item comes next: The greater the demand, the higher the price.
4. The costs of producing the item are in the middle of the list. They include advertising costs, but these are only a small percentage of overall costs. Others are the costs of production, raw materials, labor, profit margins, and other marketing and promotional efforts. So even if costs greatly influenced prices, advertising costs would play a relatively small role. For most businesses, costs are not very high on the list. The exception would be for retailers, who often base the selling price of an item on its cost.
5. The way the item is distributed also affects prices. The more steps there are in the distribution process, the more expensive the item may be. The type of store that sells the item may be important, too: The same item may sell for less in a discount store than it does in a full-service department store.
6. Various political and legal factors also affect prices. For example, if a company sets a very low price, it may gain a monopolistic position, which is discouraged by the federal government.
7. Public relations is the last pricing factor. The price level will affect the public's image of the company.[10]

Of course, the importance of each factor may vary with the particular service or product or the specific company involved, but this list gives a good idea of all the factors that affect price. The key idea to remember is that advertising costs are only a small part of overall costs, and overall costs are only one of many factors in pricing.

Some people, however, argue that advertising brings higher prices by stressing a product's differences. This product can then build up a loyal customer following. As a result, the firm may be able to charge higher prices because the customers are now willing to pay more just to keep buying their preferred product.[11] But competing products can also use advertising. In fact, many companies need advertising just to maintain a certain share of the market, rather than gain the ability to charge higher prices. And we have already seen that companies advertise to increase their sales, not because they want to raise prices but because the economies of the larger-scale production will let them lower their costs.

Finally, some people have suggested that manufacturers should lower prices instead of advertise. This, they argue, would benefit consumers and bring more sales. But suppose that retailers do not cut the price by the same amount, if at all.[12] Laws against what is called *price fixing* prevent manufac-

---

[10] Backman, *Advertising and Competition*, 117–18.
[11] Backman, *Advertising and Competition*, 123–26.
[12] Robert S. Headen and James W. McKie, *The Structure, Conduct, and Performance of the Breakfast Cereal Industry: 1954–1964* (Cambridge, Mass.: Arthur D. Little, Inc., 1966), 37–38.

turers from trying to force retailers to lower their prices by that same amount. So cutting a price instead of using advertising might not offer much if any savings to customers.

Even if an entire industry cut prices across the board, sales would probably not increase as much as they would with additional advertising. Several studies bear this out. A study of the ready-to-eat cereal industry, for example, shows that an industrywide price cut of 10 to 20 percent probably would not greatly increase the total amount of cereals people buy.[13] But more advertising might be able to increase demand.

If only one firm in an industry cuts prices, wouldn't it increase sales? Maybe it would temporarily, but its competitors would lose sales as a result. Then the competitors would cut prices to regain their former shares of the market. Eventually, all the companies would be back at about their previous market share, but each firm would be making less money for its products than it did before the price cutting started.[14]

So the evidence shows that price cuts would not increase sales either for a single company or for an entire industry. And advertising may bring other economic benefits that price cuts would not. A television advertisement for Crest toothpaste also encourages good oral hygiene, even if the customer does not buy Crest. And store brands of toothpaste that sell for less than the major brands might not sell well if the major brands' advertisements did not promote dental care.[15]

If advertised goods sell at a higher price than nonadvertised goods, it is probably because their quality is better and more consistent and their commercials provide useful information.[16] The value of this information alone may justify a higher price for the item.

Do Companies That Advertise Make More Profits?

In general, firms that advertise a lot tend to make more profits than firms that do not.[17] Of course, this may not be true in all cases, so advertising does not guarantee higher profits.

Also, the profits for firms that advertise a lot are not higher just because of advertising. In fact, studies show that the difference in the amounts of money companies spend on advertising accounts for only about *one-tenth* of the difference in profits.[18] That means that many other factors besides advertising must affect profits, too. In may be that companies smart enough to use advertising well are also smart enough to manage their resources better in general. Or it may be that companies with higher profits have more money to use for advertising.

[13] Backman, *Advertising and Competition*, 123–26.
[14] Backman, *Advertising and Competition*, 125–26.
[15] Lester G. Telser, "Advertising and Competition," *Journal of Political Economy* (December 1964): 542.
[16] Backman, *Advertising and Competition*, 149–50.
[17] Backman, *Advertising and Competition*, 154.
[18] Backman, *Advertising and Competition*, 154.

Companies that use advertising consider it an investment. They want the money they spend on advertising to bring some sort of return, just as we expect a return on money that we invest in a savings account. But the return on the advertising investment is usually lower than the return on investments in other areas such as new manufacturing equipment or research and development of new products.[19] So advertising is only a small part of the many investments a company makes in its products.

From all that we've discussed here, you can see how the economic factors such as pricing, profits, costs, competition, and other considerations are constraints for the practice of advertising.

SOCIAL CONSTRAINTS

Advertising operates under other kinds of constraints, too, because our society and our social standards influence advertising—the way it works and the ideas it uses. And advertising, in turn, affects society. Let's look at a few of the social issues that result from this relationship.

Does Advertising Help or Hurt Politics?

Some people believe that advertising and politics do not mix. Advertising should not be used in political campaigns, they say, because it increases the costs of running for political office and it oversimplifies the issues.

Political Advertising Is Expensive. It is almost impossible these days to run for political office without using advertising. Why is it so important? For the same reason that it is important in business: Advertising is the best way to reach large numbers of people. If political candidates could see as many people in person as they can by mass media advertising, they might choose that personal approach. But it takes too much time and costs too much to try for personal contacts with all the voters, so advertising makes these contacts instead. This gives the politician more time to meet with influential groups and plan campaign strategy.

But even though advertising is efficient, the cost involved makes political campaigns very expensive. Some people want to limit political advertising, but it may be more reasonable just to help political candidates pay for it. In recent years, presidential campaigns have been partly paid for by taxpayers who decide to sign over $1 of their income taxes for this purpose. Some broadcasting stations have also decided to give all candidates in their regions free time on the air, with equal time for all competing candidates, as a way to lower the cost of reaching voters. Both these methods may help solve the problems of

---

[19] Backman, *Advertising and Competition*, 154.

political advertising because they recognize that these kinds of expenses are here to stay.

Political Advertising Oversimplifies. It is impossible to take any complicated national problem and discuss it reasonably and completely in a one-minute television commercial. Even in magazines and newspapers, the amount of advertising space that the candidate can afford limits the amount of information that can be included. As a result, political advertisements tend to be very oversimplified. Even worse, they may not discuss the issues at all. Instead, they may rely on jingles or slogans that help voters remember the candidate's name. It is not unusual to hear a political advertisement say something like, "We must do something about this galloping inflation, and I intend to start right after I'm elected." That may be encouraging information but it does not tell how the candidate proposes to stop inflation, if the proposed solution will work, or if it will be worse than the problem itself.

Perhaps we will need to monitor political advertisements or set a standard that all political advertising must follow. But there are no simple or direct solutions to the problem of oversimplification in political advertisements.

Does Advertising Control the Media?

Advertising pays many of the costs of our mass media and almost all the costs of our broadcast media. But if advertising pays the bills, doesn't it also control the media? Wouldn't you expect the media to avoid publicizing any unfavorable information about advertisers' products or services? After all, why cause trouble for advertisers and risk losing some of their money?

This is a reasonable question. But it is probably not as much of a problem as it might seem. Certainly there may be small-town newspapers that avoid printing information about a large advertiser who gets into trouble with the law, just as they may avoid reporting a drunk-driving charge against an influential citizen. But keep in mind that people read newspapers and watch television for information, news, and entertainment—not just advertising. If advertisers want to reach media audiences, they need to make sure the media remain popular. If advertisers interfered with media, then maybe the audiences would no longer pay attention. That would defeat the purpose of advertising in the first place!

Also keep in mind that advertisers need the media to carry advertising messages just as much as the media need advertisers to help pay some of their expenses. An advertiser who doesn't like a certain program or news story and stops advertising because of it can no longer reach the audience as easily and cheaply as before. So it is the advertiser who is really penalized.

Should All Media Be "Common Carriers"?

We all know that we are entitled to freedom of speech: We can say what we want to as long as it does not interfere with other people's rights. One of the ways firms may express themselves is by buying an advertisement to reach a large group of people efficiently and effectively.

To protect this form of expression, the government forces radio and television stations to accept all advertisements *in the same category*. That is, they must act as **common carriers.** An example of a common carrier is a trucking firm that must carry all products of the same type. It can refuse to carry all explosives, but if it carries one company's explosives, it must carry all other companies' explosives.

common carriers Media that must accept all advertisements in the same category.

Likewise, broadcasters can decide not to accept *any* advertisements for a certain kind of product if they think the advertising is not in the public interest or not suitable for public discussion. For example, some broadcasters may not accept personal hygiene product advertising. But if they accept one brand of personal hygiene product, they cannot refuse others. So if our competitor advertises on a particular television or radio station, we can demand to buy the same kind of broadcast advertising.

The government can force television and radio stations to grant "equal time" to all advertisers because it regulates the broadcast media. You cannot simply decide to start a radio or television station of your own. There just aren't enough frequencies. So the government needs to decide who will receive a license to broadcast and who won't. Needless to say, people who don't want to act as common carriers simply don't get licenses.

But there is no limit on the number of newspapers that a community can have, so the government does not directly regulate newspapers, magazines, and other nonbroadcast media. Thus, there is nothing to force them to accept all advertisements in the same category. They can accept our competitors' advertisements and turn ours down. Many newspapers and magazines choose to operate as common carriers even though they don't have to. If they carry one firm's advertisement, then they carry competitors' advertising, too. Perhaps all nonbroadcast media should do this. It is a practice that opens up advertising to all of us and allows us to exercise our freedom of speech in advertising.

Does Advertising Show Us How to Look and Act?

The way children learn to behave in society is called **socialization.** In earlier times, most socialization took place in the family. That is where people learned how to do things and where they learned the difference between right and wrong. Later, much of this learning began to occur in the schools, so the educational system became an important part of the socialization process.

socialization The way children learn to behave in society.

Now many people rely on advertising in the mass media to tell them what fashions are in style, what music is popular, and what decorating ideas are the "in thing" for the home. The mass media have become an important part of the socialization process, telling us how to act and how to get along with other people.

The problem is that much of what we see, hear, and read in the mass media is about unusual events and outlandish styles, because things that are out of the ordinary are news. We don't want to read about things that we already know and do; we want to learn about other ways of doing things. So mass media socialization may teach us things that do not necessarily help us fit into modern society.

Television programs show lots of murders, but we do not assume that is normal behavior. Popular magazines may tell us how movie stars behave, but we cannot all be movie stars. Newspapers report on thefts, corruption, and dishonesty in government, but we don't want lots of other people imitating this kind of behavior. Too many advertisements concentrate on the need to be beautiful, or the desire for whiter teeth, or the unwillingness to have bad breath. Although these concerns may be part of the socialization process, they are hardly the most important activities for us to concentrate upon and live by.

How Should Children's Advertising Be Handled?

The problem of mass media socialization is especially important—and difficult—when it comes to advertising for children. Young children are not able to tell the make-believe of advertising from reality. For example, they cannot understand that a model racing car shown in a television close-up may not look the same in their own living rooms.

So we must protect children from advertisements that may mislead them, even though they might not mislead adults. Children's television programs no longer use the host to endorse a sponsor, because the children who watch the program trust the host. Children's programs are also careful to separate the advertisements from the entertainment part of the program so the children do not accept the commercials as part of the program.

There are still problems, though. Advertising may make children want products that may not be good for them; ready-to-eat cereals with lots of sugar have been accused of causing this kind of problem. And children may still be more easily affected by all kinds of advertising than adults are, even with many rules to regulate children's advertising. This is especially true with children's television advertising.

Because of these problems, some people want to ban all television advertising on children's programs. But there might be fewer shows with no advertising money to pay for them.

ETHICAL CONSTRAINTS

Ethical constraints may be more difficult to analyze than economic, social, and regulatory constraints, because ethics is a complicated subject.

By **ethics,** we mean the set of moral standards that most people in our society agree to follow. Some of these standards are written down in the form of laws or regulations. Others are unwritten rules that are often hard to define. For instance, most people may agree that it's wrong to be dishonest, but everyone may have a different idea of what dishonesty is and how it applies to different situations.

ethics The set of moral standards that most people in our society agree to follow.

As a result, many ethical questions are personal matters that we cannot regulate. All of us must decide what is ethically right and wrong according to our own standards. This makes ethical questions hard to answer. Ethical problems in advertising are therefore not clear-cut, but we can give a general picture of these problems here—even though we may not be able to solve them.

What Is Truth in Advertising?

Most people would agree that, for an advertisement to be ethical, it should tell the truth. But what *is* the truth in advertising? Individual standards and interpretations of truth may differ. And, even when an advertisement tells the exact truth, it may mislead people. So we must be very careful when we analyze the ethical problems of truth in advertising.

It is important to realize that truth and ethics may not be the same thing. A manufacturer of automobile tires may say, "This is a better steel-belted radial tire" and mean that it is better than other tires that the company manufactures. But consumers might think that this tire is better than tires made by other manufacturers. A dairy might advertise that its milk "has extra vitamins and minerals to make your children grow up strong and healthy," meaning that it adds the same nutrients to its milk that all dairies do. But consumers might wrongly assume that this milk is better for children than milk from other dairies. So advertisers must consider what the advertising actually says as well as what impression it creates in the minds of consumers.

Testimonials Are Legal

We have all seen movie stars urge us to use products in advertisements. Some of us might actually buy the product just to copy well-known performers, but even if we don't, we may still watch or read the advertisement more closely because of the person who appears in it. In other words, the movie star may not sell the product so much as attract attention to the advertisement.

testimonial An advertisement in which a person endorses a product, service, or idea.

Testimonial is the word we use to describe advertising in which a person endorses a product, service, or idea. Some advertisers must believe it is effective or there would not be so much of it. And it is legal as long as the person in the advertisement actually uses the product or service or believes in the idea so that he or she qualifies as what we call a *bona fide* user of that item and brand. It is impossible to know if a person really believes what he or she says about an item, so all we can judge on is actual use. But you may wonder just how ethical testimonial advertising is. Should Michael J. Fox try to make more people drink Pepsi-Cola or James Garner try to increase the consumption of beef? It's up to individuals to decide for themselves.

Puffery Is Legal, Too

material claim Any absolute statement about an advertised product.

Any absolute statement about an advertised item is called a **material claim.** An advertiser who makes a material claim must be able to back it up with research or other factual support. For example, a cleanser advertisement that claims "forty percent more cleaning power than the leading brand" must be based on real facts and research findings.

But everyone has the right to express an opinion. If an advertiser claims to have "the best-tasting pies in town," that is just an opinion. The advertiser doesn't have to prove it with research findings. Taste is an individual matter, and as long as the advertiser really believes that these pies taste best (and how could we ever find out what people really believe, unless they tell us?), the claim is legal.

This kind of unsupported opinion is called **puffery,** and although there may be doubts whether such claims are effective, they are legal. As to whether they are ethical, you must decide for yourself as you must with many ethical problems.

puffery An unsupported opinion in an advertisement.

Good Taste in Advertising

There are many problems with maintaining standards of good taste in advertising. For one thing, advertising uses the mass media to carry its messages, and the media also have problems deciding what is in good taste for their audiences. An advertisement that might be tasteful in a men's magazine might not be right for a business publication or a children's magazine, for example.

And tastes change over time. Today we find more kinds of topics acceptable for conversations, movies, and television programs than we did only a few years ago. So keeping good taste in advertising is a continuing challenge because of changes in standards and individual tastes.

Persuasion versus Information

Should advertising simply inform consumers about ideas, services, and products that are available in the marketplace? Or should advertising also persuade people to buy these items?

Actually, advertising is a blend of both persuasion and information, yet it is not completely one or the other. Advertising does not present full information, because most advertisers want to show only the positive aspects of their products. That's the normal pattern for all of us: We try to present our best attributes and hide our shortcomings. Think of what a lawyer does when defending a citizen charged with a crime. Does the lawyer tell all the positive and negative traits about the client, or does the lawyer present only positive information that may help the client? Of course, the lawyer shows only the positive side, and the opposing lawyers can present any negative views. So it is with advertising: we present positive information to help sales of the product, and competitors may tell the other side of the story.

So advertising does not contain full and complete information, nor is it entirely directed toward persuading. There is some persuasion mixed in with the information. The information serves both the advertiser and the customer, but the persuasion mainly serves the advertiser.

The Creation of New Needs and Wants

Advertising has been accused of creating needs and wants in consumers. Because consumers may not want new products and services before they see advertisements for them, critics claim that advertising *makes* consumers want things. But does advertising create new desires, or does it simply point out desires that were always there? And doesn't advertising also show ways to fulfill these new desires?

need Something you must have.

want Something you would like to have.

Actually, a **need** is something that you must have, perhaps just to survive, such as air to breathe, food to eat, shelter in which to live, and clothes to wear. A **want** is something you would like to have, but which is probably not vital to your health or survival. You might like a new color television set, but it is not a necessity. We therefore call it a want.

The needs you must satisfy were around long before advertising, so advertising did not create them, although it may show you new ways to fulfill them, such as new styles of clothes or new convenience foods. Some wants also existed before advertising, although advertising may have pointed out more wants to us. Advertising is very good at demonstrating wants to us, but very likely it only reflects the wants we already have. Advertising develops few wants by itself; instead, it finds wants that are not being fulfilled and shows us how certain advertised items will help us fulfill them. (See Figure 4–2.)

Advertising lets us recognize wants that we might fulfill by using research to uncover unfulfilled wants or wants of which we are not yet completely aware. Firms then develop and promote items that meet these desires. Look back over the material on the marketing concept and the advertising concept and see if it helps you understand how advertising looks for wants that provide an opportunity for product development and promotion.

REGULATORY CONSTRAINTS

The most obvious kinds of constraints that affect advertising are laws and regulations. Most of these laws and regulations are passed and enforced by the government. But some advertising regulation is also carried out by the advertising industry itself.

Governmental Regulation

external regulation Regulation by an outside agency.

Regulation from outside the advertising industry, called **external regulation,** can come from the federal government or from state and local governments. If the advertising being regulated is used by a firm that sells in more than one state, then generally interstate trade is involved and the federal government has the power to regulate it.

Federal Trade Commission (FTC) A government agency that prevents unfair competition and regulates interstate trade.

Federal Trade Commission. For advertising, the most important federal regulatory agency is the **Federal Trade Commission (FTC).** The Federal Trade Commission is charged with preventing unfair competition

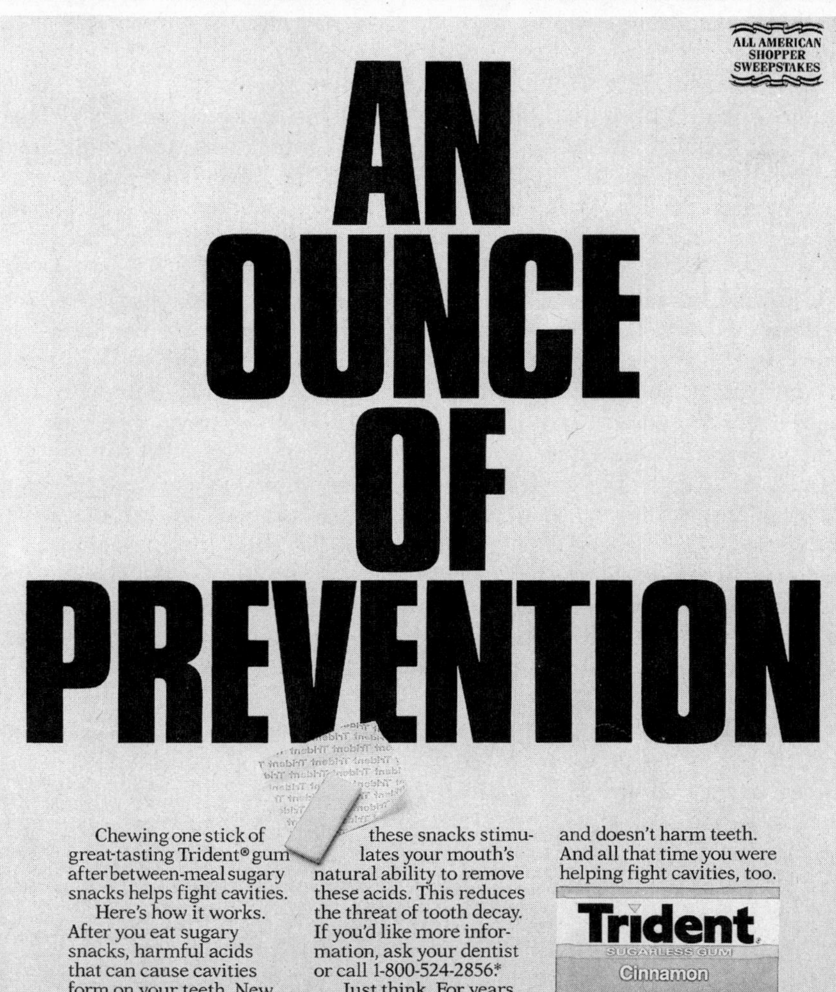

Courtesy Warner-Lambert Co.

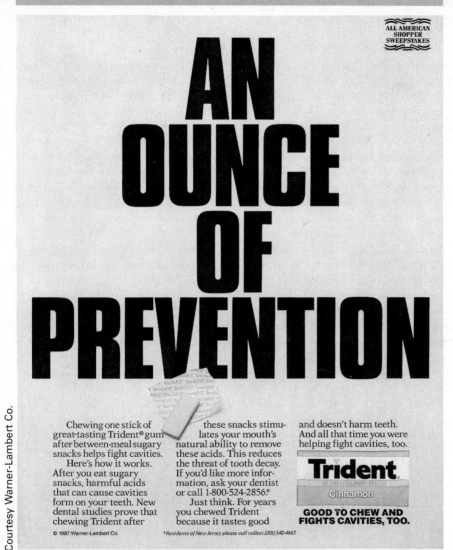

FIGURE 4–2
Notice how this advertisement suggests new uses for a product with which most readers are already familiar.

and regulating interstate restraint of trade. By **restraint of trade,** we mean any activity that keeps competition from operating freely. Because dishonest advertising might be unfair to the competition and some advertising practices might prevent open trade in the marketplace, the FTC regulates advertising when it might cause these problems.

restraint of trade Any activity that keeps competition from operating freely.

Most of the time, the FTC investigates complaints from citizens and from its own staff. The FTC may simply ask an advertiser to present research information that can support advertising claims. The commission also holds hearings to make charges public and allow the advertiser to present a defense against them.

Sometimes the FTC will get an advertiser to agree to stop the practice in question. The firm does not necessarily agree that the advertising has violated any laws or regulations, but it stops anyway in return for the commission's agreement not to prosecute the firm in the courts. This avoids long court trials and costly legal actions. Such an agreement is called a **consent decree.** If the advertiser breaks the agreement, the FTC might fine the firm or take it to court.

consent decree An agreement in which an advertiser stops a practice the FTC is questioning so that the FTC will not prosecute.

If no such agreement can be reached, the commission may issue a **cease-and-desist order** to stop the practice in question. If the firm continues the practice after such an order, then the FTC may use the evidence it has gathered for a court trial. The final judgment in this situation would be up to the courts, because every person and corporation is entitled to an open court hearing and trial before being found guilty or innocent.

cease-and-desist order An order that the FTC issues to stop an advertising practice.

In recent years, the Federal Trade Commission has also issued many **trade regulations** that set standards of business practice for various kinds of industries. The Federal Trade Commission has also required **corrective advertising** from some firms that have used advertising that the commission considered misleading. For example, when Ocean Spray cranberry marketers were found to have misled the public with some of their advertising, they were required to buy additional advertising to correct the earlier misimpression.

trade regulations Business standards set by the FTC.

corrective advertising Advertising the FTC orders to correct previous misleading advertising.

Other Federal Regulators. The **Federal Communications Commission (FCC)** regulates broadcast stations because only a limited number of stations can operate in any geographical area. Stations must be licensed before they can operate, and the licenses are reviewed every three years. The FCC does not regulate the broadcast networks, nor does it directly regulate advertising, but because advertising uses broadcast media a great deal, advertisers must be aware of FCC rules and regulations.

Federal Communications Commission The federal agency that regulates the broadcast media.

The **Food and Drug Administration (FDA)** is chiefly concerned with keeping foods pure and safe and maintaining drug quality. Certain information must be on the labels of food and drugs, and because the labels are also often a promotional tool, the labeling regulations may be of interest to advertisers. If advertising features certain product ingredients, it might be regulated by the FDA as well.

Food and Drug Administration (FDA) A federal agency concerned with keeping foods pure and safe and maintaining drug quality.

Certain industries and their advertising are regulated directly by other government agencies, and these agencies can influence advertising. The commercial airline industry is still partly regulated, for example, so the things that can be said and the approaches used in airline advertising might be important. In addition, the Congress has passed some regulations of individual industries, so any advertising in these industries might have to follow certain guidelines. Recently, when researchers discovered that using aspirin might reduce the chances of heart attacks, aspirin producers were prevented from making broad health claims for their products because they had not mentioned possible side-effects.

Some regulation has been aimed at protecting consumers. Advertisements that offer loans must follow the truth-in-lending laws, which are intended to help consumers find out all they can about a loan before they borrow.

State and Local Regulation. Even a small firm that does not operate in many states is still subject to regulation—not by the federal government perhaps, but by the laws of the state. Each state has its own standards and laws, and although the guidelines and penalties may vary from one state to another, the basic principles of truth in advertising, fair competition, and open trade in the marketplace apply in all states.

The states also help protect consumers, most of them with special consumer protection agencies, sometimes funded by the state government. As you know, problems often arise when the statements in advertisements create the wrong impression in the minds of consumers, and the states' regulations on these issues vary a great deal. In most instances, however, truthful advertising is still a safe policy to follow.

Nongovernmental Regulation

Not all regulation is conducted by the government. Some advertising is regulated by the industry itself or by voluntary organizations.

Better Business Bureaus. For a long time, businesses in many cities have operated **Better Business Bureaus,** which are voluntary groups who work against unethical and illegal business practices, including advertising. If a bureau receives a complaint about a local firm, it first investigates both sides of the problem. If the bureau thinks the firm was wrong in its operation, it asks the firm to correct the situation. If the firm refuses, the bureau has no power of its own to prosecute, but it can give evidence to the local prosecutor's office, which can take legal action. In smaller cities that do not have a Better Business Bureau, the local Chamber of Commerce often serves the same role.

Better Business Bureaus Voluntary organizations that work against illegal and unethical business practices.

Internal Regulation. In recent times, we have seen an increase in **internal regulation,** in which the advertising industry regulates itself. In most cases, the advertising industry has no real regulatory power, but a judgment by one's peers is a powerful force, and if all advertisers were to band together to follow certain standards of ethical and truthful procedures, few advertisers would be willing to risk breaking the rules.

internal regulation Self-regulation of the advertising industry.

Internal regulation also exists in the form of the **National Advertising Review Board (NARB).** Large advertisers, advertising agencies, mass media, the national Council of Better Business Bureaus and other groups worked to establish such an organization. The National Advertising Review Board examines complaints that come in from consumers and from competing advertisers.

National Advertising Review Board (NARB) A self-regulatory body of the advertising industry.

Many times, the firm that is being examined will be asked to supply information that supports the advertising claims. Much of the advertising the NARB examines is found to be accurate, truthful, and ethical, but if it is not, then the advertiser usually agrees to stop it or to modify its claims. If the firm keeps using advertising that the NARB believes is untruthful, the evidence could be turned over to government regulatory agencies such as the Federal Trade Commission. The NARB provides another place for the consumer to get help without resorting to legal suits.

Individual Efforts. It is also possible, of course, for each of us, as individual citizens, to be watchful of the advertising we see and hear. If something is wrong, we can complain directly to the advertiser. It is surprising how effective a small protest can be.

And conscientious advertisers are constantly monitoring their own advertising to be certain that it does not mislead and that it contains complete and accurate information. Sometimes two different people receive two different messages from an advertisement, so an incorrect meaning can be accidental. The advertiser has to be extra careful in preparing and editing advertising materials.

SUMMARY

Regulatory constraints are only one of four kinds of constraints that affect or limit the ways in which advertising operates; the other three kinds of constraints are economic, social, and ethical. All these types of constraints may limit the ways in which advertising is practiced. Violating these limits may bring legal penalties for nonconformity, while violating others may only bring declining sales or negative public opinions.

Some advertising practitioners have complained that all these constraints have hampered the advertising business by reducing flexibility and by reducing the opportunity for creative advertising. Yet advertising still has a great deal of freedom in the way it operates and the things it says. Perhaps the constraints bring new challenges to advertising, challenges that provide new opportunities for advertising creativity.

As you will see in the next section of the book, the need for creativity in advertising is just as great as ever. In fact, these constraints increase the challenges that face the creative person in advertising.

TERMS TO KNOW

Now that you have finished this chapter, you should understand the following terms:

constraints	need
competition	want
monopoly	external regulation
product differentiation	Federal Trade Commission (FTC)
added value	consent decree
added utility	cease-and-desist order
consumer's gain	trade regulations
economy of scale	corrective advertising
common carrier	Federal Communications Commission (FCC)
socialization	Food and Drug Administration (FDA)
ethics	Better Business Bureaus
testimonial	internal regulation
material claim	National Advertising Review Board (NARB)
puffery	

If you are not certain of the meaning of any of these terms, go back through the chapter and review them.

THINGS TO THINK ABOUT

1. Why can't advertising operate more freely and openly? Why are constraints necessary?
2. What are the major problems of political advertising?
3. How can advertising both raise and lower prices?
4. Does advertising lead to monopolies and waste? Explain why or why not.
5. What are added value and added utility?
6. Does advertising control the mass media? If so, how? If not, why not?
7. Why are ethics a personal problem?
8. What is puffery? Why is it legal? How does it compare to untrue statements in advertisements?

THINGS TO TALK ABOUT

1. What do you think advertising was like before the current constraints were developed? How did that advertising differ from today's regulated advertising?
2. Should children be more protected than adults from advertising? Why? How?
3. What are the benefits of government regulation of advertising? What are the dangers?
4. How does advertising influence product costs? Product prices? Business profits? Competition?
5. If advertising does not always increase costs and prices, then why do most companies that advertise a lot tend to make more profits?
6. How does advertising contribute to inflation? How could advertising be used to help fight inflation?
7. What parts of the socialization process depend on the family? On the educational system? On the mass media and advertising?
8. How is ethics in advertising similar to truth in advertising? How are they different?

THINGS TO DO

1. Find an advertisement that you think is unethical and/or untruthful. Find another advertisement that you think is completely ethical and truthful. Compare your advertisements with those collected by others in your class and discuss them.
2. Write out all the information that you think should be included in a political advertisement.
3. Find some children's advertising and compare it with advertising aimed at adults.
4. Find advertisements for candidates in your most recent local or state political campaign.
5. Examine testimonial advertisements and analyze their effectiveness on you.
6. Cut out some advertisements from newspapers and magazines. Underline the parts that are persuasion in red; underline information in blue.
7. Contact your state government for information on advertising regulation and consumer protection.

SECTION 2
Creative

Now that we know something about how and why advertising works the way it does, what about the advertisements themselves? How are the advertisements planned, written, executed, and produced?

You cannot just sit down and start writing an advertisement. There is much more to it. And the entire effort must be combined into a unified effort.

In this section of the book, you will learn some of the specifics of writing advertisements for newspapers and magazines, and for television and radio—and for some other kinds of advertising media, too. You'll see that much preparation is involved, and much thought and effort are required to compose an effective, efficient, enticing advertising message.

This creative section may be the most fun of all for you, because writing ads allows you to involve yourself in your work. It permits you to express yourself, too. And you may find out just how well you're doing from the results of the advertisements you write.

So, let's find out more about advertising creativity: writing, art, layout and production.

CHAPTERS

5 Creative Concepts and Approaches

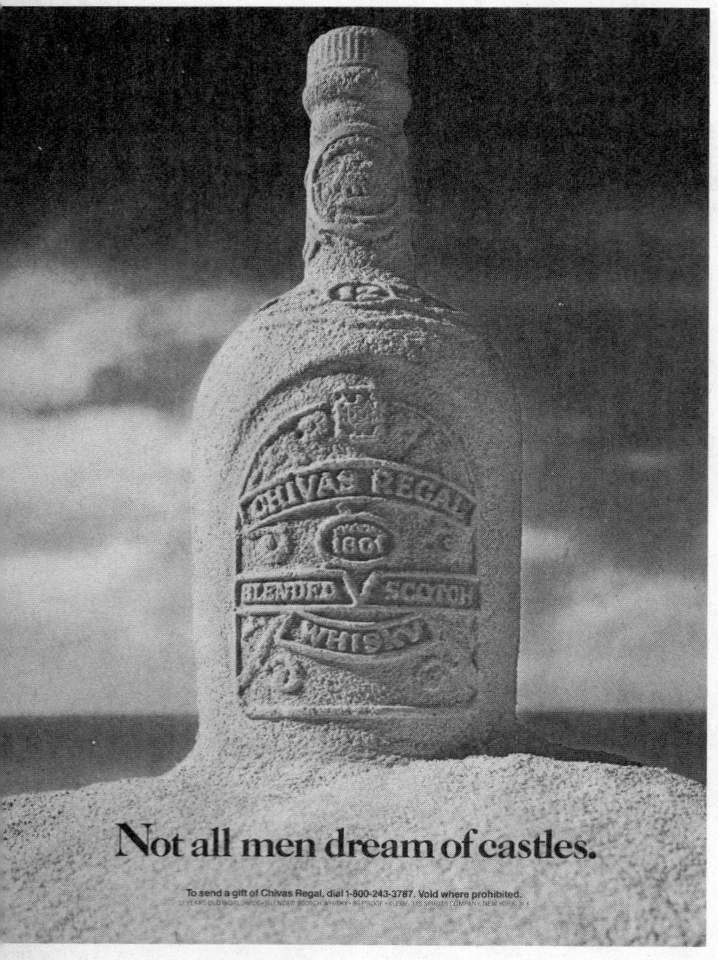

CHIVAS REGAL
1801
BLENDED SCOTCH
WHISKY
Not all men dream of castles.
To send a gift of Chivas Regal, dial 1-800-243-3787. Void where prohibited.

Courtesy of 375 Spirits Company

CHAPTER OUTLINE

By the time you finish this chapter, you should understand:

1. **Where to look for advertising ideas.**
2. **That some facts are more advertisable than others.**
3. **That advertising activities must match all other company activities.**
4. **The help to be gained from a creative strategy.**
5. **That there are some differences between communications goals and marketing goals.**
6. **That advertisers sell best when they differentiate their products from others.**
7. **That it is important to search out both marketing opportunities and marketing problems.**

The most common cry you will hear in any advertising situation is "We need an idea!" This chapter tells you how to go about getting ad ideas and how to recognize them when you see them.

First off, it's a rare ad idea that just springs into your mind—bingo!—like that. Such a happy event may occur occasionally, but most times the soundest advertising ideas come only after you have done your spadework. Almost always, ideas stem from information and research. Most professional copywriters begin by writing headlines—and you should too. But before you even try to write a headline, before you dare put pencil to paper, you must make a thorough study of your business or product, your customers, and your competitors.

WHAT INFORMATION SHOULD YOU GATHER BEFORE WRITING ADS?

Research is nothing more or less than information, gathered in an orderly manner. Research can be as simple as rereading last year's ad, as elaborate as a field survey involving many respondents, or anything in between. The kind of research needed depends on each separate business situation.

Start by Studying Your Own Product

Whether you are the advertiser or the advertising agent, the first thing for you to know is your own product or service. Ask yourself the most basic questions. What is its purpose? How is it made? Is there anything special about the materials it uses or the way it is produced? Is there anything new about the way it works? To compete with traditional pie-shaped pizza, an enterprising restaurateur offered deep-pan pizza by the slice. Is it new, does it have a new

FIGURE 5–1
Eye-stopping treatment of everyday item persuades reader to think of this advertiser as a creative innovator in the field.

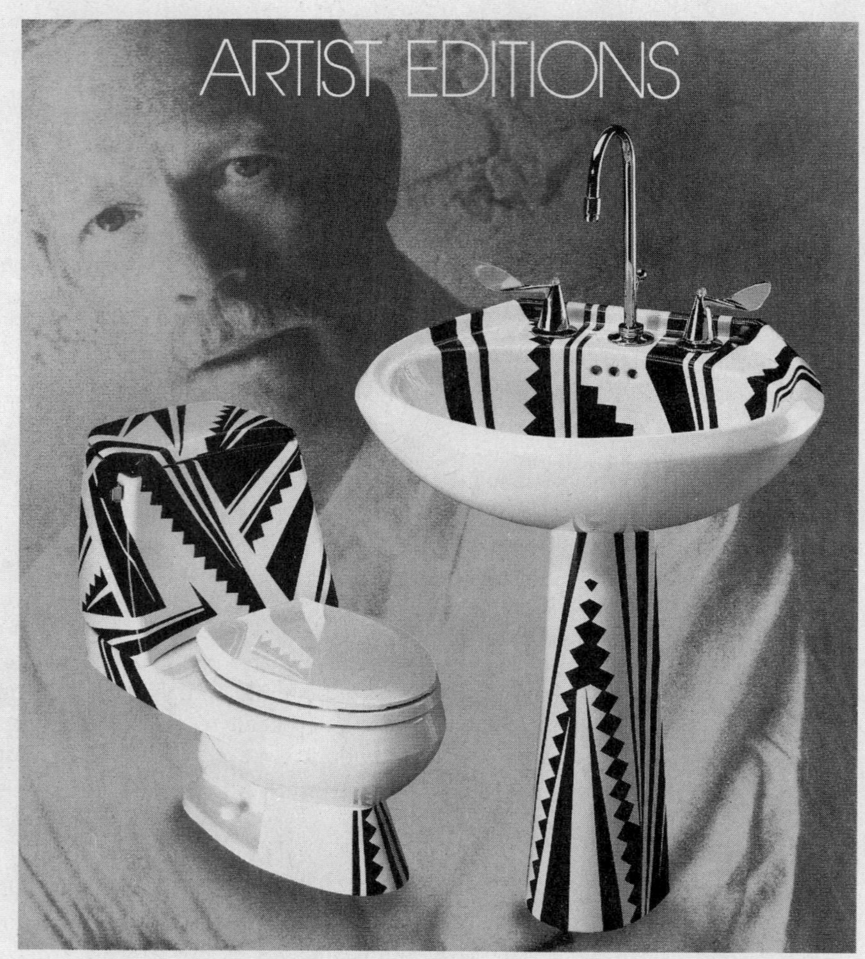

ARTIST EDITIONS
THE BOLD LOOK OF KOHLER.
Cactus Cutter™ by Art Nelson. Just one triumph of Kohler's bold design freedom challenge to renowned ceramic artists. A most original series of fixtures advancing the bath as artform. Six different limited edition designs to make your own statement of taste and penchant for unique pattern, color and texture. For a complete collection portfolio of all six Artist Editions, send $3 to Kohler Co., Dept. AU9, Kohler, Wisconsin 53044.
C6050 Copyright 1986 Kohler Co.

Courtesy of Kohler Company.

feature, or does it perform a new service? Mercy Hospital included hospice care among its unique services. U.S. Gypsum introduced "designer" ceiling tiles. What is its competition? How does it differ from its competition?

Identify Any Special Features of Your Own Product. If your product is a food item, how does it taste? What other foods does it blend with? What kind of recipes might it be used in? If you are advertising a retail store, where is its location? Is it in or out of the main traffic pattern? Is merchandise clearly displayed and marked? How do prices compare with those of similar stores? How does the store see itself—as a "price" operation or a "quality" operation?

Know Your Own Product's History. If you are advertising a small industrial manufacturing plant or a retail store, examine that organization's past. Who founded it? For what purpose? On what principles does it operate? Be a historian. Study the company archives. Study sales figures. Read the correspondence.

Remember that a retail operation, no matter how large, is strictly a local matter. The retailer is a member of the community, a neighbor to all, so to speak. The more you know about the retailer's "family background," the more you can present a unique personality to the public. For example: Suppose you built a window display around fashions this retailer sold seventy-five years ago. The display is not only interesting in itself, it punches home the fact that the retailer has been a staunch member of the community for generations and that friends and neighbors have found the retailer highly dependable over many years.

Suppose your investigation shows that the retailer has a distinctive personality—Honest John or Daredevil Dick. A popular Midwest pizza palace is operated by two partners, both pilots, who call themselves, officially, the Flying Tomato Brothers. The advertiser's personality may be a factor to use in advertising and public relations, thus differentiating the advertiser from competitors. The personality of the owner is often used in the promotion of car dealerships. And wisely so.

Know Your Producers. When you are advertising a product, look beyond the corporate producer. Talk to the inventor or designer. Who can tell you better what purpose it serves? Talk to the engineer who built it. Who better can tell you what went into its manufacture and why? Perhaps a single ingredient makes an advertising difference. Swedish steel evidently has special meaning in the razor blade world. Perhaps the way a part is designed is important or possibly the way components operate. (It beats as it sweeps as it cleans.) Engineers and plant managers are more technical and less flamboyant than ad writers, but their information is golden.

Stop now and think for a moment. The answer to any one of the questions already asked might lead to an idea. Yet each question is both obvious and simple. You can see that there is nothing very mysterious about getting ad ideas . . . and you have barely scratched the surface.

FIGURE 5–2
Well-targeted ad reaches out to young men recently finished with college but not yet "hooked" on a business career. Picture-headline combination is practically irresistible to an adventuresome youth.

It's not like sitting behind a desk.

Not when you're in the cockpit of one of our most advanced jet fighters, the F-16.

Not when you're on the flight deck of one of the world's largest transports.

Not when you've earned the silver wings of an Air Force pilot and watched your future take off with top benefits and opportunities to further your education.

The training is demanding. But, as you can see, the rewards are enormous for those who make it through.

If you're under 27 and a college graduate with the physical and mental stamina to become a pilot, join the Air Force. You can make an important contribution to your country.

Find out if you qualify. See your nearest Air Force recruiter or call toll-free 1-800-423-USAF (in California 1-800-232-USAF).

Aim High. Be an Air Force pilot.

AIR FORCE

Courtesy of United States Air Force.

Find Out What Your Customers Think

You've asked a lot of questions about what you're trying to sell. Now ask some questions about the folks to whom you are trying to sell it.

Customers' Shopping Patterns. You can learn a lot just by watching people and their shopping patterns. Say, for example, that four out of five people who come in to a store are young mothers. That alone should help shape

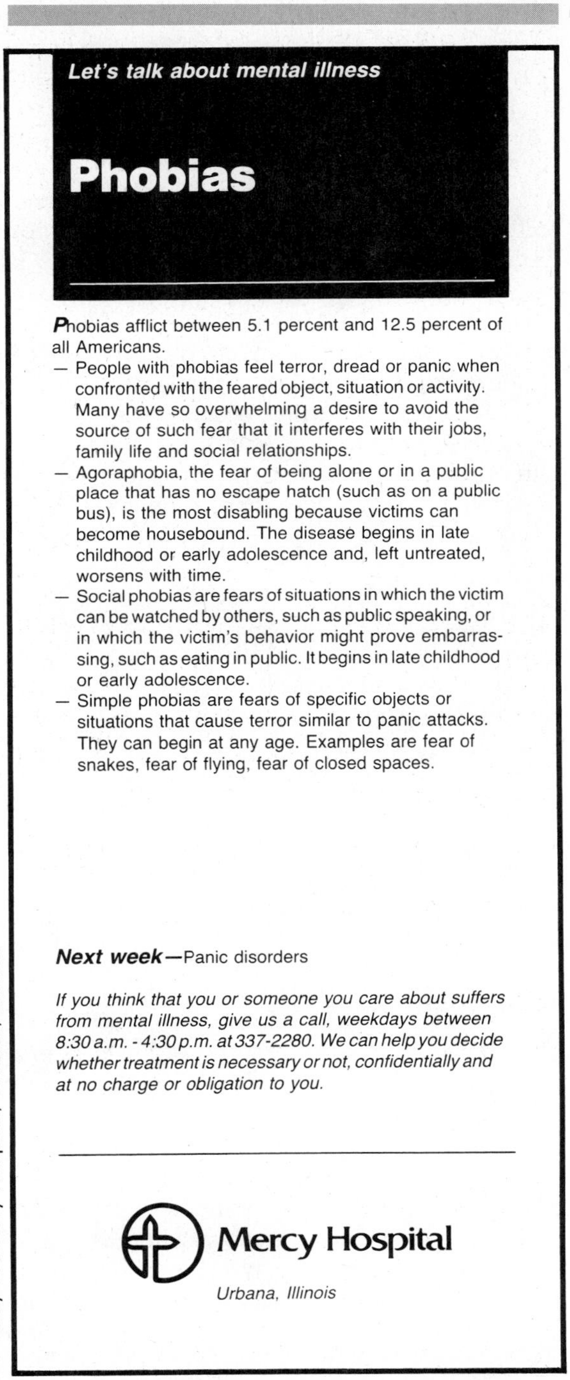

Let's talk about mental illness

Phobias

Phobias afflict between 5.1 percent and 12.5 percent of all Americans.

— People with phobias feel terror, dread or panic when confronted with the feared object, situation or activity. Many have so overwhelming a desire to avoid the source of such fear that it interferes with their jobs, family life and social relationships.

— Agoraphobia, the fear of being alone or in a public place that has no escape hatch (such as on a public bus), is the most disabling because victims can become housebound. The disease begins in late childhood or early adolescence and, left untreated, worsens with time.

— Social phobias are fears of situations in which the victim can be watched by others, such as public speaking, or in which the victim's behavior might prove embarrassing, such as eating in public. It begins in late childhood or early adolescence.

— Simple phobias are fears of specific objects or situations that cause terror similar to panic attacks. They can begin at any age. Examples are fear of snakes, fear of flying, fear of closed spaces.

Next week—Panic disorders

If you think that you or someone you care about suffers from mental illness, give us a call, weekdays between 8:30 a.m. - 4:30 p.m. at 337-2280. We can help you decide whether treatment is necessary or not, confidentially and at no charge or obligation to you.

Urbana, Illinois

Courtesy of Mercy Hospital, Urbana, Illinois.

FIGURE 5–3
Here is an example of newspaper advertising aimed at a highly specific target audience.

the store's selling appeals. Much can be learned from study and analysis of sales records. Let us say we learn that most purchases are made late in the week at a cost averaging $5.00 per sale; that the 12-ounce jar is most popular; that the greatest number of sales seem to be clustered in a particular neighborhood. This kind of information can be turned to a selling advantage.

What Customers Have to Say. There is no substitute for talking directly to a customer or prospect. But your inquiry should be more than just friendly, it should be structured. You want to talk to a number of people and end up with a composite picture. This is what is known in research circles as a survey. Seven-Up Company once conducted a survey and learned that the general public didn't consider its product a "soft drink," even though it was the third largest-selling soft drink in the world. What one person may say about you is opinion: What fifty people say about you is a test and should give you a pretty clear picture of how you stand with your customers and neighbors. Often advertisers are amazed to find that the public has quite a different image of their store or product than their own. The image that counts is the image customers hold.

How Customers Rate Your Product. It is not enough to ask people what they think of you and your merchandise. Ask what they think in comparison to alternatives, to competition—as Seven-Up did.

Ask customers why they buy, when they buy, for whom they buy. The actual purchaser may be only an "agent" for the decision maker in the family; the wife may buy the beer but not drink it.

What Media Customers Use. Ask your customers what newspapers and magazines they read, what TV channels they watch, what radio stations they listen to. A well-directed message is important in the advertising battle; you want *your* message on the station that the greatest number of your potential customers use.

Study Your Competition

Everybody agrees that the world of business in America is highly competitive. The very least you can do in a business situation is to *be aware* of what your competition is up to.

Knowing the Competition's Products. Know your competitor's product or service almost as well as you know your own. Ask the same questions about your competitor's product as you ask about your own. Do some comparison shopping. Analyze your competitor's location, service policy, pricing, and the like, as carefully as you analyze your own. Probe for strengths and weaknesses. Look for gaps in your competitor's service to the public, gaps that you might fill profitably.

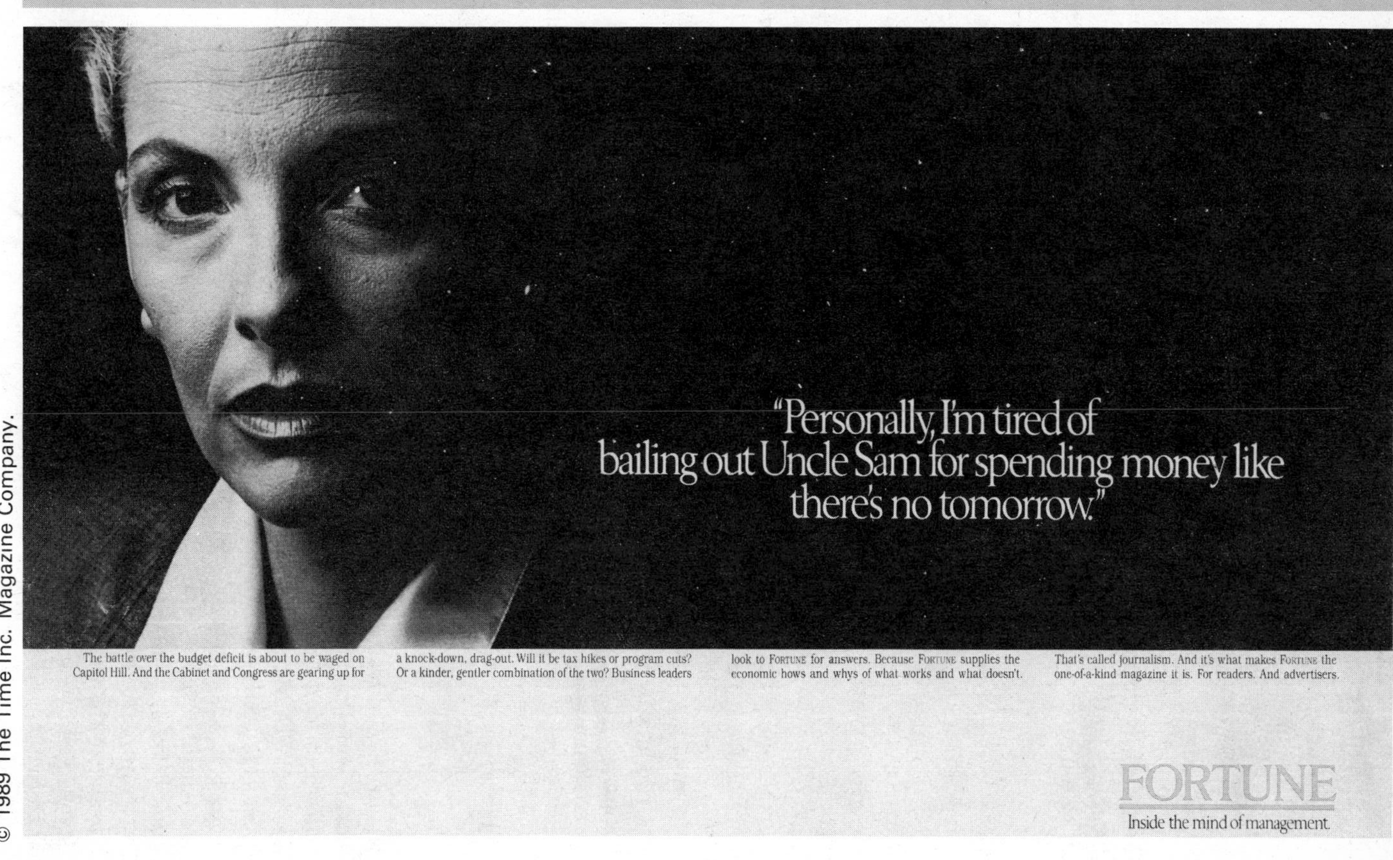

FIGURE 5–4
This full-page newspaper ad is a superb example of advertising based on an immediate but fleeting event in the news. This kind of rare message is sometimes referred to as a "one shot."

What Do People Think of the Competition? Analyze your competitor's image with the public. Find out what people think of your competitor. How do potential customers rank your product or service in comparison with your competitor's? Study the "face" your competitor presents to the world through advertising, customer relations, and public relations in the community.

At this point, can you begin to see how the answers to several simple questions begin to form a selling pattern? The more questions you ask and answer, the more you know about organizing your selling approach. You can never know too much about your product, your customers, and your competitors.

PUTTING YOUR RESEARCH TOGETHER TO WRITE AN AD

If you look hard enough you will usually find some definite customer buying patterns—whether you're a retail advertiser or a national advertiser promoting a brand of product. If a retail shop gets its greatest traffic on Thursday night, it can advertise Thursday into an even bigger event—or it can promote specials on other nights in an effort to equalize the selling burden. If orders for your product pour in during September, you might think twice about running ads in April. Many items in the marketplace survive from year to year on Christmas sales. The ad maker must know this and act accordingly. The manufacturer of a product is highly dependent on distribution. If a product is not readily available in the marketplace, advertising probably won't be much help. If you are advertising a small supermarket item, you should check its shelf position. If your budget is small, perhaps a related-item selling promotion could be worked out—say, a combination of products used at a picnic or barbecue, with each of the various products splitting the cost of the promotion.

Be Aware of Cultural Trends

Try to keep abreast of changing life styles. They've come thick and fast since World War II. If you need reminding, consider: discount houses, shopping malls, fast-food franchises, hair, beards, moustaches, blue jeans, backpacks, acid rock, country-and-western. Alert marketers and advertisers have cashed in and are continuing to cash in on the selling opportunities provided by the changes in the way our people live. Any product related to physical fitness has flourished in recent years. Keep your eyes and ears open for the newest ideas around you and hope that you will be able to tell a fad from a trend.

Naturally, all salespeople, all advertisers believe they are selling the greatest value in the world. But does your product or service actually perform as well as you think? Check the experiences of a satisfied customer (and you may find an ad that writes itself). Listen carefully to the gripes of an unhappy customer. It may save you from grievous disaster. At the least, it may win you a friend.

Satisfied customers make good advertising copy. Dissatisfied customers may help you avoid pitfalls.

List the Obvious Facts

How does your product help people most? What is its chief advantage to a consumer? Can you *convince* prospects of this benefit? They have to believe before they will buy. Can you support your claim with facts and figures—not just flowery words? Has the product been tested in the laboratory, tested in production, tested in the field? Can you demonstrate how the product has performed in use? Few prospects will rush to take an advertiser's say-so. In fact, most people take advertising claims with a grain of salt. If you can present them with solid, factual evidence, you'll be ahead of the game. *Invent* a use test, if you must. And remember, there's great conviction in a legitimate third-person endorsement. Some Mercy Hospital ads feature satisfied patients. So always be on the lookout for proof, proof, proof.

Sometimes two competing products are of similar quality, but you may be able to take advantage of the difference in the way the two parent companies *back* the product. Prompt repair service. Quick refunds. Fair exchanges. A retail operation may rise or fall on such nonproduct factors as returns and exchanges, charge accounts, deliveries. These so-called "institutional" aspects of a business enterprise often provide great subject matter for advertising copy.

How is your product priced? If it is very expensive, you may never mention price; if it is very inexpensive, you may never mention anything else. If competition is just as inexpensive, price loses its selling attraction.

Occasionally you may be fortunate enough to promote a product that has won official acclaim—a gold medal, blue ribbon, best in show, an Oscar, or Car of the Year. This can be a great talking point.

Likewise, an outstanding sales performance can be a very persuasive argument to use on reluctant prospects. Sales leadership is the most potent kind of third-person endorsement. It means not just one or two satisfied customers, but *many* of them. It says, "If we've made more people happy than any other, we must be good." This increases a prospect's confidence in what you have to sell.

Do not overlook the tons of never-ending information and suggestions that come to you through the trade journals and trade bulletins of your industry. Such trade association publications not only keep you current with the industry in general, but also offer you marketing and advertising case histories from individual operations all across the country. The Newspaper Advertising Bureau regularly reports to its members on outstanding advertising from every corner of the land. An idea used in Binghamton, New York, may also work wonders in Birmingham, Alabama.

The subject of media will be dealt with in detail in Chapter 11, but you have to be conscious of it while you are starting to grope for advertising ideas. If you advertise in a smaller community or area, you may not have many media

GRIP STRUT®

SELF-CLEANING TEETH BITE BEST THROUGH MUD AND SNOW!

SAFETY GRATING

You'll feel a gripping difference between GRIP STRUT® Safety Grating and ordinary grating. Serrated teeth combine with an open design to provide a non-slip walkway surface. Waste, mud and snow slide right through. Ice shears free underfoot for maximum slip resistance from any direction.

GRIP STRUT Safety Grating comes in a wide choice of sizes, widths, gauges and materials. Get specifics. Check the Yellow Pages for your distributor or *call toll-free: 800-621-7789 (in Illinois, call 312-321-5856). Or write to us at 101 S. Wacker Dr., Chicago, IL 60606-4385, Dept.*

Meets OSHA Standards

Metal Products Division

USG Industries, Inc.

© 1985 USG Industries, Inc.

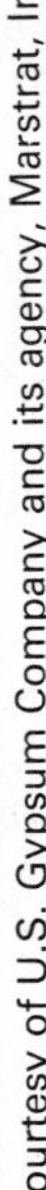

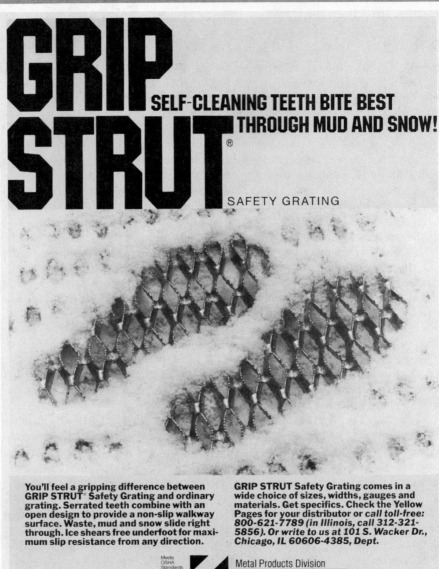

FIGURE 5–5
The concept of safety is clearly demonstrated by a simple photograph in this business-to-business magazine advertisement.

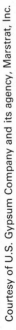

options. But even if your town has only one newspaper, you should be familiar with all its daily features. You should know which features appeal most to which members of the audience. If you are selling a kitchen product you aren't likely to ask that your ad be put on the sports page. Radio stations nowadays work at appealing to one narrow segment of the audience rather than a broad audience. You should be aware, at least, of basic differences between a "news" station, a "talk" station, and a "music" station. And keep in mind that music lovers come in many tastes and preferences; champagne waltz music, for example, may be a joy to the elderly but it is a joke to the young. Many young people will wait in line all night to hear a rock group that wouldn't be allowed past the gate in Sun City. The important point is that every detail you know about available media makes you that much better qualified to arrive at a decision.

As indicated earlier, well-prepared advertisers must know what their own customers are like. They must know why they buy the product and how they use it. They must know their interests, their activities, their backgrounds.

You have been urged to seize every opportunity to talk to your customers and prospects. Such contacts provide the most fertile ground for effective advertising and selling ideas. Important decisions and investments should be based on responses from a reasonable number of people—a "significant" number. This is not as overwhelming a task as it may first appear. You can use personal interviews, mail questionnaires, telephone calls asking structured questions—or one of the other methods detailed in Chapter 3.

If you only need the "flavor" of public opinion, you can conduct a focus group interview. A small, informal gathering of, say, beer drinkers will discuss beer and beer advertising with a minimum of prompting. They will interact with one another and may give you some new insights about your product. Because it involves so few people, this kind of research is *not* statistically significant; it is qualitative rather than quantitative. It furnishes ideas and insights rather than proof. At the very least, it can furnish you with authentic and sometimes "colorful" customer language to weave into your selling copy.

See What Other Advertising Can Tell You

Since you are a student of advertising, first be a student of your own company's advertising. Study *past* advertising— all the way back to the beginning. It will give you a smattering of human history; it may provide you with some highly distinctive material; it may save you the embarrassment of discovering in a board meeting that your "new" idea was first used by the company back in 1906. Years back, it was the practice of many agencies to start bright young prospects on their careers by having them paste ad reprints in the proof file books. This is not very elevating, but sound. Every advertiser must be familiar with the past image or "face" that the company has presented to the public. Sometimes past advertising has a particular tone or style that is well worth keeping. This is particularly true in retail advertising, where store image far outweighs all other factors. But even if all previous advertising was dreadful, you have to be familiar with it before you launch something new. Perhaps just trying to avoid past mistakes will lead you to a new avenue of creative expression. We repeat—do not attempt to prepare new advertising for your company until you have studied the old.

Familiarize yourself with your competitors' advertising too. Know what their sales propositions offer, what they look like, exactly what they say. Never imitate. Figure a way to counter their offer, or top it. Figure a way to sound different. Go out of your way to look different. If you were a cigarette advertiser would you start a new campaign based on cowboys? Often, your conscious effort to finesse a competitor's advertising will lead you into new advertising that is distinctly your own.

You must be aware of advertising in general. Obviously you'll watch the advertising of competitors, the advertising in your industry. But it pays to keep abreast of *all* advertising. Perhaps you can ride an advertising trend or even anticipate one. At the very least you can keep up-to-date in your use of graphics and illustrations. If you are trying to present yourself as a fashion leader among retailers, it would never do to run stodgy, old-fashioned, ill-balanced ads. Your own advertising visuals would give the lie to your claim—because fashion *is* news. If you have anything to do with the advertising of better clothing, regular glances at *New Yorker* magazine and at the *New York Sunday Times* magazine section will quickly let you know what is in style for advertising. If you are alert to all kinds of advertising around you, you can sometimes "borrow" or adapt an idea from a totally different field and achieve a fresh look in your own industry. It is always fun to look at advertising; it is even more fun when you can turn this pleasant activity into a profit.

Identify Highly Advertisable Facts

We stated earlier that creative ideas begin with questions. You ask, you probe, you investigate—and you never stop. You learn a jillion things about your product or service, your customers and prospects, your channels of distribution, and your channels of communication. What do you do with this mountain of information? Well, you discard most of it—for advertising purposes, that is.

First off, almost all research reveals obvious facts. It substantiates what already exists or what you logically expected.

Second, all that you may have learned about your product or service is not highly advertisable. It is up to you to custom tailor all the information you have gathered. You must have all the information, even down to the dullest detail. All this background information is like a bolt of cloth that you will fashion into a distinctive image in the marketplace. Perhaps you will match an interesting advantage of the product with a basic desire of the customer, weaving in an attractive feature from a local radio station. This is how advertising concepts come about. They are more a matter of solid work than of inspiration or imagination. You can see now that they do not just spring into being—presto!—like a magician's trick. If you can match an exclusive advantage of your product or service with a deeply felt need on the part of customers, you are well on your way to being a creative advertising genius.

At this point, however, you must remind yourself that advertising is only part of the venture with which you are involved. Perhaps only a very minor part—as it is with many industrial firms. No matter how important the advertising may be to you personally, you must plan it and organize it so that it fits in with the overall plans of the parent organization. Your advertising must be synchronized with all other facets of the marketing enterprise—the basic purpose of the product, its special design, and its suitability for certain market segments. Suppose a writer came up with a great idea for a luxury car. No matter how brilliant, it still would not fit the Volkswagen marketing plan. Your advertising plan must mesh with the activities of the company sales force and of the wholesaler sales force. Your advertising plans must be understandable to and win the cooperation of the retailers.

Going Ahead with a Purpose

Most important, you plan your advertising with a purpose. That is how advertising creativity differs from much purely artistic creativity. Advertising creativity is designed to produce results. It cannot be aimless. It must have a goal, an objective.

It is good business to have plans and objectives in writing—even if it amounts to just a paragraph or two or an outline. Any plan, no matter how crude, tends to keep you on track, obligates you to proceed logically, forces you to work toward a clearly stated goal.

Jot Down a Creative Strategy

In most professional advertising circles today, no headlines, layouts, or copy are started until management and creative people alike agree on creative strategy. The **creative strategy** is a very crisp written statement on what the advertising is going to talk about, but not how the advertising is going to say it. The creative strategy outline takes no standard form; it can vary from agency to agency, from advertiser to advertiser. But it always highlights these three key points: the **principal benefit** of the product or service; the **principal target** or group of consumers the advertisers might wish to reach; and the **principal objective** of the ad itself, that is, what the advertiser wants a person to think, feel, or do after seeing the ad.

creative strategy A written statement on what the advertising is going to talk about.

principal benefit The main advantage of a product or service.

principal target The group of consumers an advertiser wants to reach.

principal objective What you want a person to see, hear, feel, or do after seeing an ad.

Differences between Marketing Goals and Communication Goals. As an advertiser, you must learn the difference between marketing goals and communications goals. The first function of any advertisement is to communicate: the message itself has to register an impression before any result can follow. Naturally, all advertising efforts are designed to contribute to the overall marketing goals. But, in fairness, advertising must be judged primarily on its ability to communicate. For example: market share (your percentage of total sales compared with all the competitors) is a marketing goal; public recognition of a new slogan is a communications goal. When a certain Midwest supermarket chain launched a new selling line of copy or theme line for its advertising campaign, the company's marketing goal was an 8 percent increase in market share, but the communications goal was an 80 percent awareness of the new campaign copy line within the first 13 weeks. Communications goals are set because so many factors—from product to price to packaging to weather—can influence sales results that it is difficult to trace sales success or failure to advertising alone.

Agreement on a Central Selling Concept

central selling concept The core idea or main theme that ties together all advertising and promotional efforts.

Once the creative strategy has nailed down the principal benefit, target, and objective, it is well to settle on a central selling idea or theme that ties all advertising and promotional efforts together. Examples: "The Pepsi Generation" and "Fly the Friendly Skies of United." Some executives call this a core idea. In any event, this **central selling concept** states concisely the basic reason or reasons that a product or service should be selected for purchase ("Quality is Job 1") or a particular source (store, shop, office, factory) should be selected as a supplier of goods and services ("the big store with great little places to shop"). It is the basic reason management feels a product has superior want-satisfying ability and, consequently, is the basic reason prospects will buy it regularly.

This central selling concept is based on the first point of your creative strategy—principal benefit. It is anchored to the second point of your creative strategy—principal target. The creative strategy adapts the thought in a central selling concept to a specific audience. Consider how the central selling concept of United Airlines has been adapted to special advertising for business people, vacationers, and families.

The reward of a central selling concept is that it helps assure that each advertising dollar supports every other dollar. For example, that what is seen on a point-of-sale display in the supermarket relates to *the* major advertising theme seen on television instead of introducing unrelated ideas. The reward of a creative strategy is that it takes each individual piece of the total campaign and gets the best possible results out of it. Each United ad or commercial may stress a particular phase of service—more carry-on luggage space, for example—but it never loses track of the central selling concept: "Fly the Friendly Skies."

The Personal Profile

personal profile A fictional description, based on statistics, of a product or service's most likely buyer.

The creative strategy is a great aid in keeping ad makers on track. So, too, is another current advertising concept known as the **personal profile.** This is a bit of fiction based on fact, a short biographical sketch of one of your most likely prospects. You give this imaginary person a name, a home, a history, a family, a set of attitudes—all logical, but all created from the dry statistics of research reports, personal interviews, sales figures, and the like. The purpose of a personal profile is to give you a single individual to talk to in your advertising copy. This is much easier than trying to talk to some nameless, faceless set of figures provided by mere demographics. The most effective advertising copy is written as though you are having a face-to-face conversation with a single individual. The use of a personal profile aids this process.

Checking Copy for Validations and Differences

One agency man in a medium-sized Midwest city suggests that the two key words to use in reference to the function of advertising are *validate* and *differentiate*. First, the advertising **validates** or reinforces the image of the product or service that the public already has. Second, it tries to **differentiate** or show the difference between the advertised product or services and that of the competitors.

validate To reinforce the image a customer already has of a product or service.

differentiate To show how a product or service differs from its competitors.

This last point deserves special emphasis. Differentiation is the secret of a successful advertising concept. You are not being very creative if you prepare an ad that can be signed by somebody else. In fact, an acid test is to substitute *X* for *Y* and see if the copy reads the same. Pray that your product comes with its own built-in differential advantage which provides a much-needed benefit. If your product or service is similar to others, then you must seek some other way to differentiate it. Try never to be satisfied with "me too" advertising. Diligently seek that element that sets you apart.

If your advertising task seems very difficult to solve, consider the story of a young osteopathic surgeon newly settled in a small Midwest town. He was forbidden by law to advertise. Yet he found a way to differentiate himself. When older doctors got night emergency calls from the far reaches of the community, they would beg off but suggest the patient try the new Dr. *A*. Dr. *A* would respond at 3:00 A.M. but first he would go to the farmhouse just beyond the one where he was wanted. He would bang on the door, yelling "I'm Dr. *A*. Is this the Blank farm that made the emergency call?" On his way back, after treating the correct patient, he would stop at the farm on the other side, repeating his Paul Revere routine. By the time he got back to his home there were now *three* families in the community who knew who Dr. *A* was and that he could be counted on to respond to a 3:00 A.M. emergency call. We cannot vouch for the truth of the story, but we applaud the inventiveness of the advertising.

No matter how you choose to differentiate yourself, you must make a strong effort to stand out from the crowd. This is what potential customers remember. If you want them to remember *you*, it pays to be at least a little bit different.

Drawing Up a Plan

Different readers will use the advice in this book in different ways. It is designed primarily for beginners in advertising, people who are pretty much left to their own devices, or, at least, for people who are *not* backed by a big, high-powered, sophisticated advertising organization. Yet there is much to be learned from the "big boys."

At least one large national agency used a committee known as the Plans Board to review creative strategies. That Plans Board functioned at the highest executive level; its membership was often made up of the president or chairman of the agency, the creative director, media director, management supervisor, and the research director. Before this high and mighty Plans Board, the group of people who worked day-in, day-out on each major account had to present their advertising plans for the year ahead. Everything was organized into a formal Plans Book (which sometimes reached a staggering size). This Plans Book was distributed ahead of time so each member of the Plans Board could study it before the formal presentation was made in a group meeting. A copy of this same Plans Book was kept always handy at the client's office and in the agency account supervisor's office throughout the year. It was there to point the way and to help solve problems that might develop. The Plans Book was, in effect, the bible for that particular account.

In case you are wondering what was in the Plans Book, there is no great mystery. It contained much the same thing you have tucked into your advertising file or jotted down in your notebook or on your scratch pad. The language may have been fancier or more exalted (and obscure), but the content was identical. The super-duper Madison Avenue agency Plans Book contained *information:* information people got from studying and asking questions; information about the product and the company that makes it; information about customers, potential customers—their attitudes and their buying habits; information about competitors—their products, their advertising, their selling practices.

Does that all sound familiar to you by now? Of course. The only difference is one of scope.

The Plans Book also included creative recommendations, media schedule, and budget. But these were based firmly on the real foundation of the book—information.

Analysis: Watching for Problems and Opportunities

There is a crucial step in between the basic information and the final recommendation known as analysis. A well-known term in American marketing sets the tone for proper analysis: "Problems and Opportunities."

Every business enterprise has both problems and opportunities—even dominant Campbell Soup Company. In fact, Campbell's very dominance of the soup market created problems. How do you sell more soup when you already "own" the market? With beef bouillon, this problem gave rise to a communications goal: show the reader new uses for an established product. The resulting advertisement read: "Soup on the Rocks"—a can of beef bouillon poured over ice cubes in an Old-Fashioned glass. Sales increased sharply. Campbell turned the problem of custom or habit into another opportunity. Usually people served soup to kids at lunch; some served soup at a fancy dinner for guests. Campbell saw the gap in daily usage and decided to expand the use of its already familiar

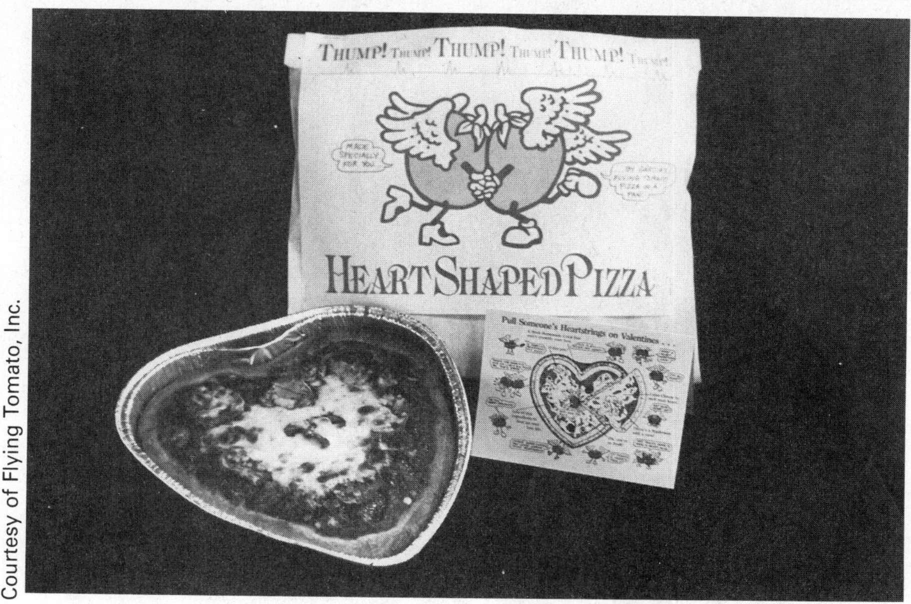

Courtesy of Flying Tomato, Inc.

FIGURE 5–6
Always innovative marketers, the Flying Tomato Brothers of Garcia's Pizza pioneered a special Valentine promotion: heart-shaped pizzas, available only from February 4 to February 14.

products with an unusual serving suggestion. The advertisement used the innovative theme "Soup for Breakfast."

To take a much smaller but very dramatic example of the analysis of marketing problems and opportunities, consider the situation of a small pizza restaurant named Garcia's, founded in 1971 just off campus at the University of Illinois. Garcia's market was composed of students who wanted fast, cheap lunches and light dinners. Its competitors were chiefly fast-food franchises offering burgers and fries. Garcia's broke the monotony, became the first to sell pizza by the slice, thus giving the students taste variety at an attractive price. Quickly Garcia's captured the market of students eating in restaurants and opened additional locations. Later on, to fight a leveling off of business and to pursue growth opportunities, Garcia's marketing and promotion activities emphasized delivery service. Later still, Garcia's began promoting a family night theme. In fact, Garcia's has quite a track record for being alert to marketing opportunities. They even offer a heart-shaped pizza for Valentine's Day.

Every business—and every one of its competitors—has problems and opportunities in the marketplace. It is up to you to take the information you have gathered and use it to maximize your opportunities and minimize your problems at the very time that you minimize your competitors' opportunities and maximize their problems.

IT'S MIDNIGHT.

(Do You Know Where Your Banker Is?)

Ours are at the Bank, Working.

From 7:00 a.m. to midnight, seven days a week, Marine American National Bank keeps its drive-up and walk-up windows open and staffed with experienced, professional tellers. These individuals can help you with loan payments, money orders, travelers checks, balance inquiries, and more.

Just stop by and talk to one . . . any time.

MARINE

AMERICAN NATIONAL BANK

P. O. BOX 3009, CHAMPAIGN, IL 61821, 217-351-1600 MEMBER FDIC

Courtesy of Marine American National Bank, Champaign, Illinois.

FIGURE 5–7
Here is a truly unique selling proposition—perhaps the only such one in the country. It is consistently and proudly promoted on television, on radio, on billboards, and in newspapers.

You are never likely to solve all your marketing problems at any one time—or exploit all your opportunities in a flash. You form a strategy that seems the best way to proceed at any given time. Football coaches call this a "game plan," but it's a rare plan that's perfect. You are well aware that one successful football coach will insist that games are won on defense while another equally successful coach will proclaim that a good offense is the best defense. Each marketer-advertiser must adopt the strategy best suited to a given situation that has been analyzed for problems and opportunities.

Take, for example, the small family-owned grocery store in a sizable community. It can't compete with the big supermarkets on price. So it competes by keeping different store hours than the supermarkets—or by offering free deliveries.

Many a small clothing store in America had to specialize in the face of traditional full-line competition and prospered recently by realizing that blue jeans were not a fad but a fact of life.

We tend to dismiss our local banks as being "all alike." But must they be? Did you know that banks used to close at 2:00 P.M.? If you weren't there when the bell rang, you were out of luck. Not so any more. Banks are becoming aggressive marketers. Most banks now feature mechanical tellers. To top such extended service competition, one bank in Champaign, Illinois, has *live* tellers to serve you from 7:00 A.M. to midnight, seven days a week.

In a city where there were several equally fine supermarkets, one of them sought a way to be unique. It offered a catering service. In one medium-sized city, a clothing merchant offered his stock at equivalent prices to a couple of big discount chain stores in the vicinity. He prospered and soon had ten stores. The differences? His merchandise consisted of first-rate brand-name goods that he bought at distress sales around the country.

A successful Chrysler-Plymouth dealer in the Midwest had several first-rate competitors. Somehow he managed to snare the Rolls Royce franchise for his area. Heaven knows how many Rolls Royce sales he'll make, but overnight his dealership has more class than anybody else's.

Suppose, for example, you were advertising a product dependent on raw materials in limited supply. You certainly would advertise to promote steady sales over time rather than strive for a rush of orders.

Suppose your product was built slowly and in small quantities by local craftsmen. You would be likely to target your advertising against "mass-produced junk."

It does not make any difference what your particular interest in advertising may be. Whether you are a small retailer, a small manufacturer, or an aspiring advertising agent, the procedure is the same. You isolate your problems and opportunities, your strengths and your weaknesses. You put your best foot forward. You make the most of what you have.

SUMMARY

A good advertising concept starts with sound creative strategy. Creative strategy is based on thorough knowledge and wise analysis of the marketplace. Knowledge stems from inquiry.

Ask questions. Get answers. Study the facts. Focus on factors that differentiate you. Concentrate on that area where you do a superior job of filling a human need.

If you will approach all these obvious steps by applying good old-fashioned common sense, you will unearth an advertising concept worthy of the most seasoned pros on Madison Avenue or Michigan Avenue. How to bring the basic advertising idea to life in headline, illustration, layout, and copy is the subject of the next chapter.

TERMS TO KNOW

Now that you have finished the chapter, you should understand the following terms:

creative strategy	central selling concept
principal benefit	personal profile
principal target	validate
principal objective	differentiate

If you are not certain of the meaning of any of these terms, go back through the chapter and review them.

THINGS TO THINK ABOUT

1. Why are not all facts about a product "advertisable?"
2. How is advertising writing unlike poetry writing or novel writing?
3. When an advertising idea springs to life, how much do you think is due to "inspiration" and how much to "perspiration?"
4. How do you feel about "borrowing" ad ideas?
5. Can you imagine the difficulties of trying to sell management an *unplanned* ad?

THINGS TO TALK ABOUT

1. Discuss why it pays to study not only your own advertising and competitive advertising but all advertising.
2. Discuss the most active advertisers in your community. Vote on which you think does the best job. Analyze why you think so.
3. It has been said that good advertising is "a believable promise to an interested audience." Why the word "interested?" Shouldn't good advertising interest everybody?
4. Discuss the various media available in your community. Which would you want most to have carrying your advertising messages?
5. If novelists must please literary critics, whom do advertising writers have to please?
6. What are the common traits in good copywriters?

THINGS TO DO

1. Select one local clothing store you would like to represent. Clip and study the advertising of all its competitors. Suggest an advertising approach different from theirs.
2. For that same clothing store, set a marketing goal for the company. Set a communications goal for its advertising.
3. Make a clip file of all the automotive ads you see in one month. Which advertising does the best job of standing out from all the others? Put your analysis into a short paragraph.
4. Learn the founding date of the oldest business in your community. Look up what happened that year in American history.
5. Analyze an ad in your favorite advertising campaign. What basic selling idea is it trying to communicate to you?

6 Copywriting for Print Media

Twenty years ago, George Hadfield discovered a broken, yet beautiful, 175-year-old grandfather clock. He also discovered that no one in all of England could repair it. So he learned how and found great pleasure in fixing it himself.

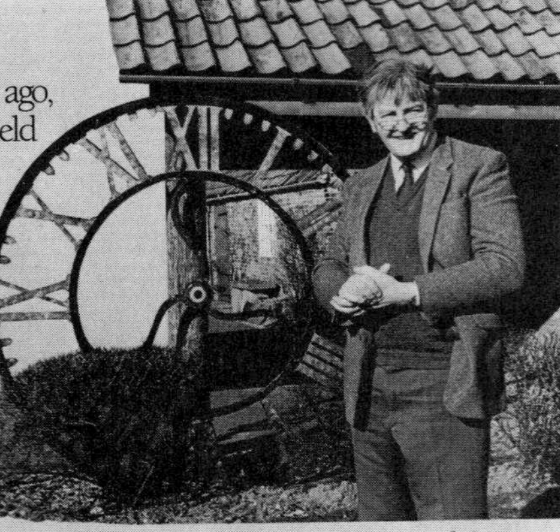

Now George Hadfield's pleasure is his business. And a visit to his unique clock shop in Shepshed, north of London, is, in many ways, a trip through time.

You can stroll the grounds among giant tower clock faces. And go inside his 18th-century farmhouse and fall in love with a meticulously restored grandfather clock.

But if you're planning to buy one, don't ask if it keeps good time. And don't forget your Visa card.

Because George won't sell anything unless it works as beautifully as it looks. *And he won't take American Express.*

VISA

It's everywhere you want to be.℠

© Visa U.S.A. Inc. 1986

Advertising courtesy of Visa USA, Inc.

CHAPTER OUTLINE

By the time you finish this chapter, you should understand:

1. That advertising copywriting involves more than just writing.
2. The importance of communicating with picture as well as with words.
3. The vital importance of the headline.
4. Which type of headline appeals are most effective.
5. The function of subheads.
6. Ways to make copy believable.
7. The reference books to be familiar with.
8. What the term *layout* means.

The information-gathering, information-sifting process discussed in the previous chapter goes on constantly. You never stop learning all you can about your product, your store, your customers, your competitors. You never stop analyzing this information to find problems and opportunities. You never stop looking for a way to put your best foot forward. Part of putting your best foot forward involves writing copy—the next step in the creative process.

COPYWRITING—AN OVERVIEW

Copywriting includes all phases of composing an advertisement. In print advertising, it is the creation of words, pictures, visuals, symbols, and graphics. In broadcast advertising—which we'll discuss in the next chapter—it is the creation of all these elements as well as music and sound effects. Everything the advertiser creates, then, comes under the general heading of "copy."

copywriting All phases of composing an advertisement.

Bridging the Gap from Research Information to Ad Copy

Exactly how you should write copy depends on the particular problem facing you. A catalog sheet for a small manufacturer needs little embellishment; it should be straightforward, clean, and well organized. A trade ad for a local manufacturer may require more imaginative skills, though it too should be straightforward. The advertising for a small retail store represents a quite different challenge. It is a day-in day-out proposition, a selling and promotion effort that never ends. A large retail operation—say, a department store—may pose a different advertising problem from the kind a small retailer poses. Types of businesses differ. You might advertise clothes one way and food in quite another way. And you might advertise a bank in a totally different way.

As an employee of a manufacturer or store, you may be asked to get out the advertising; you may own and operate your own business (including the advertising); you may wish to specialize—to make advertising your business, either through an agency or free-lance.

Using the Creative Strategy

Copywriting is basically the process of solving problems in communication—generally of a business nature. While copywriting is often called an "art," it is far from an art form. It is, for the most part, a strictly business proposition, designed to reach the consumer's pocketbook, not the Art Institute or the public library. To keep your copywriting businesslike, start with a creative strategy that shows the principal benefit of your product or service, the principal target audience you are trying to reach, and the principal goal of your message. Never touch pencil to paper until you have decided on the creative strategy.

Decide what you are going to be creative about. Your chief news. Your biggest selling point. Your proposition's greatest benefit. Decide to whom you are going to talk—high school students, homemakers, lawyers, plumbers. And, finally, decide what kind of action you want these people to take, physically or psychologically. These decisions are the basics of your creative strategy.

For example, in Campbell's "Soup on the Rocks" ad, mentioned earlier, the principal benefit was that cold beef bouillon was a healthful, bracing beverage; the target audience was homemakers interested in caring for and pleasing their families; the goal was to inform homemakers of a new way to serve an old favorite.

The shrewd advertiser begins his copywriting with a creative strategy, no matter how crude or informal or brusque it may be. Write it down. It costs you only a few minutes of your time; it may save you wasted effort later on.

Getting Started

Let us say that you wish to prepare a newspaper advertisement for a unit of space that measures 7" × 10"—a size and shape used in most magazine ads today.

You know the principal point that you want to get across, the principal impression that you want to make, and the principal reaction you want people to have. That's your creative strategy. Now take a blank piece of paper and rule in the 7" × 10" area. Then look at it. Terrifying, isn't it?

Believe it or not, that blank piece of paper staring back strikes fear into the most experienced copywriting heart. In this respect, you are no different from the most grizzled veteran on Madison Avenue.

Do you wish to fill it with words alone? Nothing wrong in that. Classified ads are filled only with words. But, as you look, do you see where a picture or pictures might help tell your story better than words? There is an old saying about a picture being worth 1,000 words. An old saying, yes, but oh, so true. A skilled advertising copywriter communicates with pictures as well as with words. The advertising writer of today cannot afford to be one-dimensional.

WORDS—THE PRIMARY MESSAGE CARRIERS

Most ads contain these five main elements:

Headline

Illustration

Subhead (if any)

Body Copy

Signature

The elements are generally arranged in that order. The most common variation would be for the illustration to come before the headline. But this is not a radical change because headline and illustration work together.

You must not have your headline and your illustrations marching off in two different directions at the same time. They must work together because they have the same basic communications function. They must capture the attention of the right audience. They must offer a reward for reading. They must tell at least part of the story. In the rest of this section, we'll talk about the many different elements the copywriter needs to consider in creating the *words* for an ad. Later, we'll discuss the visual aspects of copywriting.

Headlines: The Most Important Part of the Ad

At this point, ask yourself these questions. What is the first element you see in an ad? What is the first element your classmate sees? What is the first element almost everybody sees? The **headline.** That big, bold statement that proclaims the basic selling proposition. People read the headline and then decide whether or not to read the rest of the ad. Therefore, most advertising experts agree that the headline is the most important part of the advertisement.

headline The statement that proclaims the basic selling proposition of an ad.

If people read your headline they *may* read the rest of your story. If they do not read your headline, they almost certainly will not read the rest of the ad. A world-famous advertising agency executive insists that a headline represents 80¢ of an advertiser's dollar. He has learned through research that four out of five readers do not go beyond the headline of an ad.

It has been said that a good advertisement is a believable promise to the right audience. Keep in mind that illustrations as well as headlines can be seen in that same light.

What to Include

Be sure you get into your headline the one point that could compel the reader to buy the product or service: the chief benefit. Do not let anything—style, humor, graphics—get in the way of that point.

FIGURE 6–1
Novel one-word headline combines with rich illustration to make the benefit instantly clear.

Hush!
Fabric magic at work. SILENT™ Acoustical Wall Panels and new SILENT SQUARES® Acoustical Ceilings coordinate beautifully with selected baffles and accessories. It's all part of a full family of fabric-clad products we call our SILENT COLLECTION™—stylishly clothed surfaces synergistic with today's hard-working environments.
Appraise our fashionable palette of color and textures. Pleasing to the eye. Comforting to the ear. With NRC ranges up to 1.00.

It's yours to design with. Luxury-look fabrics in woven, plain or ribbed faces. Surprisingly affordable, too. Acquire specifics. Call 312-321-5495. Or write
USG Acoustical Products Company
101 S. Wacker Dr., Chicago, IL 60606-4385,
Dept.
USG Interior Systems
SILENT COLLECTION
© 1986. USG Acoustical Products Co

Courtesy of USG Acoustical Products Company and its agency, Marstrat, Inc.

Never be satisfied with the first headline that comes to you. It may be a dandy. It may not. But you will never know until you consider other options. Experienced ad writers scribble down twenty, forty, sixty, one hundred headlines before making a final decision. This is not a waste of time. Far from it, for two reasons. First, the ninety-eighth headline may prove the brightest of all. Second, all those carefully composed alternate headlines can provide well-written lines for use in the body copy.

The purpose of a headline is to attract attention and stir up interest. It should stand out. The shorter you keep your headline, the more likely a busy reader will notice it. Try to train yourself to write short and snappy, punchy lines.

Yet there is no hard and fast rule. The same famous advertising man, David Ogilvy, who wrote "The Man in the Hathaway Shirt" also wrote "At 60 miles an hour the loudest noise in this new Rolls-Royce comes from the electric clock." There are times when a short headline simply won't do. A headline can be as long as it has to be. But don't waste a word. Make every word count. (See Figure 6–1.)

How to Make Headlines Effective. If you wish to become a good headline writer, study the mail-order ads around you. Their headlines are tested by actual sales results. One of the greatest mail-order writers who ever lived, John Caples, a fifty-year veteran, has written a popular book called *Tested Advertising Methods*. The most recent edition came out in 1980. In that book Caples tells scores of ways to write effective headlines. It would pay you to study his methods.

The most important thing to do in a headline is appeal to the reader's *self-interest*—solve her problem, satisfy his needs. Second, give the reader *news*. Third, appeal to the reader's *curiosity*.

Most of us are rather self-centered. We tend to judge every human experience on the basis of "What's in it for me?" Since you can't very well change human nature, it's more practical to go along with it. Write self-interest headlines—the reader's self-interest, not *yours*. Put yourself in the prospect's shoes. Look at the selling proposition from the prospect's point of view. This is the most basic requirement of effective communication. Psychologists call it **empathy,** the ability to see things from someone else's point of view. Without it your efforts are almost certainly condemned to failure. Example: "We're constantly improving our Met Life prompt payment squadron."

empathy The ability to see things from someone else's point of view.

The second most effective headline approach is the news headline. This is logical. Human beings are irresistibly attracted to the new and the different. If there is something new about your product or your proposition, use it. Remember that what may be old stuff to you and your management can be intriguing news to a prospect. A new design, new feature, new use, new way of serving—take advantage of any aspect of your product that is new to the consumer. Example for sunglasses: "Vision Breakthrough."

Curiosity headlines rank a distant third in effectiveness. These are sometimes called "blind" headlines. Many copywriters get almost poetic in compos-

Courtesy of U.S. Gypsum and its agency, Marstrat, Inc.

FIGURE 6–2
News headline announces big benefit for a special audience. The sequence of small illustrations explains the process, builds belief in the headline promise.

ing curiosity headlines. There have been some memorable ones. The trouble is that the prospect has to take the time and trouble to bridge the gap, to complete the message. Alas, most readers will not bother. A communications ad is headlined: "Paradox of Power." The reader would have to read on.

Ways to Involve Readers. The best kind of headline forces the reader to participate in your ad. There are certain simple, time-tested devices that almost guarantee reader involvement.

The most common way to pull a reader into your ad is to ask a direct question. "Do You Make These Mistakes in English?" is a classic mail-order headline that ran unchanged for many, many years. A question is provocative. It talks directly and personally to a prospect. It implies a solution to the prospect's problem. Just be sure that your question has some genuine "bite" to it, some deep-down thought-provoking quality. Don't ask a question that can be answered quickly "Yes" or "No" and then ignored. When you write a question headline, make sure your question is valid.

Another device that gets readers involved in your message is the "how-to" headline. For example, "How to Redecorate Your Living Room in One Day," "How to Drive Defensively," "How to Save on Food Costs." The how-to headline is almost irresistible. It promises helpful information, a practical solution to a problem. A how-to headline "levels" with the reader; it does not waste the reader's time.

Two other much-used ways of getting readers involved in your message are the quiz and the challenge. How many times have you succumbed to such quiz headlines as "Can You Answer These Questions about Gasoline Mileage?" or "Test Your Knowledge of Airline Travel Practices"? Again, the reader is drawn in because the ad writer settled on a pertinent topic. Challenges come in many forms. A campaign of several years back challenged the reader by saying "If You Can Find a Better Bourbon, Buy It." A beer campaign was based entirely on "We Challenge You." Whether you "challenge" or "defy" with your ad, you force the reader to take an active part in your selling proposition.

While it is well to know something about what has worked for others in the past, you will find yourself adapting your approach to suit each special problem. And rightly so. If a question headline works best, use it. If a command headline works best, use it. The most intriguing—and sometimes frustrating—thing about writing the advertising message is that there is no single correct way to do it.

Subheads: Their Functions

In some ads you will see a large, bold headline followed by another line that is not so large and bold, yet is much larger and bolder than the body copy, or the main text of the ad. This line of copy—second only in importance to the headline—is called a **subhead.** It expands on the selling idea introduced in the headline and induces the reader to read the complete body text. Here's an example from an ad for acoustical wall and ceiling coverings:

subhead A line of copy that expands on the selling idea introduced in the headline.

(Headline) HUSH!
(Subhead) Fabric magic at work.

Learn to make use of subheads. They allow the casual reader to get your basic message at a glance; the interested reader will, of course, find full details in the main text.

Body Copy: Clinching the Sale

The **body copy** is the main text of the ad. Whereas the illustration and headline bring the customer in, the body copy clinches the sale. The body copy explains more fully how a product works, proves that it works, and ends up "asking for the order."

body copy The main text of an ad.

Body copy should be compelling. Who wants to read a dull, uninteresting sales story? It should also be clear. There is no room for confusion. Write simple sentences. Use simple words. And make it crisp. Each selling situation is unique, but there is never room for a wasted word. The way to insure crisp copy is to edit, rewrite, edit, rewrite, edit, rewrite. To be a good copywriter, you must work at it. The secret to success lies in the trimming and the tightening.

But above all else, your copy must be believable; it must carry conviction. You can't do this with fancy words and colorful writing. You are not trying to win a literary award; you are trying to sell merchandise.

So skip the hot air in your copy and stick to cold facts. Give information, details, prices, proof of performance. Straight talk does not bore potential customers; instead, they will thank you for it.

The Value of Specifics. The greatest weakness of beginning ad writers is the tendency to talk in generalities and cliches. Suppose you are writing a restaurant ad and you say, "Fine food at fair prices." This is a flat-out generality, so commonplace as to be totally ignored. It is meaningless. What restaurant has not claimed it? But if you say "Tonight. Tender oceanfresh scallops. $8.98," you are saying something specific and understandable. You are delivering a message that readers can sink their teeth into, figuratively and literally.

You must work very hard at this. It takes a strong, conscious effort to go beyond such a bland statement for a restaurant as, "Served graciously in a unique atmosphere" and tell the reader instead exactly how the food is served and exactly what makes the atmosphere unique. Suppose the waiters are dressed in colonial costume and wear powdered wigs. Suppose the entire room is candlelit. Suppose the food is served on Wedgewood plates. Don't these kinds of details have more meaning than an easy generality? Of course they do. But they mean you have to work harder at your job. The lazy writer tries to slide by with clever words; the salesperson digs down for solid facts. There is no comparison when it comes to packing conviction into an argument. Words are not necessarily believable; *facts* are believable. Repeat to yourself a thousand times: I will be specific. I will not use generalities.

Beginning adwriters also have a tendency to exaggerate, well-intended, no doubt. Enthusiasm runs wild. But the trouble with exaggeration in advertising copy is that it may annoy readers while failing to win belief. You don't like it when other people exaggerate; why do it yourself in your advertising? Even when you have a truly fantastic claim, you must not appear to exaggerate. In most instances, understatement is far more convincing than overstatement. An Air Force recruiting ad shows the dramatic view a fighter pilot sees, with the understated line: "It's not like sitting behind a desk."

Avoid "brag and boast" copy. It offends people. If you toot your horn too loudly, people won't listen to a word you say.

Straight Talk and Friendliness. Write your copy as though you were talking to *one* person, not to a group of people or to the whole community. Remember, most agency ad-makers first compose a highly detailed personal profile of just one prospect to whom the ad will be written. Open your plea by saying something with which the reader can mentally agree. Example: "Home cooking is great, but at today's prices—!" Example: "The largest cost in running an advertising agency is payroll." Show at once in your copy that you understand the reader's situation in life or in business. Show at once that you are really sympathetic with the reader's problems and that you think you may be able to help. Be friendly but not phony or overly familiar. Be as conversational as possible without being slangy or folksy. Do not freeze up and go formal when you start to tackle that blank piece of paper. Make believe that cold and forbidding paper is an acquaintance whom you are trying to persuade face-to-face. Try to act natural. Try just to be yourself.

The "You" Approach. As you write, drop the word *we* from your vocabulary and concentrate on the word *you*. This may seem a simple suggestion or rule, but it is broken every day by some major advertisers. When you say "we" in an ad, you are talking about yourself—the manufacturer, the retailer, the bank, the ad writer. When you say "you" in an ad, you are addressing the customer. The reader listens when you say "you"; the reader tunes you out when you say "we." Work hard at adopting the "you" approach in your thinking and writing. Readers do not especially care about pictures of your company's founder or new bottling plant. Customers are self-centered. Their interest is self-interest. Keep in mind that the ad reader is not nearly as interested in what you put in to a product as what he or she can get out of it.

Staying on Track. Organize your text in a logical way so that it will be a persuasive argument. The main thrust of the argument naturally stems from the thought or promise introduced in the headline. If the headline promises "economy" the body copy should stick to the subject of economy, putting specific arguments in order of their importance. Start with the most important claim about economy. Add enough detail to make your story believable. Then proceed to your next most important claim about economy, and so on to the least important. Do not get off the track or wander in circles. March in a straight line from the beginning of your argument about the subject all the way through. When you come to the end, tie the whole "package" up with a ribbon by making an obvious reference to the promise of your headline.

Call for Customer Action. Remember that firms rarely run ads willy-nilly. Ads are run for a purpose. Every ad you create should be planned to get a particular response from a reader. If you do a good job with your sales story, the reader will want to respond. Do not leave the prospect hanging. Give the prospect something to do. Suggest some action to take. "Send a check." "Wire your Congressional Representative." "Talk to a contractor." "Ask for the booklet." "Clip the coupon." In other words, you should ask for action—preferably immediate action. The reader not only won't resent it; the reader may indeed be grateful to you for it. The reader is saying, in effect: "You've done a good job. You've convinced me. Now what do you want me to do about it?" Telling the reader what to do is what advertising is all about. Don't neglect it. Even if all a particular ad can say is "Come in tomorrow," you have, at least, planted the seed of positive response.

The Mechanics of Finished Copy

When you type up your copy—to clear it with management and, later, send it to the typographer—there is a reasonably standard form you will find easy to follow. In the upper left corner, type the name of the advertiser, the name of the product, the name of the media, the size of the unit of space, and the date of the appearance of the ad. If an illustration comes first, describe it briefly in parentheses. (Illus: photo of school kids on jungle gym). Type the headline in capital letters. Type the subhead, if any, in capital and small letters and underscore it. The main text is usually double-spaced. This permits easier reading and leaves a bit of room for writing in revisions and corrections. The signature of the advertiser (or **logotype,** as it is also called) is typed last in an open area to indicate that it will be displayed in the actual ad. Make sure every word that will appear in the ad is typed on the copy; don't trust the typesetter to pick up words that are hand-lettered on the layout.

logotype The signature of the advertiser.

Helpful Copywriting Resources

Many advertisers are not natural-born ad writers. Many feel uncertain about their mastery of English. Many worry about their choice of words, their spelling, and their grammar. There is no reason for an advertiser to be upset because he or she is not another Shakespeare. Few advertisers are. Yet the advertiser has reason to be concerned over the image presented to the public—for that's what advertising is. A misspelled word or an ungrammatical expression is a sort of social error that puts an advertiser in a bad light with the audience. A basic blunder in print can make an otherwise splendid person look like a nincompoop.

Many of the finest advertising writers in America keep five basic reference books near at hand as they work. You can easily do likewise. No writer feels equipped for the job without a good dictionary. There are several fine paperback dictionaries available today. Don't make a move without one. Never guess about the spelling of a word. Look it up. This takes only a moment; it is enlightening, and it may save you much embarrassment later on. Like it or not, a misspelled or misused word is a sign of ignorance.

If you are not a wordsmith by nature, there will be times when you will be groping for the correct or precise term, times when you would like a more colorful or interesting way to state the obvious. Refer to Roget's *Thesaurus,* also available in paperback.

Perhaps you are not enchanted with your own way of stating things. Your language may be dull and unimaginative. There may be highly skilled literary help at hand. If, for instance, you have to write a restaurant ad, you might find it very helpful to look in Bartlett's *Familiar Quotations* and see what some of the greatest writers of all time have said on the subject of eating. The long-running campaign "Any apple worth its salt is worth Morton's" came right out of Bartlett's *Familiar Quotations*. Learn to check with this classic volume, also available in paperback. You will find it educational and entertaining. If you do not find a suitable quote for your ad, you are likely to find a witty remark for future table conversation.

If your writing is labored and hesitant, the next book can help you immensely. It is a small volume worth many times its weight in pure gold. Its title is *Elements of Style* by Strunk and White. It is a lively, instantly helpful primer on English grammar. It, too, is available in paperback at a very modest price.

The last volume recommended for the aspiring adwriter is not a literary reference book at all. It is that good old reliable Sears, Roebuck catalog. It will teach you the economy of words. You will find the Sears catalog copy lean, clean, and clear—packed with crucial selling information, stripped of every unnecessary word. Sears copy is strictly no-nonsense and a good pattern to keep in mind.

Here's a tip on another source of inspiration when you're stuck for an opening appeal in your copy. Get out a copy of *Reader's Digest,* any copy. Study the titles and the short "teaser" paragraphs that introduce each article. They stop you, capture your interest, make you want to find out more. It is an art to write tight, inviting copy like this. The *Reader's Digest* editors give you a banquet of it every month.

Whatever your sources of inspiration, whatever your models, whatever your style, always keep in mind this important principle: Readers are human beings first, prospective customers second. If you will treat them this way in your copy, you cannot go very far wrong. You will win friends.

LAYOUT/ILLUSTRATIONS: SUBTLE MESSAGE CARRIERS

Up to this point we have have been concentrating strictly on words, words, words. But we pointed out earlier that copywriting means that you are responsible for the way an ad *looks* as well as the way it reads. This brings us to the next basic step: the visual side of copywriting.

layout The overall arrangement of elements in a unit of advertising space.

The word **layout** means the overall arrangement of elements in a unit of advertising space. The number of elements differ with the assignment, but a general rule might be: Dramatic illustration. Headline. Main text. Product package. Advertiser's signature. The trick is to arrange these elements in the space, not just to create an attractive design, but to give total impact to the communication. All attention must be focused on the message.

The major agencies of America employ staffs of art directors whose main concern is to make layouts. But what if you don't know the first thing about art? What if you can't draw a straight line? Do not despair. There are ways to help yourself around these barriers.

If you are going to be responsible for making ads, you're going to have to make it a constant practice to look at ads. It won't take you long to start separating the wheat from the chaff or, at least, separating what you like personally from what you don't like. Start a clip file of outstanding ads.

Different Types of Layout

Most advertisements you see fall into one of the six layout categories shown in Figure 6–3: standard, editorial, poster, picture-caption, cartoon, comic strip. Use them as a checklist to help you think up variations as you approach a new assignment.

The Volkswagen campaign has long been admired by advertising professionals. Over time, its basic layout has consisted of a large dramatic photograph (the dominant element on the page) followed by a bold headline, followed by text, followed by signature—all in rather military 1, 2, 3, 4 alignment. This arrangement of elements, the **standard layout,** is far and away the most common layout in American advertising. Art directors have nicknamed it "Layout A." It is popular because it is functional. It channels interest through the page in a straight line—the clearest way to present most advertising propositions. This is the layout to use when you're stuck for an idea and don't know which way to go.

standard layout The most common category of layout, consisting of illustration, headline, text, and signature—in that order.

In some advertising layouts, the words dominate; either there is no illustration or it has a very minor position. This kind of layout is often called an **editorial layout.** It looks a good deal like editorial material from a publication. The editorial layout lends itself to a long, detailed copy story, as Figure 6–4 shows.

editorial layout A layout consisting mainly of words.

A **poster layout** consists of a totally dominant illustration with only a few words of copy. This type of layout is highly suitable for low-cost, frequently purchased products with which the customer is familiar. It makes ideal reminder advertising and style advertising.

poster layout A layout in which an illustration is totally dominant.

A **picture-caption layout** is composed of several illustrations, each with a short block of copy. This type of layout often looks like a page in *People* Magazine. It gets lots of people to read the copy and is an efficient way to display and discuss several features of a product in a single message. You will often see the picture-caption layout used in travel advertising.

picture-caption layout A layout composed of several illustrations, each with a short block of copy.

In the **cartoon layout,** a humorous drawing becomes the dominant element in the ad. It gets attention because everybody loves cartoons. Perhaps

cartoon layout A layout featuring a humorous drawing.

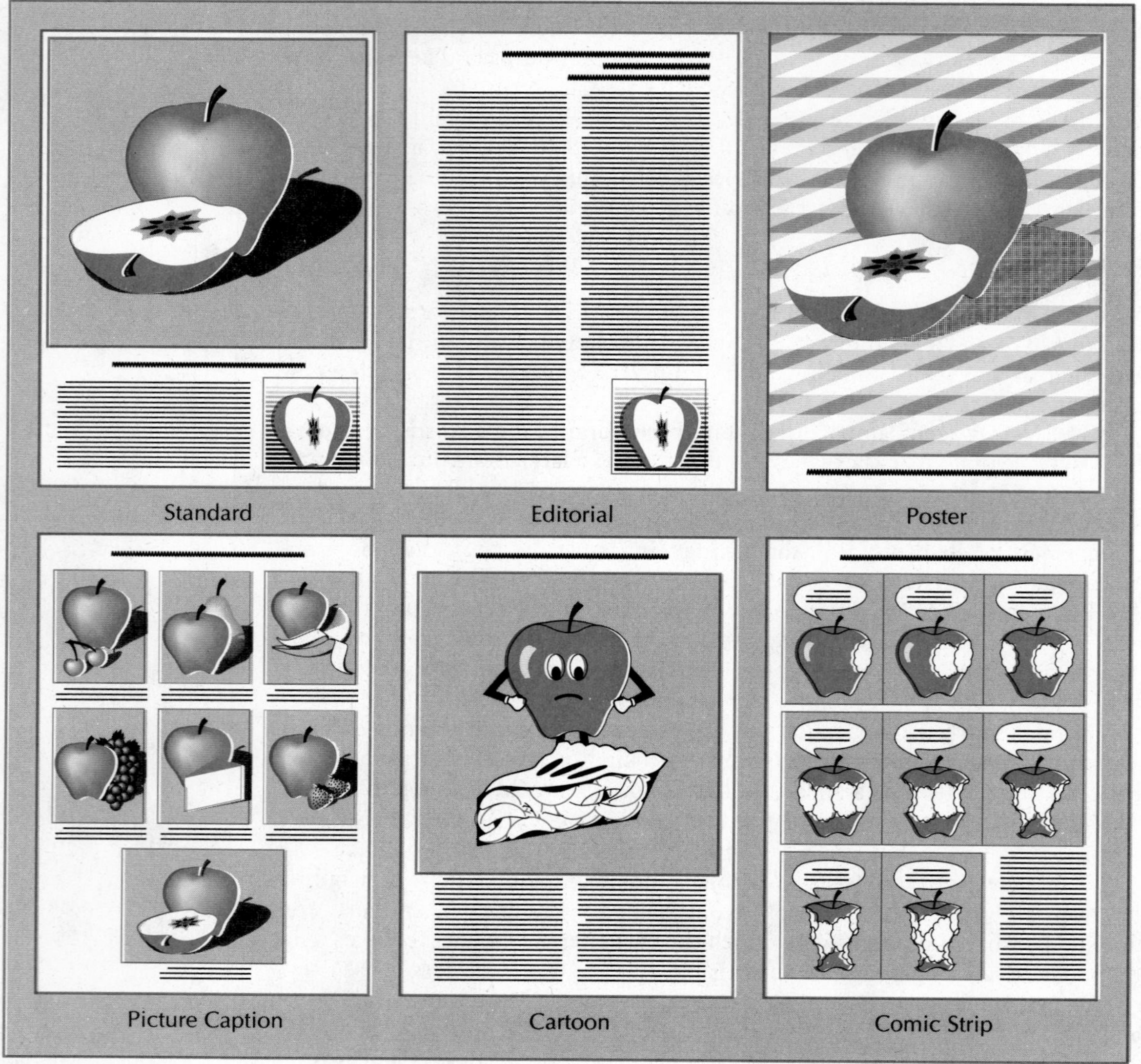

FIGURE 6–3
Most advertisements you see fall into one of the six layout categories shown here. Use these as a checklist to help you think up variations as you approach a new assignment.

Your boss wants you to do a million things at once. Tell him you'll do five.

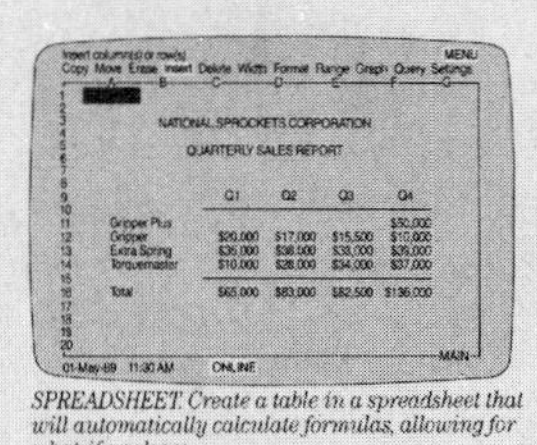

SPREADSHEET. Create a table in a spreadsheet that will automatically calculate formulas, allowing for what-if analyses.

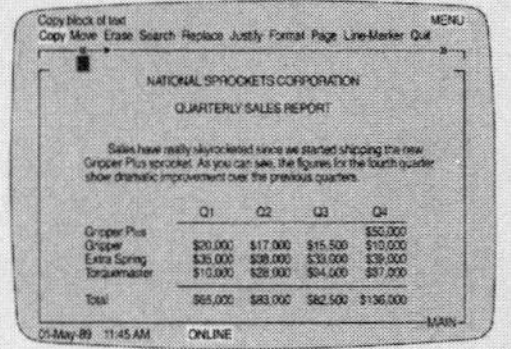

WORD PROCESSING. Write a document in the full featured word processor. Even include a spreadsheet.

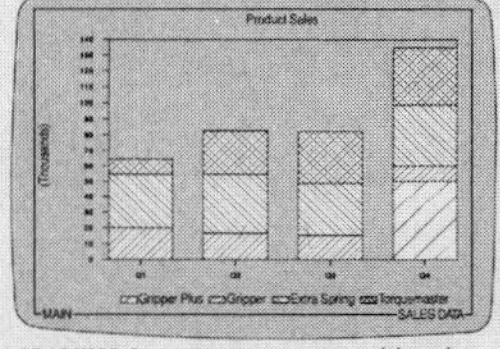

GRAPHICS. Instantly turn your spreadsheet data into a graph. Choose from six graph types.

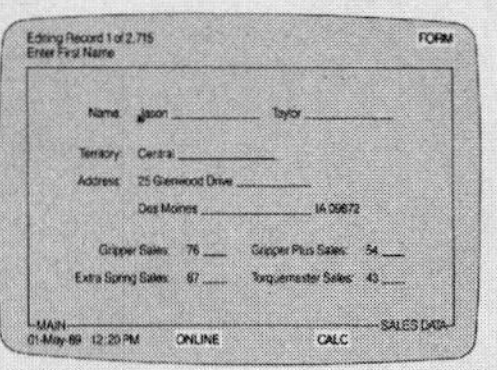

DATABASE. Store information in a powerful database that can hold over 8,000 records, with up to 256 fields.

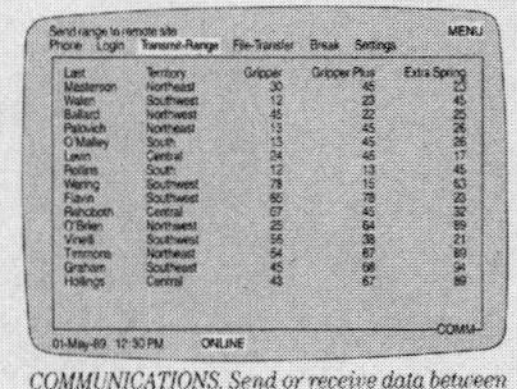

COMMUNICATIONS. Send or receive data between your PC and a mainframe, another PC or an on-line information service.

Your boss should take this quite well.

Because with Symphony* from Lotus®, you're able to easily juggle five key business applications at once: spreadsheet, word processing, graphics, database, and communications.

And if you buy now you can get Symphony with Allways, the Spreadsheet Publisher from Funk Software, all at one great price.*

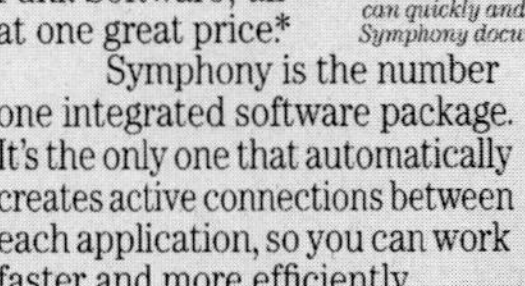

Using the Allways program, you can quickly and easily make your Symphony documents look terrific.

Symphony is the number one integrated software package. It's the only one that automatically creates active connections between each application, so you can work faster and more efficiently.

For example, you could create a table of sales data on your Symphony spreadsheet. Then, with one keystroke, switch to the word processor and write an accompanying memo. Switch to graphics and chart that same sales data, and you're done. If you need to change your data, switch back to your spreadsheet, revise it, and all your other sections update automatically.

You never have to cut and paste information or type in a formula to create a link, as in other integrated programs. What's more, the Symphony spreadsheet is based on Lotus 1-2-3,® the industry standard. As 1-2-3 advances, Symphony will incorporate the latest spreadsheet features, in addition to enhancements to the other Symphony applications.

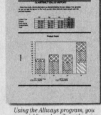

And Allways makes your Symphony reports look better than ever. Allways provides you with many advanced formatting and printing options, including laser printer support. Allways is easy to use, and works directly from within Symphony.

Take advantage of this offer. Go to your Info. Center Manager or your local Lotus reseller and ask for Symphony. With Symphony you can show your boss just how versatile you can be.

© 1989 Lotus Development Corp. Lotus, Symphony, and 1-2-3 are registered trademarks of Lotus Development Corporation. *Offer valid while supplies last. Participating resellers only.

FIGURE 6–4
This business-to-business magazine ad treats a very serious subject in a highly professional manner, with long, detailed copy and explanatory charts and graphs. A great deal of essential information is organized into this low-key editorial layout.

more important, cartoons are very useful in expressing ideas and intangibles. A cartoon is a good device to use when you wish to suggest rather than precisely portray.

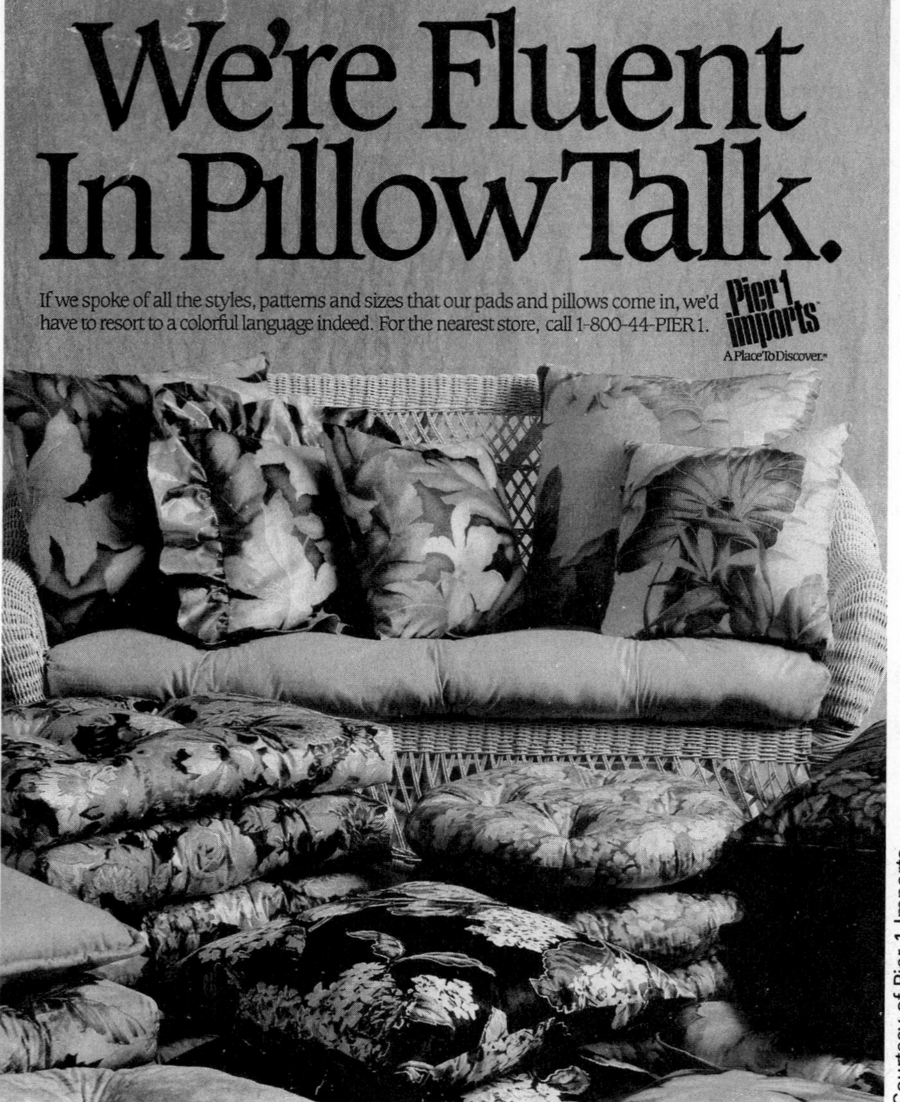

We're Fluent
In Pillow Talk.
If we spoke of all the styles, patterns and sizes that our pads and pillows come in, we'd have to resort to a colorful language indeed. For the nearest store, call 1-800-44-PIER1.
Pier 1 imports
A Place To Discover.
Courtesy of Pier 1 Imports

FIGURE 6–5
Artwork illustration shows what the headline suggests. Note play on words in the headline.

comic strip layout A layout featuring a sequence of drawings or photographs that tell a story.

A **comic strip layout** is dominated by a sequence of drawings or photographs that tell a story. The product is always the "hero" of the story line. The comic strip layout is also a strong attention getter.

By using these six layout categories, you can become your own art director. You can look a newspaper sales representative or printer in the eye and say firmly: "I want my ad to look like *that*."

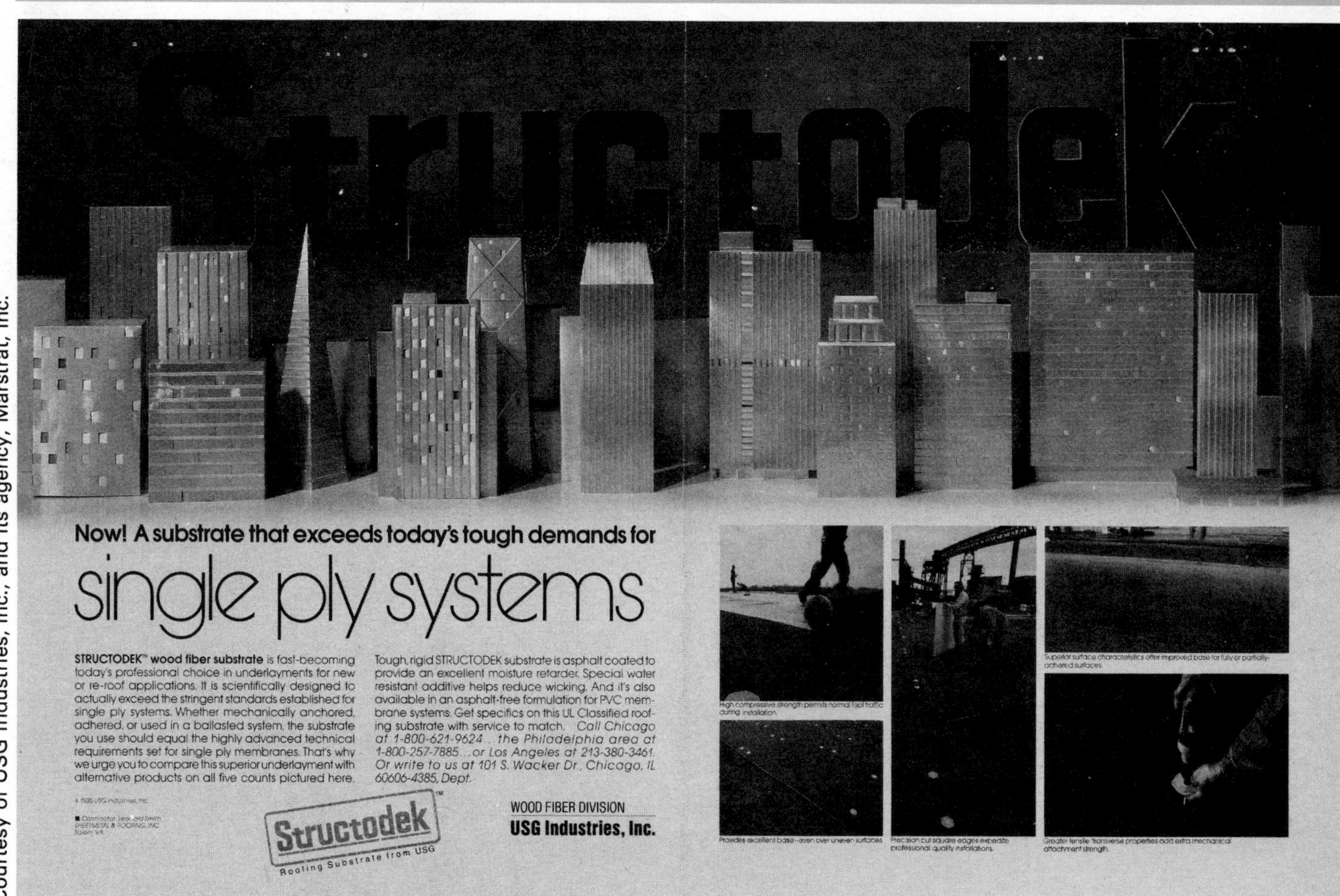

Courtesy of USG Industries, Inc., and its agency, Marstrat, Inc.

FIGURE 6–6
Highly imaginative way to illustrate the product: Use it to build a city skyline.

FIGURE 6–7
Illustration here is of the product alone, but displayed so dramatically that attention is riveted to a simple item. The conical configuration, attached plume device, and the words HERSHEY'S KISSES are trademarks of Hershey Foods Corporations.

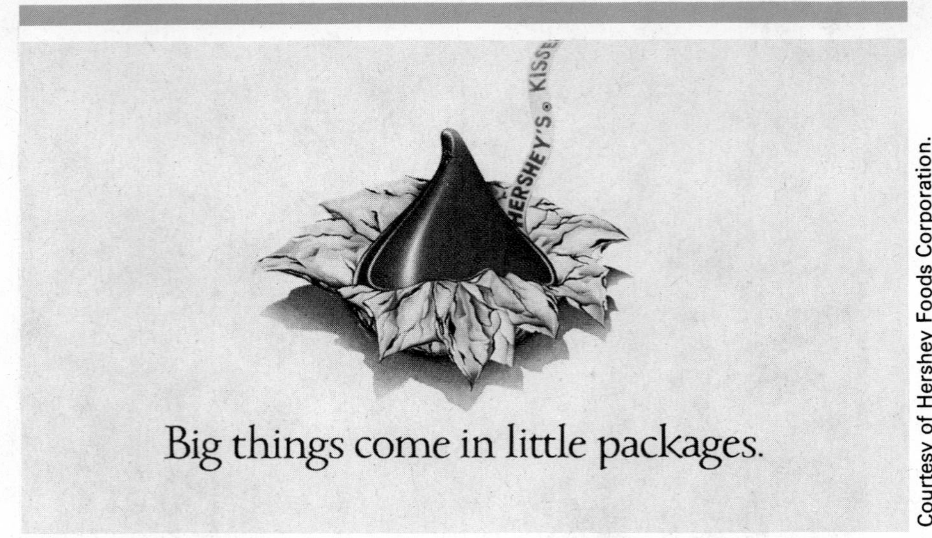

HERSHEY'S® KISSES
Big things come in little packages.

Courtesy of Hershey Foods Corporation.

Finding the Right Kind of Help

Your next problem is bringing your layout to life and you'll need help to do it. If your task is an ad for the local newspaper, reasonable help is close at hand. The local newspaper can help transform your typewritten copy into a printed message, find suitable art, and then reproduce it. This is part of the service offered to all advertisers. It is part of the newspaper's cost of doing business, covered by the standard line rate charged to all advertisers.

The Media Salesperson. The newspaper salesperson who calls on you will sincerely try to help. (In fact, some merchants simply toss some odds and ends at the newspaper salesperson and say, "Make me an ad." And, it will be done!) This is how much of the advertising in a typical community is done. But if you are somewhat sophisticated in your tastes and more demanding than the average, you may find the newspaper facilities somewhat limiting. For one thing, the local newspaper offers limited choice in type faces and sizes. For another, it relies on clip art.

Clip Art. Newspapers subscribe to clip art services—catalogs of already prepared professional art, in various sizes, covering almost every kind of occasion. The newspaper salesperson will just take a pair of scissors and snip out the art that fits your advertisement. The most notable of these art services is named *Metro*. Metro offers a panorama of art treatments covering almost every human endeavor that occurs in a year's time—weddings, births, graduations, moving, business promotions, vacations, and scads of art ideas built around every conceivable national holiday or idea for a retailer sale. Some art services offer specialized selections—in agriculture, for instance. You can look through

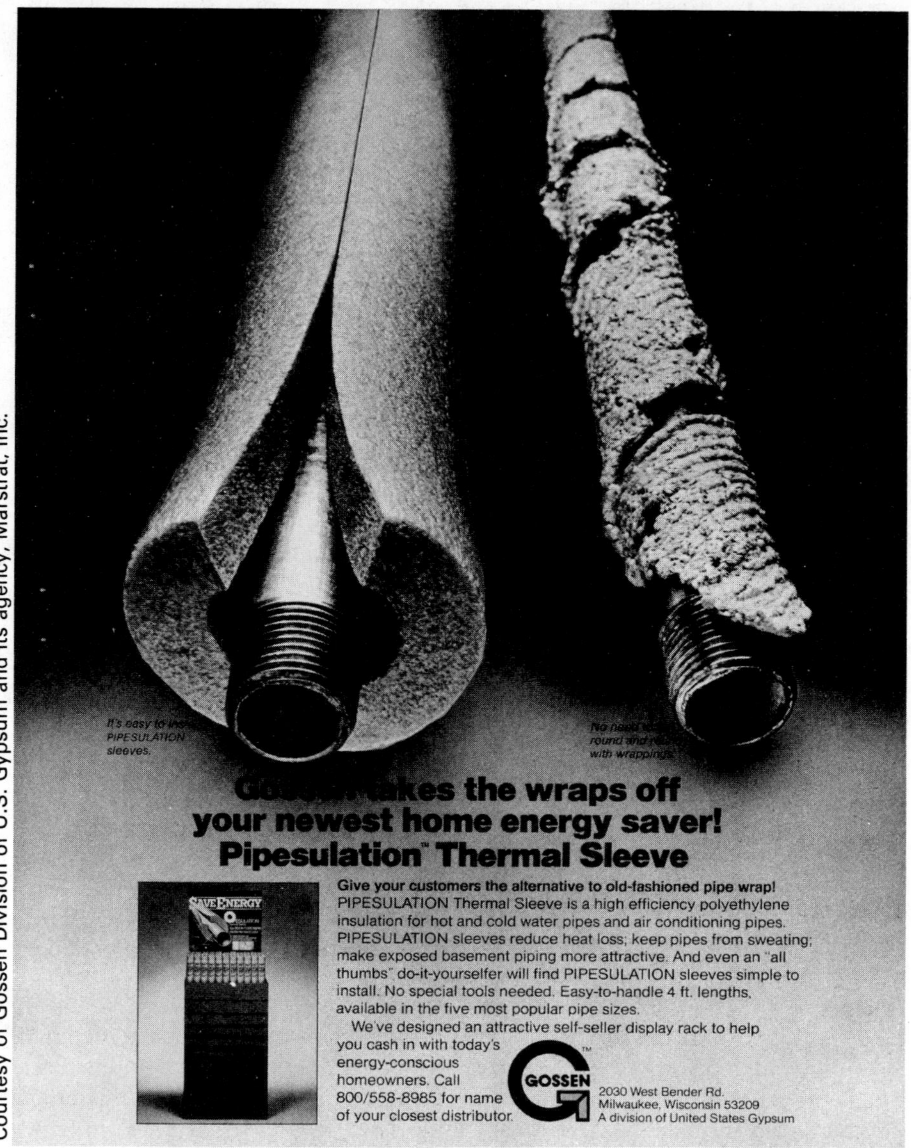

Courtesy of Gossen Division of U.S. Gypsum and its agency, Marstrat, Inc.

FIGURE 6–8
Comparison and contrast in illustration is often an effective selling device.

the clip art catalogue and pick out a pig in practically any size. There is a clip art catalogue that contains nothing but pictures (in various sizes) of national brand products of almost every conceivable description from Armstrong tires to Zest soap. There is a clip art catalog containing humorous drawings that appeal to the youth market.

FIGURE 6–9
This elaborate dealer aid kit was sent to all Hart Schaffner & Marx retailers on the 100th anniversary of the manufacturing company. The kit opens in the center to reveal 4 suggested radio commercials, 11 suggested newspaper ads with photos, 8 suggested newspaper ads with artwork, a reproduction sheet of logotypes in various sizes and shapes. Also in the kit is a folder on Dealer Aids, a folder on Display Ideas, a booklet on suggested Special Events, and a folder on a Retail Incentive Program.

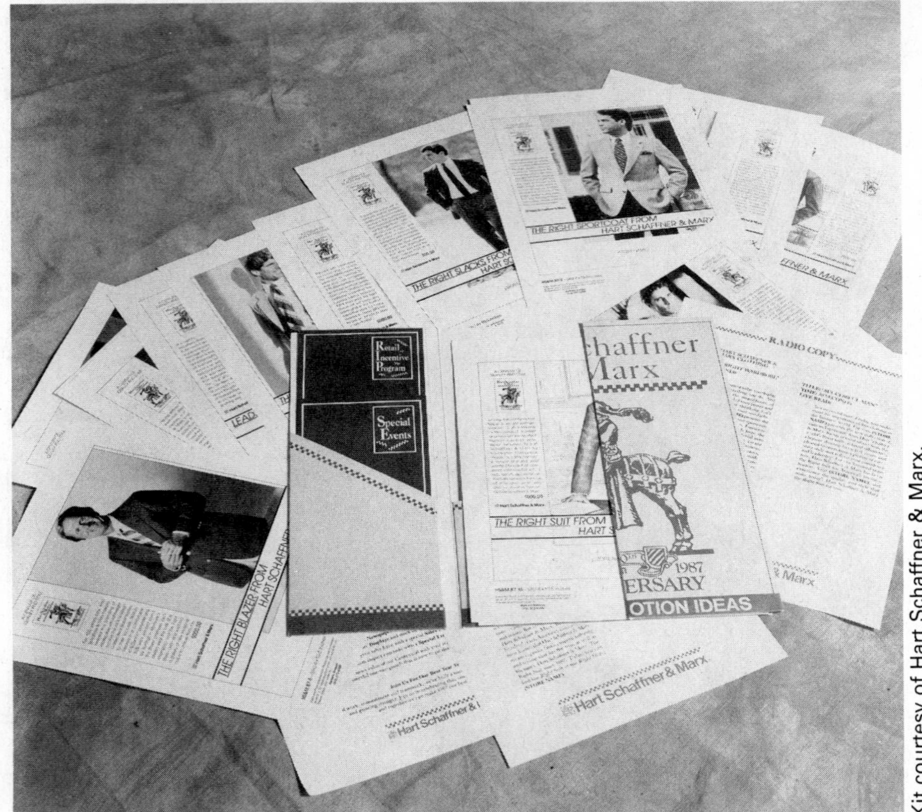

Kit courtesy of Hart Schaffner & Marx.

Clip art is perfectly good art, produced by skilled artists and photographers. It is particularly suitable for newspaper reproduction (a point to consider). But, good as it may be, it is all stock art, lacking in imagination, personality, distinctiveness.

The Manufacturer. Many manufacturers of national brand merchandise offer all kinds of advertising aid to their retailers. Brand manufacturers produce dealer ad kits that contain everything from first-rate pictures of the product used in national advertising, to trademarks of various sizes, to hand-lettered headlines, to entire advertisements that the dealer can use whole or in part. Some manufacturers will build and photograph entire window displays as suggestions for dealers. (See Figures 6–9, 6–10, and 6–11.)

Local Talent. But suppose you want something hand-tailored, some artwork done especially for you—a particular human interest situation, a scene of your place of business, a new trademark? Art talent may not be abundant

Display Your Centennial Spirit

Make the most of our Centennial Celebration with displays that convey the excitement and spirit of this event. Colorful, creative window displays notify prospects that there is a special event underway and draws them into your store. In-store Centennial displays draw special attention to your Hart Schaffner & Marx merchandise.

To help you create your own Centennial displays, we're offering a variety of display items including banners, posters and signage with a Centennial theme. Follow the display designs suggested in this folder or create your own. Centennial items can be ordered from the Dealer Aids order blank enclosed in this kit.

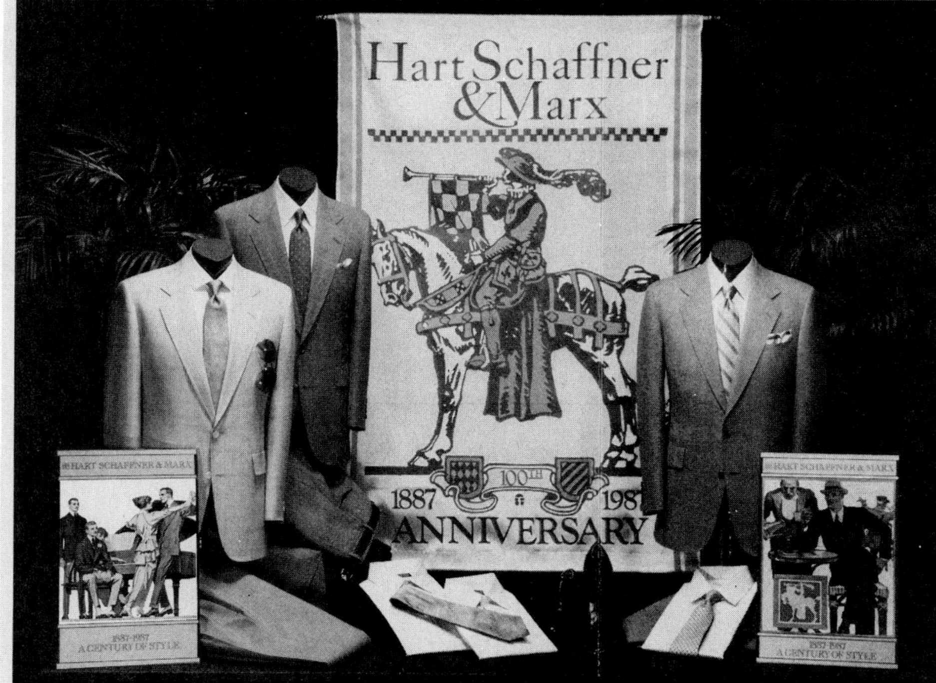

*Order Gold-Tone Letters from:
The Sign Center
5221 N. Long St.
Chicago, IL 60630

*Order free-standing acrylic Card Holders (22" x 14") from:
Janis Paterini
Impax, Inc.
3124 Gillham Plaza
Kansas City, MO 64109

Hart Schaffner & Marx.

FIGURE 6–10
The manufacturer has a display expert create window and store displays at company headquarters and photograph them there. The suggestions are sent to Hart Schaffner & Marx retailers with full details on how to obtain and use the supplementary pieces in the display.

Courtesy of Hart Schaffner & Marx.

FIGURE 6–11
This full-color mailing piece with swatch of fabric is made available to Hart Schaffner & Marx retailers at nominal cost. All retailers have to do is have their own store name imprinted on the back.

in small communities, but it exists to some degree everywhere. You have to seek it out. A shrewd local advertiser must be a bit of a Sherlock Holmes.

First off, almost every newspaper has a staff artist of sorts. Perhaps he or she can do some special work for you on a fee basis. If you live in or near a college community, you are lucky. There is fresh young talent there just waiting for an opportunity to shine. Check faculty members: check students. Schools—universities, community colleges, high schools—are an obvious source of drawing talent.

Perhaps you have seen a certain folder, brochure, or mailing piece around town that you admired. Get in touch with that advertiser and ask him who did the artwork you liked.

Large independent creative services—art and photographic studios—exist across the country. Jack O'Grady Communications in Chicago is an outstanding

Product: the Sauce Mill
Magazine: full page/4-color

ILLUSTRATION: (Frontal view of woman by her stove. She has her hands on her hips, is smiling, and looking at her range where there are two pots which are being stirred by the sauce mill.)
(a photo of the sauce mill at the bottom of the page.)

HEADLINE: Look Mom, No Hands.

COPY: You'll never have to use your hands to stir again. Because the Sauce Mill stirs all by itself: no hands. The Sauce Mill is a sturdy plastic disc that rotates by heat induction. It rotates automatically, so you'll never have to stand at the stove again.

No batteries.

No switches.

Invest in the Sauce Mill. Give yourself some extra time to do other things while you're preparing dinner, or lunch, or snacks.

The Sauce mill, it's a real helping hand in the kitchen.

FIGURE 6–12
This is the proper form for typing up the copy of a magazine or newspaper advertisement.

example. Naturally, the greatest concentration of these communication specialists is in the larger cities. But you can track them down. You are likely to find this kind of creative help more original, more experienced, more professional than what you will find in an average community. You are also likely to find it a good deal more expensive. But it's out there.

Suppose you want a special kind of photograph. A newspaper staff photographer may be persuaded to "moonlight." The local studio photographer (portraits, weddings, etc.) would probably be happy to pick up some extra money by taking a picture of your store, shop, plant, or product. And there is no law that says that you can't try your own photography. Even instant snapshots can be used if there is enough black-and-white contrast in them.

The world is full of camera fans. There may be a hidden genius developing in the darkrooms of your own home town. Check with the camera store proprietor. Maybe even run a classified ad. "Wanted. Somebody to take a picture of my office." A small investment may bring dazzling returns.

Helpful Art Resources. Just as there are books and periodicals to help the ad writer, there are guides to aid the person concerned with art and layout. One of the clearest and most down-to-earth books available is *The Design of Advertising* by Roy Paul Nelson. While basically a book on layout and art, it also contains much practical information concerning ad writing and print production.

Many advertising people who cannot even draw a straight line are regular subscribers to two brilliantly edited publications, *Communication Arts* and *Art Direction*. Even if you know nothing about art, you can see what is currently of interest to the most highly skilled professionals. This constant exposure to the finest in contemporary advertising art is bound to sharpen your own tastes. At the very least, you will find out what's new and "now" in national art circles.

For those who wish to experiment with their own hands, Crain Books (Chicago) offers a Graphics Kit that opens up all kinds of possibilities in art direction for the nonprofessional.

The point is that you are not alone—no matter how ill-equipped you may be to put together an ad. The first line of help is the media you deal with. The local newspaper wants your business. It will do everything possible to help you in order to keep your business. Small trade and industrial magazines, while not as handy as the local paper, will extend themselves in many ways to get and keep your business. Don't hesitate to rely on the skilled help that the media can provide.

If your concern is with a booklet, folder, letter, or the like, you will be dealing with a printer. Some printers set type and even offer some layout services. Some do not. But printers are professionals. They know *how* to get things done. They will guide you to the other necessary suppliers. It is to their advantage to help.

Don't be ashamed to admit your ignorance. Why should somebody who has never ever written an ad of any kind be familiar with layout, art, photography, printing, and the like? You'll learn what you need to know, more and more with each ad you work on.

SUMMARY

Just remember that all these other experts and geniuses—artists, photographers, printers, media people—look to you to supply the most vital link in the advertising communications chain. It is up to you to come up with the strong selling idea that sets you apart.

You do that by analyzing all information about your product and deciding on your creative strategy, by isolating a chief benefit, by settling on a target market and by deciding what effect your ad is to have on that target market. You write a headline and select an illustration that combine to promise the reader a benefit. You prove your point in the body copy. And you ask the reader to do something about it.

Then you seek out the available sources for technical help and you keep current with art and layout trends by reading what the professionals read.

Writing print copy is largely a matter of displaying common sense, using logical procedures. This is true, too, in writing for broadcast. But, as we shall see in the next chapter, the broadcast media do have certain fascinating peculiarities of their own, because, in a sense, broadcast advertising is business and *show* business combined.

TERMS TO KNOW

Now that you have finished the chapter, you should understand the following terms:

copywriting	standard layout
headline	editorial layout
empathy	cartoon layout
subhead	comic strip layout
body copy	poster layout
logotype	picture-caption layout
layout	

If you are not certain of the meaning of any of these terms, go back through the chapter and review them.

THINGS TO THINK ABOUT

1. What can a beginning advertising writer learn from looking through the Sears Roebuck catalog?
2. If reader self-interest is the most effective headline appeal, does this mean that the human race is beyond salvation?
3. Why are there several basic layout variations? Why doesn't *one* layout work in all situations?
4. How long should a headline be?
5. Why can you never write too many headlines?
6. What makes a good copywriter?

THINGS TO TALK ABOUT

1. How much more than *writing* goes into copywriting?
2. Do you believe the old proverb that one picture is worth 1,000 words? Defend your viewpoint.
3. Why does print advertising for soft drinks look different from, say, advertising for TV sets?
4. Why do you suppose so many ad experts consider the headline the single most important element in an ad?
5. Why does a how-to headline quickly involve readers?

THINGS TO DO

1. Pretend you have been assigned to write a magazine ad for your favorite automobile. Prepare a creative strategy for your ad.
2. From a current magazine, clip one ad with a self-interest headline, one with a news headline, and one with a curiosity headline.
3. From current magazines clip a dozen ads with a poster layout—a dominant visual and a short line of copy. Analyze the advertisers and the types of products. Do you find similarities?
4. Select the three best headlines in a current magazine.
5. Clip the advertising illustrations that have appealed to you most this month.

7 Copywriting for Broadcast Media

WHAT IF YOUR NAME IS CARSON AND YOU'RE NOT FUNNY?
DICK CARSON, TV DIRECTOR
If you make serious money by being funny, it's easy to find investment firms that will take you seriously.
Dick Carson isn't as funny as his brother, Johnny. But, he *is* a Dean Witter client, so he's just as special.
And even though he's not a big-time talk-show host, there are a host of ways in which Dean Witter is able to help him meet all of his financial needs.
In fact, we're helping Dick plan for his business and retirement.
Through his Dean Witter Account Executive, Dick has the benefit of Dean Witter's resources and expert advice, in addition to a full range of investment opportunities.
As a Dean Witter client, you can expect the same special treatment.
So call us today, or stop by to talk with one of our Account Executives.
You'll discover that you're somebody at Dean Witter.
No kidding.
You're somebody at Dean Witter.
A member of the Sears Financial Network
DEAN WITTER
© 1987 DEAN WITTER REYNOLDS INC. MEMBER SIPC.

Courtesy of Dean Witter Reynolds, Inc.

CHAPTER OUTLINE

Radio
- Radio: Good Points and Bad
- Kinds of Copy
- How to Prepare a Script
- Seeking Help from the Station

Television
- TV: Good Points and Bad
- Overall Impression Counts
- Think Pictures First
- Preparing the Script
- Using Music
- Leave Time for Others to Be Creative
- The Value of Close-ups
- Memorable Visuals
- Using a Storyboard
- Local Help with TV

By the time you finish this chapter, you should understand;

1. The good and bad points of radio advertising.
2. A number of basic radio broadcast terms.
3. How to organize a radio script.
4. The good and bad points of television advertising.
5. Some basic television broadcast terms.
6. How to organize a television script.
7. What a storyboard is.
8. The two main ways a storyboard is generally used.

In the last chapter we talked about writing copy for a print ad in the local newspaper. It may well be that you will do all your advertising from now on in the local newspaper, but that is not the only medium available to you.

In most communities of reasonable size, you can buy radio coverage and television coverage as well. Advertising in each of these broadcast media requires some special writing skills. And each has both good and bad points.

RADIO

Let us begin with the medium that is almost as popular with local businesses as newspapers—radio.

Radio: Good Points and Bad

Radio gives the writer that most effective means of communication—the warmth and personality of the human voice. Cold type on lifeless paper is no match for it. Radio also offers the opportunity to use music, which plays so readily on the emotions of us all. Sound effects add yet another dimension of drama and excitement. Radio uses the imagination of the listener in place of studio sets or location shooting. Radio is timely—copy can be changed right up to air time.

But radio does not have vivid pictures in glamorous color. The radio message "moves" rapidly; it is difficult for a listener to retain. A radio ad cannot be saved and clipped for reference at a later time. It cannot even be studied slowly. Therefore, repetition of key copy items such as a sponsor's name, is a must.

In radio, the writer does only a minor part of the work. The imagination of the listener does the rest. The writer's job has been likened to creating pictures in the mind's eye. The writer provides the barest hint; the listener's imagination completes the picture.

Kinds of Copy

straight radio copy Radio copy that includes words only, sent to the station in typewritten form to be read by an announcer.

production radio copy Radio copy that is produced in a recording studio under ideal conditions and sent to various stations.

There are two basic kinds of radio writing—straight copy and production copy. The terms are simple. **Straight radio copy** is words only, sent to the station in typewritten form, to be read by whichever station announcer happens to be on duty when it is the advertiser's turn to be on the air.

Production radio copy is produced in a recording studio under ideal conditions and captured on audio tape. Duplicates of this perfect tape are then sent to the various radio stations on the media schedule for play at the appointed time. A production spot may include several voices, music, sound effects . . . or only one voice (a very special voice, perhaps). In any event, a production spot is recorded. This means that advertisers retain perfect control of their spot every time it is heard on the air.

How to Prepare a Script

Figure 7–1 shows a sample script of a radio production commercial. The instructions for preparing such a script are quite simple and require no technical knowledge of radio broadcasting.

Note that all instructions or directions are typed in capital letters; only the words the listener hears at home are typed normally. A name typed in capitals shows who is to speak the line. The talent will read copy in a normal voice at a normal pace unless you tell them otherwise. If you wish a certain reaction from a speaker, type it in parentheses, like this:

SYLVIA (OUTRAGED): "But you said to do it!"

SFX Abbreviation for sound effects.

You can insert such an instruction anywhere you wish—even in the middle of a line of dialogue. The same is true with music and sound effects. (A commonly used abbreviation for sound effects is **SFX.**) Just type the instruction in capitals. If you want a kind of music, say so.

(WALTZ)

If you want a particular selection, specify it.

("BLUE DANUBE" WALTZ).

IN Instruction to begin.

OUT Instruction to end.

UP Instruction to increase volume.

DOWN Instruction to decrease volume.

UNDER Instruction to hold something in the background.

SEGUE Instruction to provide a segue or musical transition from one song to another.

A few basic broadcast terms will be helpful to you. **IN** means to begin. (MUSIC IN). **OUT** means to end. (SFX OUT). **UP** means to increase the volume. **DOWN** means to decrease volume. **UNDER** means to soften music or sound and keep it in the background, i.e., under a following scene. **SEGUE** (pronounced seg′-way) is a musical transition from one song to another (like a medley) to indicate a change in time or place or mood. It is a fantastic story-telling device on radio. The listener draws the correct conclusion; you save yourself time and words. Figure 7–2 illustrates a radio production spot. Since radio is a moving message, the best strategy is to try to make one strong overall impression, in different ways. Example: A commercial that said

Product: the Sauce Mill
Radio: 30 sec.

MUSIC: IN AND UNDER

WOMAN: When I start to prepare dinner - the action begins.

SFX: PHONE RINGS, DOORS SLAM, KIDS VOICES

(a photo of the sauce mill at the bottom of the page.)

SMALL CHILD: Mom, phone.

WOMAN: I can't stir this soup and talk on the phone at the same time. So I bought a Sauce Mill. The new disc that stirs and rotates by heat induction. Put it in your pan, turn on the heat, and it stirs. No batteries or switches and no hands. The Sauce Mill, it stirs up a storm on my range, and I don't even have to be there.

MUSIC, UP AND OUT

Courtesy of Norah Diedrich

FIGURE 7–1
This is the proper form for typing up a radio commercial.

"It takes two hands to handle a Whopper," also read "You've got to put down your shake to pick it up." Overriding impression: The burger is *big*.

Be far more conversational than in print copy. Talk regular talk. Use short, simple words. Use choppy sentences. Use sentence fragments. Use one-word sentences. Use the "oohs" and "ahs" and grunts and groans that are part

AFA MARKETING FACT BOOK
THEME ADVERTISING
RADIO MATERIALS (Scripts)

OLDER MAN:	Variety! I like variety.
ANNCR:	We're here at an Arby's Roast Beef Restaurant asking people why they're breaking the hamburger habit.
OLDER MAN:	You see, at Arby's I can get anything from hot ham and cheese to a delicious roast beef sandwich. Arby's is a delicious . . . change of taste.
ANNCR:	And you, Miss?
YOUNG WOMAN:	'Cause I can get turkey, ham, cheese, lettuce and tomato . . . all in the Arby's club. Arby's Club is a luscious . . . change of taste.
ANNCR:	And you, young lady?
LITTLE GIRL:	'Cause my Mom lets me have a big Jamocha shake. Arby's is a big . . .change of taste.
SINGERS:	Arby's is a . . .
OLDER MAN:	Arby's is a delicious . . .change of taste.
SINGERS:	Arby's is a . . .
YOUNG WOMAN:	Arby's is a luscious . . .change of taste.
SINGERS:	Arby's is a . . .
LITTLE GIRLS:	Arby's is a big . . .change of taste.
SINGERS:	Arby's is a big juicy fresh wholesome lean, luscious . . . Arby's is a big juicy fresh . . .wholesome lean, luscious . . . Arby's is a big, juicy delicious change of taste:

TITLE:	"Variety"
THEME:	Menu Variety
LENGTH:	60 seconds (55 commercial, 05 local tag)
CODE NUMBER:	AFA-R 122

Courtesy A1A Service Corporation and its agency, Danser-Fitzgerald-Sample, Inc.

FIGURE 7–2
Script for radio production spot, using dialogue of several characters backed up by singing group.

of our normal, person-to-person conversation. Be colloquial, even slangy—within the bounds of good taste.

Keep it in mind always that you are writing for the ear, not the eye. If you write perfect grammar—book prose—you are doing the wrong thing for radio. Give every piece of radio copy you write the acid test. *Read it out loud* (or have somebody else read it out loud to you). Your ear will quickly pick up awkward phrasing.

Time your copy carefully. If you do not have a stopwatch, use the sweep second hand of a regular watch. You cannot take liberties with broadcast time. If you contract for 30 seconds, you cannot sneak in a 35-second commercial.

Never write a commercial longer than the prescribed length. Instead try to write your commercial a wee bit shorter. Then your talent will not have to perform at a machine-gun pace to get everything in. Allow time for good pacing, for dramatic pauses, for normal reaction time. Do not cram copy into a commercial. It is a misuse of time and talent. Instead of "getting your money's worth," you are simply going to sound unprofessional.

Seeking Help from the Station

You may feel you haven't the right touch for radio; you won't even attempt to write it. If such is the case, go to the station. Tell the station manager or salesmanager your problem. Explain what idea you would like to get across to the public. Someone at the station will come up with copy ideas for you. The more money you spend on that station, the harder its staff will work to keep you supplied with good radio copy. The final say-so rests with you. You have the strong selling idea. The radio people have expertise with the medium. (A discussion of the "mechanics" of producing radio commercials will be found in Chapter 10.)

TELEVISION

Television is far and away the most potent advertising medium available to us today. It attracts large audiences. That's why it receives the highest percent of the budget of most national advertisers.

TV: Good Points and Bad

Television gives us the pictures and color we get in print advertising; it gives us the voice, sound, and music we get in radio. Television adds one magic dimension of its own—movement. No other medium sends a message with greater impact. Television is unequalled for demonstrating how a product works, what a product will do.

But television is not as readily available as newspaper and radio. Television time is expensive. Production is complicated. As with radio, the television message "moves." It cannot be called back and studied. Therefore, it is best to strive for the one strong impression. Once produced, television copy cannot easily be changed.

Overall Impression Counts

The key to all successful broadcast copy—radio or television—is utmost simplicity. Most successful television commercials are built around one idea and register one overriding impression on the viewer.

No matter how elaborate the production, the basic selling idea is simple. The Fiat car commercial shows a movie stunt driver roaring through unbelievably spectacular maneuvers, but the message is simple: This car is tough. The pictures shown on the screen demonstrate that point in a breathtaking way—but they never wander from that point.

Think Pictures First

When you come to put your ideas down on paper, keep uppermost in mind that television is a *picture* medium, not a word medium. Do not try simply to add pictures to radio words. Tell the story in pictures, not words. Try to think out your idea in pictures before you ever put anything on paper.

Preparing the Script

The sample script in Figure 7–3 shows that television is written in a form quite unlike any you've been used to. You start by dividing your paper in half vertically. All instructions for the pictures go on the left side of the line under the heading VIDEO. All instructions for voice, sound, and music go on the right side of the line under the heading AUDIO. As in radio, all instructions or directions are typed in capital letters; only the words the viewer hears are typed normally.

Describe Only Essential Action. As you write your script, describe only those scenes and changes of scene you need to get your idea across. Keep your descriptions as brief as possible, as though you were sending a telegram and had to pay for every word. Use abbreviations. Eliminate articles. You cannot highlight all the action; you can highlight only the most important story-telling action.

Words are secondary in television writing. (Some of the finest TV commercials have only one line of spoken copy at the end.) But make sure that whatever words you use match up with the pictures. Both should make the same point to the viewer. You have too big an investment to risk confusion.

Know Some Technical Language. Television scripts call for the same vocabulary used in radio commercials, plus a special vocabulary of their own. The key words are easy to learn and remember—and they will save you a good deal of typing time.

Product: the Sauce Mill
Television: 30 sec.

VIDEO	AUDIO
1. OPEN ON WAITER AS HE BURSTS INTO THE KITCHEN	MUSIC: IN AND UNDER
2. MS OF WAITER, HEAD CHEF, AND THE KITCHEN	WAITER: O.K. Pierre; a white sauce, chocolate sauce, and cheese, hollandaise, bernaise, and soup de jour.
3. PAN TO MCU OF HEAD CHEF AS HE BEGINS TO PLACE THE SAUCE MILL INTO PANS. THERE ARE EIGHT DIFFERENT PANS ALL IN A ROW; EACH HAS A DIFFERENT SAUCE INSIDE	ANNCR. VO: The head chef is using the Sauce Mill; the newest kitchen
4. CU AS CHEF PUTS EACH PAN ON THE RANGE AND TURNS ON THE FLAMES	aid. It's a disc that rotates evenly —by heat induction No plugs, batteries, or switches.
5. MCU AS CHEF BACKS AWAY FROM THE RANGE AND LOOKS PROUDLY AT THE CONGLOMERATION OF PANS	And best of all, no hands, It's amazing, but true.
6. DISSOLVE TO MS OF THE WAITER'S TRAY WHICH IS NOW PILED HIGH WITH ALL OF THE FINISHED DISHES TOPPED WITH YUMMY SAUCES	Try the sauce mill. Whether you're stirring for many
7. PAN WITH WAITER AS HE WALKS FROM KITCHEN TO A TABLE WITH ONE MAN (RATHER FAT). WAITER BEGINS TO SERVE MAN	or just one.
8. CUT TO CU OF SAUCE MILL	The Sauce Mill
9. SUPER THE SAUCE MILL IN ITS' BOX	
10. FADE OUT	MUSIC: UP AND OUT

Courtesy of Norah Diedrich

FIGURE 7–3
This is the proper form for typing up the script of a television commercial.

PAN Instruction for camera to move horizontally left or right from a fixed point.

TILT Instruction for camera to move up or down.

ZOOM Instruction for camera's Zoomar lens to move to a rapid close-up (ZOOM IN) or away to a distance shot (ZOOM OUT).

A camera will **PAN** (move horizontally left or right from a fixed pivot or central point). It will **TILT,** down or up. By manipulating a lens called the Zoomar lens, the camera may **ZOOM** in and out quickly. The camera itself does not move; only the lens is adjusted. It can ZOOM IN from a medium shot of your product to a tight close-up—as fast as a finger snap. And it can ZOOM OUT just as quickly. The camera itself can move, but this takes more

DOLLY Instruction to move entire camera forward or backward.

BOOM SHOT Instruction for camera to shoot from a boom or crane

TRUCK SHOT Instruction for camera to shoot from alongside moving object.

ECU Extreme close-up.

CU Close-up.

MCU Medium close-up.

MS Medium shot.

MLS Medium long shot.

LS Long shot.

ELS Extreme long shot.

CUT Instruction to change picture immediately.

DISSOLVE Instruction to fade out of one picture and into another.

WIPE Instruction to push one picture off screen to reveal another.

SUPER Instruction to superimpose one image over another.

VOICE OVER (VO) Instruction to provide off-screen narration.

time. To move the entire camera forward or backward, you **Dolly.** You can DOLLY IN or DOLLY OUT when it suits your dramatic purpose. You refer to a shot made by a camera mounted on a crane or boom as a **BOOM SHOT.** When a camera moves right alongside and in pace with a moving object (such as a car), that is called a **TRUCK** (or TRUCKING) **SHOT.**

There are no prescribed measurements for distances in television. You call 'em as you see 'em in your own imagination. Distance designations depend on the nature of the scene you are shooting. These are the common scriptwriter terms for various distances: **ECU** means extreme close-up, **CU** means close-up, **MCU** means medium close-up, **MS** means medium shot, **MLS** means medium long shot, **LS** means long shot, **ELS** means extreme long shot.

The term **CUT** means an immediate change of picture. It is extremely fast. A **DISSOLVE** on the other hand, is a fading out of one picture and a fading in of another. Because it takes a little more time, the DISSOLVE is often called for to show a lengthy passage of time. Overnight, perhaps. Or an office day.

A **WIPE** is just what it sounds like. One image is pushed off the screen to reveal another. There are many different kinds of wipes—particularly in videotape. For example, a CLOCK WIPE changes the picture the way the hands of a clock go around. A FLIP WIPE does it like the flip of a playing card.

In many television commercials you will see words, a package, or a trademark placed over a scene. This is called a **SUPER** (a superimposition of one image over another). Use the SUPER somewhat sparingly—to reinforce your basic selling theme perhaps. The SUPER punches home key points; it reinforces in words or symbols what your pictures are showing. But too many supers can hamper the flow of your story.

Another term unique to television is **VO** or **VOICE OVER.** This is the abbreviation for off-screen narration; the person who is speaking is not being shown in the picture. The VO treatment has proved a godsend for television commercial writers. It permits dramatic demonstration on the screen and dynamic sales presentation on the sound track without letting either get in the way of the other. Put in its simplest terms, VO means you don't have to have the announcer or store owner on camera all the time. The nightly television news programs are great users of the VO technique. Obviously, the voice should be talking about what the picture is showing.

Using Music

One of the great advantages of broadcast advertising is the opportunity it provides to use music. Music touches all but the most hardened of us; it has as many moods as the human personality. The use of music is rather obvious for radio, but it can also work wonders in television. Use it as a signature, as identification. Use it to set a mood or a pace. Use it to indicate a time or a place. Example: Young singing groups today like to poke fun at the singing style of the Andrews Sisters—a style that immediately identifies the early forties and World War II.

There is no law that says you must use music, and it's probably better *not* to use it than to use it badly. Yet you should always at least consider the use of music. It has fantastic story-telling properties, even when it is kept softly in the background.

You can produce a glorious emotional effect with the right combination of pictures and music. Consider those scenes in the movie "Rocky" where the hero was doing his predawn training through the streets of Philadelphia. Or recall the opening sequence from "Chariots of Fire," where the British athletes were running on the beach. In each case, the total effect of pictures and music practically lifted the audience out of their seats. The proper use of music in commercials can be just as effective.

Leave Time for Others to Be Creative

Timing is as crucial in television as it is in radio. You simply must stay within the limits of the alloted time. Deliberately keep your script on the scant side; think in terms of twenty-five seconds for a thirty-second commercial. Here's why. You are dealing with cameras, directors, actors, movement, sound, music, settings—a wide assortment of individual creative talents and influences, each of which can make a contribution to your idea. Give them an opportunity to make that contribution. Give them precious time to "do their thing." Your commercial will be richer and more effective for it. If your script is too "tight," the announcer cannot dramatically build up the sales argument, the actors cannot react properly to one another's dialogue, the director and camera cannot linger over a particularly effective shot. When a script is too "tight," everything loses meaning, and nothing stands out. The advice about writing scant may not mean much to you as you read it in a book—but wait until your first experience in a television studio. Then you will understand.

A television commercial only *begins* when the finished script comes out of your typewriter. The idea does not come to life until you step inside the studio. And then it comes to life in ways you never dreamed of in your office. You depend on so many different professional skills and talent. You must give those outside skills and talents room to "breathe."

The Value of Close-ups

Keep in mind always that television commercials are designed to be seen on that small screen at home, not in a movie palace. Therefore, you should make generous use of close-up shots. They let the viewer at home see what you're talking about in greater detail.

Memorable Visuals

In all your advertising efforts, you should strive to be different. In television you should strive for a memorable visual—a dramatic scene, a "twist" that people remember and talk about. Example: "Did you see those beer commercials where the different kinds of light appear?" "Have you seen the sandwiches fighting off the cheap mustard?" "Remember those commercials where babies play inside the tires?" Nobody can tell you how to come up with such an idea, but it pays to seek one. Don't be fanatic about it, don't "strain" . . . but do your best to come up with a visual "twist" that will make your television advertising stand out from all others. Just as your product or service needs to be different from your competitors', so does your advertising.

Using a Storyboard

storyboard A series of sketches used to show the action of your commercial.

You may have heard the term **storyboard** in connection with television commercials. Depending on the chain of command of your operation or the simplicity of your idea, you may not need a storyboard. A storyboard is a visual substitute for the real thing. It consists of a series of six-inch wide or four-inch wide sketches of the key action described in your script. A copy block

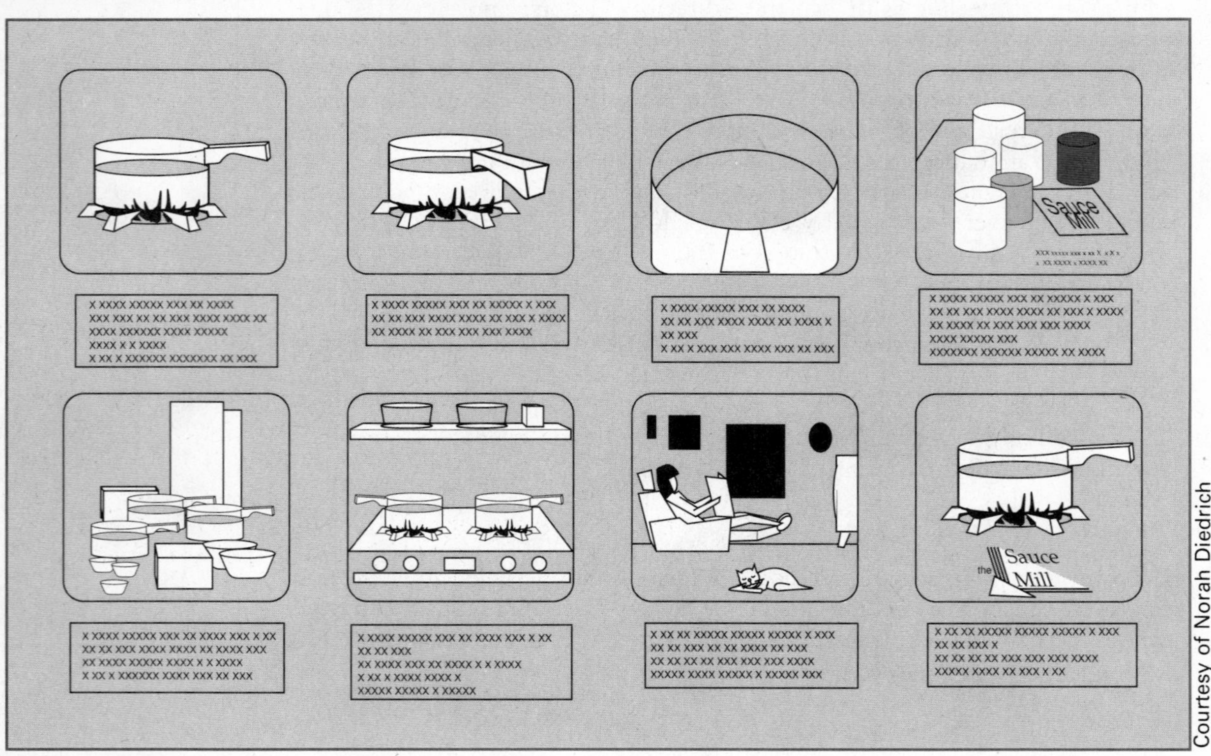

Courtesy of Norah Diedrich

FIGURE 7–4
This is the form generally followed when putting together a television storyboard.

under each sketch contains first, the video instructions, then, under that, the audio instructions. It is a sort of pictorial script. Major advertising agencies use storyboards for two main purposes: first, to make a presentation, attempting to "sell" the idea to a client; second, to send copies of the okayed storyboard to selected film or videotape production houses for bids. Figure 7–4 shows how a storyboard works.

If you are your own boss, making a commercial locally, a storyboard may be an unnecessary step. If setting and action are somewhat routine, there seems little need for a storyboard.

Local Help with TV

If there is a television channel—or several—located in your community, you are in luck. The commercial television stations offer service similar to that of the local radio stations and local newspapers. The television station has sales people—writer-producers on the staff who will take your suggestions and come up with a television commercial approach that you okay. The station staff will write, direct, cast, and produce your commercial for you. Because they are professionals and want your continued business, they will do the best they can for you, within the limitations of their facilities. You will be charged for the production, and possibly for the writing. Most local advertisers work this way. It may have some limitations, but you have to do the best you can with what's available. The trick is to come up with such a strong selling idea, stated in such a distinctive way that nothing keeps your message from shining through.

If you are preparing television commercials for a national advertiser with a substantial budget, you operate under a different set of rules for television production (which will be discussed more fully in Chapter 10.)

SUMMARY

In the previous chapter, we reviewed writing copy for print media—mainly newspapers. In this chapter, we have reviewed writing copy for radio and television. While the broadcast media use different communication elements and call for a different script form, they still demand single-minded emphasis on a consumer benefit directed to the right audience. The principles of creative strategy remain constant regardless of the media, as we shall see in the next chapter when we discuss direct mail, outdoor billboards, and other methods of communicating to the target audience.

TERMS TO KNOW

Now that you have finished this chapter, you should understand the following terms:

Straight radio copy	TILT	MLS
Production radio copy	ZOOM	LS
SFX	DOLLY	ELS
IN	BOOM SHOT	CUT
OUT	TRUCK SHOT	DISSOLVE
UP	ECU	WIPE
DOWN	CU	SUPER
UNDER	MCU	VOICE OVER (VO)
SEGUE	MS	storyboard
PAN		

If you are unsure about the meaning of any of these terms, go back through the chapter and review them.

THINGS TO THINK ABOUT

1. Why are key elements of copy repeated so often in radio? What might *three* of these "key elements" be?
2. It has been said that a copywriter's script—no matter how brilliant—is only the "bare bones" of a filmed commercial. Why do you think this might be so?
3. Why is the writer of radio copy urged first to read it out loud?
4. Why is it desirable to write short television copy?
5. What time of day is radio advertising most effective?

THINGS TO TALK ABOUT

1. Nominate your favorite presenter or actor in a TV commercial. Nominate your least favorite. Discuss the reasons you feel this way.
2. It has been said that advertising's most effective medium—television—may end up being advertising's greatest enemy. Discuss why you think this might be so.
3. Discuss why the imagination of the listener might be an essential ingredient in radio copy.
4. Discuss several reasons that writing for the ear is different from writing for the eye.

THINGS TO DO

1. Tonight between 7:00 P.M. and 9:00 P.M. analyze every TV commercial you see. How many use music? How many use SUPERS?
2. Find out how many advertising copywriters are employed by each of your local broadcast stations.
3. List the key elements of copy which are repeated for several "spots" you hear on your favorite radio station tonight.
4. Rough out a 30-second TV script extolling the virtues of your own watch or of the shoes you are wearing.

8 Copywriting for Other Media

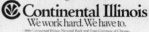

CHAPTER OUTLINE

Direct Mail
- The Good Points of Direct Mail
- Uses of Direct Mail
- Forms of Direct Mail

Direct Marketing Advertising
- Direct Marketing Copy Is Complete
- All Direct Marketing Copy Is Tested

Specialty Advertising

Point-of-Purchase and Window Displays

Yellow Pages

Outdoor Posters (Billboards)

Business-to-Business Advertising

To a Continental banker, this is a sweatsuit.
The New Continental Illinois is using a remarkably effective weapon in today's banking battlefield.
We call it hard work.
While the whole notion may seem foreign in a business known for its short hours, we've found that a little extra effort can go a long way.
For example, before we give advice we'll look at the way cash moves within your company, the way you buy services and materials, how you pay your debts, and how you invest your money.
Then, after asking the right questions, we'll make informed recommendations about loans, investment products, raising capital and managing cash.
So when you come to The New Continental, you can count on a bank that will make an extra effort to find creative ways to meet your financial challenges.
Because we're willing to do more than simply dress for success.
We're willing to work for it.
Continental Illinois
We work hard. We have to.

Continental Illinois National Bank and Trust Company of Chicago

By the time you finish this chapter, you should understand:

1. Some uses and forms of direct mail.
2. The key ingredients of a good direct marketing ad.
3. How direct marketing ad copy is tested.
4. The great variety of specialty advertising forms.
5. How point-of-purchase and window displays work.
6. Why billboards can carry so few words of copy.
7. How executives read business-to-business advertising.

When we think of advertising media, most of us think of newspapers, magazines, radio, and television. But there are other ways to get messages to our audience. Most advertisers, large or small, use direct mail to some extent. Outdoor billboards are nearly everywhere. So are the Yellow Pages. Specialty advertising abounds. You can reach even the smallest community by direct mail, window exhibits and modest point-of-purchase displays. Each method can be effective and each has its own special characteristics.

DIRECT MAIL

Direct mail is advertising mailed directly to the homes or businesses of target customers. The smallest advertisers use direct mail; the largest advertisers use direct mail. And they both use it for the same reason—it has no equal for targeting a specific market. You can see the particular advantage of direct mail for a small retailer with a modest number of customers or for a small manufacturer with a limited number of prospects. For example: A manufacturer of diesel engines does not have remotely the number of customers as the manufacturer of Wheaties. Why use a big-circulation medium?

direct mail Advertising mailed directly to the homes or businesses of target customers.

The Good Points of Direct Mail

Direct mail goes to a specific person or group of persons. There is little waste circulation. The message reaches the person you want to reach. It goes when you want it to go and in the shape you want it.

From the point of view of the copywriter, direct mail offers glorious advantages. The writer can talk very personally to the reader—even using the reader's name. The approach can be highly personalized to the reader's business situation. You can talk in terms of real job problems—be the reader purchasing agent, maintenance engineer, or personnel director.

The message can be as long or as short as the writer would like, as large or as small. A direct-mail piece can use any kind of paper or material. It can be built around a model of the product you're selling. Or a sample. Or a "gimmick" of some kind.

The creative person is really free to be creative. The mailing can be as modest as a postcard or as elaborate as a die-cut booklet on metallic paper. Even the most expensive direct-mail items (and they can get quite expensive) reach only the prospects you want to reach. Money is not wasted on people who are not potential customers.

Uses of Direct Mail

Most retailers, no matter how small, have long known about direct-mail advertising and promotion. Every retailer with charge account customers makes regular mailings. It costs little to insert an envelope stuffer—a single slip of paper or simple folder promoting a particular item—in with the monthly statement; it may lead to additional sales. Often such envelope stuffers are already available, preprinted from the national manufacturer of merchandise the retailer markets.

If a business draws most of its customers from the east side of town and would like more trade from folks on the west side, direct mail will do the job precisely and efficiently. Advertisers can make up their own **direct mail list;** can buy or lease one of many specialized lists, e.g., the subscribers of a technical journal or the members of a professional association. They can do their own mailing and tabulating or hire a firm that will take over the entire project.

direct mail list A list of prospective customers to be reached by direct mail.

Often direct mail is used for information gathering. It is relatively easy to send out a simple survey by mail. (And this lets you know that the right people are being questioned.)

The most widely used form of direct mail is the letter. Something provocative should be on the envelope to get the consumer to look inside. The opening sentence of the letter should act as the headline of the ad. It should get attention, offer a benefit, get the consumer to read further.

Forms of Direct Mail

Direct mail can take almost any form and be used for almost any purpose. You can send printed proofs of advertisements to selected customers before they appear in the magazines, send annual reports to stockholders, send calendars to regular customers, and try out new merchandising ideas on a select sample. From greeting cards to booklets to broadsides (a multifold piece that unfolds to a very large message), the only limits on your use of direct mail are your budget and your imagination. Many an advertising copywriter finds greater fulfillment working in direct mail than in any other medium.

DIRECT MARKETING ADVERTISING

Among the greatest users of direct mail are companies that sell directly to the customer without intermediaries. There is usually no retail store or sales person involved. The prospect reads an ad, likes the proposition, and orders directly from the advertiser. This kind of business is called **direct marketing advertising.** In addition to direct mail, direct marketing advertisers use many media—newspapers, magazines, radio, and television. (Direct marketing advertising is often called **direct response advertising** or, more traditionally, **mail-order advertising.**)

direct marketing advertising Selling directly to the customer without using an intermediary.

direct response advertising Another term for direct marketing advertising.

mail-order advertising A traditional term for direct marketing advertising.

Direct Marketing Copy Is Complete

The writer of direct marketing or direct response copy follows certain fairly rigid procedures. First, the copy gets the attention of a specific, interested audience. For example: "Money-saving News for Car Owners." Not an artistic headline, but notice several points. It singles out car owners. (The ad is not interested in people who are not car owners.) It promises a basic benefit. It uses time-tested selling phrases: "Money-saving" and "News."

Direct marketing copy must do the complete selling job. This one message may be your only shot at the prospect. At least, it would be wise to assume that. You must put all convincing arguments in line and in order, starting with the most important, and leave no stone unturned. You must play the role of the prospect, anticipating doubts and questions. Remain a step ahead, and keep offering added inducements. (If the item for sale is a history book, you might offer an authentic map of that period . . . a protective jacket . . . a bookmark.) You must support your argument with detailed information, highly specific and lots of it. ("This history book has 27 chapters, 1,102 pages, 42 maps, and 300 illustrations.") And reinforce your own arguments with the testimony of others—laboratory tests, field tests, use tests, satisfied users and endorsers, all identified. In the case of a book, don't forget the comments of literary critics.

Above all, the direct marketing copy must include some assurance of satisfaction, a guarantee of some kind. Through such long-used selling machinery, the advertising writer builds conviction in the minds of the readers. Then the writer closes with a strong urge for action. ("If you send in your check by July 10, your book of poetry will be specially bound in Moroccan leather with your name embossed in gold on the cover.") Last, insert some kind of action device if at all possible. A coupon, at the very least. A postal reply card. A self-addressed, stamped return envelope.

All Direct Marketing Copy Is Tested

To find out how well a particular appeal worked in the marketplace, all return addresses are keyed or coded. The "key" is a sort of secret code number or name used to trace the response back to a particular ad. This system is call **keyed response.** The key may be a particular post office box number or number in a street address. More and more companies today are using 800 phone numbers. The prospective customer is urged to phone Ms. Brady or Mr. Howe, for example. The name itself is a key—used only for *one* ad appeal.

keyed response Testing the appeal of a particular ad by providing a key or code to identify the people who respond to it.

Replies to direct marketing show not only the strength of various appeals but also the pulling power of various media. There *are* differences. That's why direct marketing merchandisers keep complete records, why they are constantly testing.

Direct marketing advertisers are not quick to change a winning combination. But they always put aside a part of their budget for judging new approaches. If they get a strong reaction to a new appeal, *it* becomes the new champion and is backed by the bulk of the budget.

According to historical sources, one of the most effective of all direct marketing headlines was: "Do You Make These Mistakes in English?" It was written by Maxwell Sackheim for the Sherwin Cody Home Study Course in English. It ran unchanged for over twenty-five years; yet during all that time the advertiser was constantly testing alternatives.

Since every insertion must give a complete sales story, direct marketing copy tends to run long. This is natural and proper. Do not be persuaded by the siren song of those who proclaim "People won't read long copy." Perhaps they won't—in a Coca-Cola ad. But when they're in a buying mood, and you have an interesting proposition that promises a benefit, potential customers will read every word of long copy and beg for more.

To repeat, if you are sending your direct marketing appeal in a letter, follow this checklist:

1. Have some provocative "teaser" on the envelope.
2. Back your letter with supporting evidence—pictures, swatches, samples.
3. Include an action device that makes response easier.

Advertising that does the job right will win tangible and immediate rewards. But the task is demanding. It is hard enough to get a reader even to glance at advertising, much less sit down and write a check on the spot.

SPECIALTY ADVERTISING

specialty advertising Advertising by placing the advertiser's name and selling message on a useful article given to consumers.

A unique medium called specialty advertising may offer an ideal solution to the advertiser who cannot logically make great use of newspapers, magazines, radio, or television. **Specialty advertising** carries the advertiser's name and very short selling message on an article that a customer might use over and over again for a long time. Specialty advertising items can take many forms: ballpoint pens, desk lighters, desktop sets, attache cases, glassware, paperweights, rulers, key holders, luggage tags, balloons. While the message on such items is limited, the number of exposures can be fantastic.

There are thousands of advertising specialties to choose from and new ones can be created to order. Entire promotional campaigns have been built around specialty items. The Crocker National Bank of California offered stuffed dogs called Crocker Spaniels. Manufacturers Hanover Trust in New York once did a special mailing of a silk scarf with a Van Gogh reproduction printed on it. Chances are, one of the many specialty advertising items can be

Courtesy of Fourth Investment Advisors, Tulsa, Oklahoma, and Specialty Advertising Association International.

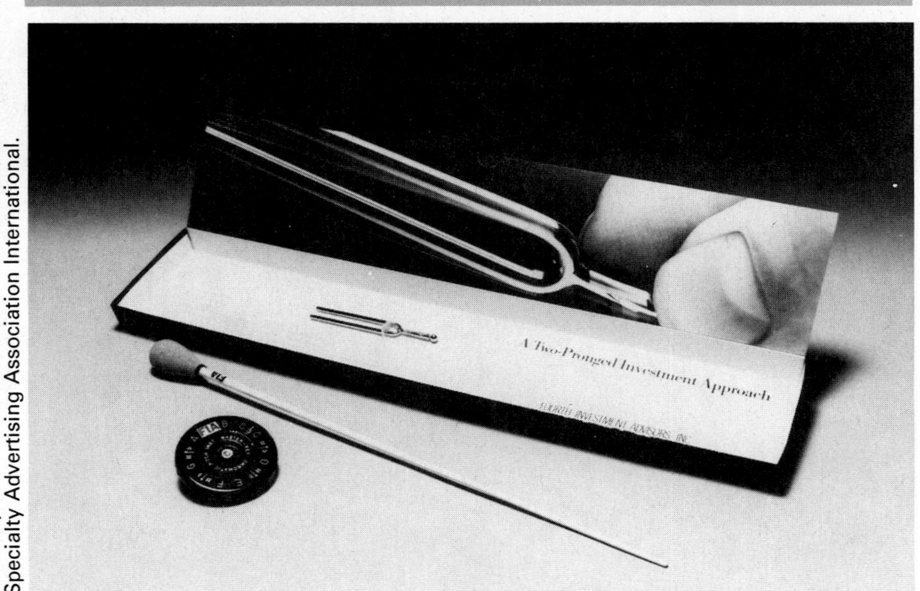

FIGURE 8–1
A musical theme and three specialty advertising items were used by Fourth Investment Advisors to help pave the way for sales presentations to 150 financial executive/investors. Three mailings were sent a week apart. First, a conductor's baton. Second, a pitch pipe. Last, a tuning fork promoting a "two-pronged investment approach." The series of mailings opened many doors that were difficult to open.

almost tailor-made for your specific problem. Suppose, for example, you sent a plastic ruler marked in inches and meters. You might word your copy in this manner: "By any measure, Grant Gaskets give a tight seal."

POINT-OF-PURCHASE AND WINDOW DISPLAYS

Some small retailers are on a tight budget that does not permit newspaper, radio, television, poster advertising, and the like. Even they have one of the world's great media available to them at all times—free. That medium is display space—shelf, aisle, counter, and window displays—past which in-store traffic and sidewalk traffic is constantly moving.

A remarkable number of purchases are made on impulse. In many cases, all people have to do is see an item and they want it. You can create awareness by shrewd use of the retail facilities at hand. Inside the store, you can get people's attention simply by putting merchandise in full view. Up front. At the check-out counter. In an end-aisle display. On an eye-level shelf.

Counter cards, shelf strips, light pulls, and the like may speed up customer reaction. The message should be extremely brief: possibly a key word like "New" or "Introducing." At most, it should repeat the basic selling theme of the campaign for the product displayed or the service being promoted.

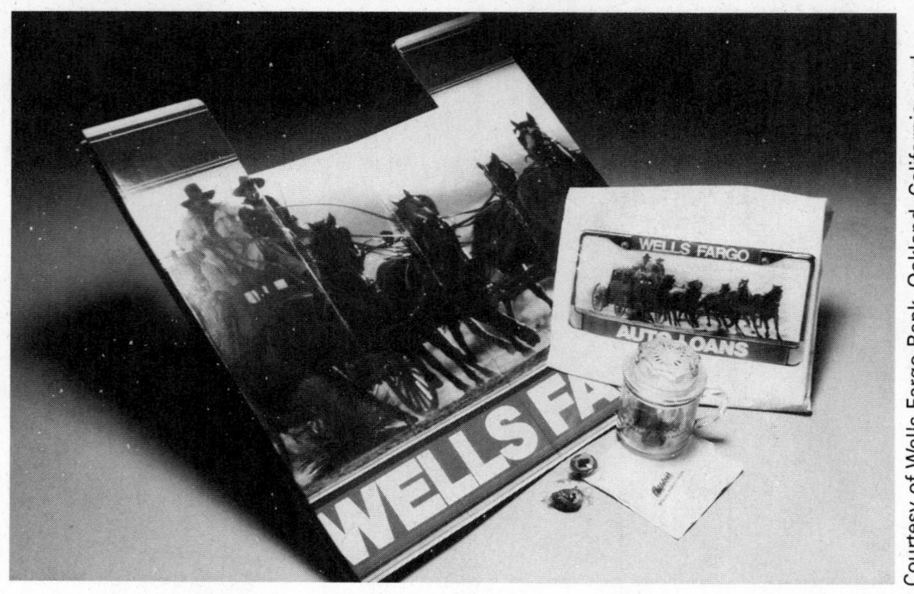

Courtesy of Wells Fargo Bank, Oakland, California, and Specialty Advertising Association International.

FIGURE 8–2
To build traffic at its booth in the San Francisco International Auto Show and to promote auto loans, Wells Fargo Bank turned to specialty advertising items. At a VIP preview party, apothecary jar/coffee cups filled with imprinted salt water taffy were given to auto dealers. Visitors to the auto loan booth received a 4-color photographic auto sunshade depicting the Wells Fargo stagecoach. Also distributed were plastic shopping bags imprinted "Auto Loans" in the license plate graphic. Response was overwhelming: more than 4,000 handwritten leads for auto loans.

Many national manufacturers have a wide selection of point-of-purchase material available for their dealers. Some of it can be specially adapted for local use.

Windows, of course, are the major medium for many small retailers. A constant flow of traffic moves by. What a pity not to give those passing eyes something new and different to look at from time to time. Retailers without an extra dime in their pockets can freshen up their store windows—even if all they do is change the groupings of merchandise. If they sell branded merchandise, they can receive much in the way of props, designs, and suggestions from the national advertiser's home office. They can use ideas created by the highest-priced display people in the business—being careful, of course, not to let the national brand material overshadow their own operation.

The finest window displays are usually keyed to a focal idea or theme such as "Spring Colors" or "Vacation Values" or "Spruce Up the Old Homestead." The better department stores are expert at building interest and drama into window displays. An occasional jaunt to Michigan Avenue or Fifth Avenue can supply imaginative advertising ideas that will serve for years. The Bonwit Teller windows in New York have long been a "must" for tourists. In recent years, Bloomingdale's windows in New York have been praised in the national press.

But even the barest budget and the drabbest merchandise should not discourage a shrewd merchant from taking full advantage of this fantastic adver-

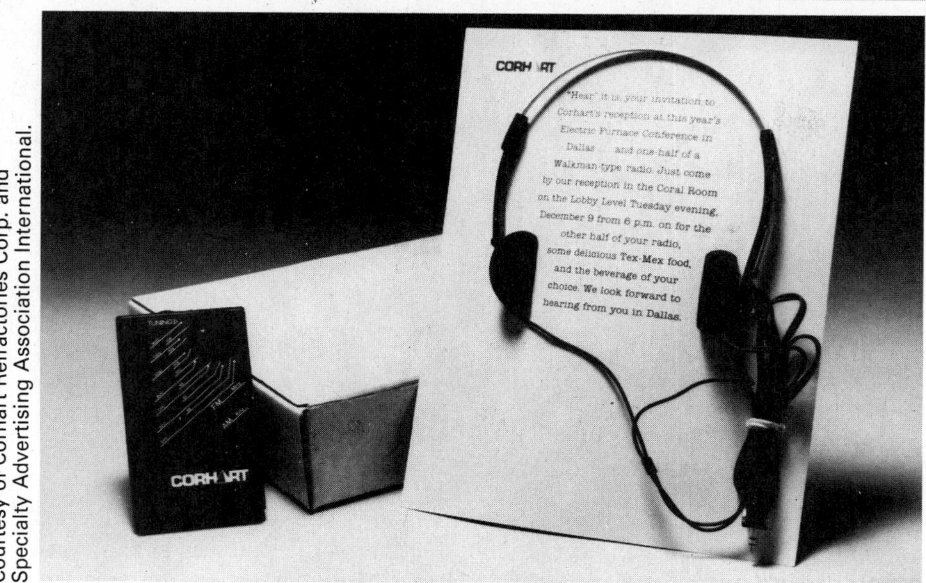

Courtesy of Corhart Refractories Corp. and Specialty Advertising Association International.

FIGURE 8–3
Specialty advertising boosted attendance at the Corhart reception during the Electric Furnace Convention. An unusual invitation was sent to 240 metallurgical steel executives with buying power. The invitation came in a box containing *earphones only* for a pocket AM/FM radio. All the recipients had to do to pick up the radio itself was attend the reception. The results: an overflow crowd.

tising medium. All it takes is a little time and elbow grease. Keep freshening up the groupings of merchandise. Freshen up the props. Keep that window neat and tidy. An uncared-for window gives off strong negative vibrations.

YELLOW PAGES

To many small merchants, the word *advertising* is synonymous with the Yellow Pages. It is a tremendously important form of advertising because it guides consumers to the actual point of sale for a needed product. Most Yellow Pages ads are monotonously alike. Dull and drab. A few simple touches may make your ad leap off the page. Examples might be a strong headline, symbol, or illustration to get attention, clear information, complete details, exact location, or a touch of color. Try to keep your typography well spaced, with a little "air" around it so that the total effect looks well organized and tasteful. You want the directory reader to get the impression that your shop is equally well organized and attractive. And, as in all advertising, always stress the features that make you special.

OUTDOOR POSTERS (BILLBOARDS)

You can buy as many—or as few—outdoor posters (or billboards) as you wish. You can even buy only *one*.

FIGURE 8–4
This billboard's highly imaginative visual treatment of the product ties in wonderfully with the promised benefit.

Courtesy of California Milk Advisory Board and Institute of Outdoor Advertising.

Most small retailers and infrequent users of posters try to pack too much on them. True, the space is large. But a poster is meant to be seen at a distance from a moving car. The viewer must become involved with and comprehend your message at a glance. Thus, a billboard is a visual medium. The illustration should dominate—whether it is a human-interest situation, a trademark, a picture of the product, or a store front. The words should be held to a minimum—seven or eight at the most. Five would be ideal.

Simple illustration and design are a must. All extra materials must be stripped away. Your visual should focus on key action and key elements. If, for example, your poster message involves people camping out, you do not have to show the entire forest. Perhaps a close-up of a tent flap will do. In discussing the problem of creating billboards, a leading advertising agency said that if your idea wasn't small enough to fit on a postage stamp, it wasn't big enough for a poster.

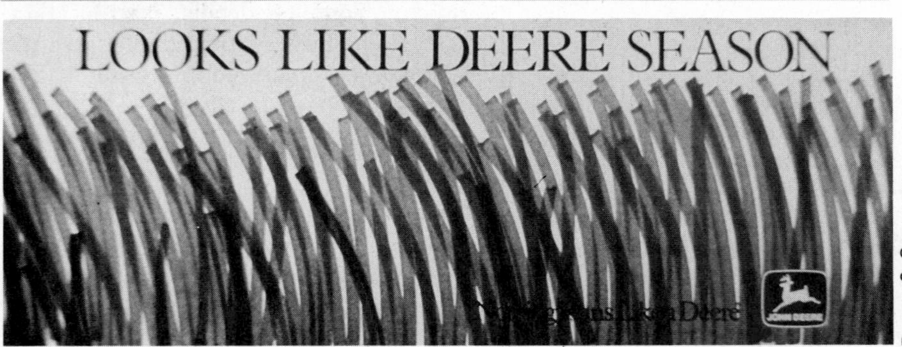

FIGURE 8–5
Utter simplicity in design and illustration of this billboard makes the benefit obvious instantly.

Deere & Company

Zoological Society of San Diego and Institute of Outdoor Advertising

The joint is jumpin'.
The San Diego Zoo

FIGURE 8–6
In this dramatic billboard for the San Diego Zoo, notice how every background detail has been stripped away to focus full attention on the animal.

Billboards are used mainly as reminders. Often outdoor ads are the last reminders a prospect sees before going into the store. And, like any other medium, posters should be used in a way that separates your selling approach from all others.

BUSINESS-TO-BUSINESS ADVERTISING

Advertising writers trying to sell a product or service to industry or agriculture had best be extremely straightforward. They are dealing with professionals: people who are strictly business when they read advertising in their business publications. They are not reading for fun. Often, their companies buy the business publication subscriptions for them. Hence, they are seeking new products, new uses, new ideas that can help them in their own field of endeavor. Wise ad writers talk straight from the shoulder, stress news, and offer proof of performance. They talk facts. They talk results. And they realize that the story of a satisfied user speaks most eloquently. Nothing intrigues a business reader more than the case history of an actual product installation or adoption.

Many industrial transactions involve **specified purchases,** products created especially to solve one manufacturer's problem. Consequently, your advertising is likely to stress your company's capabilities rather than a product line.

specified purchases products created especially to solve a particular manufacturer's problem.

Graphically, business-to-business advertising today looks more like consumer advertising, often with a dominant, dramatic visual element accompanying the copy.

Try to make your business publication advertising look as straightforward as possible. Keep it orderly and informative. Write low-key copy. Be sure your advertising is businesslike in appearance and tone. Readers of industrial and trade publications are actively seeking the help you can offer. Just don't try to dazzle them or hoodwink them. They can spot a phony on sight.

FIGURE 8–7
Stark simplicity of illustration on these public service billboards registers copy point with chilling impact.

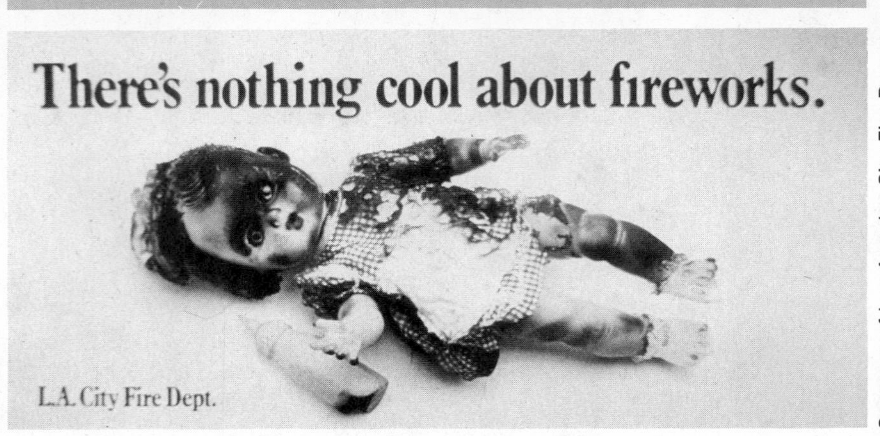

There's nothing cool about fireworks.
L.A. City Fire Dept.

Courtesy of Los Angeles City Fire Department and Institute of Outdoor Advertising

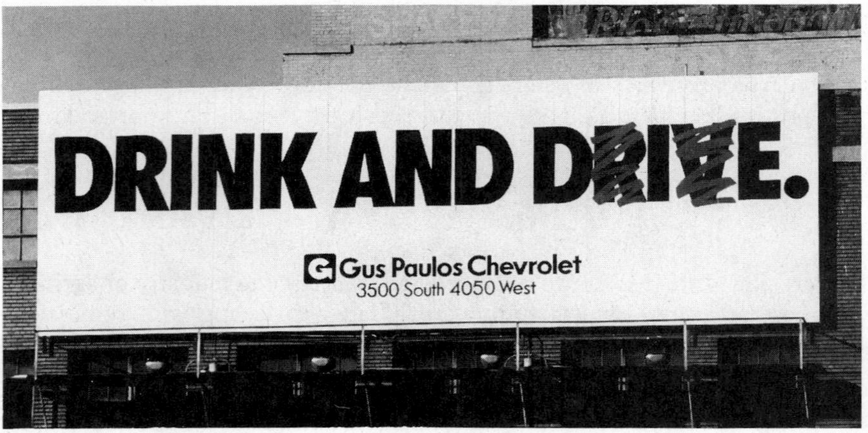

Evans/Salt Lake - Dick Brown, Art Director, Writer

SUMMARY

In previous chapters, we reviewed copywriting for print and for broadcast. In this chapter, we have reviewed copywriting for several other media. We have seen that each individual medium has its own advantages. Each has certain characteristics that you must adapt to in writing your copy.

Use the various media as they suit your purpose and problem. Just make sure that you never permit the peculiarities of a particular medium to get in the way of your basic selling message. First, be certain that you have a good concept, a strong central selling theme. You'll find that such a concept will adapt to any medium.

In the next two chapters we shall discuss how your selling idea, your typewritten copy, gets into print or on the air. That subject is called production.

TERMS TO KNOW

Now that you have finished this chapter, you should understand the following terms:

direct mail	direct mail list
direct marketing advertising	keyed response
direct response advertising	specialty advertising
mail-order advertising	specified purchase

If you are unsure of the meaning of any of these words, go back through the chapter to review them.

THINGS TO THINK ABOUT

1. Even though an outdoor billboard is very large, why should you try to hold the number of words down to five?
2. Businesspeople will not read their trade publications the same way they read *People, Cosmopolitan,* or *Sports Illustrated.* Why?
3. It has been said that with outdoor billboard art the trick is to take things out rather than put things in. Why might this be so?
4. Why would a businessperson be particularly interested in an ad featuring an actual product installation?
5. An attractive window display might be compared to the headline/illustration element of a print ad. Explain.

THINGS TO TALK ABOUT

1. What is the most common mistake made by small retailers who are infrequent users of outdoor billboards?
2. A store that cannot afford newspaper, radio, television, billboards, Yellow Pages, specialty advertising, or direct mail still has a potent advertising medium available to it. Which?
3. Perhaps the greatest billboard ever created showed a group of nuns loading into a VW Van with the caption "Mass Transit." What made it so good?
4. Suppose you wanted a Halloween promotion and all you could afford were printed balloons. What images or messages might you print on the balloons?
5. In the early days of television, direct marketing advertisers could not make very effective use of that medium. Nowadays they can. What caused the change?

THINGS TO DO

1. Save all the pieces of direct mail that come to your home and/or office in the next month. Examine and analyze them. Notice all the different kinds. Notice all the different lead-in devices that capture a reader's attention.
2. Clip the same direct marketing ad from each of two different publications. Then examine the coupon or hidden offer. How does the advertiser keep track of where the responses are coming from?
3. For the same product or service, clip a consumer ad and a trade ad. Analyze the differences in copy.
4. Check ten outdoor billboards in your community. Count the number of words of copy on each.
5. Compare a direct marketing ad that uses a coupon and a direct marketing ad that does not use a coupon. Do you see differences?

9 Print Advertising Production

Courtesy of Hilton Hotels Corporation

CHAPTER OUTLINE

Typography
- Families of Type
- Be Practical with Type
- Points and Leading
- Pica Measurements
- Metal or Photo
- Where to Seek Help Locally

Printing and Reproduction
- Basic Forms of Printing
- Reproducing Artwork

Where to Seek Help

Desktop Miracle

By the time you finish this chapter, you should understand:

1. What the term *print production* covers.
2. That type comes in families.
3. How to tell roman from italic type.
4. A little about how type and printing areas are measured.
5. That there is more than one important form of printing.
6. The difference between line and halftone reproduction.
7. That a full-color ad actually involves several colors.
8. How computers are used in ad making.

Print production is what happens between the time your ad idea is okayed and the time it finally appears in its proper medium. In other words, it includes all the processes involved in turning typed copy and layout into a finished piece.

It is only fair to warn you that you cannot learn print production by reading a book. This chapter cannot teach you how to set type or reproduce an illustration. Those skills are learned by doing, not reading. ("Hands-on" learning, as some educators say.) The most this chapter can do is introduce you to the subject, tell you a little bit about print production, acquaint you with a smattering of the terminology. Put it this way—after reading this chapter you will not be expected to recognize the various typefaces but simply to know that there are a number of different ones.

So proceed unafraid. Print production is a fascinating phase of advertising—but you can be a great advertising person without knowing much about it. Many people drive a car without having much idea of how the machinery operates. You see, the production process is mechanical, technical. It may seem a great mystery to you at first. Do not worry about that. Time will take care of it. As you actually work with making ads, you will soon learn about production—enough to know your way around. It won't take you long to discover that the real trick is not necessarily knowing how to do it personally, but how to get it done.

Production of print ads embraces the separate technical skills of typography, reproduction, and printing. Since production may, indeed, be a strange new world for you, it is best to take it in easy stages. This discussion will begin with a look at **typography**—the printing of words.

typography The printing of words.

TYPOGRAPHY

It could be that you have spent your entire lifetime up to now without once giving a thought to the many differences in type. With the exception of newspaper headlines, type or printing probably all looked alike to you.

FIGURE 9–1
Typeface differences.

Little did you dream of all the shapes and sizes and thicknesses designed to delight the human eye. If you are not familiar with type differences and are ready to be dazzled, call on your local newspaper or print shop and ask if you may glance through a type-specimen book. Flip through a few pages. You can accept the various sizes from small to large, the two basic styles (slanted and vertical), the choice of capital or small letters. But all those different shapes and thicknesses—it's enough to make the head spin.

Be of good cheer. Each is different from the other. Once you start making ads, you will learn to tell typefaces apart—at least, the most important ones.

Families of Type

type families Groups of type with distinguishing characteristics.

All typefaces (or type fonts) come in families, just as human faces do. Just as the Kennedys, the Rockefellers, the Barrymores, and the Osmonds have distinguishing characteristics, so do the **type families.** Many of them have proud family names, too, usually inherited from the original designer of the typeface. Here are a few: Bodoni, Garamond, Baskerville, Caslon, Goudy.

With a bit of concentration, you can recognize distinguishing family features. As shown in Figure 9–1, Bodoni is a bold type with a delicately thin horizontal line in the small *e*. Goudy is a handsome, gutsy typeface with a diamond-shaped dot over the *i*.

Certain families offer all kinds of variations. Take Franklin Gothic, for example. It is a thick, eye-catching type that you can see most often in newspaper headings and subheads. You can order this distinctive face with several options—Franklin Gothic Bold, Franklin Gothic Extra Condensed, Franklin Gothic Extended, and the like. All come from the same family roots, yet each has a slight facial distinction that makes it especially suitable for a given situation.

ascenders Upstrokes in letters.

descenders Downstrokes in letters.

Certain letters of the alphabet have parts that extend above or below the "body" of the letter. The letter *o* is unadorned, but the letter *d* has a stem that goes above the line and the letter *p* has a stem that goes below. The upstrokes are called **ascenders** and the down strokes are called **descenders.** In some type families, certain combinations of letters may be joined (*fl* for example). Such a joint treatment of two letters is called a **ligature.**

ligature The joining of two letters in print.

Traditional Type/Serifs. Most traditional types have tiny extensions on the ends of letters called **serifs.** Serifs not only add to the beauty of design, they also make a typesetting much easier to read.

serifs Tiny extensions on the ends of letters.

Modern Type/Sans-Serif. Some of the more modern type designs do not have these tiny extensions on the ends of letters. Such typefaces are called **sans-serif** (which is French for "without serifs.") Most sans-serif faces are crisp and bold and look very good in display; that is, when they have lots of white space around them. But the sans-serif faces do not work very well in a solid block of reading matter. They are tiring to read.

sans-serif Type that does not have serifs.

Basic Styles–Roman and Italic. Each family offers capital letters and small letters (referred to by typographers as "upper and lower case" or u & lc) as well as two basic styles—roman and italic. Most of the type you see in textbooks, novels, newspaper stories, and magazine articles is **roman.** That is, the type stands straight vertically, featuring heavy stem strokes along with light strokes. This sentence, for example, is set in roman.

roman A vertical type style.

The other basic style is **italic** which is slanted or sloped. It is used chiefly for emphasis: as a subhead; as a short lead-in to a new copy topic; to punch out key words and phrases in copy. *This sentence is set in italic.* But italic is rarely used for long text because it is too hard on the eyes.

italic A slanted type style.

Be Practical with Type

The best way to use type is with restraint. Stated another way, type should never get in the way of the message. Do not use type for its own sake; use it only to enhance the advertising message.

Stick to the Tried and True. The human eye is used to certain common practices in typesetting. It is best to follow the tried and true: Use capital and lower-case letters (rather than all capitals); have copy run horizontally from left to right; space letters and words evenly. It rarely pays to be different. Avoid setting type at an angle; avoid the stacked headline with one word over another. Use capital letters chiefly for headlines and do so sparingly. A long line or a block of copy set all in capital letters is extremely difficult to read. Figure 9–2 shows an especially good use of type.

The most common printing of type is black on white. Occasionally great emphasis can be achieved by doing just the reverse—showing white type on a dark background. This is called, appropriately, **reverse.**

reverse Printing in white on black rather than black on white.

Avoid Mixing Faces. Use good sense in "mixing" typefaces. Often it is better to use just one basic typeface in a message, getting drama and

FIGURE 9–2
Type selection seems especially appropriate to announce this industrial product, which is so handsomely presented.

Courtesy of USG Industries, Inc. and its agency, Marstrat, Inc.

emphasis through all the basic variations available in that face—capital, lowercase, italic, condensed (thin), and expanded (thick) letters.

Points and Leading

Type is measured in **points.** There are 72 points to 1 inch vertically. Most families of type offer sizes from tiny 6-point to giant 72-point and larger. You may hear a typographer say "We'll set that 10 point on 12 (or 10 over 12) Garamond." The two numbers refer to **leading** (pronounced "led'-ing") or use of thin (1-pt) strips of spacing between the lines of type. A sensible use of leading "opens up" the typesetting and makes it ever so much easier to read. Too much leading, however, can make the setting look "loose" and "jittery" to the eye. Type that has no leading between lines is said to be set "solid."

points Units used to measure type.

leading The spacing between lines of type.

When fairly long text is being set in type, 10-point, 12-point or 14-point size makes for good reading. With any type much larger than that you are into display or headline sizes. The text you are reading, for example, is set in 10-point type with 2 points of leading.

A very long line of normal-size type is hard to read. That is why you see type broken up into vertical columns. (Think how difficult your *Time* magazine would be to read if every line of type ran clear across the page.) Of course, the use of larger-size type permits a wider column.

You will need to be able to tell the typographer how long you want your lines of print to be. You will also need to specify such things as the space you want between a headline, a subhead, and your text, and the actual length and width of the advertisement itself.

Pica Measurements

In typography the unit of area measurement is called a **pica.** There are 12 points in a pica, 6 picas to an inch. A copy block might be termed 16 picas wide by 36 picas deep. There are short cuts to "casting" or estimating type, and whoever sets type for you can teach you simple tricks of the trade. Basically, on the type-specimen sheet you count the number of characters (single letters) permitted by your selected face, say 10-pt. Century Schoolbook, in the number of horizontal picas available to you. Let us say one line will take 50 characters. Then you see how many 50-character lines are in your typed manuscript (remembering to allow for the spaces between words). If this comes to more picas than your layout allows, you had better cut some copy.

pica Unit used to measure area in print.

Metal or Photo

For many years each letter of type was "carved" on metal set on a lead slug. Only the raised surface of the sculptured letter held ink and printed a mark on paper. In recent years, phototype has taken over the center of the stage. Phototype has changed the names of typefaces but still offers the same wide range of choices. It is also flexible; it can be shaped to add a dimension that was unavailable in rigid metal type. Modern typesetting machines can add up to five variations on one typeface: slanting backward, slanting forward, expanding, condensing, or reversing.

A somewhat primitive form of type is a transfer process whereby you press down certain characters in place from a pre-printed sheet of letters. You can buy such presstype in almost any dime store. This is all right for simple display work—a short headline or key word—but is far too tedious and imprecise for long typesetting.

Most advertising messages today are typed on a typewriter-style keyboard that feeds a tape into a computer-operated system. Letters on an alphabet film strip or disk are then photographed at high speed onto a strip of sensitized film paper. The complete message comes out at one end of the machine precisely printed on the strip of film paper. This printed strip is then pasted into exact position on the mechanical layout. One of the most prominent manufacturers of photocomposition equipment is the Compugraphic Corporation of Wilmington, Massachusetts. Some active advertisers who like in-house control of their graphics have invested in their own on-premises headline-setting photocomposition machines.

Where to Seek Help Locally

If you have never had anything to do with type, you will have to lean on the expertise of others. If there are typographers in your community, consult them. You'll find them artists of sorts, sensitive to the proper balance of display weight and body-text "color." You may pay a little premium for their services.

Not all printers set type, but many printers do have a number of type selections available. Figure 9–3 shows a list of phototype choices available from one printer. The printer is a craftsman and will do everything possible to guide you into a final product of which you'll both be proud.

Local newspaper advertising offers fewer typography options. Most newspapers have a very limited choice of typefaces. Within those limitations, however, the newspaper will do everything possible to produce your ad with all the style and punch you want. When the type choices are limited, simplicity becomes a greater factor than ever in effective advertising.

No type, metal or photo, can give you the *beauty* of superb hand lettering. This is called **calligraphy.** In many national ads, the display headline will be hand lettered.

calligraphy Hand lettering.

PRINTING AND REPRODUCTION

While you might someday dabble with your own phototypesetting facilities, printing and the reproduction of artwork are best left to the professionals.

There are really two parts to the printing process: creating the plates that hold the material to be printed and printing the number of copies desired (the "run"). A quality printer can do both, but sometimes you'll need to have your plates made by your own printer and delivered to the newspaper or

Avant Garde Gothic Ex. Lt. Roman
Avant Garde Gothic Ex. Lt. Italic
Avant Garde Gothic Book Roman
Avant Garde Gothic Book Italic
Avant Garde Gothic Med. Roman
Avant Garde Gothic Med. Italic
Avant Garde Gothic Bold Roman
Avant Garde Gothic Bold Italic
Baskerville Roman
Baskerville Italic
Baskerville Bold Roman
Baskerville Bold Italic
Bodoni Roman
Bodoni Italic
Bodoni Bold Roman
Bodoni Bold Italic
Bookman Roman
Bookman Italic
Bookman Bold
Bookman Bold Italic
Caledonia Roman
Caledonia Italic
Century Expanded Roman
Century Expanded Italic
Century Bold Roman
Century Bold Italic
Clarendon Light Roman
Clarendon Light Itaiic
Clarendon Roman
Clarendon Italic
Clarendon Bold Roman
Clarendon Bold Italic
Garamond 3 Roman
Garamond 3 Italic
Garamond Bold 3 Roman
Garamond Bold 3 Italic
Helvetica Lt. Roman
Helvetica Lt. Italic
Helvetica Roman
Helvetica Italic
Helvetica Bold Roman
Helvetica Bold Italic
Helvetica Black Roman
Helvetica Black Italic
Helvetica Black Roman No. 2
Helvetica Compressed
Melior Roman
Melior Italic
Melior Bold Roman
Melior Bold Italic
Optima Roman
Optima Italic
Optima Medium Roman
Optima Medium Italic
Optima Bold Roman
Optima Bold Italic
Optima Black Roman
Optima Black Italic
Pabst Extra Bold Roman
Palatino Roman
Palatino Italic
Palatino Bold Roman
Palatino Bold Italic
Times Roman
Times Italic
Times Bold Roman
Times Bold Italic
Trade Gothic Light Roman
Trade Gothic Light Italic
Trade Gothic Roman
Trade Gothic Italic
Trade Gothic Bold Roman
Trade Gothic Bold Italic
Trade Gothic Bold 2 Roman
Trade Gothic Bold 2 Italic
Trade Gothic Condensed Roman 18
Trade Gothic Condensed Italic 18
Trade Gothic Bold Condensed Roman 20
Trade Gothic Bold Condensed Italic 20

FIGURE 9–3
This gives some idea of the variety of typefaces available from one printer.

magazine your ad will appear in. The publication's own printing facilities will then include your plate in the run of a specific edition.

This chapter cannot teach you all the technical material involved in these processes. It will simply give you a sketchy idea of the most basic differences in reproduction and printing processes. It will also teach you a smattering of terminology. After reading this chapter, you will not be expected to recognize offset printing but simply to know that there is such a thing. Likewise, you will not be expected to recognize one halftone screen from another but simply to know what a halftone screen is and that it performs an essential function in reproducing artwork. So plunge right in. If some of the strange terms baffle you a bit, don't worry. Remember, this is one phase of the advertising process that the technical experts take care of for you.

Basic Forms of Printing

All three basic forms of printing follow a similar process. The printer photographs your ad using a special sensitized film, then transfers the image on the negative to a plate by a chemical process. Basically, the printing processes differ in the kinds of plates they use.

letterpress printing A printing process that uses plates with a raised surface.

gravure printing A printing process that uses plates with a recessed surface.

offset printing A printing process that uses plates with a flat surface.

Letterpress printing uses a plate with a raised surface. It gives the clearest image, but it is rather expensive to produce.

Gravure printing uses a plate with tiny reservoirs or ink wells sunk below the surface. The porous paper sucks up the ink as it goes through the presses. Gravure printing is not as precise as letterpress but it is great for very large print runs. For example, gravure is used for printing large quantities of boxes. Many grocery store free-standing inserts are printed by gravure.

Offset printing has become far and away the most popular process in recent years because it is fast and inexpensive. It is really *the* printing process today. Offset printing does not use a raised surface or a recessed surface but a flat surface of inexpensive aluminum to which the final photographic image has been transferred through a chemical process. (See Figure 9–4.)

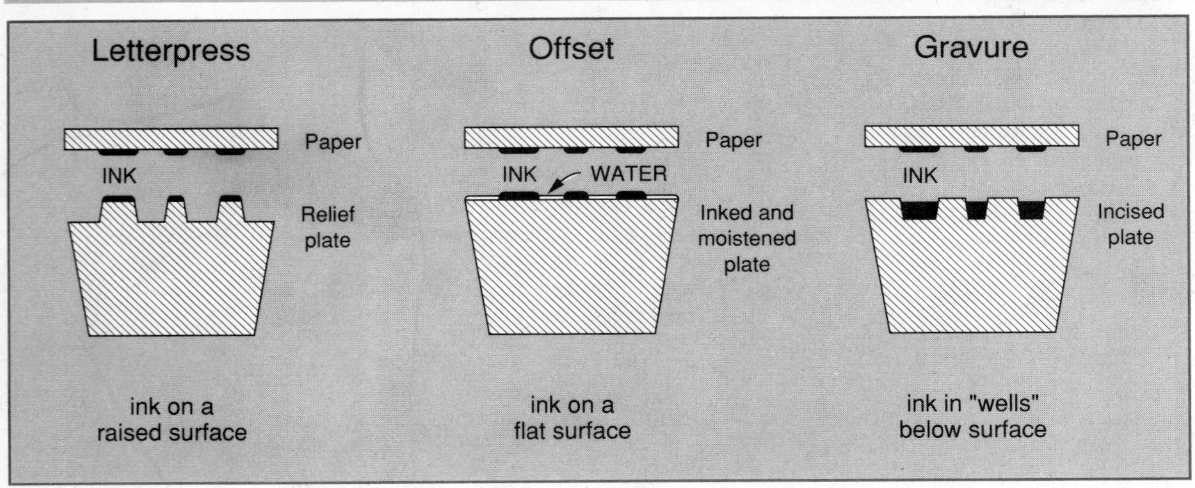

FIGURE 9-4
The three basic engraving-printing methods: letterpress (ink on a raised surface); offset (ink on a flat surface); and gravure (ink in "wells" below the surface).

Well-targeted ad reaches out to young men recently finished with college but not yet "hooked" on a business career. Picture-headline combination is practically irresistible to an adventuresome youth.

Courtesy of United States Air Force.

To produce a full-color advertisement for a magazine, you, as an advertising manager, will oversee the work of many different people—the copywriter who writes the ad, the photographer who takes the product shot, the production artist who puts all the elements of the ad together, and last but not least, the separator, who prepares a cromalin or proof for the ad. The cromalin shows you what the ad will look like when it is printed. On this proof, you check that the copy, art, and photograph are correctly placed and that the colors are true.

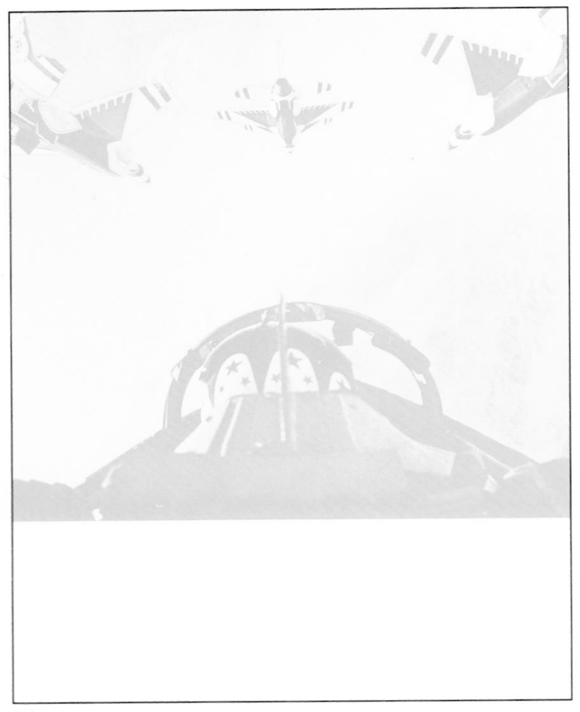
(a)

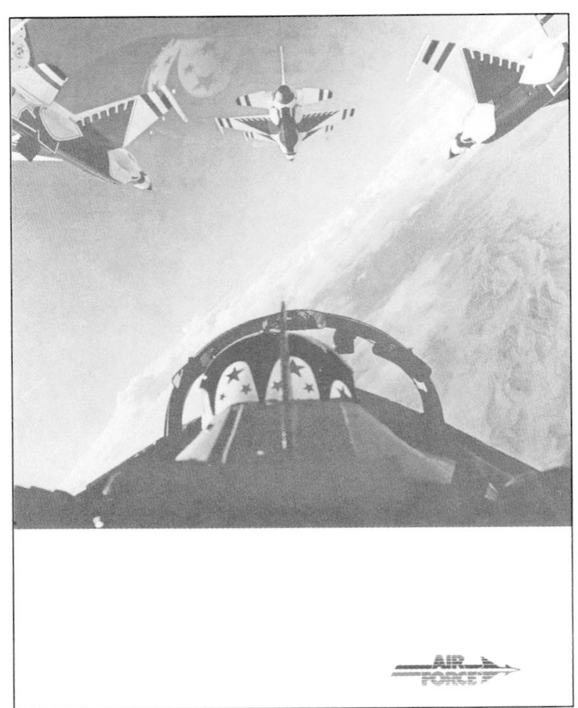
AIR
FORCE
(b)

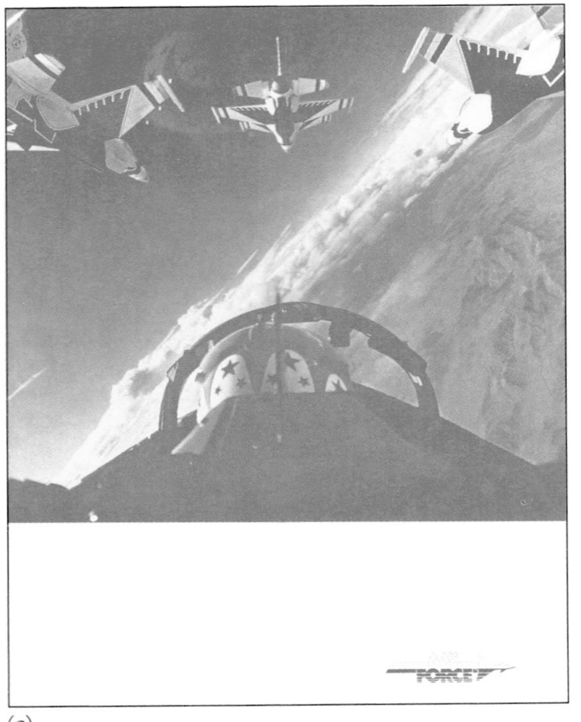
(c)

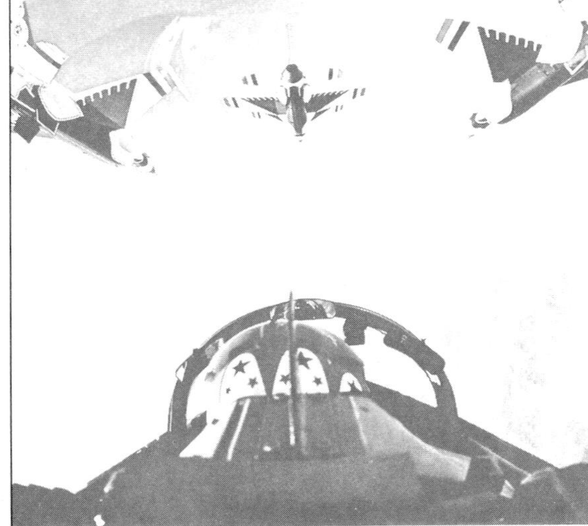
It's not like sitting behind a desk.
(d)

(e)

(f)

It's not like sitting behind a desk.

Not when you're in the cockpit of one of our most advanced jet fighters, the F-16.

Not when you're on the flight deck of one of the world's largest transports.

Not when you've earned the silver wings of an Air Force pilot and watched your future take off with top benefits and opportunities to further your education.

The training is demanding. But, as you can see, the rewards are enormous for those who make it through.

If you're under 27 and a college graduate with the physical and mental stamina to become a pilot, join the Air Force. You can make an important contribution to your country.

Find out if you qualify. See your nearest Air Force recruiter or call toll-free 1-800-423-USAF (in California 1-800-232-USAF).

Aim High. Be an Air Force pilot.

AIR FORCE

(g)

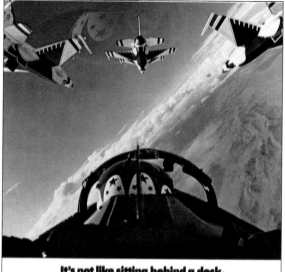

To print a color ad, the colors are first separated into four colors—yellow, magenta, cyan, and black—by photographing the original art for the ad, as seen in Figures (a), (b), (c), and (d). These colors are called "process colors" and represent the ink colors used in four-color printing.

After the colors are printed in yellow, cyan, magenta, and black from four corresponding printing plates, they are combined as seen in Figures (e), (f), and finally, (g). As you can see, the inks blend to provide an optical illusion of full, natural color.

(a)

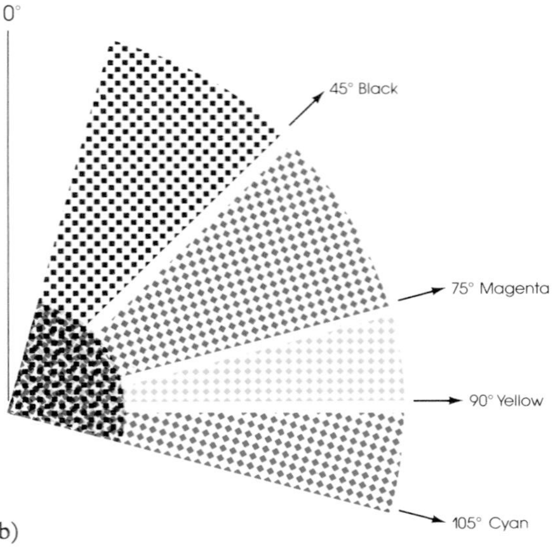

(b)

The optical illusion in four-color printing is achieved by combining the photographic screens, which are made up of many dots, as shown in Figure (a). Screens must be placed at angles for each of the four colors. When the dot patterns are placed at the proper angles, as seen in Figure (b), a correctly registered ad results.

In most instances today, when you prepare an ad for offset printing you furnish the printer with artwork, typeproof, and a layout showing precisely how all elements are positioned. The printer does the rest, shipping light, flat photographic negatives to the newspaper or magazine your ad will appear in. As we'll discuss later, full-color offset printing calls for four separate sheets of film. Such films are lighter to handle, easier to store, far less expensive to ship than the letterpress metal-on-wood printing plates. Incidentally, this very book is printed by the offset process.

The publications take the final step. For example, newspapers photograph each assembled page (of retail ads and editorial matter). They send this master negative to their printer, who employs a rotary offset press. The printer takes the newspaper's master negative and makes an aluminum press plate that can be curved around the cylindrical press. After this process, the publication can return the photographic plates to the advertiser or advertising agency.

We mentioned in-house advertisers that have their own photocomposition headline machine. Some of these same busy advertisers also have their own photomechanical transfer (PMT) machine for film enlargements or reductions of their own camera-ready artwork.

Another process used for very small runs is called **silkscreen printing.** A pattern or "frisket" is cut out of paper and laid over fabric, exposing only those parts that will print. The ink is forced through the fabric onto the printing surface. Different patterns are cut for the different colors in the design. Silkscreen printing is highly suitable for small posters such as those in store windows all over a community.

silkscreen printing A type of printing that uses paper and fabric.

Reproducing Artwork

Most ads contain both type and artwork. Printers reproduce art in much the same way as they reproduce type. They photograph the art to produce a negative. That negative and the negative of the type are then stripped together to produce a single printing plate. There are three types of art: line art, halftone art, and color art. Printers handle each kind in a different way.

Line Art. Art that is made up of solid blacks and whites is called **line art.** Type itself is therefore a form of line art. So are many cartoons. It is just as easy to transfer a black-and-white cartoon to a printing plate as it is to transfer type. When line art has been transferred to a printing plate, it is called a **line cut.**

line art Art made up of solid blacks and whites.

line cut Line art that has been transferred to a printing plate.

Just because line art is easy to reproduce doesn't mean it limits you to primitive drawings. Perspective, contour, and the like, are created by the way the artist positions black strokes on white paper. Closely spaced strokes show more detail than widely separated strokes. Exquisite drawings and designs have been done in scratchboard and in pen-and-ink. Yet they are still simple line cuts in the reproduction process—solid black lines and solid white areas. (See Figure 9–5.)

To add tone to a solid black-and-white line drawing the printer can use a Ben Day tint (named after its inventor). Your printer can show you Ben

Courtesy Norah Diedrich

Figure 9–5
To a printer, each of these pictures is simple line art—solid black and white. To the artist, the variation lies in *where* those solid black lines are placed.

Day tints in many patterns and degrees of darkness. Some tints are quite simple (regular dots, for example); some tints are quite elaborate (wavy lines, for instance). These tints are printed on a filter and applied to your basic artwork in the reproduction process. Also available are some preprinted plastic tint patterns that can be pasted directly on to your basic artwork *before* it is photographed onto a printing surface.

halftone art Art that is printed in a continuous tone.

halftone screen A screen or filter used to produce halftone art.

Halftone Art. Art that is not solid black and white but done in a continuous tone is called **halftone art.** To capture a variety of tones on a printing surface the artwork is photographed through a glass screen or filter called a **halftone screen.** On the glass screen is a grid of perpendicular lines. The closeness of the lines to one another indicates the designation or title of the screen. An 85-line screen has 85 vertical lines crossing 85 horizontal lines in a square inch. When photographed through such a screen, your artwork appears on the printing surface not as criss-crossing lines but as a series of separate dots. (Next time you see a photograph printed in your newspaper, look at it through a magnifying glass. You will see hundreds of tiny dots.)

An 85-line screen is termed a “coarse” screen suitable for newspapers, which have rough and porous paper. Because newspaper pulp stock soaks up the ink, the dots must be widely spaced. Or, put another way, the lines on the halftone screen must not be too close together.

Magazines, however, are printed on much finer paper stock that has a smooth, slick finish. Perhaps you've heard the term "slick magazines"? On this "slick" paper stock, the printing dots can be much closer together because the ink does not run. Most magazines specify a 120-line screen; some specify a 133-line screen or higher. (Extremely fine printing capabilities exist today. For fine art books, printers in Japan and Spain have reproduced halftones in 300- and 400-line screens. Such fine screens make the dots almost impossible to find.) Put a newspaper illustration and a magazine illustration side by side under the glass and you will instantly see the difference in sharpness of image produced by the difference in size of the individual dots.

Picture definition or sharpness is also affected by the spacing between the dots. Closely spaced dots give a dark picture area; widely spaced dots give a light picture area—sometimes almost, but never quite, white. No matter how light the picture area, the dots are still present. And the ink that every dot is printed in is in solid color, usually black.

A halftone picture that is squared off at the edges is called a **square halftone**—regardless of its actual dimensions. A halftone that follows the exact shape of the object photographed is called a **silhouette halftone.** A halftone with edges that fade into the paper is called a **vignette halftone.** A picture that has both halftone art and line art is called a **combination.** A halftone that drops out some tone and prints areas of stark white is called a **highlight** or **dropout halftone.**

square halftone A halftone squared off at the edges.

silhouette (or outline) halftone A halftone that follows the shape of the object photographed.

vignette halftone A halftone with edges that fade into the paper.

combination A picture that has both halftone and line art.

highlight (or dropout) halftone A halftone that drops out some tone and prints areas of white.

Color Art. To get "full" or authentic color, the printer uses three primary colors—yellow, magenta (red), and cyan (blue)—and black in the high-speed printing process. A full-color picture requires four separate printing surfaces: one for each color. These primary inks are standard—the same in all printing plants and on all publications, in all parts of the country. Full-color reproduction requires four separate photographs of your artwork, using a different color filter for each shot. These four shots must be the same in every detail so that the four finished printing surfaces will be in perfect fit or **register.** If not, the colors will overlap, thus becoming muddy and indistinct. Few things in advertising production are more disappointing than a four-color proof that is "out of register" or "off-register."

register The extent to which the four separate photos for each of the four colors in full-color printing fit or match up.

The printer may give the advertiser a set of color keys made of four films. Each film, with its multitude of halftone dots, shows one of the four basic colors used in the standard printing process—yellow, magenta, cyan and black. When the four are stacked together, you see how the final full-color reproduction will appear in print. The color insert following page 158 shows the four separate color keys for an ad. Such a set of color keys gives the printer and art director an opportunity to catch errors and make needed changes.

WHERE TO SEEK HELP

If you are a little overwhelmed by type, printing, and art reproduction at this point, relax. Obviously there is no way an "outsider" can learn all the ins and outs of print production overnight. You will learn by doing, and there is actually no need for you to be expert at it. The professionals will guide you all along the way. Put yourself in their hands. If some of those hands disappoint you, change hands.

If you insist on becoming more personally expert, there are sources of help. Check with Crain Books in Chicago (the same people who publish *Advertising Age* magazine). They offer several helpful volumes. One is called *Graphics Master,* which they term a "do-it-yourself graphics kit."

DESKTOP MIRACLE

Speaking of do-it-yourself, computers have now made it possible for you to create finished ads, suitable for reproduction, right at your own desk.

With certain sophisticated software, you can do incredible things at lightning speed. You have your choice of several typefaces, several styles such as Bold, Outline, and Italic, and a wide range of sizes. You can create your own illustrations and logotypes. You can enlarge or reduce them. You can install all kinds of patterns of dots (like Ben Day screens). You can draw lines, thin to thick. You can call up borders, frames, shapes. You can erase. You can lasso objects on the screen and move them to another location. You can "cut" an item from the page and store it in a scrap book. You can select illustrations from a computer catalog of clip art.

Most wondrous of all, you can experiment and improvise with all these elements until you get the page exactly the way you want it. What you see on your computer screen is what you'll get on the printed page.

If you have a laser printer, you'll get high-resolution reproduction with 300 dots per inch. Using a digitizer or scanner, the laser printer will reproduce photographs and drawings with remarkable sharpness and clarity. The result is camera-ready advertising that can save a bundle in art and production costs.

If you find this report of desktop publishing just a little hard to believe, we suggest you visit a nearby computer store for an actual demonstration. It almost defies description.

SUMMARY

This chapter has given you a short peek at what happens between the time your basic idea is okayed and the time it finally appears in print. The process is called print production. For the most part, print production is mechanical, technical. It cannot be learned from reading a book. This chapter can give you only the sketchiest kind of background. Production can only be learned by doing, by actually getting involved in making ads and commercials.

In print production, your idea is "set" before you start; your only interest is to reproduce that okayed idea accurately. In broadcast production, your okayed idea is only the beginning. Broadcast production is quite a different world from print production, as we shall see in the next chapter.

TERMS TO KNOW

Now that you have finished this chapter, you should understand the following terms:

typography	points	line cut
type families	leading	halftone art
ascenders	pica	halftone screen
descenders	calligraphy	square halftone
ligature	letterpress printing	silhouette or outline halftone
serif	gravure printing	vignette halftone
sans-serif	offset printing	combination
roman	silkscreen printing	highlight or dropout halftone
italic	line art	register
reverse		

If you are uncertain of the meaning of any of these terms, go back through the chapter and review them.

THINGS TO THINK ABOUT

1. Somebody once said that "being different" is no great advantage where typography is concerned. What do you think that means?
2. Why do you think the size of the type should increase as the length of the line increases?
3. Why does it take four separate colors to make a full-color ad?
4. What do you think is the significance of the word *half* in the reproduction term *halftone*?

THINGS TO TALK ABOUT

1. Each of you clip an ad you think demonstrates a good use of typography. Compare them in class and see if you recognize some common principles running through them.
2. Clip an ad for a local woman's dress shop and an ad for a local garage. Compare the type in each and speculate on why there should be differences.
3. The text says that serifs aid readability. Does the class agree? Have the class vote on the readability of a serif paragraph versus a sans-serif paragraph.
4. Make a similar experiment with a block of type which is all in capital letters versus a block of type using upper- and lower-case letters.

THINGS TO DO

1. Visit the composing room of your local newspaper. Get a sample sheet showing the number of different typefaces available for advertisers.
2. Visit a local printer and ask to see a type specimen book published by one of the major national type suppliers.
3. Pick a typeface and size (like 12 pt. Bodoni) and count the number of characters you can fit on a line that is 24 picas wide.
4. Ask a local printer to let you handle an unused aluminum printing plate. Notice how thin and light it is.

10 Broadcast Advertising Production

BOY: Hey Mr.? Can I have a Mr. Goodbar, Mr.?
ANNCR: (VO) Back in the old days, Mr. Goodbar discovered the magic of peanuts and chocolate.
Ten years later...
MAN: Another Mr. for the Mrs.!
ANNCR: (VO) ...people still loved the combination of crunchy peanuts and creamy chocolate.
Even in the forties...
SAILOR: Mr. Goodbar, SIR!
ANNCR: (VO) ...even in the sixties...
FLOWER CHILDREN: Peace.
ANNCR: (VO) And even now, one thing's still true:
GOOD PEANUTS
Good peanuts...
GOOD CHOCOLATE
and good chocolate...
GOOD BAR
mr. Goodbar
make a very good bar.
MAN: Good-Good-Good. Mr. Goodbar!

Courtesy of Hershey Chocolate Company

CHAPTER OUTLINE

Radio
- Making a Straight Commercial
- Making a Production Commercial
- Finding Help
- Being a Talent Scout

Television
- At the National Level
- Three Basic Kinds of TV Production
- How to Get It Done

By the time you finish this chapter, you should understand:

1. **How straight radio copy and production radio copy differ.**
2. **Why the preproduction meeting is the key to success in TV production.**
3. **That there are three basic kinds of production for television.**
4. **Why film can be the most expensive kind of television production.**
5. **Which kind of television production is easiest on your nervous system.**
6. **Which kind of television production has made it possible for local advertisers to use the medium more.**

Broadcast production is, indeed, a different world from print production. You'll need to deal with audio tapes, sound effects libraries, recordings, film or videotape, camera operators, performers, directors, and editors. While mechanical in a sense, broadcast production involves lots of creativity, imagination, and individuality. In broadcast production, your okayed idea is like an embryo that grows as the various talents in the production process affect it. Broadcast production is, to a great extent, "show biz," pure and simple. It's an exciting world, but there are pitfalls for the beginner.

RADIO

You are likely to enter the world of radio with more background than you realize. Few young people today are unfamiliar with record players and stereo equipment. The electronic tape recorder is now commonly used. Records and tapes are staples of the radio production business. Proceed with reasonable confidence.

Making a Straight Commercial

As mentioned in Chapter 7, there are two basic types of radio copy—straight copy and production copy. You may recall that *straight copy* consists of nothing but a typewritten script read by whichever regular station announcer is on duty at the time your commercial is to be broadcast. Basically, then, it's just one voice (any voice) reading words only. The only things the advertiser really controls are the words themselves. A good and careful writer squeezes as much character, drama, and warmth into those "words only" as is humanly possible. You can be creative with straight copy, but that creativity takes place at the typewriter and may involve rhyme, rhythm, simple dialect, or unique wording. It's a real challenge.

If you are advertising on several stations or in several regions, you'll send duplicate copies of the typewritten script to the various stations. Then you pray that whoever steps up to the microphone and reads your copy is in good voice and good spirits.

Making a Production Commercial

With *production copy* you won't get a sloppy job from the station announcer. You record your message ahead of time under ideal conditions and send a duplicate to each of the stations on your list. Thus your commercial has the same quality every time people hear it and everywhere it's played.

Infinite Possibilities. You can make a production commercial as simple or as elaborate as you wish by using one voice or several, a personality (like a certain disk jockey) or a celebrity (like a famous actor). Maybe you'll want a musical spot, a jingle, or you may just use music in the background. You can certainly make use of sound effects. You can make it straightforward, dramatic, or humorous. You have no end of options. The advertiser with the big budget, in the big city, can get just about any effect. Some famous owners of distinctive voices have gotten rich just reading radio commercial copy anonymously—Lloyd Bridges, Burgess Meredith, Sally Kellerman, James Garner, and Bill Cosby to name a few.

Low-budget Music. The local or regional advertiser has to work within a more limited range. Musicians, for example, cost money. The more musicians, the greater the cost. The more famous the musicians, the greater the cost. Take your idea to the sales manager of your local radio station. Ask if the station can come up with a solution. You will be amazed at the amount of already recorded material that is available at modest cost. Every radio station has a music and sound effects library to cover almost every conceivable invention of a copywriter. There are even prerecorded musical "themes" you can rent on an exclusive basis in your marketing area. This exclusive theme music can run before and after your copy (a sort of "doughnut" effect) or it can play softly in the background under your copy. Organizations that offer much superb music for local rental are TM Productions (Dallas), Media General (Memphis), The Network (San Diego), Century Twenty-one (Dallas), First Com (Dallas), and American Business Consultants, an associate of Pat Patrick Productions (Nashville).

Local Inventiveness. Staff members at a local radio station have to be very inventive. When a standard sound effect from the library does not cover a particular situation, they know how to do tricks with simple sounds and objects. They can increase or decrease the speed at which an audiotape is being played and alter the sound completely. They can make two metal bridge chairs sound like an automobile wreck. (You may already be aware that the sound of a forest fire is made by crinkling a piece of cellophane.) If your writer asks for the sound of "fifty caterpillars playing tug-of-war," the sound engineers will give you something dazzling. Who knows what they'd actually sound like anyway?

Finding Help

As we've said before, local radio stations will write commercials as well as produce them. They will make every effort to please you because they want to sell you the time on their station. One major Midwest restaurant owner challenged the two radio stations in his particular target market. He would expand his schedule to include every good idea they could bring him. He got some remarkable quality in writing and production. He found it a pleasure to keep his end of the bargain.

But local stations aren't your sole source of help. Independent production houses exist across the land. Certainly you would be wise to check out any regional or local independent production houses that seem practical to use.

Being a Talent Scout

Where announcing and acting talent are concerned, you must first rely on the resources of the local station. They know the good voices around town or within reasonable reach. They know who's good on a news-type announcement, who can deliver a funny line, who has a sense of drama. Not everybody can talk for a microphone. In smaller communities, the talent pool may be limited—but it's there. Teachers know how to talk; preachers know how to talk. A choir singer may have a resonant voice. The high school drama coach knows how to express emotions, and so do members of the little theater groups. The person who "chairs" the Rotary Club meetings may have an engaging voice. Enlist the aid of the talent scouts at your local station, and learn to be a talent scout yourself. Often the owner or manager of a business makes an excellent spokesperson. Always be on the lookout for the voice that has quality but is "different." And always keep in mind that the main purpose of your commercials is to sell merchandise, not to showcase theatrical talent. It's great to be imaginative and inventive, but you should never fall in love with radio production for its own sake.

TELEVISION

Television production holds great fascination for everybody. Even at its simplest, it is a form of show business. There are few people who are not awestruck at the thought of setting foot in a studio or theatre. It is glamorous. It is exciting. There is a special kind of thrill to seeing your advertising idea come to life on the screen, even if it is only a 10-second ID employing a printed slide.

Before letting television overawe you, consider this: Most of us have grown up with television. It's no stranger. Certainly all of us have grown up with the movies. And we have all seen movies about making movies. There's no business like show business— and there's no business that offers more gripping program material for the cameras. We've seen the lights, microphones, and cameras of television studios; we've seen the bank of monitor picture screens on the scoreboard shows; we've seen the handheld cameras on the news telecasts.

You are not likely to be nearly as mystified in a television studio as in a printer's shop. However, it does take time to become fully expert in the ways and means of television production. This chapter can give you only a peek inside—a rough idea of procedure, a bit of basic terminology, and some awareness of the main options.

At the National Level

For the big national advertiser with a big agency and a big budget, the television production process begins the moment the storyboard is okayed by management. (You read about storyboards in Chapter 7 on Copywriting.) At the same time that the idea is okayed, a tentative budget is approved. It's "tentative" because, by the very nature of the medium, it is impossible to be absolutely precise about productions costs. A fairly routine 30-second film commercial today might cost $30,000–$50,000 to produce. Back in the 1970s the television world was agog when comedy genius Stan Freberg spent some $200,000 to produce a high-powered musical minute for soup. By the mid-1980s, a computer company was rumored to have spent over $1,000,000 for a single commercial.

Getting Bids on Storyboards. At the advertising agency, a producer is assigned to the just-okayed idea. It is the agency producer's task to "herd" the idea all the way through to its appearance on the air. The commercial is not produced in the agency. Instead, photostatic copies of the storyboard are first sent to several independent production companies selected by the agency producer. (The agency producer must know which production "houses" are best suited to interpret a particular idea. For example, some are good on close-up product shots; some are good on outdoor spectacles.)

The independent production companies then study the storyboard and submit bids to the agency and advertiser. By no means is the job always awarded to the low bidder. It may go to the production company which has exclusive rights to a particular director or camera operator. Any number of such "quality" considerations could influence the awarding of the contract.

Function of Independent Producer. Once this decision is made, the boss of the independent production company becomes "The Producer" on this particular project, and the agency producer assumes the role of liaison person or consultant. The head of the independent production company, or The Producer, then takes responsibility for all details large and small. The producer chooses the director, the talent, the camera operator, the technicians,

BOY: Hey Mr.? Can I have a Mr. Goodbar, Mr.?
ANNCR: (VO) Back in the old days, Mr. Goodbar discovered the magic of peanuts and chocolate.
Ten years later...
MAN: Another Mr. for the Mrs.!
ANNCR: (VO)...people still loved the combination of crunchy peanuts and creamy chocolate.
Even in the forties...
SAILOR: Mr. Goodbar, SIR!
ANNCR: (VO)...even in the sixties...
FLOWER CHILDREN: Peace.
ANNCR: (VO) And even now, one thing's still true:
GOOD PEANUTS
Good peanuts...
GOOD CHOCOLATE
and good chocolate...
GOOD BAR
HERSHEY'S
mr. Goodbar
PEANUTS IN MILK CHOCOLATE
make a very good bar.
MAN: Good-Good-Good. Mr. Goodbar!

Courtesy of Hershey Chocolate Company.

FIGURE 10–1
Nostalgia is an effective tool used to promote the product.

the studio or location, and is responsible for such crucial items as coffee breaks and box lunches.

Production Chain of Command. The "chain of command" is interesting, particularly where film is involved. The producer is the boss in the sense that he or she hires the director, but the director is boss in the studio floor once the cameras start to roll. A good head camera operator is deferred to by everybody and is treated like a little tin god on wheels. Yet many experts will tell you that the final quality of a commercial largely depends on the artistic taste of the film editor.

Importance of Preproduction Meeting. Once an independent production company is hired, the next major step is the preproduction meeting. Here the producer, director, set designer, talent director, and various other key people meet with the agency producer and copywriter to iron out a hundred-and-one details that must be settled before going into the studio to shoot film. It is incredible the number of questions that must be answered in detail even on the most simple idea. For example, the "young woman" in a script has to become a specific human being, and she has to be dressed a certain way.

Major and minor problems solved in the preproduction meeting can save literally thousands of dollars in studio costs. A studio is hired on a time basis, and the operating costs include those of the most skilled and expensive talent imaginable—directors, camera operators, actors, musicians, lighting experts, sound experts, stage hands. It is exciting to see them all work together on your idea, but it is sobering to think of the costs mounting up as every minute ticks away. The more questions you have settled ahead of time, the better off you are. But questions continue to come up.

Importance of Every On-Camera Detail. Large advertiser or small advertiser—a commercial idea depends on the people who appear in it and the setting in which they appear. Minor "talent" should be chosen as carefully as major talent. If, for instance, the lady on camera is stewing over a clogged sink, she should look like a homemaker and not some glamorous Hollywood starlet. Nor should she be dressed in a fancy gown. The people in a commercial must be believable or the message cannot be believable. The homes they live in, the offices they work in, the kitchens they cook in, must be believable. The sad part is that it takes only one false note to jar the public consciousness. No detail is too small to be overlooked. (If the wallpaper design "clashes" with the lamp shade, it can hurt your commercial.) Think of how many times you have been turned off, not so much by what a commercial says, but by the person saying it.

Three Basic Kinds of TV Production

All production for television broadcast involves certain basic principles regarding the use of cameras, talent, studio, and other technical facilities. Those principles of good television "theatre" don't change. What does vary is the *type* of production an advertiser chooses.

There are three basic types of production in television—live, film, and videotape.

live TV production A production in which the action is shown as it takes place.

Live Production. **Live TV production** is action as it takes place. Dan Rather on the evening news is "live." He is literally right there sitting in the studio as he talks to you. (In the early days of television, entire ninety-minute drama shows were done live.) Most advertisers—local as well as national—prefer the assurance of videotape. Yet live commercials, rare as they are, do have some advantages.

Live commercials are the least expensive. They take the least time to produce—largely because they are simple in concept and action. Picture quality is excellent. Copy ideas can be changed right up until air time. Because things can (and frequently do) go wrong in live commercials, they have a certain human appeal for a public that is bored with the slick professional product. One bad feature of live production is that it's over and done with the moment the commercial hits the airwaves. The live commercial offers almost no reuse value.

Film Production. Since the first television commercial was made, film has been the most popular form of TV production. If you have ever made home movies, you have held film up to the light and looked through it. What you see is an actual photograph in each frame, which is enlarged as it is projected onto a large screen. Movies are shot anywhere and everywhere in the world, but the bulk of America's commercial film production for national advertisers is done in Hollywood and New York.

film TV production A production that is put on film and aired at a later date.

Time is Money. Film TV production tends to be the most expensive kind of production because of the time involved. Film shot one day is sent to the lab to be developed and is not seen until the next day. If a mistake has been made, you learn about it a day late. In many instances, sound is recorded separately and is "mixed" with the picture later. The transition effects discussed in Chapter 7 on copywriting—cuts, dissolves, wipes—are done in a laboratory after the basic film footage has been shot. The last step is editing.

Editing is the Key Step. Producers of movies and commercials always shoot far more footage than will appear on the theatre or home screen. For example, a dramatic argument between a husband and wife may be covered by three cameras. One camera takes a "two-shot" of both participants. One camera takes a continuous close-up of the wife and her reactions. The third camera gives close-up coverage to the husband. At the end, the film editor decides how much footage to use from each source to "milk" the scene of its full dramatic potential. All these essential steps in film production take time, and time is tremendously expensive.

Advantages. In spite of its costs, film offers many advantages. It can shoot anything, give you any effect. Film offers you live action (regular movies), animation (a la Mickey Mouse), or a combination of animation and live action (Charlie the Tuna). Film producers can knock the world apart ("Earthquake") or create new ones ("Star Wars").

Film offers good picture quality, precise control of lighting. (Sometimes a crew will spend a couple of hours lighting an object that will be filmed for a few seconds.) Film is excellent for "spectacular" production effects, big outdoor scenes.

It is rather complicated to get a final okay on film (often special interlock projection equipment must be hired to synchronize the sound track with the film track). Effects will be indicated on the rough film by hand-drawn symbols that don't have great meaning for nonfilm people.

But one of the great advantages of film for any advertiser is its reuse possibilities. It is easy to duplicate into a rather compact unit for carrying and shipping. A 16mm print of a 30-second commercial can easily be tucked into a jacket pocket. The spot can be played time and time again at sales meetings, at trade exhibits, and for school or civic groups.

Videotape Production. But the most wondrous development in television production is videotape (VT). The picture effect on your home screen is so perfect that you think you are seeing the action live. Actually, what is being transmitted is not a picture at all, like movies, but an electronic signal recorded on magnetic tape. Originally videotape was available in a 2-inch wide strip. It is now also available in 1-inch, 3/4-inch, 1/2-inch, and 1/4-inch cartridges or cassette strips. One side of the magnetic tape strip is very shiny; the other side is dull. The electronic impulse is recorded on the dull side. Don't bother to look. You see nothing with the naked eye.

videotape TV production A production that is recorded live on videotape.

In **videotape TV production,** all elements—cameras, microphones, turntables, slide projectors, film projectors—are wired into a central electronic control panel. The director is not out on the studio floor, but at the control panel where monitors (small TV pictures) show exactly what each camera is shooting. As the three (or more) cameras continue shooting on the studio floor, the director "calls" the shots in the control room, mixing camera shots as picture and sound are recorded simultaneously. Not only that, but the director records effects at the same time—"Wipe to Camera Three," "Dissolve to Camera One," "Fade to Black." Wonder of wonders, everything is done all at once. Then, greatest wonder of all, the director asks to see an instant playback of what has just been recorded. If something is wrong, it is reshot immediately.

Without question, the bulk of local television production today is recorded on videotape.

Videotape can also go on location, particularly with handheld cameras. And it can give some interesting electronic animation effects. Duplicates can be quickly recorded and sent to all channels on schedule. Videotape stock can be erased and reused. But the greatest advantage of videotape is that the commercial can be completed in one sitting. A few hours in the studio can give you your commercial exactly as it will go on the air, complete with client approval. Compare this with the rigmarole of film and you can see why costs differ greatly.

As for replay facilities, it's a rare company, organization, or school today that does not have the equipment to show videotape. It's fair to say that videotape has become a universal phenomenon.

As with film production, an advertiser can deal with an independent videotape producer or with a television station. The bigger the television station, the more extensive its facilities are likely to be.

How to Get It Done

The small local advertiser must depend almost entirely on the production facilities of the nearest television station. If there are two or three in town, the advertiser has some choice. If there is only one station in town, that's it, unless the advertiser takes the more expensive option of going elsewhere to an independent production company.

There are wonderful talents and facilities spread across the nation, but the small advertiser must search them out. They tend to cluster in population centers. But you don't have to go all the way to Hollywood or New York.

The local TV station will charge a modest fee for production. Some stations will include the service of a writer to help prepare your message. In one medium-sized Midwest city, the local CBS affiliate station has a staff of six full-time television writers to serve small local and regional advertisers.

No matter how big—or small—television production is, try to be present during the process. First, it's fun. Second, it pays to look after your own interests all down the line.

SUMMARY

This chapter has given you some insight into how your basic creative idea evolves from management okay to polished broadcast suitability. It's a rather complicated process involving many artistic talents. Broadcast production is a process you'll learn by doing—not by reading.

Actually, no matter how much you learn over time, you will always depend on the professionals, the technicians. Fortunately for all of us, the men and women who have chosen to make a career of print or broadcast production are skilled and creative, dedicated to the highest professional standards.

Once the ads and commercials have finally been produced, they are then turned over to the media for showing to the public. And that is the subject of the next chapter.

TERMS TO KNOW

Now that you have finished this chapter, you should understand the following terms:

live TV production
film TV production
videotape TV production

If you are unsure of the meaning of any of these terms, go back through the chapter to review them.

THINGS TO THINK ABOUT

1. Radio and television are both broadcast media, yet the copywriter must approach each in a different way. Why do you think this is so?
2. What kind of school, work, or hobby activities might give a young writer a good background for using the television medium?
3. In a movie the actors and director get reams of publicity, but the producer gets "top billing" in the credits. Why do you think this is so?
4. Think of all the people you know in town. Which of them has a voice you would like to use in a radio commercial? Why?

THINGS TO TALK ABOUT

1. Television can be nerve-wracking for the writer. Which of the three basic kinds of TV production is easiest on the ad writer's nerves? Why?
2. Discuss the way advertisers in your community use television. Do you notice differences between local and national TV production? Why might this be so?
3. Discuss the kind of questions that could arise in a TV preproduction meeting over the simple script designations BOY and GIRL.
4. Discuss why many experts consider editing to be the key step in film production.

THINGS TO DO

1. Using only popular songs of past and present, see if you can tell a thirty-second radio "story" in music.
2. As a group, rent or borrow a Super 8mm movie camera and see if you can film a sixty-second commercial for the Hershey Milk Chocolate Bar. Cut an audio tape to work in reasonable synchronization with it.
3. Visit the nearest videotape studio. Ask to be shown how the director at the control board "mixes" pictures and adds effects.
4. Ask your radio station to show you its sound effects library.

SECTION 3

Channels

After an advertisement is written and prepared, it must be run in the proper places. We will call these places the "channels" that carry the advertisements. Most of these channels are the mass media, so this is usually referred to as the media aspect or function of advertising.

Actually, the decisions as to what channels to use may not be made *after* the advertisement is written. That decision may come *before* the advertisement is written, because the copywriter must know for what media the ads are to be prepared. The media selection may also be going on at the same time as the creative effort.

This channel selection and purchasing is sometimes complex—and it is becoming even more complicated. But these complications may make the media more selective in the future, so we may be able to direct our ads to even more specific target groups. And that would mean that the use of advertising channels would become more efficient as a result.

Our discussion on channels will start with the print media, then go on to the broadcast media, and finally to other kinds of channels that may be available to us in certain advertising situations.

CHAPTERS

11 Print Media

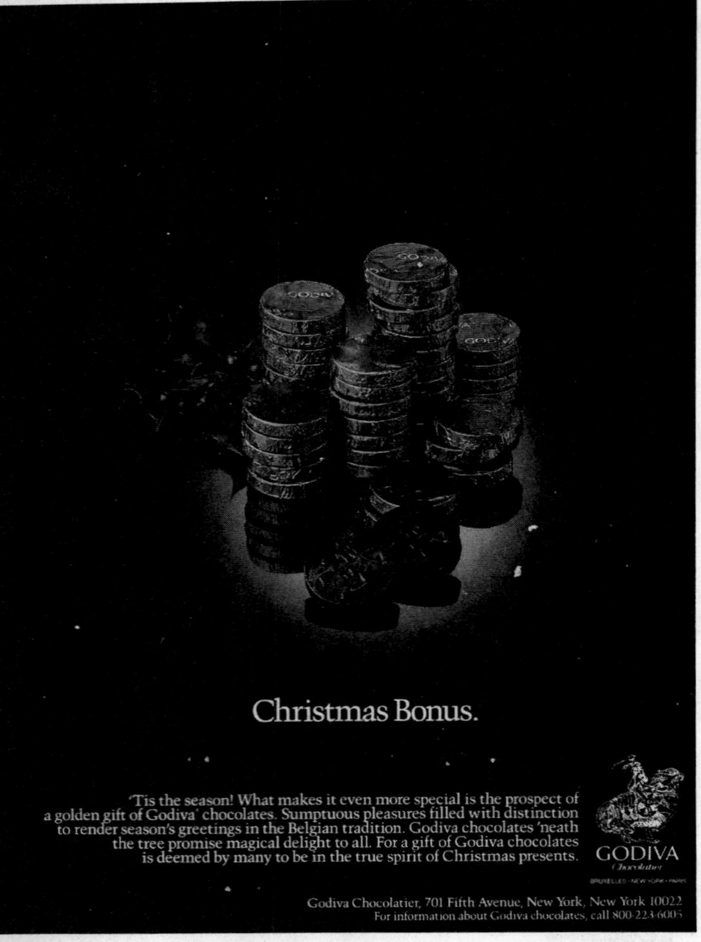

Christmas Bonus.
'Tis the season! What makes it even more special is the prospect of a golden gift of Godiva chocolates. Sumptuous pleasures filled with distinction to render season's greetings in the Belgian tradition. Godiva chocolates 'neath the tree promise magical delight to all. For a gift of Godiva chocolates is deemed by many to be in the true spirit of Christmas presents.
GODIVA
Chocolatier
BRUXELLES · NEW YORK · PARIS
Godiva Chocolatier, 701 Fifth Avenue, New York, New York 10022
For information about Godiva chocolates, call 800-223-6005

Courtesy of Godiva Chocolatier, Inc.

CHAPTER OUTLINE

By the time you finish this chapter, you should understand:

1. **The importance of choosing the right advertising channel.**
2. **The advantages and disadvantages of newspaper advertising.**
3. **How newspaper ads are bought and used.**
4. **How to compare the efficiency of two newspapers.**
5. **The special situation of Sunday supplements.**
6. **The advantages and disadvantages of magazine advertising.**
7. **How magazine advertising is bought and used.**
8. **The special situations of business and farm publications.**
9. **How to compare the efficiency of two magazines.**

Once we know how to create the right advertisements to help sell our ideas, products, and services, then we must get these creative messages to the right customers. We call the communications channels we use to carry our advertisements to prospective customers **advertising media.** Notice that the word *media* is plural. There are many different media. A single channel such as radio is called a *medium.*

advertising media Communications channels used to carry advertisements.

Most of the money spent on advertising goes for media. Think about it: About 85 percent of an advertising budget goes to the media; the other 15 percent goes to the advertising agency. And a part of the advertising agency portion is also spent for media. The rest goes to research, creative work, administration, general expenses, and profit.

The key problem in choosing advertising channels is to make sure that the advertisements reach the prospective customers. We can use research to find the best prospects, but when we use a mass medium to reach these prospects, we are sending our message to the medium's **audience,** the group of people who listen to or see a medium. We therefore try to choose media with audiences that include our best prospects.

audience The group of people who listen to or see a medium.

NEWSPAPERS

Even though many media—such as television—are becoming more and more popular, more advertising money is spent on newspapers than on any other medium. There is a good reason for this: Retailers use newspapers more than any other medium in their local advertising, and retailers spend a great deal of money on advertising. Of the hundreds of thousands of retail stores in the United States, most use advertising to help promote their goods and services. The greatest portion of that advertising goes into newspapers.

Why Retailers Prefer Newspaper Advertising

Newspaper advertising is a versatile and important channel for all kinds and sizes of advertisers, but especially for retailers. Retailers like to advertise in newspapers for several reasons:

1. The advertising does not need to be very expensive.
2. Because the advertising is in print, the audience can read it over again.
3. It is easy to buy the advertisements because sales representatives for the newspapers go to the stores to pick up the advertisements and also help write them.
4. **Circulation,** the number of copies distributed, often covers a community.
5. Most people see a newspaper almost every day.

circulation The number of copies a newspaper distributes.

daily newspapers Newspapers that come out every day or almost every day.

weekly newspapers Newspapers that come out one or two days a week.

zoned editions Special editions of big-city newspapers intended for certain parts of the metropolitan area.

Newspapers that come out every day, or nearly every day, are **daily newspapers** but there are also many **weekly newspapers** that come out only one or two days each week. Some specialized newspapers appeal to certain ethnic groups, nationalities, or people who work in certain occupations, for example, the *Christian Science Monitor,* the *Jewish Standard* or the *Army Times.*

In recent years, many newspapers have been started just for certain suburban areas of large cities. Some big-city newspapers also publish several different editions, called **zoned editions,** for different parts of their metropolitan areas. Table 11–1 sums up the advantages and disadvantages of newspaper advertising.

Newspaper Advertising Rates

advertising rate The amount charged by newspapers for advertising space.

classified advertising Want ads.

display advertising Nonclassified ads.

column-inch A space one inch high and one newspaper column wide.

The amount charged by the newspaper for advertising space is the **advertising rate.** If you buy **classified advertising** (commonly called "want ads"), the advertising rate depends on the number of words in your advertisement. For **display** (non-classified) **advertising,** the rate depends on the amount of space used for each advertisement. It doesn't matter whether anything is printed in all the space; the newspaper has only space to sell, and the size of the advertisement determines the cost of the advertisement.

There are two ways to measure newspaper advertising space—by the column-inch and by the agate line. The **column-inch** is a space one inch high and one newspaper column wide. So an advertisement that measures three columns wide and nine inches high would have 27 column-inches in it. And if the newspaper advertising rate was $1.40 per column-inch, that advertisement would cost $37.80. (The 3 columns × 9 inches = 27 column-inches, and 27 column-inches × $1.40 per column-inch = $37.80).

In the early days, newspapers used very small type to print advertisements, so the paper (which was very expensive in those days) could fit in lots of them. About 14 lines or this small type, called *agate type,* would fit into each column-

TABLE 11–1 Advantages and disadvantages of advertising in newspapers.

Advantages

1. Newspaper advertising is timely; the paper comes out every day.
2. It guarantees good readership, because the news is of vital interest.
3. It can appeal to all kinds of people.
4. Localized circulation permits advertising in certain areas.
5. It provides complete coverage, because almost everybody reads newspapers.
6. Continuous impressions are possible with continuous advertising.
7. It's good for emergency situations.
8. It can tie the advertising in with the news
9. It's easy to direct customers to stores.
10. All sizes of advertising budgets can use it.
11. Results are quick.
12. Many different items can be included in a single advertisement.

Disadvantages

1. The advertiser must have separate dealings with each newspaper, and each newspaper may have a different page size.
2. There is great variation in printing and color quality.
3. Advertisements have a short life.
4. People may read newspapers hastily.

inch, and the advertising rate was based on how many lines of this type were used. And each line was called an **agate line,** which was one column wide and one-fourteenth of an inch high. Advertisements are sometimes still measured by agate lines, although we often just used the term *line* rather than *agate line.*

agate line A space one column wide and one-fourteenth of an inch high.

Our 27-column-inch advertisement would be 378 agate lines (27 column-inches $\times$ 14 lines per column-inch $=$ 378 agate lines). If the advertising rate is ten cents per line, then the cost of the advertisement would total \$37.80. That's the same cost as we got with the column-inch rate, because our earlier advertising rate of \$1.40 per column-inch is the same as a rate of ten cents per line (fourteen lines in a column-inch).

In recent years, however, national advertising rates in newspapers have been based solely on the column-inch measurement, so most newspapers use the column-inch instead of the agate line for measuring the size of an advertisement. Figure 11–1 shows how both of these measurements work.

Discounts Are Usually Available

flat rate The same advertising rate no matter how much advertising a single client buys.

Some newspapers charge the same advertising rate no matter how much space a single advertiser buys; this is called a **flat rate.** Most newspapers, however,

FIGURE 11–1
A comparison of the two ways to measure newspaper advertising space.

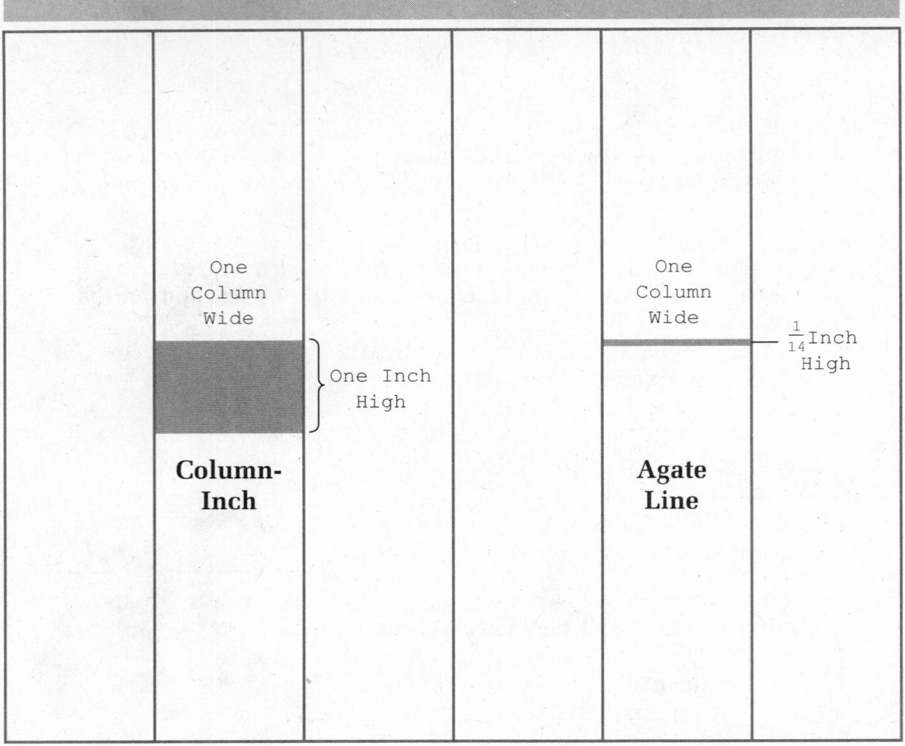

discount rate A lower rate for advertisers who regularly buy space in a newspaper.

open rate The highest advertising rate, used for advertisers who do not earn a discount.

frequency discount A discount earned for buying advertising space often.

quantity discount A discount earned for buying a lot of advertising space.

offer a lower rate, a **discount rate,** for advertisers who buy space regularly or in large amounts. An **open rate** is the highest advertising rate. It is used for advertisers who do not earn a discount. An advertiser who buys space very often earns a **frequency discount.** An advertiser who buys a lot of advertising space may earn a **quantity discount.**

Many retail advertisers sign contracts with their newspapers showing how much advertising they intend to buy and the discount rate to be earned. These contracts help retailers plan out their advertising for a long period and let them pay the discount rate that would otherwise apply only *after* they had bought a certain amount of space. Newspapers also benefit. They don't have to send out sales representatives for repeated selling efforts with retailers who have contracts. And they know in advance approximately how much advertising they will have.

But what happens if the retailer's prediction is wrong? Let's say the retailer uses less advertising than predicted in the contract and therefore earns a higher rate than the contract states. Then the retailer must pay the newspaper the difference between the contracted rate and the rate actually earned. This amount of money is called a **short rate.**

On the other hand, a retailer who uses more advertising than predicted in the contract may earn an even lower advertising rate. Then the newspaper pays the retailer a **rebate,** the amount of money the retailer gets back for having paid a higher rate than the one actually earned. Figure 11–3 shows how to find out if a retailer has earned a contract discount or if a short rate or rebate applies.

short rate The difference owed by an advertiser between a contracted advertising rate and the rate actually earned.

rebate The amount of money returned to an advertiser who paid a higher advertising rate than the one actually earned.

monthly earned rates

At the end of each month, advertising is charged at the earned rate according to the amount of space used during the calendar month. Bills not paid within 30 days will be subject to a service charge of 1½% each month (18% each year).

	per col. inch
open local rate	$3.00
25 inches/month	$2.25
50 inches/month	$1.95
100 inches/month	$1.80
200 inches/month	$1.70
300 inches/month	$1.60
500 inches/month	$1.45
1000 inches/month	$1.35

classified rates

	one time	two times	three times	four times	five times
15 words or less	$2.00	$2.25	$2.50	$2.75	$3.00
additional words	.01	.02	.03	.04	.05

words set in all caps count 2 words
words set in bold face count 3 words

business card rates

daily for one month (20 insertions) — $36.00 per column inch

no more than one copy change per month

other rates

national ad rate	$3.92 per column inch (.28 per agate line)
classified display rate (max. one column wide)	$3.50 per column inch
political ad rate (cash in advance only)	$3.00 per column inch
pre-printed inserts	estimates available on request

FIGURE 11–2
A sample of a newspaper advertising rate card.

A retailer signed a contract with a newspaper to use 55,000 column-inches of advertising in a year. The newspaper's advertising rates offered a quantity discount, like this:

Amount of space used per year	Advertising rate
0–10,000 column-inches	$2.50 per column-inch
10,000–25,000 column-inches	2.40
25,000–50,000 column-inches	2.30
50,000–75,000 column-inches	2.20
75,000–100,000 column-inches	2.10
More than 100,000 column-inches	2.00

So the retailer contracted to pay $2.20 per column-inch, because that is the advertising rate he would earn if he uses 55,000 column-inches in the year and that is the rate he pays during the year. But at the end of the year, the retailer found that he had used only 45,000 column-inches, so he should have been paying $2.30 per column-inch, which is 10¢ per column-inch more than he had been paying. So he owes the newspaper a short rate of 10¢ for each column-inch of advertising *that was actually used* (not the number of column-inches that were originally contracted for), which means the retailer must pay the newspaper a short rate of $4,500.

45,000 column-inches used
× .10 per column-inch
$4,500 short rate

FIGURE 11–3
This is an example of how to find out if you have earned a contract discount or if a short rate or rebate applies.

Comparing Two Newspapers

Suppose you are considering two newspapers to use for your advertising, but you have only enough advertising money to buy space in one of them. You must decide which newspaper to use. Of course, you want to use the newspaper that reaches the most people for your money. But you cannot simply use the newspaper with the larger circulation, because it will also charge more for its advertising space. And you don't simply select the newspaper with the lower advertising rate, because it will probably have a smaller circulation, too.

You need to find out what the advertising rate would be for both newspapers if they had the same circulation. And that is exactly what advertisers used to do. For each newspaper, they took the advertising rate per agate line and divided it by the actual circulation of the newspaper. Then they multiplied this by one million. The result was called the **milline rate,** the cost of

milline rate The cost of advertising in a newspaper if its circulation were one million.

The Tribune

Circulation = 84,000
Advertising rate = \$0.42 per line

The Gazette

Circulation = 90,000
Advertising rate = \$0.44 per line

$$\text{Milline rate} = \frac{\text{Line rate}}{\text{Circulation}} \times 1{,}000{,}000$$

$$\text{Milline rate} = \frac{\$0.42}{84{,}000} \times 1{,}000{,}000$$
$$\text{Milline rate} = .000005 \times 1{,}000{,}000$$
$$\text{Milline rate} = \$5.00$$

$$\text{Milline rate} = \frac{\$0.44}{90{,}000} \times 1{,}000{,}000$$
$$\text{Milline rate} = .0000048 \times 1{,}000{,}000$$
$$\text{Milline rate} = \$4.80$$

So *The Gazette* is more efficient. If it had a circulation of 1,000,000, its advertising rate would be \$4.80 per line, while *The Tribune* would have an advertising rate of \$5.00 per line if its circulation were 1,000,000.

FIGURE 11–4
This is an example of how to find the milline rate for comparing the advertising rates of two newspapers.

advertising in a newspaper if its circulation were exactly one million. This calculation is illustrated in Figure 11–4. But it is not used much anymore because most newspapers no longer use the agate line rate for figuring how much space an advertisement will use. Perhaps newspapers will someday adopt a different kind of calculation called *cost per thousand*. Other media use this method for their cost comparisons. It is explained later in this chapter.

Buying Newspaper Advertising

If you were placing an advertisement in a newspaper, you would want to know how many people in the audience might see your advertisement. This number is called the **reach** of an advertisement. Not everyone who reads a newspaper will see every advertisement, so the reach may be smaller than the audience.

reach The number of people who might see an advertisement.

If some people miss your advertisement, you may want to run it again so they can see it next time. And even though some people already saw your advertisement, you may have to repeat the message until you really convince them. So you may run your advertisement more than once. The number of times you run your advertisement or the number of times people see it, is the **frequency** of that advertisement. (The terms *reach* and *frequency* can apply to all advertising media.)

frequency The number of times people see an advertisment.

Generally, you want a lot of people to see your advertisement, so you would like to have a large reach. However, a single advertisement (or even two or three advertisements) will not do a good selling job. So high frequency is important, too. But remember that a newspaper with a larger circulation will charge more for your advertisements than a newspaper with a smaller circulation. If you spend more on each advertisement, then you won't be able to buy as many advertisements—or you will be forced to buy smaller ones. Basically, if you have a set amount of advertising money, every time you increase reach, then you must decrease frequency; every time you increase frequency, you must decrease reach.

We have already seen that retailers use newspapers for most of their advertising. But they still have to choose among many options. Keep in mind that many newspapers published in large cities may be read by commuters who are riding buses, trains, and subways to and from work. These commuters are more likely to read morning papers. Also, a smaller newspaper page size, called a **tabloid**, is sometimes popular among commuters. The tabloid page is about half the size of a full-size, or **broadsheet,** newspaper page, so it is easier to hold and read while commuting. Figure 11–5 shows the difference between a tabloid and a broadsheet.

tabloid A newspaper page about half the size of a full-size, or broadsheet, page.

broadsheet A full-size newspaper sheet.

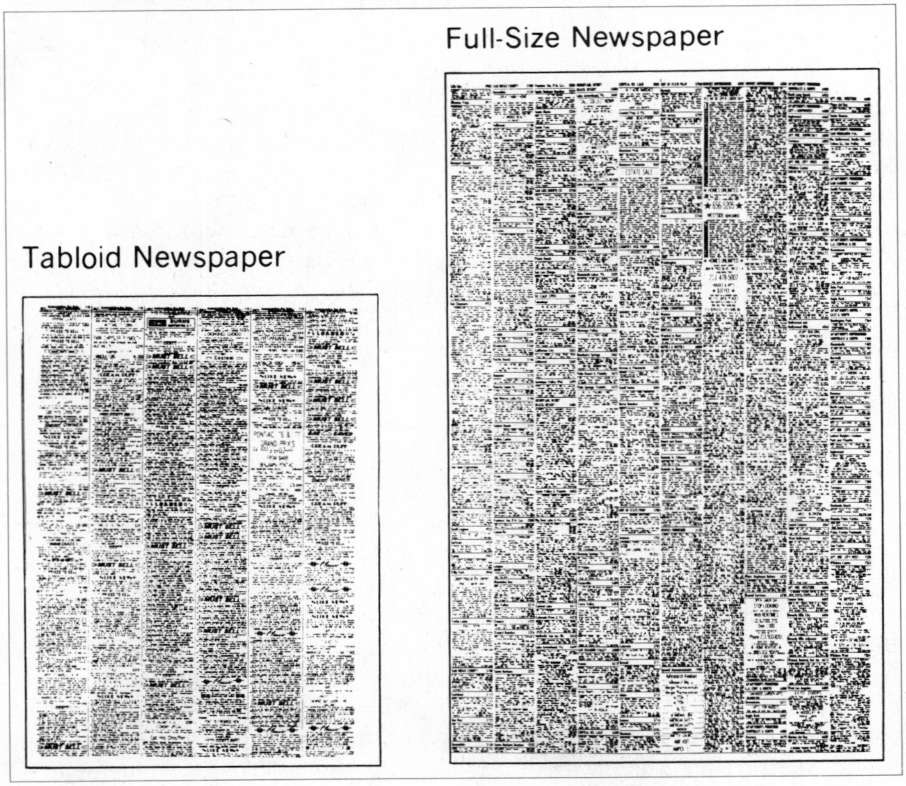

Full-Size Newspaper

Tabloid Newspaper

FIGURE 11–5
Even though these pages have been reduced, you can still see the relative comparison between the full-size broadsheet newspaper page and a tabloid newspaper page. The original size of the broadsheet was approximately 23 inches high and 14 inches wide; the tabloid page was about 15 inches high and 11 inches wide.

Because people may not always read carefully, newspaper advertising must attract the readers' attention while it supplies useful information. Retailers often include prices, store locations, hours, credit cards accepted, and information about delivery and other services. They also tend to feature more than one item in each advertisement.

When advertisers want to experiment with two different creative approaches, some large newspapers will print an ad using one approach in half its papers, then stop the printing presses to substitute an ad using the other approach for the second half. This is called a **split run.** It allows half the audience to see one advertisement and a second half to see the other. By using coupons that have been **keyed** or specially coded in the advertisement, the retailer can tell which advertisement produced the greater response.

split run A newspaper run or printing that is stopped halfway through to substitute one advertisement for another. Two separate advertisements therefore go out in one run.

keyed Specially coded to show response to an ad.

Timing Is Important. Newspaper advertising must be run when the customers are most likely to be interested in buying the advertised item. Grocery advertising, for example, may be in newspapers almost any day of the week, because somebody always needs to buy groceries. But most grocery advertising appears on Wednesdays and Thursdays for consumers who are preparing to do their weekly grocery shopping on Fridays and during the weekend.

Cooperative Advertising Can Save Money. Sometimes a manufacturer will pay part of the cost of a retailer's advertising. The reason is that newspapers may charge a higher advertising rate to national and regional advertisers than they charge to local retailers. If the retailer places the advertisement and a manufacturer pays part of the cost, both sides save money. This is called **cooperative advertising** (or "co-op").

Retailers also use newspaper advertising to support their own merchandising efforts. They can clip the advertisements from the newspaper and display them in the store to remind customers of the featured merchandise.

cooperative advertising Retail advertising that is partly paid for by the manufacturer.

Inserts

Some advertisers use newspapers without buying advertising space. They prepare **free-standing inserts,** or advertising sections, which are then inserted into the newspaper and delivered along with it. Usually, advertisers have their inserts printed and then deliver them to the paper. In this case, all the advertisers have to pay for is the privilege of having their insert delivered along with the paper. They are "buying" the newspaper's circulation. If the insert is printed by the newspaper, there would be an additional printing charge.

Advertisers who want to reach every household in a market often use inserts because many newspapers aim for **total market coverage (TMC)** at least once a week. This is the ability to reach *every* household, even those that do not subscribe to the newspaper regularly.

free-standing inserts Advertising sections delivered with a newspaper but not considered a part of it.

total market coverage (TMC) The ability to reach every household in a market at least once a week.

NEWSPAPER SUPPLEMENTS

supplement The magazine section of a newspaper.

Many newspapers insert a **supplement** that looks like a magazine; in fact, it is often called the "magazine section" of the newspaper. Because it is most often distributed with the Sunday edition of the newspaper, "Sunday supplement" is another common name for it.

There are a few national supplements, such as *Parade* and *USA Weekly*, that are carried in several newspapers. Some newspapers group together to cooperate in selling their supplement advertising space to advertisers, although each cooperating newspaper may edit its own supplement section. Supplements tend to use color illustrations and feature stories rather than the black-on-white format and news emphasis that the newspaper uses.

In some ways, then, the supplement is very much like a magazine. It looks like a magazine and may be read like a magazine—but it is still part of the newspaper.

CONSUMER MAGAZINES

consumer magazines Magazines sold directly to the consumer.

specialization A magazine's appeal to special interests or hobbies.

The magazines you probably see most often are **consumer magazines** sold directly to consumers for their education, entertainment, and information. Hundreds of consumer magazines are for sale in the United States, and the trend in recent years is for more to be developed. The reason behind this growth of consumer magazines is their increasing **specialization,** that is, their appeal to special interests or hobbies. Several general magazines have stopped publishing, for example *Look, Collier's,* and for a while *Life* and *The Saturday Evening Post*. These magazines appealed to all kinds of people, and advertisers used them to carry messages about products and services of general interest. But now television can perform that task more easily and less expensively, so there are few general magazines remaining. *Reader's Digest* is a large general consumer magazine that is still very successful, but it condenses many articles from other publications. Another widely circulated magazine, *TV Guide,* is itself the result of the growth of the television medium.

Several of the other large consumer magazines are much more specialized. *Better Homes & Gardens, Family Circle,* and *Women's Day* are oriented toward family service and homemakers. *National Geographic* is a very specialized but very popular magazine. The success of such magazines shows how the popularity of specialized publications has increased. We now have more magazines for consumers than ever before, but they are specialized rather than general in their appeal.

Because magazines have become more specialized, advertisers can use them to communicate to certain interest groups. Magazines may not be used as much as they once were for general mass-appeal products, but they are very good at reaching certain kinds of consumer segments—what we called target groups in Chapter 2.

There Is More than One Kind of Specialization

Magazines are also becoming better at reaching certain geographic areas and target markets. Many magazines that are sold throughout the country publish **regional editions** that are distributed only in certain parts of the country. Advertisers can use these regional editions to advertise only in certain areas or to change the advertising messages from one region to another.

There are even **metropolitan editions** (commonly called "metro" editions) so an advertisement can run only in the magazine copies that will be sold and distributed in and near certain cities. Retailers can use these magazines to advertise their stores in large cities without the **waste circulation** that results from advertising in areas where the customers are not prospects because they are too far away.

Table 11–2 sums up the advantages and disadvantages of advertising in consumer magazines.

regional editions Magazine editions distributed only in certain parts of the country.

metropolitan editions Magazine editions distributed only in and near certain cities.

waste circulation Advertising directed to customers who are not prospects.

The Mechanics of Magazine Advertising

Color printing is very good in most magazines—usually better than in most newspapers. Magazines use full-color, or four-color, printing, which you learned about in Chapter 9. A four-color advertisement like the ones reproduced in the inserts of this book will get more readership than a black-and-white advertisement; on the average, such an advertisement may receive about half again as much readership as the same advertisement just printed in black.

TABLE 11–2 Advantages and disadvantages of advertising in consumer magazines.

Advantages

1. Readers take longer to read magazines, so there is more time to sell in the advertisements.
2. Magazine ads have very good printing and color quality.
3. Magazines come out at various times, so there is flexibility in scheduling.
4. More specific magazines allow market segmentation.
5. Advertising reflects the prestige of magazines.
6. Magazines are kept in the home for a long time.
7. Good information is available about magazine audiences.
8. Flexible formats permit different sizes of advertisements, as well as foldouts, inserts, color, and even smell.

Disadvantages

1. General consumer magazines may have waste circulation.
2. Advertisements are easy to ignore, simply by turning the page.

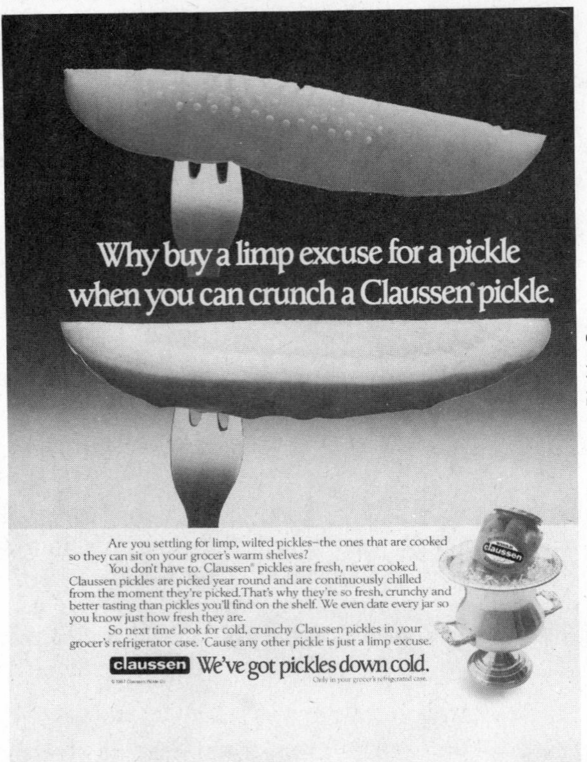

Courtesy of Kitchenaid and Claussen Pickle Co.

FIGURE 11–6
These magazine advertisements are examples of nonbleed and bleed illustrations. Bleed ads seem to go off the edge of the page. Nonbleed advertisements have an unprinted border around the edges.

border A margin of unprinted white space around an advertisement.

bleed illustration A magazine advertisement that seems to be printed off the edge of the page.

Therefore, a four-color advertisement will cost about half again as much as a black-and-white advertisement of the same size. Printing with extra colors also costs more than printing with only black ink, so increased production costs also add to the higher rates for color advertising.

The actual size of a standard magazine advertisement is smaller than the page it is printed on; there is a **border** of unprinted white space around the advertisement. This is what you get for the standard price. But most magazines are also able to print right up to the edge of the page in what is known as a **bleed illustration** as shown in Figure 11–6. Actually, the printing goes beyond the size of the page on a slightly larger sheet of paper; then the sheet is trimmed back to the regular page size. Bleed advertisements may receive about one-tenth more readership than nonbleed advertisements, and since the extra readership is worth more to the advertiser, magazines charge about one-tenth more for a bleed advertisement than for the same size nonbleed advertisement. Some magazines charge even more.

More than one person may read a copy of a magazine. Because these extra readers represent a larger audience for the advertising message, they are important to advertisers. The readers who buy the magazine or subscribe to it are the **primary audience,** and the "pass-along" readers are the **secondary audience.**

For small advertisements, magazines charge for advertising space by the column-inch, as newspapers do. But most magazine rates are based on a page of advertising and are quoted for a full page of advertising as well as for partial units such as a half page, quarter page, third page, sixth page, two-thirds page, and the like. Usually it will cost more to advertise in two half-pages than in a single full page, even though the total amount of space used is the same. Magazines must sell the two remaining half-pages separately, and they must run two separate advertisements in the printing press run of the magazine. It is also more tedious to arrange the magazine with two half-pages than with a single full page. Therefore, the smaller units of advertising usually cost proportionately more than the larger units.

primary audience People who buy or subscribe to a magazine.

secondary audience People to whom a magazine is passed along.

Comparing Two Magazines

As with newspapers, we may want to compare two magazines to find out which is more economical. But only newspapers use the milline rate. In magazines and most other advertising media, we use the **cost per thousand** or **(CPM).** Here M stands for the Roman numeral M, a thousand.

cost per thousand (CPM) The formula used to compare advertising rates in magazines and most other media.

$$\text{Cost per thousand (CPM)} = \frac{\text{Page rate}}{\text{Circulation}} \times 1{,}000$$

What we are comparing is the cost of advertising for each thousand copies of circulation for both magazines. All we need to do is start with an advertising rate, usually the rate for a full magazine page of space. If you knew that your advertisement was to be some other size, you might start with that rate. And if you plan to use bleed or color, you might use those higher advertising rates to make your calculations more accurate.

First, we divide the advertising rate by the circulation of the magazine to find out how much it would cost for that advertisement in each copy of the magazine. Then we take that figure and multiply it by 1,000 to find out what the advertisement would cost for each 1,000 copies circulated. The magazine with the lower cost per thousand will be the more economical. Figure 11–7 shows how the cost per thousand method works.

Newspapers and magazines both provide rate cards that show how much they charge for their advertising. But what if you don't live near the magazine or newspaper office? How would you get a rate card? The answer is, you don't need one. You can look up the advertising rates for most consumer magazines in the appropriate volume of a source called **Standard Rate and Data Service (SRDS).** A sample SRDS listing is shown in Figure 11–8. SRDS has advertising rate volumes for weekly newspapers and magazines, too.

Standard Rate and Data Service (SRDS) A source that lists advertising rates for consumer ad media.

SRDS contains more than just advertising rates: You can also find out how often the publication comes out, when you should get your advertisement

Magazine X
Circulation = 629,000
Advertising rate = \$7,000 per page

Magazine Y
Circulation = 742,000
Advertising rate = \$8,900 per page

$$\text{CPM (magazines)} = \frac{\text{Page rate}}{\text{Circulation}} \times 1{,}000$$

$$\text{CPM} = \frac{\$7{,}000}{629{,}000} \times 1{,}000$$
$$\text{CPM} = .0111287 \times 1{,}000$$
$$\text{CPM} = \$11.13$$

$$\text{CPM} = \frac{\$8{,}900}{742{,}000} \times 1{,}000$$
$$\text{CPM} = .0119946 \times 1{,}000$$
$$\text{CPM} = \$11.99$$

So Magazine X is more economical. It costs \$11.13 to advertise in each 1,000 copies of Magazine X, while it costs \$11.99 to advertise in each 1,000 copies of Magazine Y.

FIGURE 11–7
This is an example of how to compare the advertising rates of two magazines, using the cost per thousand (CPM) method.

there for a certain issue, the sizes of the pages and of the advertising space available, an estimate of the circulation, addresses and telephone numbers of magazine offices, and much more valuable information. So for planning advertising and determining the costs involved, SRDS is a valuable advertising tool.

BUSINESS PUBLICATIONS

business publications Magazines directed to business and industrial purposes.

There are hundreds of consumer magazines, but *thousands* of magazines are directed to certain kinds of business and industrial purposes. These **business publications** have many of the same characteristics as consumer magazines, and they operate in much the same way. However, business publications are less likely to be sold at newsstands and their news and advertising is usually oriented toward specific business interests.

Some business publications appeal to all kinds of business interests: *Business Week, Fortune,* and *Nation's Business* are examples. Others concentrate on certain operations within business, such as *Purchasing* magazine for purchasing agents and *Sales and Marketing Management* for marketing executives. Still others cover only a certain kind of business, for example, *Progressive Grocer, Package Engineering, Welding Journal,* and *Advertising Age.* Some of these publications may appeal to all the people who work in a certain business, while others such as the *Journal of Advertising* and *Medical Economics* are narrower in their scope.

	Herald	News
1/6 page	1,668.00	232.00
1/8 page	1,248.00	174.00
1/12 page	832.00	118.00

Herald/News TV comb. available at Herald rates above plus 10%.

COLOR RATES AND DATA
No extra charge for color on back cover page or inside cover pages. Color not available on any other pages inside.

CLOSING TIMES
Thursday, 3:00 p.m. 11 days prior to publication.

MECHANICAL MEASUREMENTS
PRINTING PROCESS: Heatset Offset.
Page size; 6-7/16" wide x 10-3/8" deep. 3 cols. to page.

20. CIRCULATION
Established 1910. Per copy, Morn .25; Eve .20; Sun .75.
Net Paid—A.B.C. 9-30-87 (Newspaper Form)

	Total	CZ	TrZ	Other
Morn	398,612	249,501	95,041	54,070
Eve	55,458	50,647	4,691	120
M&E	454,070	300,148	99,732	54,190
Sun	501,001	315,102	116,405	69,494

Max-Min CPM rate: M&E Max 14.71; Min 6.10.
For county-by-county and/or metropolitan area breakdowns, see SRDS Newspaper Circulation Analysis.

Naples

Collier County—Map Location G-6
See SRDS Consumer market map and data at beginning of the state.

NEWS

1075 Central Ave., Naples, FL 33940.
Phone 813-262-3161.

newsplan
DISCOUNTS FOR CONTINUITY

Media Code 1 110 6110 7.00 **Mid 016322-000**
EVENING (except Saturday) AND SUNDAY.
Member: INAME: NAB, Inc.; ACB, Inc.

1. PERSONNEL
Publisher—Corbin A. Wyant.
Advertising Director—J. Patrick Berling.
Nat'l. Adv. Rep.—James R. Murray.

2. REPRESENTATIVES and/or BRANCH OFFICES
Publisher's Representatives of Florida, Inc.
Sawyer-Ferguson-Walker Company, Inc.

3. COMMISSION AND CASH DISCOUNT
15% to agencies; 2%—15th following month.

4. POLICY-ALL CLASSIFICATIONS
30-day notice given of any rate revision.
Alcoholic beverage and tobacco advertising accepted.

ADVERTISING RATES
Effective December 1, 1987.
Received October 29, 1987.

5. BLACK/WHITE RATES

	Eve.	Sun.
SAU open, per inch	15.05	15.42

Inches charged full depth: col. 21.5; pg. 129; dbl truck 279.5.
NEWSPLAN—SAU

Pages	Eve.	Sun.
3	14.55	14.92
6	13.55	13.88

See Newsplan Contract and Copy Regulations—items 1, 2, 4, 5, 6, 9, 11, 12, 14, 15, 17.

7. COLOR RATES AND DATA
Minimum 45 inches.
Use b/w rate plus the following applicable costs:

	b/w 1 c	b/w 2 c	b/w 3 c
Daily, extra	210.00	330.00	450.00
Sunday, extra	300.00	420.00	540.00

Closing dates: Reservations and printing material 1 week in advance. Cancellation date: 4 days before publication.

11. SPECIAL DAYS/PAGES/FEATURES
Best Food Days: Wednesday and Sunday.
Travel, Business, & TV Sections, Sunday.

12. R.O.P. DEPTH REQUIREMENTS
Ads over 19 inches deep charged full col.

13. CONTRACT AND COPY REGULATIONS
See Contents page for location of regulations—items 1, 2, 3, 5, 6, 7, 8, 9, 10, 11, 13, 14, 15, 16, 17, 18, 19, 21, 22, 23, 25, 26, 27, 28, 29.

14. CLOSING TIMES
Daily: 72 hours before publication; Sunday: Noon, Wednesday before publication.

15. MECHANICAL MEASUREMENTS
For complete, detailed production information, see SRDS Print Media Production Data.
PRINTING PROCESS. Offset.
6 col; ea 2-1/16"; 1/8" betw col.
Inches charged full depth: col. 21.5; pg. 129; dbl truck 279.5.

16. SPECIAL CLASSIFICATIONS/RATES
Political (cash in advance)—general rates apply.

17. CLASSIFIED RATES
For complete data refer to classified rate section.

20. CIRCULATION
Established 1923. Per copy .25.
Net Paid—A.B.C. 9-30-87 (Newspaper Form)

	Total	CZ	TrZ	Other
ExSat	26,117	17,244	8,207	666
Sun	34,900	21,452	10,993	2,455

Max-Min CPM rate: Eve Max 17.84; Min 16.06.
For county-by-county and/or metropolitan area breakdowns, see SRDS Newspaper Circulation Analysis.

Ocala

Marion County—Map Location F-2
See SRDS Consumer market map and data at beginning of the state.

STAR-BANNER

Box 490, 819 S.E. 1st Terrace, Ocala, FL 32678.
Phone 904-629-0011.

Media Code 1 110 6345 9.00 **Mid 016323-000**
MORNING AND SUNDAY.
Member: INAME; Newspaper Advertising Bureau, Inc.; ACB, Inc.

1. PERSONNEL
Publisher—Paul Brooks.
Advertising Director—Foy Maloy.
National Co-ordinator—Susan Wiley.

2. REPRESENTATIVES and/or BRANCH OFFICES
Branham/Newspaper Sales.
Publishers' Representatives of Florida, Inc.

3. COMMISSION AND CASH DISCOUNT
15% to agencies; 2% 15th following month.

4. POLICY-ALL CLASSIFICATIONS
30-day notice given of any rate revision.
Alcoholic beverage advertising accepted.

ADVERTISING RATES
Effective January 1, 1988.
Received November 30, 1987.

5. BLACK/WHITE RATES
SAU open, per inch 19.69
Inches charged full depth: col. 21.5; pg. 129; dbl truck 279.5.
NEWSPLAN—SAU

Pages	% Disc.	M or Sun.	Inches
6	1	19.49	774
13	5	18.71	1,677
26	10	17.72	3,354
52	18	16.15	6,708

See Newsplan Contract and Copy Regulations—items 1, 2, 3, 4, 6, 9, 10, 14, 15.

6. GROUP COMBINATION RATES-B/W & COLOR
Central Florida Golden Markets Group—See listing at beginning of State.

7. COLOR RATES AND DATA
Available daily and Sunday Leeway required.
Use b/w rate plus the following applicable costs:

	b/w 1 c	b/w 2 c	b/w 3 c
Extra	330.00	495.00	618.00

Closing dates: Reservations 5 days prior to publication; Cancellation 5 days in advance.
Printing material 3 days in advance.

11. SPECIAL DAYS/PAGES/FEATURES
Best Food Day: Thursday & Sunday.

12. R.O.P. DEPTH REQUIREMENTS
Ads over 19-1/2 inches deep charged full col.

13. CONTRACT AND COPY REGULATIONS
See Contents page for location of regulations—items 1, 2, 4, 6, 8, 9, 10, 13, 14, 15, 16, 22, 23, 24, 25, 29.

15. MECHANICAL MEASUREMENTS
For complete, detailed production information, see SRDS Print Media Production Data.
PRINTED PROCESS: Offset.
6 col; ea 2-1/16"; 1/8" betw col.
Inches charged full depth: col. 21.5; pg. 129; dbl truck 279-1/2.

16. SPECIAL CLASSIFICATIONS/RATES
Political (cash with order), per col. inch 15.35
(Non-commissionable; no cash discount.)
POSITION CHARGES
Next to reading—not sold; special position 25%.

17. CLASSIFIED RATES
For complete data refer to classified rate section.

18. COMICS
Effective January 1, 1988.
Received November 30, 1987.
COLOR RATES AND DATA
1 page .... 1,160.00 1/4 page 350.00
1/2 page 600.00
Daily Comic Page—B/W
35 lines by 3 to 4 columns accepted in cartoon style at regular black and white rate. Minimum 13 times.
CLOSING TIMES
4 weeks before publication.
MECHANICAL MEASUREMENTS
PRINTING PROCESS: Rotary Letterpress.
Page size 8-3/4" wide x 13" deep. 4 cols. to page.
Colors available: ANPA/AAAA: 4 Colors.
Send printing material to Greater Buffalo Press, 302 Grote St., Buffalo, N. Y. 14207.

19. MAGAZINES

TV Week

SATURDAY.
POLICY—ALL CLASSIFICATIONS
60-day notice given of any rate revision.
Alcoholic beverage advertising accepted.
Effective January 1, 1988.
Received November 30, 1987.
BLACK/WHITE RATES
Flat, per inch 19.69
COLOR RATES AND DATA
Use b/w rate plus the following applicable costs:

	b/w 1 c	b/w 2 c	b/w 3 c
Extra	58.82	100.00	147.06

CLOSING TIMES
Wednesday, 10 days prior to publication.
MECHANICAL MEASUREMENTS
PRINTING PROCESS: Offset.
Trim size: 7-1/8" wide x 10-1/2" deep.
4 cols. to page; col. width. 9 picas
Process colors only (red, blue or yellow).
Sold in 1/16, 1/8, 1/4, 1/2 and page sizes only.
Inches charged to col. 9.5; pg. 38".

20. CIRCULATION
Established 1866. Per copy, daily .25; Sunday .50.
9-30-87
A.B.C. Statement not received by press time.
Publisher guarentees: "Effective with October 5, 1987 issue, Morning net paid circulation average is 44,586."
For county-by-county and/or metropolitan area breakdowns, see SRDS Newspaper Circulation Analysis.

Orange Park

Clay County—Map Location F-2
See SRDS Consumer market map and data at beginning of the state.

CLAY TODAY

1564 Kingsley Ave., Orange Park, FL 32073.
Phone 904-264-3200.

Media Code 1 110 6580 1.00 **Mid 016324-000**
EVENING (except Saturday).

1. PERSONNEL
Circulation Manager—Glenn Watson.

2. REPRESENTATIVES and/or BRANCH OFFICES
Thomson Newspapers, Inc.

3. COMMISSION AND CASH DISCOUNT
15% to agencies; no cash discount.

4. POLICY-ALL CLASSIFICATIONS
30-day notice given of any rate revision.
Alcoholic beverage advertising accepted.

ADVERTISING RATES
Effective April 1, 1988.
Received March 9, 1988.

5. BLACK/WHITE RATES
SAU open, per inch 6.39
Inches charged full depth: col. 21.5; pg. 129; dbl truck 279.5.

ANNUAL BULK RATES

	Per inch
85"	6.10
150"	5.99
235"	5.83
385"	5.73
750"	5.61
2,250"	5.47
3,750"	5.34
6,000"	5.23
9,000"	5.09

6. GROUP COMBINATION RATES-B/W & COLOR
Also sold in combination with Clay Countain (Wed.), extra per inch 1.50.
Circulation—Sworn 9-30-87: Total Non-Paid 18,000.

7. COLOR RATES AND DATA
Available daily.
Use b/w rate plus the following applicable cost:

	b/w 1 c	b/w 2 c	b/w 3 c
Extra, net	75.00	145.00	215.00

Closing times: Reservations 3 days before publication.

11. SPECIAL DAYS/PAGES/FEATURES
Best Food Days: Monday and Wednesday.

12. R.O.P. DEPTH REQUIREMENTS
Ads over 20 inches charged full column.

14. CLOSING TIMES
Noon, 2 days before publication.

15. MECHANICAL MEASUREMENTS
For complete, detailed production information, see SRDS Print Media Production Data.
PRINTING PROCESS: Offset.
6 col; ea 2"; 3/16" betw col.
Inches charged full depth: col. 21.5; pg. 129; dbl truck 279.5.

17. CLASSIFIED RATES
For complete data refer to classified rate section.

20. CIRCULATION
Per copy .25.
Net Paid—Sworn 9-30-87 (P.O. Stat. Att.)

	Total	CZ	TrZ	Other
ExSat	4,518	2,001	2,390	127

Max-Min CPM rate: Eve Max 44.55; Min 35.49.
For county-by-county and/or metropolitan area breakdowns, see SRDS Newspaper Circulation Analysis.

Orlando

Orange County—Map Location G-3
See SRDS Consumer market map and data at beginning of the state.

SENTINEL

Box 2833, 633 N. Orange Ave., Orlando, FL 32801.
Phone 305-420-5266.

Media Code 1 110 6638 7.00 **Mid 016325-000**
ALL DAY, SATURDAY MORN. AND SUNDAY.
(Evening editions not published Saturday, Labor Day, Thanksgiving, Christmas, New Year's Day, Memorial Day, Independence Day.)
Member: INAME; NAB, Inc; ABC Coupon Distribution Verification Service; ACB, Inc.

1. PERSONNEL
V.P./Dir. of Adv.—Raymond P. Dallman.
Retail Adv. Mgr.—Joe Del Rocco.
Gen. Adv. Mgr.—David White.
Credit Mgr—William Griffith.

2. REPRESENTATIVES and/or BRANCH OFFICES
Cresmer, Woodward, O'Mara & Ormsbee, Inc.
Publishers Representatives of Florida, Inc.

3. COMMISSION AND CASH DISCOUNT
15% to agencies; no cash discount.

4. POLICY-ALL CLASSIFICATIONS
Alcoholic beverage advertising accepted.

ADVERTISING RATES
Effective January 1, 1988.
Received December 9, 1987.

5. BLACK/WHITE RATES

	Daily	Sun.
SAU open, per inch	126.37	152.53

Inches charged full depth: col. 21; pg. 126; dbl truck 267.75.

BULK CONTRACT DISCOUNTS

Pages	Daily	Sun.
1	111.44	134.50
3	108.54	132.20
6	106.30	129.49
13	101.83	124.04
26	99.58	121.30
39	97.35	118.58
52	95.11	115.85
72	89.51	109.04
88	85.04	103.59
104	80.56	98.14
106	79.45	96.77
110	78.32	95.40

APPLICATIONS OF DISCOUNTS
Advertiser billed at contract rate, less agency commission. Color charges are not included in discounts. Advertiser may extend or revise contract upward to take advantage of higher discounts. No contract to extend more than 52 weeks. Advertisers who do not fill terms of contract will be rebilled at lowest rate actually earned under the plan. Contracts will be accepted from an individual advertiser, or may be drawn to include his subsidiaries.

7. COLOR RATES AND DATA
Available daily and Sunday.
Use b/w rate plus the following applicable costs:

	b/w 1 c	b/w 2 c	b/w 3 c
Daily, extra	1,442.20	1,854.00	2,155.00
Sunday, extra	1,481.00	1,904.00	2,216.00

Closing dates: Reservations 1 week in advance when printing material is furnished; 14 days when publisher makes plates from art work; 4 weeks when publisher originates color. One spot color in a primary ink available only for ads 280 lines to 839 lines; 7 days leeway required. Process or spot color available on ads of 840 lines or more; leeway desired but not required.

9. SPLIT RUN
Minimum space 31 col. inches rop and full page Florida Magazine.
General rates plus 15% apply.
Available Thursday "Food". Sunday "Florida Magazine" and Sunday "Travel".

11. SPECIAL DAYS/PAGES/FEATURES
Best Food Day: Thursday.
Fashion, Wednesday; Entertainment. Saturday; Real Estate, Saturday & Sunday; Gardening & Decorating Saturday; Business Section: Sunday. & Monday thru Friday; Travel, Sunday.

12. R.O.P. DEPTH REQUIREMENTS
Ads over 19 inches deep charged full col.

13. CONTRACT AND COPY REGULATIONS
See Contents page for location of regulations—items 1. 3. 5, 6, 7, 8, 9, 10, 11, 12, 13, 14, 15, 16, 18, 23, 25, 26, 28, 29.

14. CLOSING TIMES
Daily 5:00 p.m. 2 days before publication. Sunday 5:00 p.m. Thursday before publication. Food & Travel, Monday noon; Wednesday Style Monday noon; Sunday Style Wednesday 11:00 a.m.; Friday Style Wednesday 11:00 a.m.; Saturday Style Wednesday 5:00 p.m.

15. MECHANICAL MEASUREMENTS
For complete, detailed production information, see SRDS Print Media Production Data.
PRINTING PROCESS: Offset.
6 col; ea 2-1/32"; 5/32" betw col.
Inches charged full depth: col. 21; pg. 126; dbl truck 267.75.

16. SPECIAL CLASSIFICATIONS/RATES
Travel Section

	1 ti.	4 ti.	13 ti.	26 ti.	39 ti.	52 ti.
Per inch	152.53	130.37	123.59	114.73	100.38	86.94

17. CLASSIFIED RATES
For complete data refer to classified rate section.

18. COMICS
POLICY—ALL CLASSIFICATIONS
When orders are placed through Metro Sunday Comics Network Group—See that listing.
Effective January 1, 1988.
Received December 9, 1987.
COLOR RATES AND DATA

Black and 3 colors:	Open	6 ti	13 ti
1 pg	8,920.60	8,361.98	8,189.57
2/3 pg	6,855.34	6,649.68	6,512.58
1/2 pg	5,336.51	5,176.41	5,069.68
1/3 pg	4,104.99	3,981.84	3,899.74
1/6 pg	2,873.49	2,787.28	2,729.81

Black and 3 colors:	26 ti	52 ti
1 pg	8,017.16	7,758.54
2/3 pg	6,375.47	6,169.81
1/2 pg	4,962.95	4,802.86
1/3 pg	3,817.64	3,694.49
1/6 pg	2,672.34	2,586.14

SPECIAL CLASSIFICATIONS/RATES
STRIPS
6 columns x 1 col. inch, per inch 95.21
CLOSING TIMES
Space: 5 weeks before publication.
Copy: 4 weeks before publication.
MECHANICAL MEASUREMENTS
PRINTING PROCESS: Heatset Offset.
Standard page size: 13" wide x 21" deep.
For ad sizes see Metro Sunday Comics listing.
Colors available: Ad Pro.

19. MAGAZINES

Florida Magazine

SUNDAY.
POLICY—ALL CLASSIFICATIONS
When orders are placed through Metropolitan Sunday Newspaper Magazine Group—see that listing.
Effective January 1, 1988.
Received December 9, 1987.
BLACK/WHITE RATES

2-page spread	19,358.75
Full page	9,679.38
7/10 page	6,777.51
3/5 page	5,808.59
1/2 page	4,839.69
9/20 page	4,304.38
2/5 page	3,870.79
3/10 page	2,904.30
1/5 page	1,935.40
3/20 page	1,448.51
1/10 page	971.33
1/20 page	477.20

COLOR RATES AND DATA
Use b/w rate plus the following applicable costs:

	b/w 1 c	b/w 2 c	b/w 3 c
Extra	1,487.00	1,913.00	2,225.00

Back page 200.00 premium.

DISCOUNTS

Units		Units	
3 pages	6%	12 pages	20%
6 pages	12%	24 pages	24%

continued

FIGURE 11–8
Sample listing from, SRDS "Newspaper, Rates and Data."

TABLE 11–3 Advantages and disadvantages of advertising in business and farm publications. These kinds of publications have many of the same characteristics as consumer magazines, but there are some special traits, as shown here.

Advantages

1. Advertisments appeal to business and farm interests.
2. Farm publications are often read during working hours, so the readers' minds are on business and farming.
3. There are few distractions, because the news and information is oriented toward the same topics as the advertisements.
4. They reach directly to the persons responsible for the items being promoted.

Disadvantages

1. There may be a lot of competing advertising.

free circulation Circulation delivered to readers without charge.

paid circulation Circulation in which readers pay for their own magazines.

controlled circulation Circulation limited to qualified readers.

uncontrolled circulation Circulation open to all.

Some audience members may get certain publications free; advertisers pay for the magazine, and the publishers send it without charge to specific kinds of readers. This is called **free circulation.** Most business publications, however, have **paid circulation** just as most consumer magazines do.

To get some business publications, the readers must qualify as being genuinely interested in the subject of the magazine. Outsiders cannot receive these **controlled circulation** publications even if they want to. As an example, *Marketing & Media Decisions* magazine is circulated free to people in the advertising business who are in charge of selecting and buying media space and time. This free circulation is controlled. If just anyone may receive a publication, it is **uncontrolled circulation.**

Planning how to advertise in business publications can be complicated. Because there are so many of these publications, it is difficult to be familiar with all of them. Many of these magazines issue small summaries of what they do, to whom they are circulated, and what their editorial policies are, so that advertising media planners and buyers can learn about them. Advertising rates for business publications may be found in a volume of SRDS.

FARM PUBLICATIONS

farm publications Magazines for farmers and agriculture business; containing specialized as well as general interest articles.

The last category of magazines is **farm publications,** which are magazines for farmers, containing specialized as well as general interest features. These are really a combination of consumer magazines and business publications. Their specialized articles and features are intended to help farmers become more efficient and profitable, but they also offer some material that is more like the entertainment features of consumer magazines. The advertising in farm publications may be split, too; most of it is related to farming and agriculture, but there is some general consumer advertising.

In most other respects, farm publications are like consumer magazines and business publications, and their advertising rates are listed along with those of consumer magazines in SRDS.

Some advertisers overlook the farm publication marketplace. And if they do use farm publications as an advertising medium, they may not use them well. Critics suggest that the creative efforts in farm publication advertising are not as strong as they should be. Yet it only makes sense to do the best possible job with this medium, just as you would with any other medium for any other audience.

SUMMARY

So now you have learned about the uses of the major print advertising media: newspapers and magazines. Try to remember how advertisers use these print media for their comparative advantages. Also keep in mind how advertising rates are set and how advertisers can save money through frequency and quantity discounts.

Newspapers are the most widely used medium among retail advertisers because newspapers are local and their advertising preparation is relatively simplified. Magazines offer more variations, such as better color, bleed advertisements, multiple-page units, and so on, but they are less selective and much more expensive.

There are also specialized magazines such as business publications and farm publications. They reach special audiences for advertisers who have items targeted toward those groups.

TERMS TO KNOW

Now that you have finished this chapter, you should understand the following terms:

advertising media
audience
circulation
daily newspapers
weekly newspapers
zoned editions
advertising rate
classified advertising
display advertising
column-inch
agate line
flat rate
discount rate
quantity discount
short rate
milline rate
reach
frequency
tabloid
broadsheet
split run
keyed
cooperative advertising
free-standing inserts
total market coverage (TMC)
supplement
regional editions
metropolitan editions
waste circulation
border
bleed illustration
primary audience
secondary audience
cost per thousand (CPM)
Standard Rate and Data Service (SRDS)
business publications
free circulation
paid circulation
controlled circulation

open rate	consumer magazines	uncontrolled circulation
frequency discount	specialization	farm publications

If you are not certain of the meaning of any of these terms, go back though the chapter and review them.

THINGS TO THINK ABOUT

1. What is the difference between audience and circulation? Between reach and frequency?
2. What service is performed by Standard Rate and Data Service? How is this service used in planning advertising?
3. What are the advantages and disadvantages of newspapers to advertisers? Of magazines?
4. What is the difference between classified and display advertising in newspapers? Then what is classified display advertising?
5. How do regional and metropolitan editions of magazines make magazine advertising more competitive and attractive?
6. How do business publications differ from consumer magazines? How would you classify farm publications?
7. What are free and paid circulation? What is controlled circulation?

THINGS TO TALK ABOUT

1. What are the uses of milline rate and cost per thousand?
2. What is the purpose of discounts in advertising rates? How do the discounts work?
3. Why are there rebates and short rates? What are the advantages of contracts, both for the newspaper and for the advertiser?
4. How does cooperative advertising work? What potential problems are involved in cooperative advertising?
5. What are split runs and how and why are they used? What is "keying" and how and why is it used?
6. Why have general magazines declined in popularity while specialized magazines have become more popular?
7. Why is it a good idea to compare the efficiency of one magazine with that of another?

THINGS TO DO

1. Calculate the number of column inches in a newspaper page that has six columns, each 21 inches long.
2. Visit a local newspaper and get an advertising rate card. Calculate the costs of various advertisements that appear in that newspaper.
3. Talk to various local retailers and find out what days of the week they consider best for advertising their products and services.
4. Compare regular daily newspaper advertising with that in a Sunday supplement.
5. Look at the advertisements in some farm publications and business publications. How do they differ from advertisements in general magazines?

12 Broadcast Media

Issues of the Information Age:

The paradox of power.

The Information Age, for all its potential, has brought with it a new kind of problem. Often, the machines that contribute so much to the flood of information do little to help most of us cope with it. They are difficult to use, rigid in their demands, almost arrogant in their inability to work with any but their own kind. They are the muscle-bound tools of specialists.

In our view, the problem is not that the machines are too powerful for the rest of us. They are not powerful enough.

This is the paradox of power: the more powerful the machine, the less power it exerts over the person using it. We define a more powerful machine as one that is more capable of bending to the will of humans, rather than having humans bend to its will. The definition is deeply ingrained in AT&T. The telephone is such a powerful device precisely because it demands so little of its user.

AT&T foresees the day when the Information Age will become universal. People everywhere will participate in a worldwide Telecommunity. They will be able to handle information in any form—conversation, data, images, text—as easily as they now make a phone call.

That day is coming closer. One example: scientists at AT&T Bell Laboratories are developing "associative" memories for computers, further enabling the machines to work with incomplete, imprecise, or even contradictory information. That's perfectly natural for a human. What makes it a breakthrough is that these computers won't ask you to be anything else.

Telecommunity is our goal. Technology is our means.

We are committed to leading the way.

Courtesy of AT & T

CHAPTER OUTLINE

By the time you finish this chapter, you should understand:

1. **The advantages and disadvantages of television advertising.**
2. **How television advertising is bought and used.**
3. **The complications of determining audience sizes.**
4. **How advertising patterns are used on television.**
5. **How cable stations are affecting television advertising.**
6. **How radio advertising is bought and used.**
7. **How retailers should use the broadcast media channels.**

Advertisers have been spending more and more in recent years mainly because of the growth of the broadcast media: television and radio. Most of this growth comes from television—although radio continues to succeed and profit, as we shall see later in this chapter. First, though, let's take a look at the complex situation that faces a broadcast advertiser.

THE COMPLEXITY OF BROADCAST MEDIA ADVERTISING

There are fewer broadcast media (that is, radio and television stations) than there are print media (newspapers, consumer magazines, and business and farm publications). But it is more complicated to choose and buy broadcast advertising time.

The audiences for broadcast networks and stations change minute by minute. Advertisers cannot be sure how many and what kinds of people might have seen or heard their commercials within a broadcast program.

The information provided by broadcast advertising is gone as soon as it is seen and hard to save for future reference. Even though people get the advertising message, they may not bother to remember it.

The prices for broadcast advertising are always shifting. As a result, the *Standard Rate and Data Service* (discussed in Chapter 11) now gives few actual advertising rates for broadcast media. To complicate the situation even more, these rates are usually worked out between the advertiser and the broadcaster; different advertisers, or even the same advertiser in separate situations, may pay different prices for advertising times of equal value. Large discounts for advertisers who buy lots of time also change the advertising rates.

Also, each station lists its rates in unique formats. No two stations use exactly the same terms and forms. The term "Class A," for example, might mean the top-rated time on one station but the lowest-rated time on another station.

In addition, broadcasters respond to audience reactions and program popularity. They base their plans on audience size more than other media do. Programming shifts and schedule changes are commonplace, so it is sometimes hard to plan advertising. As you can see, then, choosing and buying broadcast advertising is a complex situation that takes knowledge and experience to master.

TELEVISION ADVERTISING

Television advertising has been getting more popular for several reasons. As you learned in Chapter 11, magazines are becoming more and more specialized. But television is still an excellent way to reach a general audience with advertising for common products. So television has gained where general magazines have declined.

Another important plus for TV advertising is that the number of homes with televisions has been increasing. Now almost every home in the United States has at least one television set—in fact, more homes have television than telephones, indoor plumbing, or central heating! And more and more homes now have more than one television set. And television itself has been branching out, adding cable networks, satellite transmissions, and independent stations (that is, stations not connected with major networks) to the traditional broadcast stations.

But television has only a certain amount of time to sell for advertising: There are limits to the number of commercials that may be shown in an hour on television, and there are limits to the number of hours in the broadcast day. So, as more advertisers want to use television, the costs of television advertising have increased to offset this demand. Table 12–1 outlines the advantages and disadvantages of television advertising.

network television A form of television broadcasting in which an independent business, or network, joins individual stations together to broadcast its programs and advertising.

local television Individual television stations broadcasting in a limited geographic area.

Two categories of television broadcasting are important to us in advertising: network and local. In **network television,** an independent business called a *network* joins individual television stations together to broadcast its programs and advertising. The stations neither own nor control the networks. Television stations may voluntarily contract to carry a network's programs. In this case, the network pays the stations for carrying the programs. Some stations are owned by a network, but each network may own only a limited number of television stations. Usually only one station per market carries each network's programs.

Rather than go through the networks, advertisers may also deal directly with **local television,** individual stations broadcasting within a small geographic area. In fact, few advertisers are large enough to afford expensive network advertising time, so most of them deal with local stations.

TABLE 12–1 Advantages and disadvantages of advertising in television.

Advantages

1. Television allows demonstration of the products or service.
2. It combines sight and sound to increase impact.
3. It covers all kinds of people, who spend a lot of time watching.
4. Good repetition of message is possible.
5. It is versatile, allowing the combination of sounds, color, and motion.
6. It is hard for viewers to tune out a commercial.
7. The audience becomes personally involved with television.
8. The cost-per-thousand method can be efficient.

Disadvantages

1. The broadcaster and the audience control television, and the advertiser may not have much control.
2. The cost is very high.
3. Commercials may get old quickly.
4. Print advertising may seem more authentic to the audience, because television advertising may seem too much like personal selling, which some people distrust.
5. The general audience does not permit selectivity.

Categories of Television Time

The larger the audience a medium can reach, the higher the price of the advertising. So the highest cost of advertising on television networks is during the evening hours when the most people are viewing television. This is called **prime time.** In most of the country, prime time is 8:00 to 11:00 in the evening, but in the central time zone (and sometimes in the mountain time zone) prime time is 7:00 to 10:00.

The network advertising time just before and just after prime time is called **fringe time** because it is on the fringes of the highest audience viewing times. There is also **daytime** and **late night time,** which tend to have smaller audiences and lower advertising rates than prime and fringe times.

An advertiser who buys all the advertising on a certain program is called the **sponsor** of that program. Because television advertising is very expensive, however, few advertisers want to spend all their advertising money on only one or two sponsored programs. Instead they buy commercials on a variety of programs. These advertisers participate in supporting the programs along with other advertisers. So one advertisement among others in a program is called a **participation.**

At one time, advertisers who did not want to sponsor or participate in programs had to buy their television advertising from the individual stations.

prime time The evening hours when most people are watching TV.

fringe time Just before and just after prime time.

daytime The time of day that comes before early evening fringe time.

late night time The time of night that follows a night fringe time.

sponsor An advertiser who buys all the advertising on a certain program.

participation One advertisement among others within a program.

Because these stations were located at various geographic spots around the country, this became known as "spot" advertising. Most spot commercials went on the air during the station break between network programs, so gradually **spot advertising** came to mean any broadcast advertising that is not within a program. Today, networks as well as individual stations sell spot television advertisements between programs. We therefore have two general kinds of broadcast advertisements: spot announcements between programs, and participating announcements within programs.

spot advertising Any broadcast advertising that is not within a program.

Shorter Commercials

Early television advertising followed the patterns begun by its forerunner, radio. So the standard length of a broadcast advertisement was one minute, although it is often called a "sixty" for its sixty-second length. Eventually, advertisers wanted to save money by using shorter commercials and the television industry wanted to make more commercials available. So the standard commercial is now thirty seconds long, and sometimes commercials on television are as short as twenty or even ten seconds.

In the last few years, stations and even networks have begun to accept "stand-alone" fifteen-second commercials—that is, commercial announcements that are fifteen seconds long and not connected with any other commercials from the same advertiser. Keep in mind that buying shorter commercials may mean that an advertiser can afford more commercial announcements. This means added repetitions in the advertising schedule.

Measuring the Broadcast Audience

Not many years ago, most homes had only one television set. If anybody in that household was watching television, that television set was on and operating. It was convenient to know what percentage of all the television sets were turned on; this percentage was called **sets-in-use.**

sets-in-use The percentage of television sets that are turned on at a given time.

Sets-in-use does not serve us very well any more, though, because so many homes have more than one television set. Members of the household may all be watching one set, or they may be watching different programs on two or three television sets. So now we use the percentage of **households using television** or **HUT,** that is, the percentage of households with one or more sets operating at any one time.

households using television (HUT) The percentage of households with one or more television sets operating at any one time.

Sets-in-use and households using television both simply measure the percentage of television use, no matter what station, program, or network the sets are tuned to receive. But we would also like to know what percentage of those television sets are tuned in to the program or station where our commercials will appear. Of the households with television on, the percentage tuned to a certain station is the **share of audience** for that station. It is usually just called that station's *share.*

share of audience Of the households whose televisions are on, the percentage tuned to a particular station at a given time.

What if half of all the households using television are watching our program? Is that good? Usually it is, but not always. During prime time, when there is a lot of viewing (so the households using television percentage is high), then a share of 50 percent (one-half) is probably quite good. But early in the morning, few households may be using their television sets, so the same share of 50 percent would mean that many fewer television sets are tuned to our station.

So we need some way to show what percentage of households are watching our station, out of all television households, whether or not their sets are on. This is the **program rating** (usually called the *rating*). Figure 12–1 shows how ratings and shares are determined.

program rating Of the households that own televisions, whether their sets are on or not, the percentage tuned to a particular station at a given time.

Ratings are very useful because they show us the reach of each television program, station, or network. If we have advertisements scheduled on several programs, we can add up the ratings of each program and get the **gross rating points (GRP).** Let's say we have commercials scheduled on four different television programs: The rating of the first program is 18 percent, the rating of the second program is 14 percent, the rating of the third program is 11 percent, and the rating of the fourth program is 9 percent. If we simply add these ratings, we get the gross rating points.

gross rating points (GRP) The combined ratings of several programs that show the same advertisement.

	Rating
1st program	**18**
2nd program	**14**
3rd program	**11**
4th program	**9**
	52 gross rating points (GRP)

Now notice that the average rating of these four programs is 13 percent (52/4 = 13), and since the rating is really the same as the percent of the audience that we reach, our average reach is also 13 percent. Our frequency is the number of times the advertisement appears—in this case 4. If we multiply the frequency by the average reach, we again get gross rating points.

Average reach	**13**
Frequency	**×4**
	52 gross rating points

Gross rating points are valuable advertising tools because they combine both reach and frequency into a single figure. This makes it easier to buy broadcast advertising time.

Of course, we cannot go around to every household to find out if the television set is operating and what station it is tuned to. Instead, we use a sample of the population. Because the sample may not exactly represent the entire population, our figures for HUT, share, and ratings are *percentages,* not numbers of people. We only know what percent of our sample was tuned in to a particular station. But we might like to use those percentage figures to estimate how many people are really in the station's audience. That estimated number of people is called the **projected audience.**

projected audience The estimated number of people watching a station at a given time.

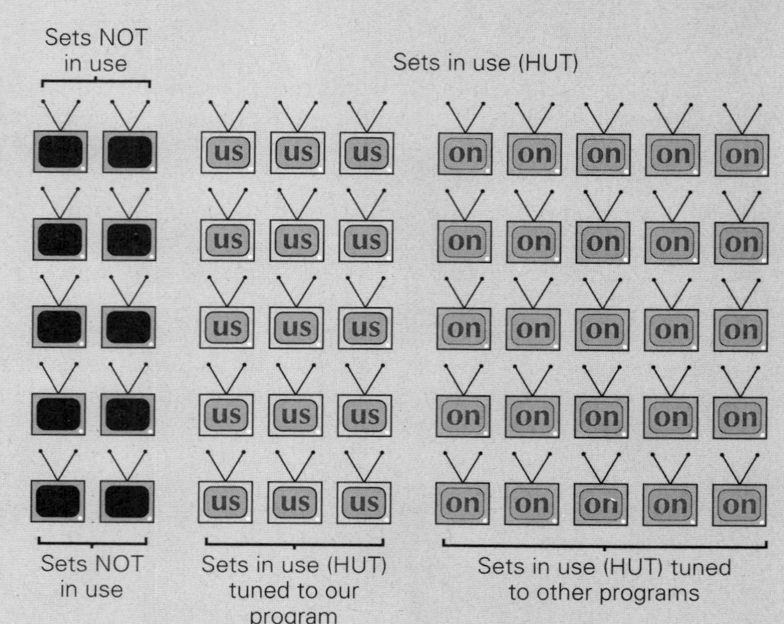

Let's suppose there are fifty television households in a community, represented by the television sets pictured here. Twenty percent of the households are not using their television sets at this particular time. The other 80 percent of the households are using their sets, so the households-using-television (HUT) percentage is 80 percent.

Our program has 30 percent of all television sets, whether they are operating or not, so our rating is 30 percent. But to figure share-of-audience, we must take our 30 percent rating and find out what percentage it is of the 80 percent HUT; 30/80 = 37.5% share.

If you want to count the individual sets in the illustration, here are the totals you get:

40 of 50 sets are operating, so 40/50 = 80% HUT;
15 of 50 sets are operating and turned to our program, so 15/50 = 30% rating;
15 of the 40 operating sets are tuned to our program, so 15/40 = 37.5% share.

Do these calculations for yourself to see how we got the answers. If you have questions, go through the definitions in this chapter again.

FIGURE 12–1
Estimating a rating and a share in broadcast media.

Costs of Buying Television Advertising

To compare two or more television stations' advertising costs, we use the same *cost per thousand (CPM)* method we used for magazines. However, CPM is not quite as simple to use in broadcast as it is in print media, mainly because TV doesn't have a clear-cut circulation (number of copies distributed) as magazines and newspapers have. Instead, we must estimate the number of people in the audience.

Another problem is that the sixty-second commercial was once the standard television advertising unit, but thirty-second commercials are now more common. Therefore, we must decide what length of commercial we may use before we know which advertising rate to enter into our CPM calculations.

Basically, however, the CPM formula does not change very much. It reads:

$$\text{CPM (Broadcast)} = \frac{\text{Cost of a commercial}}{\text{Audience size}} \times 1{,}000$$

To figure our broadcast cost per thousand, we start with the cost of a commercial of the length we intend to use (sixty-second, thirty-second, or whatever). Then we divide by the size of the audience to find out how much it costs to advertise to each listener, and finally we multiply by 1,000 to get the advertising cost per thousand listeners. Figure 12–2 shows how CPM is used in television advertising.

Like magazines and newspapers, television and radio station also have complex systems of rate discounts. There are *quantity discounts* for buying a lot of advertising time and *frequency discounts* for buying a lot of commercials. These discounts work in much the same way as the discounts from magazines.

There are other ways to save money with television advertising, too. The regular price of advertising time is called the **fixed rate,** because it does not change. But some advertisers risk buying advertising time for which no other advertiser is willing to pay the fixed rate. Then a lower **pre-emptible rate** is charged. But if an advertiser reserves a certain advertising time at the pre-emptible rate, another advertiser may come along and pre-empt that advertising time by offering to pay the fixed rate.

fixed rate The regular price of a commercial.

pre-emptible rate A lower rate applied to commercial time for which no one is willing to pay the fixed rate.

Buying Television Time

As we noted earlier in this chapter, relatively few advertisers can afford the expensive network television commercials. There are only three major television networks (plus some smaller special-purpose and cable networks) and perhaps only 150 to 200 advertisers who regularly use network television. The networks and advertisers therefore negotiate their advertising rates. Larger advertisers may be able to get more economical discounted rates than smaller occasional advertisers can negotiate. Because each rate is negotiated, there is no source of information such as the *Standard Rate and Data Service* (SRDS), discussed in Chapter 11, to help you find advertising rates for network television. You must contact the networks to begin buying advertising time and negotiating on the prices.

You are advertising in a market that has about 400,000 people. Suppose you are considering two television stations for a 30-second commerical that is to appear at 8:30 p.m.

Station A	**Station B**
8:30 p.m. rating = 18%	8:30 p.m. rating = 16%
Cost of a 30-second commercial at 8:30p.m. = $530	Cost of a 30-second commercial at 8:30p.m. = $470
(18% of 400,000 people = 72,000)	(16% of 400,000 people = 64,000)

$$\text{CPM} = \frac{\text{Advertising rate}}{\text{Audience size}} \times 1{,}000$$

Station A	Station B
$\text{CPM} = \frac{\$530}{72{,}000} \times 1{,}000$	$\text{CPM} = \frac{\$470}{64{,}000} \times 1{,}000$
CPM = 0.0073611 × 1,000	CPM = 0.0073437 × 1,000
CPM = $7.36	CPM = $7.34

So Station B is more economical. It costs $7.34 to reach each 1,000 people with your 30-second commercial on Station B, while it costs $7.36 for each 1,000 people on Station A.

FIGURE 12–2
Using cost per thousand (CPM) to compare the cost of advertising on two television stations.

rate card A card published by television stations that lists their advertising prices.

However, SRDS can help you find local advertising rates on individual television stations. Each station bases its rates on the demand for its advertising time and the size of its audience. The station usually publishes a **rate card** of advertising rate information; this same information may also appear in the SRDS volume for "spot television." In addition, SRDS can provide the location, telephone number, and other information you need to buy television advertising time from the station. Figure 12–3 shows a sample SRDS listing for a television station.

Television stations may not use the same terms the networks use for various time categories. Instead of prime, fringe, and similar terms, the stations often use letter categories, such as A, B, and C. When this system started, Class A was the highest rated (and most expensive) commercial time, Class B was next, and so on. Some stations compound the problem by using Class AAA for the best time, Class AA for their next best time, and then Class A, Class B, and so on. As we noted at the beginning of this chapter, stations have no standard time categories; some stations use numbers instead of letters for

KENTUCKY

Lexington—cont

WLEX-TV—cont

3. FACILITIES
Video 1,104,000 w., audio 220,800 w.; ch 18.
Antenna ht.: 649 ft. above average terrain.
Operating schedule: 6-2 am. EST.

4. AGENCY COMMISSION
15% to recognized agencies on time only, except as specified in contract.

5. GENERAL ADVERTISING See coded regulations
General: 2a, 3d, 4a, 5, 6a, 7b, 8.
Rate Protection: 10m, 11m, 12m, 13m, 14m, 15.
Contracts: 20a, 21, 22a, 25, 26, 27e, 29, 30, 31b, 32b, 34e.
Basic Rates: 40b, 41a, 41c, 41d, 43a, 45a, 46, 47a, 47g, 47i, 47j, 47k, 51.
Comb.; Cont. Discounts: 60a, 62b.
Cancellation: 70b, 70j, 72, 73a.
Prod. Services: 80, 83, 84, 86, 87b.
Affiliated with NBC Television Network.

6. TIME RATES
No. 55 Eff 3/1/88—Rec'd 3/9/88.
No. 35 Prog. rates eff 10/1/87—Rec'd 10/1/87.

7. SPOT ANNOUNCEMENTS
30 SECONDS

	Section 1	2	3	4	5	6	7
MON THRU FRI, AM:							
6-6:30, NBC Sunrise	75	60	50	45	35	30	25
6:30-7, Kentucky Sunrise	100	90	75	60	50	45	35
7-9, Today Show	125	100	90	75	60	50	45
9-10, Phil Donahue	90	75	60	50	45	35	30
10-noon, AM Rotator	90	75	60	50	45	35	30
PM:							
Noon-12:30, Noon Today	125	100	90	75	60	50	45
1-4, Soap Rotator	125	100	90	75	60	50	45
4-4:30, The Judge	100	90	75	60	50	45	35
4:30-5, Superior Court	100	90	75	60	50	45	35
5-5:30, People's Court	175	150	125	100	90	75	60
4-5:30, Judge/Superior Court/People's Court	125	100	90	75	60	50	45
5:30-6:30, 18 News	250	225	200	175	150	125	100
7-7:30, Newlywed Game	300	250	225	200	175	150	125
7:30-8, New Dating Game	300	250	225	200	175	150	125
7-8, Newlywed/Dating Game	300	250	225	200	175	150	125
11-11:30 Mon thru Sun, 18-News	300	250	225	200	175	150	125
11:30 pm-12:30 am, Tonight	150	125	100	90	75	60	50
12:30-1:30 am, Letterman	75	60	50	45	35	30	25
1:30-2:30 am, Friday Night Videos	75	60	50	45	35	30	25
1:30-2 am Mon thru Thurs, Sally Jessy Raphel	75	60	50	45	35	30	25
2-2:30 am Mon thru Thurs, 18-News Repeat	75	60	50	45	35	30	25
2:30-3 am Fri, Cats, Cox & Combs	75	60	50	45	35	30	25
3-3:30 Fri, Sally Jesse Raphael	75	60	50	45	35	30	25
3:30-4 am Fri, 18-News Repeat	75	60	50	45	35	30	25
SAT, AM:							
6:30-7, Farming w/ Jack Crowner	75	60	50	45	35	30	25
7-7:30, Young Universe	75	60	50	45	35	30	25
7:30-8, Muppet Show	75	60	50	45	35	30	25
8-10:30, Kid-Vid	175	150	125	100	90	75	60
10:30-11:30, Championship Wrestling	175	150	125	100	90	75	60
11:30-noon, Winner's Circle	150	125	100	90	75	60	50
PM:							
Noon-12:30, Lorne Greene's New Wilderness	175	150	125	100	90	75	60
12:30-1, In The Know	175	150	125	100	90	75	60
1-6, Movies/Sports	75	60	50	45	35	30	25
6-6:30, 18 News	150	125	100	90	75	60	50
6:30-7, NBC News	175	150	125	100	90	75	60
7-8, Specials	150	125	100	90	75	60	50
11:30 pm-1 am, Saturday Night Live	125	100	90	75	60	50	45
1-2 am, G.L.O.W.	75	60	50	45	35	30	25
SUN, AM:							
6-6:30, Education Notebook	75	60	50	45	35	30	25
6:30-10, Religion	75	60	50	45	35	30	25
10-10:30, In The Know	175	150	125	100	90	75	60
10:30-11:30, Religion	75	60	50	45	35	30	25
11:30-noon, Public Affairs	100	90	75	60	50	45	35
PM:							
Noon-12:30, Your Government	150	125	100	90	75	60	50
12:30-1, Meet The Press	100	90	75	60	50	45	35
1-6:30, Sports/Movies	75	60	50	45	35	30	25
6:30-7, NBC News	175	150	125	100	90	75	60
11:30 pm-12:30 am, Big Valley	75	60	50	45	35	30	25
12:30-1 am, 18 News Repeat	75	60	50	45	35	30	25
PRIME TIME							
MON:							
8-9, Alf/Valerie	1500	1000	800	600	500	400	300
9-11, NBC Movie	1500	1000	800	600	500	400	300
TUES:							
8-9, Matlock	1500	1000	800	600	500	400	300
9-10, Heat of the Night	1500	1000	800	600	500	400	300
10-11, Crime Story	1500	1000	800	600	500	400	300
WED:							
8-9, Aaron's Way	1500	1000	800	600	500	400	300
9-10, A Year In The Life	1500	1000	800	600	500	400	300
10-11, Bronx Zoo	1500	1000	800	600	500	400	300
THURS:							
8-9, Cosby/Different World	2500	2000	1500	1000	800	600	500
9-10, Cheers/Night Court	1500	1000	800	600	500	400	300
10-11, L.A. Law	1500	1000	800	600	500	400	300
FRI:							
8-9, Highway Man	1500	1000	800	600	500	400	300
9-10, Miami Vice	1500	1000	800	600	500	400	300
10-11, Sonny Spoon	1500	1000	800	600	500	400	300
SAT:							
8-9, Facts/227	1500	1000	800	600	500	400	300
9-10, Golden Girls/Amen	1500	1000	800	600	500	400	300
10-11, Hunter	1500	1000	800	600	500	400	300
SUN:							
7-8, Our House	1500	1000	800	600	500	400	300
8-9, Ties/Day By Day	1500	1000	800	600	500	400	300
9-11, NBC Movie	1500	1000	800	600	500	400	300

60 sec: twice the 30 sec.
10 sec: 50% of 30 sec, rounded up to nearest dollar.

10. PROGRAM TIME RATES
AA—Mon thru Sun 8-11 pm.
A—Mon thru Sun 6-8 pm.
B—Mon thru Sun 1-6 pm & 11 pm-midnight.
C—Mon thru Fri sign-on-1 pm.
D—Sat & Sun sign-on-1 pm; Mon thru Sun midnight-sign-off.

	1 hr	1/2 hr	1/4 hr	10 min	5 min
AA	4500	2700	1620	1295	1035
A	3630	2180	1305	1045	835
B	2860	1715	1030	825	660
C	2200	1320	795	635	505
D	935	560	335	270	215

11. SPECIAL FEATURES
COLOR
Schedules network color, film, slides, tape and live.
Equipped with high and low band VTR.

13. CLOSING TIME
48 hours prior film slide; 72 hours artwork.

WLKT-TV

(Airdate January 1, 1988)
LEXINGTON

Media Code 6 218 0162 0.00 **Mid 043980-000**
Family Group Broadcasting Operating, L. P.
124 New Circle Rd., N.E., Lexington, KY 40505.

WTVQ-TV

(Airdate June 2, 1968)
LEXINGTON

Katz Continental

NAB TvB

A Shamrock Broadcasting Co.

Media Code 6 218 0175 2.00 **Mid 007449-000**
WTVQ-TV Inc.
2940 Bryant Rd., Lexington, KY 40509. Phone 606-233-3600. TWX, 510-476-8806.
Mailing Address: Box 5590, Lexington, KY 40555.

1. PERSONNEL
Vice-Pres. & Gen'l Mgr.—William Service.
General Sales Manager—Jeb Baker.
Station Manager—Jerry W. Fox.

2. REPRESENTATIVES
Katz Television. Continental.

3. FACILITIES
Video 2,150,000 w., audio 215,000 w.; ch 36.
Antenna ht.: 1,002 ft. above average terrain.
Operating schedule: ———. EST.

4. AGENCY COMMISSION
15/0 to recognized agencies on time only.

5. GENERAL ADVERTISING See coded regulations
General: 2a, 2b, 3a, 3d, 4a, 5, 6a, 7b, 9.
Rate Protection: 10h, 11h, 12h, 13h, 14h, 15, 16c.
Contracts: 20a, 21, 22a, 25, 26, 27e, 31b, 31c, 32b, 32d, 34b, 34d.
Basic Rates: 40b, 41a, 41c, 41d, 45a, 46, 47a, 47c, 47j, 47k, 49, 51.
Comb.; Cont. Discounts: 60a, 62b.
Cancellation: 70b, 70g, 71, 72, 73b.
Prod. Services: 80, 83, 84, 85, 86, 87a, 87b, 87c.
Affiliated with ABC Television Network.

6. TIME RATES
Rates have been temporarily withdrawn by station.

11. SPECIAL FEATURES
COLOR
Schedules network color, film, tape, slides and live.
Equipped with high and low band VTR.

13. CLOSING TIME
48 hours prior to scheduled telecast.

WYMT-TV

(Airdate October 20, 1969)
HAZARD

NAB TvB

Media Code 6 218 0187 7.00 **Mid 038551-000**
U.S. 15 By-Pass, Hazard, KY 41701. Phone 606-436-5757.
Mailing Address: Box 1299, Hazard, KY 41701.

1. PERSONNEL
Vice-Pres. & Gen'l Mgr.—Ralph Gabbard.
Station Manager—Wayne M. Martin.
General Sales Manager—Kevin Kidd.

2. REPRESENTATIVES
Mutual Telesales, Inc.

3. FACILITIES
Video 1,350,000 w., audio 675,000 w.; ch 57.
Antenna ht.: 1,029 ft. above average terrain.
Operating schedule: 6-1:30 am. EST.

4. AGENCY COMMISSION
15/0 to recognized agencies on time; 10th of month.

5. GENERAL ADVERTISING See coded regulations
Affiliated with CBS Television Network.

6. TIME RATES
No. 2/A Eff 3/28/88—Rec'd 3/15/88.

7. SPOT ANNOUNCEMENTS
30 SECONDS

	F1	*D1	*D2	*D3
MON THRU FRI, AM:				
6-9, CBS Morning News	30	28	24	22
6-noon, AM Rotator	38	34	30	26
9 am-4 pm, Daytime Rotator	45	40	36	34
PM:				
Noon-12:30, Noon News	60	55	50	45
12:30-5:30, PM Rotator	52	48	44	40
4-4:30, My Three Sons	50	45	41	39
4:30-5, Leave it to Beaver	55	50	44	42
5-5:30, I Love Lucy	60	55	47	43
5:30-6:30, Mountain News	160	150	140	135
7-8, Gunsmoke	90	85	80	75
7-11 Mon thru Sun, Prime Rotator	115	110	105	100
11-11:30 Mon thru Sat, Mountain News	110	100	95	90
11-11:30 Sun, Mountain News/CBS News	85	75	70	65
11:30 pm-1 am Mon thru Sun, Late Night	40	32	24	22
SAT, AM:				
8-11:30, CBS Cartoons/Kids Songs	30	28	24	22
11:30-noon, Goins Brothers Show	85	83	81	79
PM:				
Noon-1, USA Wrestling	75	65	55	45
1-6, Various Sports	75	70	65	60
6-7, Hee Haw	75	70	65	60
SUN:				
7 am-noon, Religious/Public Affairs	25	23	21	20
PM:				
Noon-7, Various Sports	75	70	65	60
PRIME TIME				
MON:				
8-9, Kate & Allie/Designing Women	160	150	140	130
9-10, Newhart/Eisenhower & Lutz	130	125	120	115
10-11, Wiseguy	130	125	120	115
TUES:				
8-9, Trial & Error/The Dictator	100	95	90	85
9-10, Coming of Age/Frank's Place	120	115	110	105
10-11, Cagney & Lacey	130	125	120	115
WED:				
8-9, Magnum P. I.	140	135	130	125
9-10, Jake & the Fat Man	130	120	110	100
10-11, Equalizer	140	135	130	125
THURS:				
8-9, 48 Hours	100	90	80	70
9-10, Simon & Simon	155	150	145	140
10-11, Knots Landing	225	200	175	150
FRI:				
8-9, Beauty And The Beast	175	170	145	140
9-10, Dallas	360	330	250	200
10-11, Falcon Crest	225	200	175	150
SAT:				
7-8, WWF Wrestling	100	95	90	85
8-9, High Mountain Rangers	100	95	90	85
9-10, Tour of Duty	120	115	110	105
10-11, West 57th	140	135	130	125
SUN:				
7-8, 60 Minutes	250	200	150	100
8-9, Murder She Wrote	200	175	150	100
9-11, CBS Sunday Movie	170	165	160	155

(*) 2x/wk use D1, 3x/wk use D2, 4+x/wk use D3.
60 sec: 2x 30 sec.
10 sec: 50% of 30 sec.

11. SPECIAL FEATURES
COLOR
Schedules network color, slides, tape and live.
Equipped with 3/4" cassette only.

Louisville

Jefferson County—Map Location E-4
See SRDS Consumer market map and data at beginning of the state.

WAVE-TV

WAVE 3

(Airdate November 24, 1948)
LOUISVILLE

MMT SALES DIVISION

NAB TvB

A Cosmos Broadcasting Corporation Station

Media Code 6 218 0200 8.00 **Mid 007450-000**
Cosmos Broadcasting Corp.
725 S. Floyd St., Louisville, KY 40203. Phone 502-585-2201, TWX, 810-535-3142.
Mailing Address: Box 32970, Louisville, KY 40232.

1. PERSONNEL
Vice-Pres. & Gen'l Mgr.—Guy W. Hempel.
General Sales Manager—Steve Langford.
National Sales Manager—Nick Ulmer.

2. REPRESENTATIVES
MMT Sales, Inc., MMT Sales Division.

3. FACILITIES
Video 100,000 w., audio 20,000 w.; ch. 3.
Antenna ht.: 914 ft. above average terrain.
Operating schedule: 6-2 am. EST.

4. AGENCY COMMISSION
15/0 to recognized agencies.

5. GENERAL ADVERTISING See coded regulations
General: 2a, 3a, 3d, 4a, 5, 6b, 7b, 8.
Rate Protection: 10f, 11h, 14c, 15, 16, 16a, 17.
Contracts: 20c, 21, 22a, 22c, 23, 25, 26, 27d, 28, 31a, 31b, 31c, 32a, 32d, 34g.
Basic Rates: 40b, 41a, 41c, 42, 45a, 46, 47a, 51, 51f, 52, 52a.
Comb.; Cont. Discounts: 60b, 60f, 62b.
Cancellation: 70a, 70j, 71, 72, 73a, 73b.
Prod. Services: 81, 83, 84, 86, 87c.
Advertising of hard liquors not accepted.
Priority of Station Break Announcements
Station will accept spots in lengths from 60-sec down to station id's in specified locations as designated by the station. Spots sold in positions that differ from the station designated for that location will be subject to move with 1 wks notice to a location designated to accommodate the type spot in question.
Affiliated with NBC Television Network.

6. TIME RATES
Rates have been temporarily withdrawn by station.

11. SPECIAL FEATURES
COLOR
Schedules network color, film, slides, tape and live.
Equipped with 1" high and low band VTR plus 3/4" cassette.

13. CLOSING TIME
72 hours prior commercial copy, either film, slides or audio copy.

WDRB-TV

(Airdate February 28, 1971)
LOUISVILLE

PETRY

NAB TvB

Media Code 6 218 0225 5.00 **Mid 007451-000**
Independence Broadcasting Co.
Independence Sq., 624 Muhammad Ali Blvd., Louisville, KY 40203. Phone 502-584-6441, TWX, 810-535-3328.

1. PERSONNEL
Pres. & Gen'l Mgr.—Elmer F. Jaspan.
General Sales Manager—Jerry Staggs.
Local Sales Manager—Jack Flatterman.

2. REPRESENTATIVES
Petry National Television.

3. FACILITIES
Video 1,146,000 w., audio 114,600 w.; ch 41.
Antenna ht.: 1,280 ft. above average terrain.
Operating schedule: 6-3 am Mon-Fri; 8-1 am Sat; 6-12:30 am Sun. EST.

4. AGENCY COMMISSION
15/0 to recognized agencies on time; 10th of month.

5. GENERAL ADVERTISING See coded regulations
General: 2a, 3a, 4a, 5, 6a, 7b, 8.
Rate Protection: 14f, 16a.
Contracts: 20a, 21, 22a, 26, 27a, 32a.
Basic Rates: 40b, 41b, 41c, 41d, 42, 43a, 46, 50, 51.
Comb.; Cont. Discounts: 60c, 60f, 62b.
Cancellation: 70b, 70f, 71, 72, 73b.
Prod. Services: 83, 84, 85, 86, 87c.
Product Protection
Station uses its best efforts to separate competitive products.
For children's, political and motion picture advertising, station will endeavor to provide separation, but none is guaranteed.
Affiliated with Fox Broadcasting Company.
Member of INTV.

6. TIME RATES
Prog. rates eff———Rec'd 10/12/84.

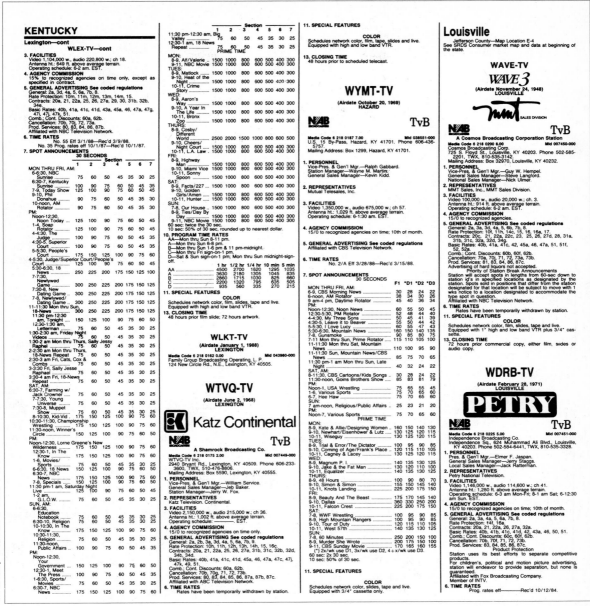

FIGURE 12–3
Sample listing from SRDS for a television station.

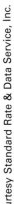

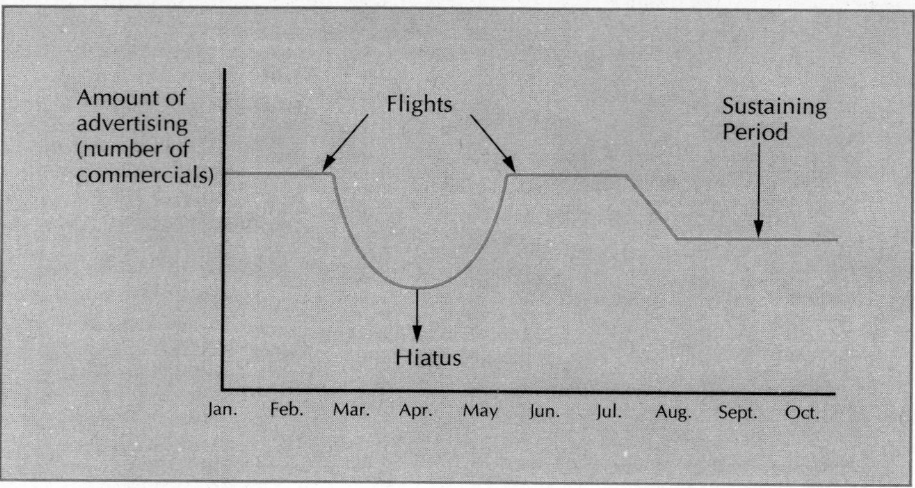

FIGURE 12–4
Diagram of a typical advertising schedule in a wave pattern.

their rate designations. This means that we must be sure we know what we're buying when we consider using local television stations for our advertising.

Advertising Patterns

Because almost everybody watches television, it is easy to achieve a lot of frequency by repeating commercials over and over. But there can be *too much* frequency. If people see your commercial too often, they may become irritated with it. This **irritation factor** can "turn off" your audience and keep them from buying your product or service. Irritation is not as critical with most other media, because it is easier for the audience members to avoid seeing or reading an advertisement over and over again simply by turning the page or paying attention to something else. In television, however, we must constantly be wary of irritating our audience with our advertising.

irritation factor The irritation caused by a commercial that is repeated too often.

flight A period of heavy advertising.

hiatus A period of no advertising.

wave pattern A pattern of alternating flight and hiatus periods.

sustaining period A period of reduced advertising following a period of heavy advertising.

One way to reduce irritation is by advertising in *waves.* Instead of using the same amount of advertising for a long period of time, we may run a lot of commercials at first and then advertise less for a while. The heavy advertising period is the **flight** and the period of no advertising is the **hiatus.** Because of the way the advertising patterns look when we diagram them, as shown in Figure 12–4, the use of alternating flight and hiatus periods is called a **wave pattern.** For a new product, we might advertise heavily for a while and then reduce our advertising a bit to economize and to avoid irritating our audience, but we still keep advertising; this would be a **sustaining period** of advertising.

Cable Television

Because some areas of the United States do not receive regular television broadcasts very well, a community antenna television (CATV) system was devised to use a tall tower to pick up television broadcasts from far away; these signals are then distributed throughout the community on wired cables. Cable systems can also bring many stations' signals into a community, making cable television popular even in areas with strong television reception. Many communities can now subscribe to special noncommercial cable television networks, such as HBO and Showtime, for a monthly fee, as well as to commercial networks such as ESPN and USA.

The extra listeners that a station gains over cable systems may be a bonus for the advertiser. But advertisers must also be wary of towns that have television stations and cable systems in the same community; the audience may watch television programs from faraway stations instead of from the local stations, so an advertiser on the local station may not be reaching a substantial portion of the television households in that locale. Another potential problem is that the ratings estimates of the size of the cable television audience are incomplete and still relatively new, so it is impossible to know precisely how many persons viewed a cable advertisement. Cable and other changes in television bring increasing complications to our use of television as an advertising channel.

RADIO ADVERTISING

We use radio advertising in much the same way as we use television advertising. There are, of course, some important differences. Local radio stations often originate their own programs rather than rely on network programs, so networks have become less important in radio while they have become more important in television. But in the way advertising rates are set and the ways audience sizes are researched and calculated, radio is similar to television.

Comparisons with Television

There is no prime time in the evenings on radio. Most radio listening occurs during **drive time** when people are driving to and from work. Usually the morning drive time lasts from about 7:30 until 9:30, and the afternoon drive time lasts from 4:30 until 6:00. These times may vary from one area to another, depending on work patterns and schedules. In some communities with lots of industrial plants, the **shift time** when factories change their working shifts may have more in-car radio listening than the normal drive times. Figure 12–5 compares radio-listening and television-viewing patterns.

drive time The radio-listening period when people are driving to and from work.

shift time The radio-listening period when factory workers are changing shifts.

Other popular radio-listening times occur during morning and noon news and special sports broadcasts. Some radio stations have talk shows or call-in shows that may attract a late-night audience, too. Radio ratings information resembles the share of audience and program-rating information used for television. We use the term **households using radio** (**HUR**) to show what percent of the homes have a radio in operation.

households using radio (HUR) The percentage of households with a radio in operation.

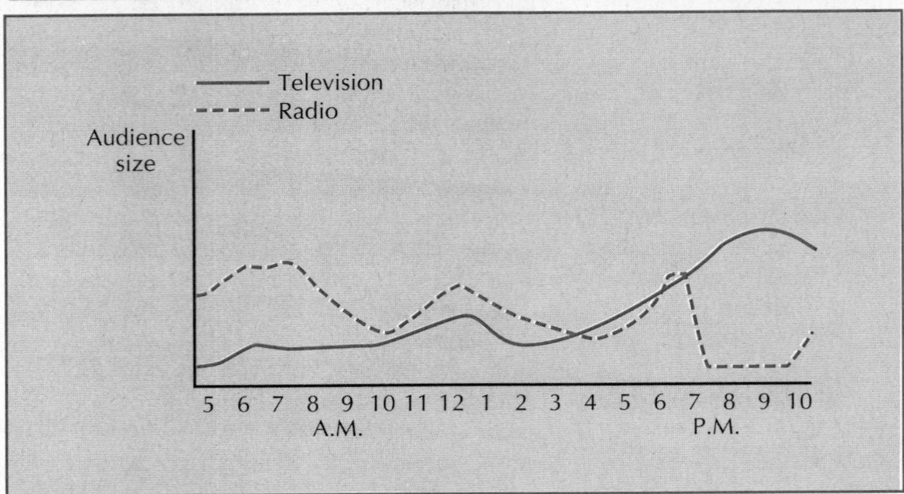

FIGURE 12–5
Typical patterns of radio listening and television viewing throughout a normal broadcast day.

For spot (local) radio advertising rates, we can usually refer to *Standard Rate and Data Service* or to the stations' own advertising rate cards. But, as with television, network radio advertising rates are negotiated directly with the networks.

Advertisers Should Use Radio Properly

We already know that newspapers are the most popular advertising medium for local retailers. Radio is popular for local retail advertising, too, because of its relatively low cost and its localized coverage.

Many retailers use newspapers quite wisely for advertising. They advertise on certain days of the week to reach the audience at the best shopping time for their particular merchandise. With radio, however, many retailers mistakenly buy steady blocks of the same amount of advertising each day instead of on the best selling days. Actually, the best retail use of radio should resemble advertising patterns in newspapers: Put most of the budget into the biggest selling days instead of using the same amount of advertising day after day.

If retailers use radio properly for promoting their best selling days, the store will benefit from advertising that is low in cost and that provides good coverage of the local area. In addition, the proper patterns will also provide good frequency of advertising on the most important selling days without wasted advertising on poorer selling days. Table 12–2 sums up the advantages and disadvantages of radio advertising.

Radio as a Supplement to Other Media

Both retailers and other advertisers can use radio to supplement their other advertising efforts. Instead of spending all their advertising budget in televi-

TABLE 12–2 Advantages and disadvantages of advertising on radio.

Advantages

1. Radio is flexible, because advertisements can run almost any time and on short advance notice.
2. It is economical.
3. It can be listened to in all rooms and locations.
4. It can reach specialized and ethnic markets.
5. It provides good daily continuity.
6. It can make good use of slogans, jingles, and music.
7. It covers the cities and suburban areas, often better than newspapers do.
8. There is no competition with the advertisement when it is on the air.

Disadvantages

1. The message is gone as soon as it is over, so it is perishable.
2. You must deal with each individual station, and the rate policies may all be different.
3. It is easy for listeners to ignore the advertisements.

sion, for example, they may be able to shift some of their money into radio advertising. Some people may hear radio advertisements who do not watch much television, so this will increase the overall reach. And at the same time, advertisers may be able to increase frequency as well because radio advertising is usually much less expensive than television advertising. So in this way, advertisers can achieve lots of impact with television and gain additional reach and frequency by combining television with radio.

Radio often works well with newspaper and magazine advertising, too, as well as with the other kinds of advertising channels that we shall discuss in the next chapter. Radio can be a strong advertising asset when used by itself, but as with many kinds of advertising media, radio can contribute quite well when used in a **media mix** or combination of advertising media.

media mix A combination of advertising media.

SUMMARY

Broadcast media are much more complicated than print media. Not only can an advertiser choose a particular day, but also the time of day and the type of program environment in which an advertisement will appear.

Broadcast media are relatively inexpensive on a cost-per-thousand basis, but because of the large audience sizes involved, advertising in radio and especially television can be an expensive decision for an advertiser. The calculations involved in figuring the sizes of the audiences can also complicate the situation. These two media have so many competitive advantages, however, that they are widely used by many kinds of advertisers.

New developments, such as cable television and home video viewing, make the broadcast industry an ever-changing part of the advertising media business.

TERMS TO KNOW

Now that you have finished this chapter, you should understand the following items:

network television
local television
prime time
fringe time
day time
late night time
sponsor
participation
spot advertising
sets-in-use
households using television (HUT)
share of audience
program rating
gross rating points (GRP)
projected audience
fixed rate
pre-emptible rate
rate card
irritation factor
flight
hiatus
wave pattern
sustaining period
drive time
shift time
households using radio (HUR)
media mix

If you are not certain of the meaning of any of these terms, go back through the chapter and review them.

THINGS TO THINK ABOUT

1. Why are time periods (such as prime time in television, and drive time in radio) important?
2. What is a rating? A share? HUT? How are they related to one another?
3. Why is the projected audience important? How does it differ from rating and share?
4. Describe the differences between local spot broadcast advertising and network broadcast advertising?
5. How does the discount system work with broadcast advertising rates?
6. What are the advantages and disadvantages of television to advertisers? Or radio?

THINGS TO TALK ABOUT

1. Why has television been growing in popularity? In advertising revenue? In number of channels available? What has been happening to radio at the same time?
2. Why is rating an easier concept to use than share of audience? How are these two concepts similar, and how are they different?
3. What does the irritation factor mean to broadcast advertisers?
4. How can local retailers best make use of broadcast advertising?
5. Why is it difficult to determine the size of broadcast audiences?
6. Why is it both an advertising advantage and disadvantage that the broadcaster controls what is programmed by each station?
7. What are gross rating points? Why is the concept of gross-rating points so useful in advertising?

THINGS TO DO

1. Visit a nearby radio or television station and get an advertising rate card.
2. Invite a local broadcaster to talk with you about the importance of ratings in broadcast advertising.
3. Make a list of the major radio stations in your area, along with the kind of programming (kinds of music, use of news, sports emphasis, and so on) that each station features. What kinds of people do you think listen to each station? What products and services are advertised on each station? Do you see any patterns?

13 Other Media

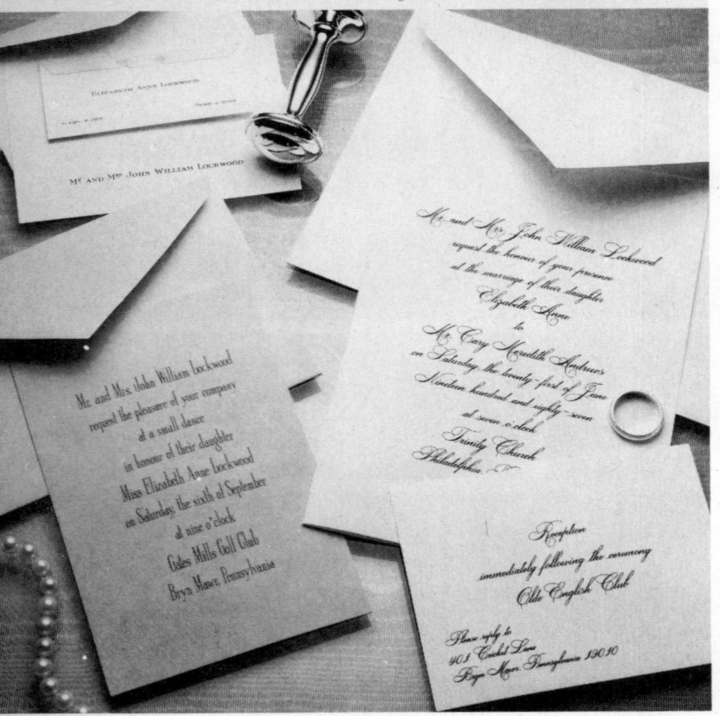
When it happens only once in a lifetime, it should be indelibly engraved for all time.
A child is born and a lifetime of special events begins. Some so important, they are etched in one's memory forever. These are the occasions that deserve to be recorded on nothing less than Crane.
Crane announcements and invitations are as distinctive as the events they help celebrate. Like all Crane papers they are made of 100% cotton fiber which makes them not only beautiful but enduring.
Thus, it comes as no surprise that when the event is unforgettable, Crane is so often chosen to be the paper the memories are made of.
Crane & Co., Inc., Dalton, Mass. 01226.
Crane
We've been taking your words seriously for 186 years.
Mr and Mrs John William Lockwood
request the pleasure of your company
at a small dance
in honour of their daughter
Miss Elizabeth Anne Lockwood
on Saturday, the sixth of September
at nine o'clock
Gates Mills Golf Club
Bryn Mawr, Pennsylvania

Courtesy of Crane and Company, Inc.

CHAPTER OUTLINE

By the time you finish this chapter, you should understand:

1. **How direct mail advertising is bought and used.**
2. **How specialty advertising is bought and used.**
3. **How outdoor advertising is bought and used.**
4. **How transit advertising is bought and used.**
5. **How point-of-purchase advertising is bought and used.**
6. **That many other kinds of channels are available to advertisers.**

You probably know more about newspapers, magazines, radio, television than you do about any other advertising media, because you may not see these other media as often. But they are important communication channels that represent a large and ever-growing part of the advertising business.

DIRECT MAIL

The term **direct mail** is the traditional term for both advertisements and merchandise orders sent directly through the mail. Now we use **direct marketing** to talk about all kinds of selling that go directly to the consumer or buyer instead of through some other channel. And we use this same term to talk about advertising in another medium that asks the customer to order directly through the mail or by telephone rather than buy from a retail store or elsewhere. We also call this direct marketing advertising, as you learned in Chapter 8, "Copywriting for Other Media." Table 13–1 lists some advantages and disadvantages of direct mail advertising.

direct mail The traditional term for advertising and merchandise orders sent directly through the mail.

direct marketing Selling directly from seller to buyer.

Many Factors in Direct Mail Costs

There are many costs involved in direct mail advertising: printing and paper, postage and design, preparation or purchase of a mailing list, and even fulfillment (that is, responding to inquiries, filling orders, and so on). When we think about direct mail costs in this way, our cost per thousand (CPM) is rather high when compared with other media. But keep in mind that we can use the mail to direct each advertisement to people we know are prospective customers, so there is little waste circulation in a good mailing. And reducing waste means that our **cost per prospect** may actually be less in direct mail than in media that are not this selective.

Some people think of direct mail advertising as "junk mail." However, junk mail is usually advertising that reaches lots of people who are not good prospects for the offer. Advertisements sent to people on a selective mailing list will be less likely to seem like "junk" to the people who receive them.

More important than the cost of the mailing is the **cost per return**, the amount of advertising costs spent for each order we receive from our mailing.

cost per prospect The cost of advertising to each prospective customer.

cost per return The amount of advertising costs spent for each order received.

TABLE 13–1 Advantages and disadvantages of advertising in direct mail.

Advantages

1. The advertiser selects who will receive advertisments.
2. The advertiser completely controls speed and timing.
3. Flexible formats are possible, with color, premiums, smells, samples.
4. The direct mail advertiser can involve the customer, by including a pencil or return card.
5. No waste circulation is necessary.
6. Message can be personalized.

Disadvantages

1. Direct mail can be expensive.
2. It is difficult to maintain mailing list addresses.
3. There is no editorial or entertainment to attract audience.
4. Customers may think of it as "junk mail."

Because we can be quite selective with direct mail, and thus reduce waste circulation, we may get more returns per thousand people who receive our mailing than we might from less selective media. So our cost per return from direct mail can be economical. Of course, the more expensive the product or service being offered, the lower the rate of orders that will come in for that offer. But that is true in any medium.

bulk rate The postal rate for third class mail.

Another cost to consider is the postage itself. Some advertisers try to save money by using the **bulk rate** available for third-class mail. This bulk rate is much less expensive than regular first-class letters, but it is delivered more slowly, and it is more likely to be discarded by the recipient because it looks like junk mail. For these reasons, it may actually be more economical to use first-class mail rates, because the receiver of the letter is more likely to open it and read it. And third-class mail must be presorted by the sender, whereas first-class mail will be sorted by the postal service.

Building a Mailing List

list brokers People who prepare and rent out mailing lists.

There are several ways to get mailing lists that have the names and addresses of certain kinds of people who may be good prospects. One way is to get mailing lists prepared by **list brokers** who will rent the names and addresses to you for a certain amount; usually there is a charge for each thousand addresses, and you must pay each time you use the mailing list. You can locate these lists by contacting the list brokers, or you can refer to the *Standard Rate and Data Service* volume on direct mail that provides much of the same information.

Retail stores often get their mailing lists by using their list of customers, which they may be able to prepare by going through sales receipts. Many retailers use lists of their charge account customers, and they may reduce the costs of direct-mail advertising by inserting the advertising materials with the monthly bills they send to customers. You can also build a mailing list from a simple contest that requires entrants to fill in an entry blank. But you must take care to see that the contest relates directly to the merchandise line so the prospects are really interested in what is for sale. Contests also have legal restrictions that vary from state to state, and you must consider these laws when planning a contest promotion.

When to Mail

When you mail an advertisement is not as important as when your customer receives it. For example, Monday is the heaviest day for receiving mail; the preceding weekend's mail arrives then, along with many magazines. So Monday would be a poor day for a direct-mail advertisement to arrive because it must compete for attention with all the other mail. If mail is sent to a business office, then try to time it for Tuesday or even later in the week. And if you send mail to people's homes, time it to arrive toward the end of the week, if possible. Of course, it is easier to predict when first-class mail will be delivered than third-class.

Certain times of the year are better for using direct mail, too. The winter months of January and February provide fewer outside distractions, so a direct-mail advertisement may receive more attention. But the spring months from April through June are not good times to use direct-mail. These patterns should be weighed against the best times for selling certain kinds of merchandise, of course. An offer to sell overcoats will not be as successful in April as it might be in October.

Frequency is just as important with direct mail as it is with other advertising media. A single mailing may not bring much response. In fact, you may need three or four mailings to convince people of the value of an offer. In some cases, you may need nine or ten.

As you learned in Chapter 11, sometimes a local retailer and a manufacturer will get together for cooperative (co-op) newspaper advertising. They also do this with direct mail. The retailer may supply the mailing list of customers and the manufacturer supplies the materials to be sent. Another kind of cooperative direct-mail advertising involves several advertisers who share a single mailing to distribute coupons and other promotional materials. In this way, they share the costs of postage and mailing lists.

SPECIALTY ADVERTISING

People spend a great deal of money on specialty advertising—more than $2 billion each year in the United States. And that's more than the money advertisers spend yearly on consumer magazine, business publication, radio, or outdoor advertising.

Just what are advertising specialities? Chances are that you own at least one right now! It might be a pen or pencil with a local store advertised on it, or a telephone shoulder rest from an answering service, or a calendar from your local service station, or a key chain from a car dealer. Or it could be any one of many gift items with advertising on them: match book, comb, appointment book, nail clipper, briefcase, ruler, letter opener, note pad, coffee mug, thermometer, rain cap, or windshield scraper.

specialty advertising Usually a gift that carries a simple advertising message.

self-liquidating offer An advertising specialty for which the customer pays a small amount.

Specialty advertising is usually a gift that carries a simple advertising message. Sometimes, with a **self-liquidating offer**, the customer pays for the item, but the advertiser usually pays for most of the cost involved. Generally specialty advertising only reminds the consumer of the business's name and maybe a slogan. Sometimes it is a useful tool the customer will use regularly.

Most advertisers would not rely on specialty advertising to bear the entire promotion burden. Instead, specialities reinforce promotional efforts that use other media by complementing the regular advertising campaign and keeping it fresh in the customer's minds.

Many advertising specialties are personalized with the name of the recipient, which encourages the consumer to keep the item as a memento. Then the consumer will use the item and see it often—along with the advertiser's name. This approach establishes a feeling of goodwill.

The business of specialty advertising is generally divided between two institutions: suppliers and distributors. Suppliers are the printers, pen manufacturers, plastic molders, and other firms that make the items used as advertising specialties. Distributors work with the actual advertisers to help find, choose, and buy the specialties from the suppliers. Table 13–2 summarizes the pros and cons of advertising in specialty media.

Dozens, even hundreds, of successful promotional campaigns have used specialty advertising. Some are shown in Figure 13–1. Specialty advertising is especially good at identifying prospective customers, expressing gratitude, reminding customers of the firm's name and address, increasing the number of store customers, introducing sales representatives, and creating good feelings among customers. Specialty advertising items are also often used as premiums or prizes in contests or giveaway promotions, as well as employee incentives, gifts, and even occasionally as items to be sold.

OUTDOOR ADVERTISING

outdoor advertising Any sort of advertising displayed outside.

Outdoor advertising is any sort of advertising displayed outside. It uses store signs, roadside posters, highway billboards, lighted spectacular sign displays in big cities, and series of small signs alongside a road. The principles of outdoor advertising are also used in many political posters, circus announcements (sometimes called *broadsides*), and perhaps even notices on your school bulletin boards.

TABLE 13–2 Advantages and disadvantages of advertising in specialty media.

Advantages
1. Specialty advertising can build good will by giving customers gifts.
2. Items may be retained for a long time.
3. The advertising message may be seen several times a day.
4. Advertising can be tied to useful items that customers want.
5. Customers recall the name of the business very well.
Disadvantages
1. Customers may discard items.
2. It can be expensive.
3. Only short sales messages can be used.

Courtesy Specialty Advertising Association International

FIGURE 13–1
Here are some advertising specialties that have been used effectively by large and small advertisers.

Two kinds of outdoor signs are used most often. Outdoor signs that can be changed by putting up new printed sheets of paper are called **posters; painted signs** are more permanent messages that present an unchanged message for a longer period of time. Posters are usually placed on large billboard backings, which take several printed sheets of paper to cover. There are many poster companies around the country, but one primary company usually serves

posters Outdoor signs that can be changed.

painted signs Relatively permanent outdoor signs.

each city and metropolitan area. Many cities, however, have more than one poster company. The poster companies rent many sign locations and maintain billboards in those locations, in turn renting the billboard space to advertisers for a monthly fee. Poster companies' advertising rates are not available in any *Standard Rate and Data Service* publication; instead, a regularly published list of **Outdoor Advertising Rates** contains information on the costs of outdoor poster advertising for most of the country. Painted signs, on the other hand, stay in the same location for months or years at a time. Their cost of production for each sign is usually greater, and the location of the sign must be rented.

Outdoor Advertising Rates A publication listing the rates for outdoor poster advertising for most of the country.

As with other media, the costs of outdoor advertising are related to the size of the audience that will see the advertising. Another important factor is **coverage,** which is how well the signs are distributed throughout a metropolitan area. Outdoor advertising rates have traditionally been set according to the number of billboards needed to reach the entire mobile population of an area. This number of billboards was called a **Number 100 showing**, and the billboard plant guaranteed enough billboards to reach 100 percent of the mobile population of the area at least once within a thirty-day period. Other levels of advertising included such options as a Number 50 showing, with half as many billboards as in a Number 100 showing, or a Number 200 showing, with twice as many.

coverage How well signs are distributed throughout a metropolitan area.

Number 100 showing Enough billboards to reach 100 percent of the mobile population in an area at least once every thirty days.

Recently, the outdoor advertising industry has begun to borrow the concept of gross rating points (GRPs) from television advertisers. In most larger cities, outdoor advertising is sold by 25 GRPs, or multiples of 25 such as 50, 75, 100, 125, or more. A Number 100 showing cannot be directly compared with 100 GRPs in outdoor advertising. Instead of reaching the entire mobile population, an outdoor advertising level of 100 GRPs would reach only about 90 percent of the *adult* population. In return for this reduction in reach, the frequency increases to slightly more than once a day for the average audience member. And the billboards are sold for a 28-day period, which means that each billboard can be used 13 times a year instead of only 12 times under the old monthly selling periods. It is probably not possible, however, to make direct comparisons between the way GRPs are used in outdoor advertising and the way they are used in other media.

Outdoor advertisers are concerned about competition for the audience's attention, just as advertisers are in other media. Each location where billboards face in a certain direction is called a **facing**, and advertisers do not want many billboards per facing (that is, not very many other billboards side-by-side at the same location competing for audience attention).

facing A location where billboards face in a certain direction.

Outdoor advertisers also like their billboards scattered throughout a market area rather than concentrated only in certain neighborhoods. Of course, if a certain store owner wants to buy billboards just in the immediate vicinity of the store, that is also possible.

The locations of billboards also may be influenced by the changes in audience traffic levels during certain times of the year. In the summer many people are traveling long distances on vacation, so rural billboard locations may

TABLE 13–3 Advantages and disadvantages of advertising in outdoor media.

Advantages

1. Outdoor advertising reaches potential customers on their way to buy.
2. Communication can be quick and simple.
3. Repetition is easy to attain.

Disadvantages

1. Only very short messages can be used.
2. There are many legal restrictions.
3. The advertiser may not have full control over where signs appear.

be important. But in the winter, billboards in cities may get larger audiences because of the in-town traffic for Christmas shopping, attending theaters, and going to nearby recreational facilities. Table 13–3 sums up the pros and cons of outdoor advertising.

TRANSIT ADVERTISING

Transit advertising is any advertising placed on or in a mass transit vehicle or station. Like outdoor advertising, transit advertising reaches people who are on their way somewhere, perhaps on their way to a store to buy merchandise like that being advertised, but maybe traveling to work, school, or home when they are not necessarily thinking about shopping.

transit advertising Any advertising placed on or in a mass transit vehicle or station or bench at a bus stop.

Transit advertisers use the term *full run* to mean that a poster has been placed inside each bus, subway car, or elevated train car in a transit system. The advertiser can buy half runs, quarter runs, or double runs in which the prices and the number of advertisements vary accordingly. The transit audience includes just about everybody who lives and travels in the area at some time or other—although the most frequent users of transit systems within cities are likely to be lower-income earners and blue-collar workers. In transit advertising aimed at commuters, however, the audience is often composed of suburban dwellers who may very well be in all levels of jobs, incomes, educational levels, and interests. So transit advertising audiences may differ according to the type of transit involved. See Table 13–4, page 221, for the advantages and disadvantages of advertising in transit media.

Advertisements inside train cars and buses are called **car cards**. They are usually arranged in rows above window level inside the vehicles. Transit advertisements may also appear on the outside of the vehicles. And if there is an elevated or subway train system, poster advertisements are usually available

car cards Advertisement inside train cars and buses.

FIGURE 13–2
Specific appeals help to make transit advertising effective.

in the stations. In many cities, taxicabs carry transit advertisements on their roofs or trunks, too.

POINT-OF-PURCHASE ADVERTISING

point-of-purchase (POP) advertising Displays in stores.

Point-of-purchase (POP) advertising consists of displays in stores, usually prepared for retailers by manufacturers and wholesalers. Displaying merchandise inside stores is a kind of point-of-purchase promotion. In some ways, POP is more than an advertising medium: It is a merchandising tool for retailers and marketers. Because the paid media advertising effort is so often supplemented by point-of-purchase promotions that remind customers of the advertising message, and because the advertising planning often includes these in-store aspects of the promotional campaign, it is important to understand this channel.

TABLE 13–4 Advantages and disadvantages of advertising in transit media.

Advantages

1. Transit advertising is very economical.
2. It is good for repetition.
3. There is continuous day and night advertising exposure.
4. The audience has nothing else to look at.

Disadvantages

1. The audience is often hurrying and not thinking about advertising.
2. Advertisements may be vandalized or mutilated.
3. The audience may not be in high economic category.

Modern self-service stores where customers select their own purchases and pay for them at a checkout stand have reduced the influence of store clerks. As a result, other ways of helping and influencing the customers have developed, primarily through the use of point-of-purchase or in-store displays and exhibits. And because so many of today's shoppers are looking for additional information about the items that are for sale, point-of-purchase advertising has a great deal of impact: In fact, more than two-thirds of shoppers report that they saw and reacted to such advertising, and almost one-third of the shoppers say they bought something because of an in-store promotion. Figure 13–3 illustrates two award-winning point-of-purchase displays.

Some advertisers are hesitant to use point-of-purchase advertising, because it takes up aisle space in the store and because it is associated with "discount" stores. Many large full-service department stores and other retail stores prefer to prepare their own displays rather than use point-of-purchase advertising from their wholesalers or other suppliers; this permits the stores to maintain their own sales themes for all their merchandise and to retain their own quality images. But keep in mind that a large share of consumer purchases are made in self-service stores, and that is where point-of-purchase advertising is most effective.

Perhaps the most common type of self-service store is the grocery. These stores have four "power" or "draw" departments that attract nine of every ten grocery shoppers. The traditional power departments are bakery, produce, meat, and dairy—and in recent years the frozen food department has begun to take on the characteristics of a draw department. These departments are usually located around the perimeter aisles of the grocery so that customers will be drawn through the store past other products to get to the draw departments. And a point-of-purchase display near one of these departments can attract many more buyers than the display of items in their regular locations in the store.

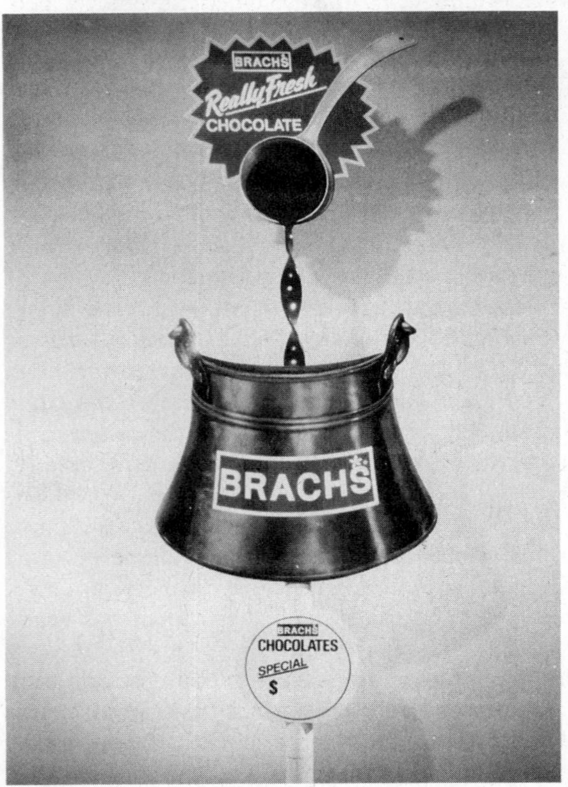

FIGURE 13–3
These award-winning point-of-purchase displays help consumers select their own merchandise and reduces the retailer's need for sales help.

TABLE 13–5 Advantages and disadvantages of advertising in point-of-purchase displays.

Advantages

1. Point-of-purchase displays may secure better locations for merchandise in stores.
2. They reach people who are ready to buy.
3. They can trigger impulse buying.

Disadvantages

1. It may be difficult to get store cooperation.
2. It is hard to control quality or location of displays.
3. Displays may not reach people who do not already shop in the kind of store that carries the merchandise.

Self-service drugstore supermarkets such as Walgreen's or Treasury Drug do not have certain draw departments, even though they carry more different items than do most grocery stores. And self-service discount stores such as K-Mart have even more items in stock, so it is more difficult to select draw departments. In these situations, deciding where to put a point-of-purchase display is not as simple as it is in grocery stores.

A capable manager of a retail self-service store will know how much profit and sales can be gained from each square foot of floor space and shelf space in the store. So an advertiser who wishes to place a point-of-purchase display in a store may need to guarantee certain minimum sales from that promotion to repay the store for the space; if that minimum sales level is not achieved, the advertiser might have to pay for the difference.

In some cases, the advertiser might offer a premium or payment to the store manager or owner in return for locating the in-store display in a good part of the store. This payment is referred to as "push" or "spiff" money.

Table 13–5 sums up the advantages and disadvantages of point-of-purchase advertising.

MISCELLANEOUS CHANNELS

There are several other ways to reach customers with your promotional messages, and all of them have their appropriate uses and benefits. We don't have room to discuss all of them in detail, but they deserve their share of consideration when you plan your promotional campaigns.

package inserts Coupons or other premiums enclosed with a purchased product.

free samples Samples of new or revised products provided free to consumers.

Yellow Pages Classified telephone directory for businesses.

Package inserts may be coupons or other premiums that are enclosed with a purchased product. Usually they work best if they relate directly to the application or benefit of the product with which they are enclosed.

Free samples are often used to familiarize consumers with new products or with products that have been drastically revised. Of course, this kind of promotion is expensive if it is used for large groups of people.

Because road maps are expensive to print, some gasoline companies now sell advertising space on their maps, even if the customer must pay for the map. You can also advertise in some paperbound books, or on shopping bags, in motion picture theaters, on weight scales, at trade show exhibits, and in industrial catalogs. You may also be familiar with skywriting advertising and with towed banners that airplanes pull over large sports arenas.

Transportation media include advertising in rail or airline timetables, in airports and railway stations, and on ticket folders. This is separate from transit advertising, which we discussed earlier. And an important advertising investment for many firms is in telephone **Yellow Pages** classified directories that most of us use to find who sells what in our localities.

Some of these miscellaneous media are more likely to be considered public relations, sales promotion, or publicity channels rather than advertising media channels, but their uses still must tie in with the overall promotional effort and should supplement advertising campaigns in the more traditional and better-known channels.

SUMMARY

There are so many kinds of media and vehicles used for advertising that we could not mention them all in this section, but we did discuss some of the major advertising media that are used.

Direct mail is evolving into direct marketing, meaning that advertisers can communicate with potential audiences through a variety of means, including mail and telephone.

Speciality advertising is surprisingly large and is used by a wide variety of businesses and institutions.

Outdoor and transit advertising are not strong at reaching specific audiences, but their cost efficiencies compensate.

Point-of-purchase advertising may not really be a part of advertising, and is more like sales promotion, but it is so closely aligned with advertising that we need to know about it.

There are many other kinds of advertising channels, too, all of which can be used in a particular advertising situation or to meet a particular advertising goal.

TERMS TO KNOW

Now that you have finished this chapter, you should understand the following terms:

direct mail	outdoor advertising	transit advertising
cost per prospect	posters	full run
cost per return	painted signs	car cards
bulk rate	*Outdoor Advertising Rates*	point-of-purchase (POP) advertising
list brokers	coverage	package inserts
specialty advertising	Number 100 showing	free samples
self-liquidating offer	facing	Yellow Pages

If you are not certain of the meaning of any of these terms, go back through the chapter and review them.

THINGS TO THINK ABOUT

1. What is the difference between cost per prospect and cost per return in direct marketing advertising?
2. What are the two kinds of cooperative advertising in direct mail?
3. How can mailing lists be prepared?
4. What is the difference between a supplier and a distributor in specialty advertising?
5. What is a Number 100 showing in outdoor advertising? What are gross rating points in outdoor advertising?
6. How is transit advertising like outdoor advertising? How is it different?
7. What are "power" or "draw" departments, and why are they important?
8. What are the advantages and disadvantages of direct-mail advertising to an advertiser? Of specialty advertising? Of outdoor advertising? Of transit advertising? Of point-of-purchase advertising?

THINGS TO TALK ABOUT

1. How can direct-mail advertising be both more expensive and more economical than other advertising media?
2. How does "direct marketing" differ from "direct mail" advertising?
3. Why is specialty advertising so large an advertising medium, yet not very well known?
4. Why is outdoor advertising now using gross rating points?
5. Why is transit advertising so low in cost, compared to other advertising media?
6. How do point-of-purchase promotions supplement advertising in the regular mass media?

THINGS TO DO

1. Visit a large local grocery or discount store and observe how point-of-purchase promotion is being used.
2. Find out how many advertising specialties the members of your class have with them on any given day.
3. Visit a nearby outdoor advertising poster plant and observe how several sheets of printed paper are pasted together to form a whole billboard.

14 Media Planning and Buying

WHAT WE COULD TELL YOU ABOUT THE SAAB 900
IN THE SPACE BELOW IS NO SUBSTITUTE FOR TEN MINUTES
IN THE SPACE ABOVE.

Visit your nearest Saab dealer for a test drive.
SAAB
The most intelligent cars ever built.

Courtesy of Saab-Scania of America, Inc.

CHAPTER OUTLINE

- Objectives, Strategies, and Tactics
- Getting the Information You Need
  - Marketing Data
  - Sources of Media Planning Information
  - Media Tactical Sources
- Deciding What You Want to Accomplish
- Dealing With the Competition
- Budgeting
  - Percentage-of-Sales-or-Profit Method
  - Competitive-Spending Method
  - Formula Method
  - Objective-and-Task Method
  - Share-Point Method
  - Preparing a Media Budget
- Media Planning Decisions
  - Target Selection
  - Media Selection
- Putting Your Media Plans Into Action
- Making a Media Buy

By the time you finish this chapter, you should understand:

1. How objectives, strategies, and tactics fit together.
2. The sources of media planning information.
3. Approaches to dealing with competitive advertising.
4. The methods used in media budgeting.
5. How to put media plans into action and make a buy.

To use advertising media effectively, it is important to understand not only what these media are but how best to plan for and buy the media space or time you need. The responsibilities involved in media planning and buying include evaluating the various media options, estimating costs, and selecting the medium, vehicle, and advertising unit to use in a specific situation.

Remember, the *media* are the channels themselves, such as television, radio, newspapers, outdoor, magazines, direct mail, and specialty advertising. The *vehicles* are the individual media outlets, such as the *New York Times,* a particular radio station, a certain television program, or an individual magazine such as *Newsweek*. The **advertising unit** is the specific space or time used in an advertising vehicle, such as a 15 column-inch newspaper insertion, a full-page, four-color, nonbleed magazine advertisement, a ten-second television spot or a sixty-second radio announcement. Table 14–1 shows the estimated amounts spent for each advertising medium each year.

advertising unit The specific space or time used in an advertising vehicle.

TABLE 14–1 Estimates of yearly expenditures in U.S. advertising media.

Medium	Annual Expenditures	Percentage
Newspapers	$29,400,000,000	26.7%
Television	$24,100,000,000	21.9
Direct Mail	$18,000,000,000	16.4
Radio	$ 7,400,000,000	6.7
Consumer Magazines	$ 5,900,000,000	5.4
Specialty	$ 3,500,000,000	3.2
Business Publications	$ 2,800,000,000	2.5
Outdoor	$ 1,100,000,000	1.0
Farm Publications	$ 200,000,000	0.2
Miscellaneous	$17,000,000,000	16.0

Projections are based on figures from the Newspaper Advertising Bureau, Inc.

With all the choices involved, this is a complicated topic. Media buyers and planners need much experience and training to succeed in their responsibilities. We can cover only the basics in this chapter.

OBJECTIVES, STRATEGIES, AND TACTICS

objective The goal that advertising should accomplish.

strategy The plan to accomplish an objective.

tactics The specific steps needed to carry out a plan.

logistics The support activities needed to complete the objective, strategy, and tactics.

A plan for any marketing situation, including advertising, must have several stages. The first stage is setting an **objective**—the goal that the advertising should accomplish. The next stage is developing a **strategy**, the plan to accomplish that objective. Then you work out the **tactics**—the specific steps that will let you carry out your plan. If you wish to carry the series of steps even further, there would be **logistics,** the various support activities needed to complete the objectives, strategies, and tactics.

In advertising, someone high up in the organization may set the objectives. Usually, a business firm will have certain organizational objectives that the marketing objectives must fit in with. The advertising objectives must then work with the higher-level marketing objectives. And our media objectives must contribute to the advertising objectives. An example of a media objective might be to reach the primary target group at least twice a week during the 13-week course of an advertising campaign.

Advertising strategies must be consistent with the objectives. Each strategy should work toward meeting one or more objectives, and each objective should have at least one strategy aimed at it. An example of a media strategy might be to select newspaper and radio advertising to reach the primary target group.

Tactics involve following the steps established in the strategies or plans. Tactics include the activities necessary to implement plans. For example, a media tactic might be to place advertisements twice a week in the principal newspaper that serves a target market area.

As a complete example, one advertising media objective might be to reach a certain target group, such as adult males, with your advertising message. Using cable television sports programming to reach that audience would be a strategy. And buying a cable TV advertisement aimed at that specific target would be the tactic. Conducting the research to provide information about your target group and the available media would be a logistic intended to support your other advertising media activities. (See Figure 14–1.)

Let's go through a sample of the media planning and buying process and see what is involved.

GETTING THE INFORMATION YOU NEED

You may already be familiar with some advertising media, because you read certain magazines or watch some television programming. But no one can possibly know enough about all the available media and vehicles to make

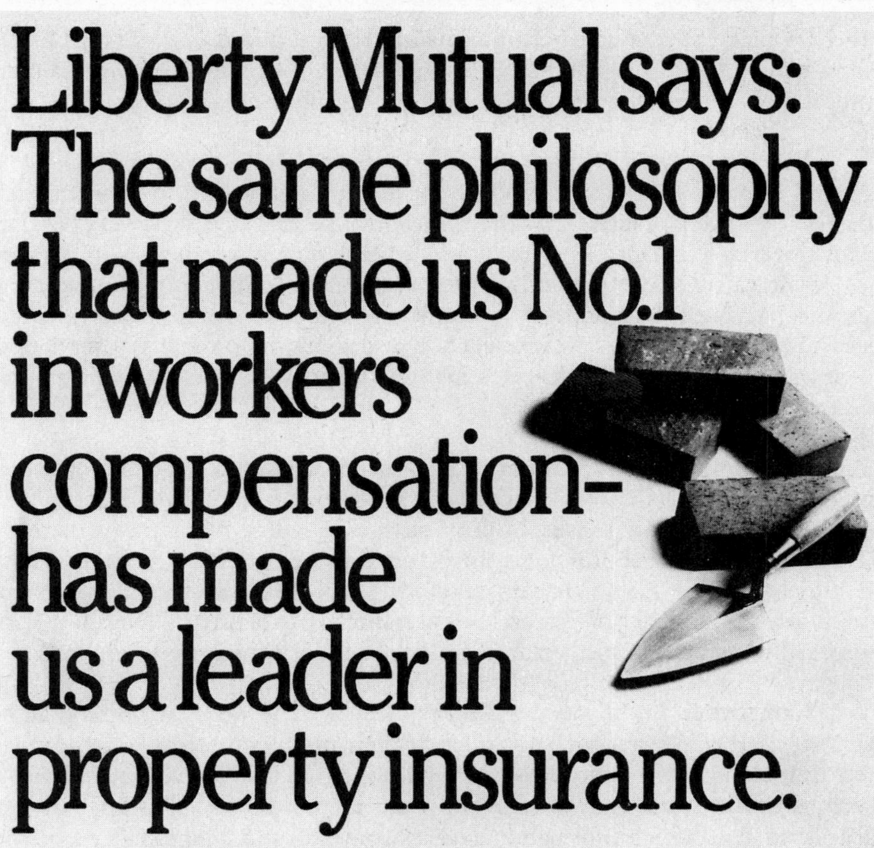

Liberty Mutual says: The same philosophy that made us No.1 in workers compensation– has made us a leader in property insurance.
That philosophy is simple: teamwork. We believe in today's complex insurance world, that it takes more than one person to make sure your business property is insured properly.
We believe—as with all business insurance we write—that it takes the combined effort of sales, loss prevention and claims professionals as well as underwriting and financial experts, all working directly with you.
Teamwork means working together to determine which of our wide variety of property coverages is right for your business. Teamwork means working with you early on to develop an action plan should a loss occur.
We have a philosophy that works. One that over 100,000 American businesses believe in for their many insurance needs. A philosophy that has made us No. 1 in Workers Compensation and a leader in Business Property insurance.
AMERICA BELIEVES IN LIBERTY MUTUAL INSURANCE.
LIBERTY MUTUAL.

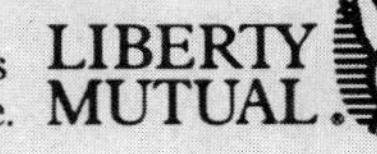

Courtesy Liberty Mutual Insurance Group / Boston.

FIGURE 14–1
This advertisement was intended for a very specific group of businesses. It may not be as flashy as much consumer advertising, but the important message will help attract the attention of the intended readers.

intelligent choices for advertising a product, service, or idea. Certainly this task will be easier if you are dealing only with media in your local community. But even in that situation, and certainly when you are handling a regional or national task, you *always* need more information than you have.

Marketing Data

To help make all the research information sources more understandable, we shall divide them into the resources we use in each stage of the planning process. We use marketing data to help set our objectives.

Sales and Market Sources. Syndicated research services provide background information on how products have been selling and in what markets they sell best or worst. You will recall from Chapter 3 that these services conduct research for many subscribers on a wide variety of products and services.

Syndicated sales research concentrates on how much of a product or service has been sold and the patterns of sales over time. This includes information about your own product and also about the products or services of your main competitors. Syndicated market data includes profiles of geographic markets.

Competitive Advertising. Media planners need to know not only how well their products are selling, but also what kind of promotional activities their competitors are using. Research firms such as **Leading National Advertisers (LNA)** continually monitor competitors' advertising patterns—how they spent, in which vehicles, and in which markets. Because so much data collection is involved, this kind of research information is expensive. However, it is essential to successful media planning, especially for large national advertisers.

Leading National Advertisers (LNA) A research firm that monitors competitors' advertising patterns.

Consumer Data. Media planners also need to know something about current users and potential consumers of their product or service. Syndicated research about consumers provides information on the economic situation—such as how much money consumers make and what their spending patterns are—as well as social information such as consumers' demographic characteristics.

The Simmons Market Research Bureau, which we discussed in Chapter 3, offers a prime example of this kind of research data, as does **Selling Areas—Marketing, Inc. (SAMI)**.

Selling Areas—Marketing, Inc. (SAMI) A research firm that provides information on consumer's purchases.

With all this information in hand, media planners can decide how best to counter the competition's advertising, where to advertise, and what target group to reach.

Sources of Media Planning Information

Once you know where and to whom you wish to advertise, you must decide on the actual advertising media and vehicles that will do the most effective job for you at the lowest cost.

For the most part, this is a process of estimation. One way to estimate cost and effectiveness is to calculate the approximate amount of advertising that you could afford to do, based on how much money is available for advertising and also on your preliminary decisions about which media to use. Another approach would be to outline the media that you might use along with the patterns and amounts of advertising that you want for each one and then estimate how much money you would need in your budget to do this advertising.

Estimating Guides. Because only rough figures are needed, many media planners make use of an **estimating guide** or **cost guide**. This is a printed summary of advertising rates for various media and vehicles, which an individual advertising agency prepares for its staff to use or purchases from a publisher. The rates are not exact; they are usually rounded off to give you an idea of how much advertising you can afford or how much your desired advertising is likely to cost. (See Figure 14–2.)

estimating guide A printed summary of advertising rates for various media vehicles.

cost guide The same as an estimating guide.

The first time you make this kind of estimate, you may find that you cannot afford the kind or amount of advertising you would like to have. That is why this estimating step is necessary, so that you do not get too far along with your advertising media plans only to find out that you must start over.

What do you do when estimates exceed the amount of money available? The most common process is to alter your goals or plans somewhat to bring the amount of advertising you want into line with the resources you have.

Audience Size Estimates. Besides estimating how much money you will need or how much advertising you can afford, you may also want to calculate about how many people will be exposed to your advertising (the *reach*) and how many times the average audience member will see your advertising (the *frequency*). Reach and frequency were also discussed in Chapter 11.

To do this, you need a guide that will tell you how many people read or see each particular advertising medium or vehicle. An advertising agency may prepare such a guide for its media planners or get the information from Simmons Market Research Bureau or a similar research source, Mediamark Research, Inc. (MRI). In those sources, you may also find data about **audience accumulation,** which is the total number of persons who might see your advertisement if it appears in a certain vehicle more than once. For example, more people will see your advertisement in three consecutive issues of *People* magazine than in just a single issue.

audience accumulation The total number of people who might see an advertisement if it appears in a certain vehicle more than once.

There is also information about **audience duplication**, which is the total number of people who will see your advertisement in a combination of vehicles. More people will see your advertisement in both *People* and *Us* magazines than would see it if it were run only in *People*. And some members of the audience will be duplicated because they will see the advertisement in both publications.

audience duplication The total number of people who will see an advertisement in a combination of vehicles.

Media Tactical Sources

Once you have chosen the media you want to use and can afford and you have a general idea of which vehicles might be included and covered by your budget, you can begin with the actual media selection or **buy**. Here, again, you will need research information.

buy Media selection.

ELECTRONIC MEDIA

NETWORK TELEVISION

PRIME TIME
I. Unit Costs and Efficiencies

	Avg. 30-Second Commercial			
	Unit Cost	CPM Homes	Women 25-54	Men 25-54
Fall	$81,950-104,300	$5.50-7.00	$13.00-15.50	$17.00-18.00
Winter	66,150- 88,200	4.50-6.00	11.00-13.50	12.80-14.50
Spring	76,050- 81,900	6.50-7.00	16.00-17.50	17.90-18.50
Summer	54,000- 70,200	5.00-6.50	13.50-16.00	15.70-16.25

II. Audience Delivery

		Delivery (MM)		
	HH Rtg.	Homes	Women	Men
Fall	17.9	14.9	15.5	13.9
Winter	17.7	14.7	15.2	13.8
Spring	14.1	11.7	12.1	11.0
Summer	12.0	10.8	10.4	9.3

III. Audience Composition

	Men V/HVH*	Women V/HVH	Teens V/HVH	Children V/HVH	Total V/HVH
Regular Programs 7-11 p.m.	61	80	15	22	178
Feature Films	66	80	16	19	181
Situation Comedy	56	78	18	31	183
Suspense & Mystery Drama	64	80	15	17	176
General Drama	53	86	12	18	169

*Viewers per 100 viewing households (HVH)

DAYTIME (M-F)
I. Unit Costs and Efficiencies

	Avg. 30-Second Commercial		
	Unit Cost	CPM Homes	CPM Women 25-54
Fall	$11,600-15,950	$2.00-2.75	$5.50-6.40
Winter	10,980-13,730	1.80-2.25	4.50-5.50
Spring	9,400-13,160	2.00-2.80	5.25-7.00
Summer	7,950-14,840	1.50-2.80	4.50-6.75

II. Audience Delivery

		Delivery (MM)		
	HH Rtg.	Homes	Women	Men
Fall	7.0	5.8	6.0	5.4
Winter	7.3	6.1	6.3	5.7
Spring	5.6	4.7	4.8	4.4
Summer	6.4	5.3	5.5	5.0

III. Audience Composition

	Men V/HVH*	Women V/HVH	Teens V/HVH	Children V/HVH	Total V/HVH
M-F 10 a.m.-4:30 p.m.	25	85	12	14	136
Daytime Drama	23	90	11	10	134
Quiz & Aud. Participation	30	79	11	17	137

* Viewers per 100 viewing households (HVH)

EARLY EVENING NEWS (M-F)
I. Unit Costs and Efficiencies

	Avg. 30-Second Commercial		
	Unit Cost	CPM Homes	CPM Women 25+
Fall	$36,400-39,200	$3.25-3.50	$11.75-12.50
Winter	28,500-31,920	2.50-2.80	8.50- 9.25
Spring	31,500-38,250	3.50-4.25	12.75-13.75
Summer	24,900-35,280	3.00-4.25	11.75-12.50

Courtesy The Sunflower Group.

FIGURE 14–2
This kind of estimating guide is used by media planners and buyers to estimate the costs for an advertising media schedule. These figures are compiled from the actual costs and audience figures for individual media vehicles.

Vehicle Audience Information. To get data about the audience for a specific vehicle, you might use broadcast ratings information. The best-known ratings companies are **A. C. Nielson Company** and **Arbitron, Inc.** There is similar information about print media vehicles, but it is not as detailed or extensive as the information about broadcast vehicles.

A.C. Nielson Company A well-known ratings company.

Arbitron, Inc. A well-known ratings company.

Ratings information is much more detailed than the summaries provided in estimating guides. At this point, you are beyond the estimation stage into the actual vehicle selection process.

Vehicle Cost Information. Before selecting the actual media, vehicles, and units you will use in an advertising campaign, you must know exactly how much each unit will cost. You also need this cost information to set the timing patterns of your advertising, because there may be lower costs for advertising at certain times or in certain combinations. Table 14–2 shows the impact inflation has had on media costs since 1976.

As we learned in Chapter 3, the primary source of cost data is *Standard Rate and Data Service*, which provides advertising rates for most major media. Many individual vehicles also publish rate cards that include only their own advertising rates. This is helpful to local advertisers because the local rates may be lower than the prices for national advertisers.

DECIDING WHAT YOU WANT TO ACCOMPLISH

Advertising goals cannot be set until after you have gathered competitive information and consumer data, because this information will affect the goals. Setting goals is a combination of art and science. There is no easy way to learn except through experience. Setting goals and then finding out if they have been met will add to that experience. It is also interesting to find out that, in many cases, a planner may set goals and then work very hard to make sure that the objectives are indeed accomplished.

Advertising is not an objective, and advertising media cannot be an objective, either. An objective is what you want to accomplish, and you do not

TABLE 14–2 The effects of inflation on the costs of advertising media per thousand audience members.

	1976	1981	1986	1991
Network television	$100	$142	$184	$226
Spot television	$100	$136	$172	$208
Spot radio	$100	$169	$238	$307
Consumer magazines	$100	$135	$170	$205
Daily newspapers	$100	$124	$148	$172

want to acheive advertising as your end result. Because it is a tool to be used to help achieve an objective, advertising is usually considered a *strategy*, not an objective.

Usually, your advertising objectives involve changing consumers' attitudes, giving them information about your product or service, or simply making them aware of what you are selling. An overall objective might involve selling the item at some certain volume level, but that is more likely to be considered a marketing objective rather than an advertising objective. In setting objectives, you should remember that an objective is usually expressed as an infinitive verb such as *to sell*, *to communicate*, or *to persuade*.

DEALING WITH THE COMPETITION

Once you have your objectives in mind and you also have the research information you need, including information about your competitors and their advertising, you must consciously decide how to deal with the competition.

Basically, there are two approaches in dealing with competitors. You can try to match the competition, at least in some ways. Or you can try to avoid the competition and find your own niche. In a way, this is a kind of market segmentation, which we discussed in Chapter 2.

You must also decide in advance how you will deal with competitors' inroads into your own markets and targets. For example, what will you do if some competitor introduces a new product or service that is better that what you are trying to sell? What will you do if a competitor decides to spend much more money on advertising than you can afford? How will your advertising media plan change if your sales do not meet your expectations? What will you do if sales exceed expectations?

All these questions require important decisions. And there is little specific, concrete information on which to base your competitive decisions. But you must still gather as much information in advance as you can. You cannot make good competitive decisions without having the best available information on your side.

BUDGETING

Budgeting is something of an art and something that you do better with experience. It may be helpful, though, to learn about the approaches to budgeting that are most often used in advertising. These are not all the budgeting methods by any means, but only some of the commonest ones.

Percentage-of-Sales-or-Profits Method

The most common budgeting approach is to set aside some percentage of one year's sales or profit dollars to use on next year's advertising budget. However, using figures from the preceding year assumes that things will continue as they have been in the coming year.

Using a set percentage of the future year's profits or sales dollars may be better, but there is still an erroneous assumption. The level of sales or profits should not contribute to the amount of advertising. Instead, the amount of advertising should contribute to sales and profits. So a **percentage-of-sales-or-profits budget** is, in a way, backward.

percentage-of-sales-or-profits budget An advertising budget based on a percentage of sales or profits for the preceding or future year.

Competitive-Spending Method

A **competitive-spending budget** tries to match the amount some leading competitor spends on advertising media. By doing this, we are assuming that we want to be just like the competitor, that we can do exactly what the competitor does and be successful, and that being like the competitor is desirable.

competitive-spending budget A budget that tries to match the advertising budget of a leading competitor.

But keep in mind that copying a competitor ignores some of the best strategies of advertising, such as developing your own market segments, finding your own product or service differentiation, servicing overlooked or previously underserved markets, and aiming at your own best targets.

Formula Method

Some advertisers seek a scientific method of budgeting by trying to develop a mathematical formula to derive the best budget level. Such a **formula budget** would have to take in all the variables (of which there are many), account for everything that might change, allow for differences from one budgeting period to another and permit using only the information and data that are available to us.

formula budget A budget based on a complex mathematical formula.

Most important, we would have to know how much emphasis to place on each figure and variable, calculating in advance whether a certain factor should be counted double or triple or half as much as another. We should also need to find a way to balance all the data so that all our measurements are made in comparable ways—but that is very unlikely in real life.

Objective-and-Task Method

In an **objective-and-task budget**, we first decide what we wish to accomplish, then determine the amount of money we need to complete the task. Instead of starting with the amount of money that we have for advertising media and then calculating how much advertising media time and space we can afford, we reverse the order of that process.

objective-and-task budget A budget that uses the desired goal to determine the amount of money needed.

For example, we estimate a reasonable amount of our product or service that we would like to sell, how many outlets it might be available in, how many people would have to purchase certain amounts to meet our sales goals, and how much each person might buy. Then we estimate how many people we would have to reach with our advertising, and with what frequency, to get that purchase level. Finally, we calculate how much advertising we might need to do that, what media in what kind of combination would do it best, and how much that is likely to cost.

Share-Point Method

share point budget A budget based on the expenditures of all competitors.

The **share point budget** is similar to the competitive-spending budget except that it considers all competitors, not just one. In this method, we try not to rely on one competitors' situation. Instead we attempt to match the average of our entire industry, thus overcoming some of the weaknesses that we noted with some other budgeting methods.

In a share-point budget, we total the amount of advertising dollars we and *all* our competitors spend—that is, the industry total, including ourselves. Then, based on the percentage of the industry's sales that we might have as our sales objective, we assume that we must do a like percentage of the advertising. For example, to achieve 4 percent of our particular industry's sales, we should have to produce 4 percent of the industry's advertising. If our industry spends $10 million annually on advertising, we would need an advertising budget of 4 percent, or $400,000 a year.

This approach assumes that all advertising is equal; that is, we assume that our advertising quality is just as valuable as everyone else's, no better and no worse than average. We also assume that there is a direct relationship between the advertising budget and the sales results.

Preparing a Media Budget

No matter which budgeting method you use, you must be prepared to make changes as the situation varies during the advertising campaign. You must also realize that there is no single perfect method of determining an advertising budget.

In fact, one way to make the budgeting process more certain is to use at least two or more different budgeting methods, comparing the results of each and seeing where similarities and differences may arise. You must also realize that there are weaknesses in the budgeting process and watch out for shortcomings in any method you use.

MEDIA PLANNING DECISIONS

There are several important items in the advertising media planning process. Sometimes an experienced planner may alter the order of the process; there is no single "right way" to prepare a media plan. An experienced planner may also seem to skip some steps, not because they are not needed but because the planner has done this before and knows what decision should be made without going through the specific processes involved.

Target Selection

As we learned in Chapter 2, target markets are the geographic territories where you will advertise. You must set both size and scope for these markets.

Then you must determine the target groups, usually demographically, but sometimes psychographically. Again, you must calculate the number of people to include in these groups so you know how many people your advertising has to reach.

Media Selection

It might seem that selecting the types of media to use is all that media selection involves. It *is* an important step, but it is only one step in the overall process. You must first rank the media in their order of importance in relation to the groups and markets to be reached and the creative approaches to be used. Most often, the budget simply will not permit using all the media you might like, so you rate the relative importance of the various media considerations and begin to eliminate some of the lower-rated media. In selecting individual media vehicles, you may also use cost comparisons such as cost per thousand (discussed in Chapters 11 and 12) to help you judge cost efficiencies.

No matter what list of media you use, you must make certain that the combination of media you select will meet all the objectives. You should provide your rationale for the media you have decided to use and for those that you may have eliminated.

You will want to analyze the ability of each medium that you are considering to reach the target markets and groups. You will also want to estimate the size of audience for each medium, its effective reach to your prospects, the quality of each one's audience, and its cost-efficiency.

In selecting media, you will pay special attention to reach, frequency, impact, and continuity. As you will recall, *reach* is the number of people in your media audiences or the percentage of your target group whom you are able to contact and communicate to with your advertising. *Frequency* is the number of times you run your advertisements (although, for the audience, frequency is the average number of times an audience member will be exposed to your advertising). **Impact** is the strength of your advertisement and its messages. In media terms, this is usually determined by how large or how long the advertisement is, whether it is in color or has a lot of action, and similar characteristics. **Continuity** is the long-term consistency of the advertisements over time. Even though there may be changes, successive, similar advertisements should contribute to the campaign and build on the same base that you originally established.

impact The strength of an advertisement and its message.

continuity The long-term consistency of your advertisements over time.

PUTTING YOUR MEDIA PLANS INTO ACTION

As we suggested earlier in this chapter, tactics involves more doing and less planning because now you are ready to carry out your advertising media plans.

You will select the vehicles, patterns, and timing you will use for each medium. Cost comparisons and audience figures can aid you in these selections. Most often, you will try various combinations of vehicles. And in the case of broadcast media, what you would like to buy may already have been purchased by some other advertiser. There can be only one commercial on a station at a given moment, and you must select from the **availabilities (avails)** that have not already been reserved by another advertiser. This is not as much of a problem in print media because a newspaper or magazine can usually add another advertisement insertion even though it may need to increase the number of pages to do so. But there is only a limited amount of broadcast time each day, and the number of commercial minutes is finite.

availabilties (avails) Broadcast times not reserved by other advertisers.

Placing the advertisements in the media will also depend on the schedule that you have decided to follow. Sometimes you can outline this schedule on a media calendar, but that may be too specific because the actual timing of the advertising depends in part on the availabilities. So advertising media planners often use a **flow chart** that shows how much advertising will be purchased for each week or month of the campaign without providing specific dates and times that may not actually be possible (see Figure 14–3). This extra flexibility also lets the media buyer consider combinations of media, various discount offers, and other packages and plans that may reduce costs.

flow chart A chart that shows how much advertising will be bought during each week or month of the campaign, but not the specific dates or times.

Also, some of your media buying activities may involve negotiation with the media. The broadcast media are more likely to be sold through negotiation, which may depend on buying certain amounts of advertising, special patterns of advertising, particular times of the day or days of the week, specially priced "packages" of advertisements, and other factors.

You may also consider what kinds of contracts or discounts the media and vehicles offer, as we discussed in the earlier chapters about each particular kind of advertising medium.

MAKING A MEDIA BUY

When you make a media buy, you are reserving the time or space that you want to use for your advertisements. Then you usually send your advertisement to the vehicle: a film, videotape, or script to broadcast media; and a printing plate, "paste-up," or layout to print media.

Along with the advertising materials, you will send an **insertion order**, which gives detailed information about when and where the advertisement is to appear. A sample is shown in Figure 14–4. And many media vehicles will send back a **confirmation** of your order, to be certain that both sides agree on what is wanted. A print advertising vehicle may supply you with a proof of the advertisement, or **tearsheet**, before the advertisement appears to permit you to check it for mistakes. And, of course, after the advertisement is published or broadcast, you must pay for it.

insertion order A form that gives detailed information about when and where an advertisement is to appear.

confirmation A form the media sends back to the advertiser to confirm plans.

tearsheet Proof that an advertisement has appeared.

But there is even more involved. If you work for an advertising agency, the entire agency and all its departments must present a coordinated effort to get everything ready, on time, and up to standard. You must clear your

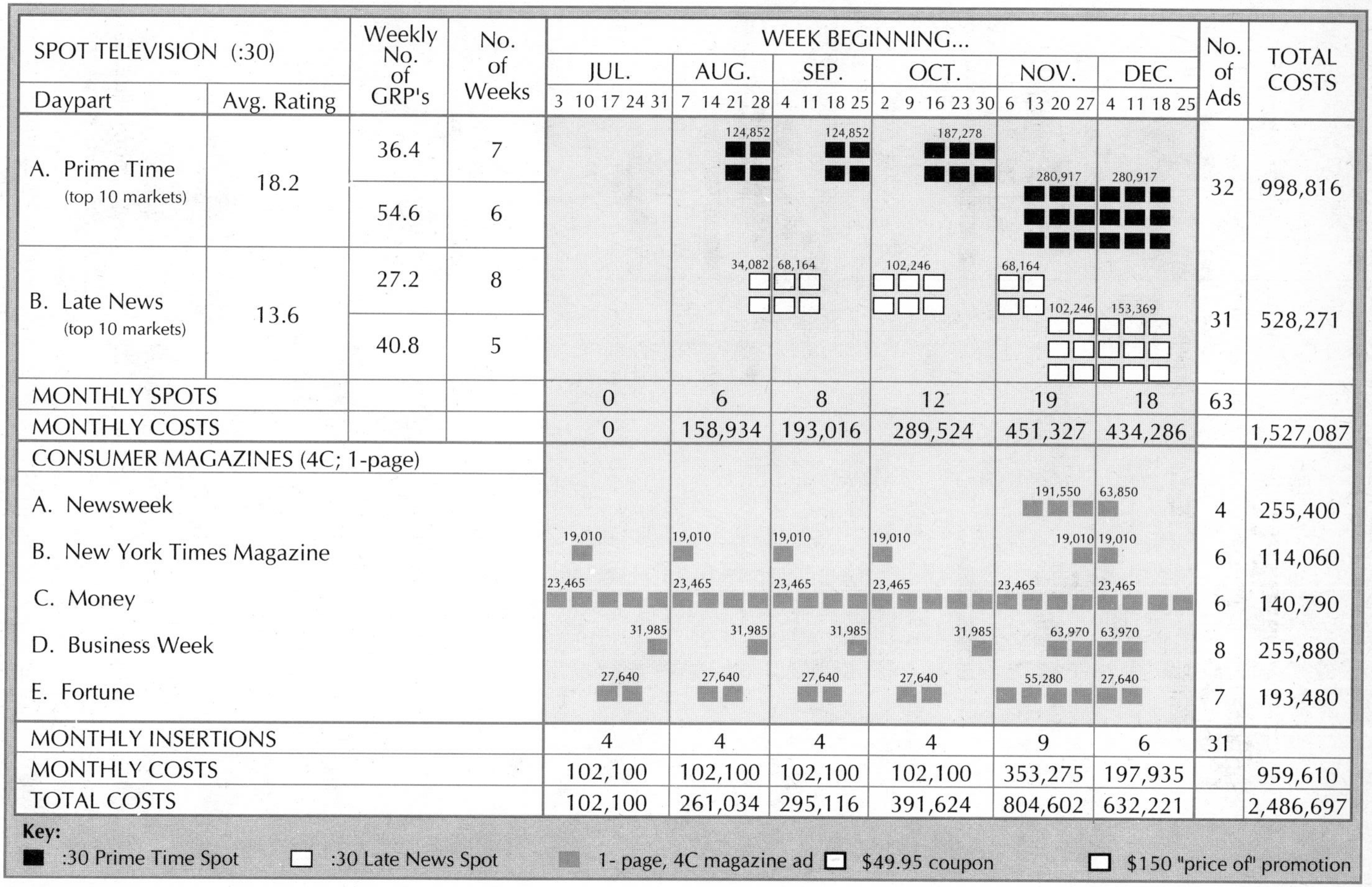

SPOT TELEVISION (:30) Daypart	Avg. Rating	Weekly No. of GRP's	No. of Weeks	WEEK BEGINNING... JUL. 3 10 17 24 31	AUG. 7 14 21 28	SEP. 4 11 18 25	OCT. 2 9 16 23 30	NOV. 6 13 20 27	DEC. 4 11 18 25	No. of Ads	TOTAL COSTS
A. Prime Time (top 10 markets)	18.2	36.4	7		124,852	124,852	187,278	280,917	280,917	32	998,816
		54.6	6								
B. Late News (top 10 markets)	13.6	27.2	8		34,082	68,164	102,246	68,164; 102,246	153,369	31	528,271
		40.8	5								
MONTHLY SPOTS				0	6	8	12	19	18	63	
MONTHLY COSTS				0	158,934	193,016	289,524	451,327	434,286		1,527,087
CONSUMER MAGAZINES (4C; 1-page)											
A. Newsweek								191,550	63,850	4	255,400
B. New York Times Magazine				19,010	19,010	19,010	19,010	19,010	19,010	6	114,060
C. Money				23,465	23,465	23,465	23,465	23,465	23,465	6	140,790
D. Business Week				31,985	31,985	31,985	31,985	63,970	63,970	8	255,880
E. Fortune				27,640	27,640	27,640	27,640	55,280	27,640	7	193,480
MONTHLY INSERTIONS				4	4	4	4	9	6	31	
MONTHLY COSTS				102,100	102,100	102,100	102,100	353,275	197,935		959,610
TOTAL COSTS				102,100	261,034	295,116	391,624	804,602	632,221		2,486,697

Key:
■ :30 Prime Time Spot □ :30 Late News Spot ▪ 1- page, 4C magazine ad □ $49.95 coupon □ $150 "price of" promotion

FIGURE 14–3
This flow chart illustrates how the advertising impact may be scheduled during the course of an advertising campaign.

FIGURE 14–4
This insertion order is used by an advertising agency to place advertising in media on behalf of the agency's client, the advertiser.

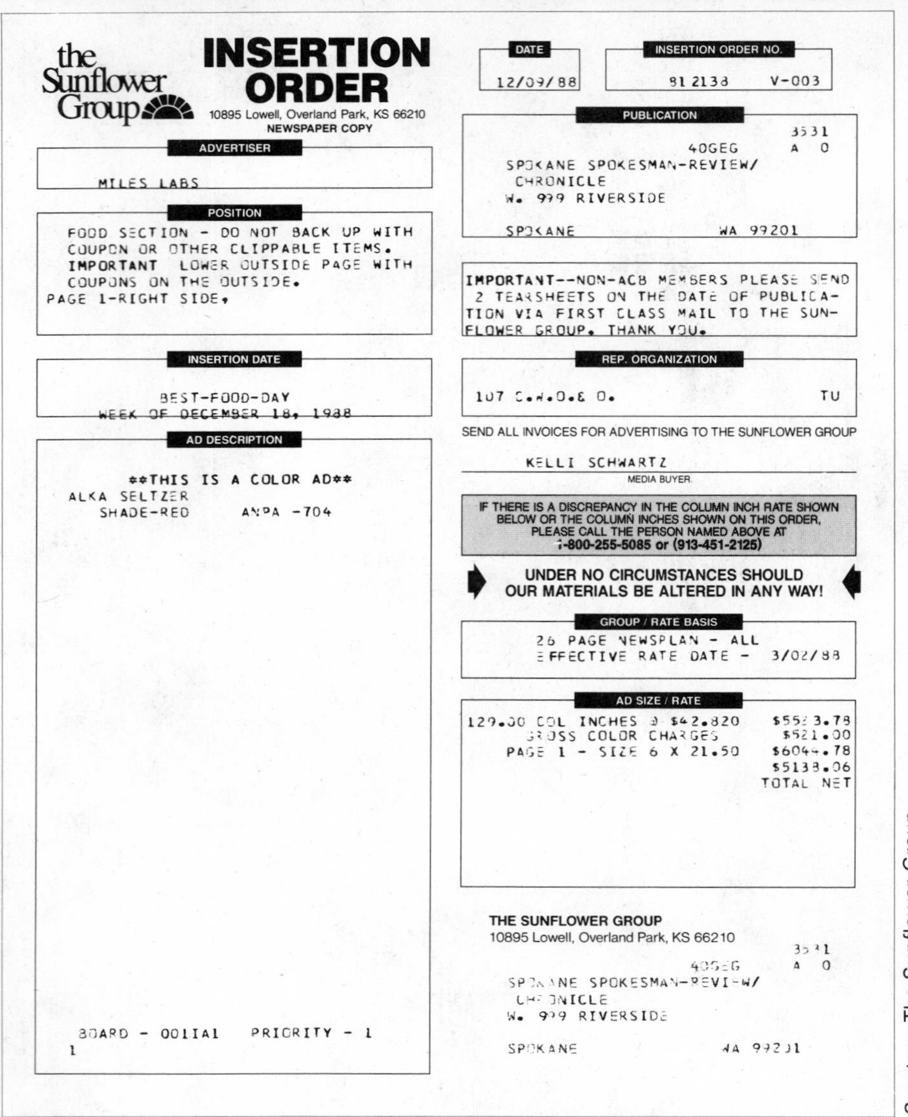
the Sunflower Group

INSERTION ORDER

10895 Lowell, Overland Park, KS 66210
NEWSPAPER COPY

DATE: 12/09/88

INSERTION ORDER NO.: 81 2138 V-003

ADVERTISER: MILES LABS

PUBLICATION:
3531
40GEG A 0
SPOKANE SPOKESMAN-REVIEW/
CHRONICLE
W. 999 RIVERSIDE
SPOKANE WA 99201

POSITION:
FOOD SECTION - DO NOT BACK UP WITH
COUPON OR OTHER CLIPPABLE ITEMS.
IMPORTANT LOWER OUTSIDE PAGE WITH
COUPONS ON THE OUTSIDE.
PAGE 1-RIGHT SIDE,

IMPORTANT--NON-ACB MEMBERS PLEASE SEND 2 TEARSHEETS ON THE DATE OF PUBLICATION VIA FIRST CLASS MAIL TO THE SUNFLOWER GROUP. THANK YOU.

INSERTION DATE:
BEST-FOOD-DAY
WEEK OF DECEMBER 18, 1988

REP. ORGANIZATION:
107 C.W.O.& O. TU

SEND ALL INVOICES FOR ADVERTISING TO THE SUNFLOWER GROUP

KELLI SCHWARTZ
MEDIA BUYER

AD DESCRIPTION:
THIS IS A COLOR AD
ALKA SELTZER
SHADE-RED ANPA -704

BOARD - 001IA1 PRIORITY - 1
1

IF THERE IS A DISCREPANCY IN THE COLUMN INCH RATE SHOWN BELOW OR THE COLUMN INCHES SHOWN ON THIS ORDER, PLEASE CALL THE PERSON NAMED ABOVE AT 1-800-255-5085 or (913-451-2125)

UNDER NO CIRCUMSTANCES SHOULD OUR MATERIALS BE ALTERED IN ANY WAY!

GROUP / RATE BASIS:
26 PAGE NEWSPLAN - ALL
EFFECTIVE RATE DATE - 3/02/88

AD SIZE / RATE:
129.00 COL INCHES @ $42.820 $5523.78
GROSS COLOR CHARGES $521.00
PAGE 1 - SIZE 6 X 21.50 $6044.78
$5138.06
TOTAL NET

THE SUNFLOWER GROUP
10895 Lowell, Overland Park, KS 66210
3531
40GEG A 0
SPOKANE SPOKESMAN-REVIEW/
CHRONICLE
W. 999 RIVERSIDE
SPOKANE WA 99201

Courtesy The Sunflower Group.

traffic department The part of an advertising agency that coordinates interdepartmental efforts.

production department The part of an advertising agency responsible for getting advertisements into print or broadcast form.

media buying plans with the advertiser or client, who will be expected to pay for what you purchase. The agency **traffic department** will coordinate all these interdepartmental efforts and make certain that the advertisement is prepared on time and reaches the media on schedule. A **production department** may be involved to get the advertisement into print or broadcast form and in sufficient number to provide to all the vehicles that will be presenting it.

Courtesy International Business Machines Corporation.

Suddenly, brilliant stereo sound and dazzling video images are coming out of IBM Personal System/2® computers with Micro Channel.™
They're opening people's eyes and ears to more involving presentations. More stimulating classes and training programs. More interesting demonstrations.
IT ROCKS, IT ROLLS, IT RIVETS THE ATTENTION.
With PS/2® MultiMedia hardware and software, you can combine full-motion video, slides, photographs, illustrations, text, graphics, animation and narration, as well as your existing data base.
You can also capture and manipulate sounds and images from video cameras, disks and tapes, from CD and audio players, and from an IBM CD-ROM player.
Show them right on your PS/2. Share them across a network. Or project them on a big screen.
Instead of passively reading a report or hearing a lecture, your audience can experience what you communicate.
An auto mechanic can hear the sounds made by a failing brake and see how to replace the part in animated sequence. A travel agency client can surf Hawaii's waves. Or a real estate prospect can stroll through houses for sale.
CREATE, EDIT, PRESENT RIGHT AT YOUR DESK.
The possibilities of PS/2 MultiMedia are limited only by the imagination.
You can do everything we've just described right at your desk, on the PS/2 with Micro Channel you already own. Thanks to two remarkable products: the IBM Audio Visual Connection™ (which PC Magazine gave their Technical Excellence Award for 1989) and the IBM Motion Video Adapter.
But they're just the beginning. New multimedia applications are emerging all the time. And with Micro Channel's expandability, you're ready for them. From the latest DVI™ (Digital Video Interactive) technology, which brings full-motion video to your hard disk or CD-ROM, to interactive touch displays and much, much more.
BEFORE YOUR NEXT PRESENTATION, SEE OURS.
To see and hear what PS/2 MultiMedia can do, contact your IBM Authorized Dealer or IBM marketing representative. For a free demonstration videocassette or a dealer near you, call 1 800 255-0426, ext. 38.
Words alone simply can't describe it.
How're you going to do it?
PS/2 it!
IBM

FIGURE 14–5
This magazine advertisement supports an advertising campaign that also appeared in another medium, television. The two media efforts complement one another to reinforce the sales message.

Eventually, the media will send the advertising agency a bill or **invoice**, usually attached to an extra copy of the insertion order and confirmation. In the case of a printed advertisement, a copy of the actual advertisement, called a **checking copy**, will be sent along with the bill to prove that the advertisement was run as intended. Broadcast media cannot send a copy, so instead a legal document called an **affidavit** will accompany the invoice and insertion order, certifying that the advertisement actually ran at a certain time and that no mechanical problems occurred.

invoice A bill.

checking copy A copy of a printed advertisement sent with an invoice to the advertiser.

affidavit A legal document used as proof that a broadcast advertisement was run.

This may appear to be a long and complicated process, especially if your advertising campaign appears in several media and if some of the advertising is being used to support a campaign that uses some other medium as its principal channel. This kind of campaign requires special attention to timing and to media compatibility, as illustrated in Figure 14–5.

But these are only the main points of the media planning and buying process. In reality, there is more to it, with more details and more decisions to be made. But as is true with so many complicated processes, it becomes easier as you gain experience and get accustomed to it.

SUMMARY

Media planning and buying are complicated processes but should be understood for the total media function to fit into the overall advertising campaign. Objectives involve what is to be accomplished, while strategies are the plans to meet those objectives and tactics are the implementations of those strategies.

Before beginning the media plan, it is important to discover what the competition is doing with its advertising. The amount of money budgeted for advertising must also be considered. Finally, the plan can be established. Estimating the cost of the plan is an essential part of the process.

Only after the media plan is approved can the actual process of buying media begin. This involves contacting individual media and vehicles and negotiating for the best rates, advertisement placement, timing and discounts. Other miscellaneous steps finish up the media planning and buying procedure.

TERMS TO KNOW

Now that you have finished this chapter, you should understand the following terms:

- advertising unit
- objective
- strategy
- tactics
- logistics
- Leading National Advertisers (LNA)
- Selling Areas—Marketing, Inc. (SAMI)
- estimating guide
- exposure
- audience accumulation
- audience duplication
- buy
- A.C. Nielsen Company
- Arbitron, Inc.
- percentage-of-sales-or-profits budget
- competitive spending budget
- formula budget
- objective-and-task budget
- share-point budget
- availabilities (avails)
- flow chart
- insertion order
- confirmation
- tearsheet
- traffic department
- production department
- invoice
- checking copy
- affidavit

If you are not certain of the meaning of any of these terms, go back through the chapter and review them.

THINGS TO THINK ABOUT

1. What is the difference between an objective, a strategy, and a tactic?
2. What are the differences between advertising media, vehicles, and units? Give an example of each.
3. What is reach? Frequency? Impact? Continuity? How would they be used with a combination of media in successful advertising media plans?
4. What are the advantages of the five basic types of advertising media budgeting? What are the disadvantages?
5. What are the differences between marketing objectives, advertising objectives, and media objectives?
6. Why is media selection only a part of the overall media planning and buying process?
7. In what ways is finding an advertising niche that differs from the competition a form of product differentiation?
8. Why is the frequency of exposure (the average number of times that an audience member is exposed to an advertisement) likely to be a smaller number than the frequency of insertion (the number of times that the same advertisement was run)?

THINGS TO TALK ABOUT

1. Why is it so important to have reliable research information before you begin media planning?
2. Why is it often easier to carry out media tactics (implementation) than media strategies (planning)?
3. Why are print checking copies and broadcast affidavits necessary before a media invoice can be paid?
4. In what ways is the potential impact of the competition so crucial to an advertiser's media plan?
5. Why is it difficult to make direct comparisons between the various types of available advertising media? Why is it also difficult to compare one vehicle with another?
6. Why is the coordination of all advertising agency departments desirable? Why must the prior approval of the advertiser (client) be gained before actual media buys are contracted?
7. Why is an insertion order needed in addition to the buy (reservation) and contract? Why are an invoice and confirmation also required for payment?
8. Why are broadcast media more likely to have negotiated rates than are print media?

THINGS TO DO

1. Visit a retailer and find out how the advertising budget is set and why that approach is used.
2. Read a copy of *Advertising Age* magazine and find out how much one or two large advertisers may be spending on advertising. Consider why the amounts invested in advertising differ so much.
3. Try to determine how much advertising rates for various media have increased during the past year or so and compare those trends with the general economic inflationary index.
4. Invite an advertising media planner to speak to your class about how a current media effort was planned.
5. Visit a local media vehicle and ask for copies of blank media invoices, confirmations, and affidavits.

SECTION 4

Campaigns

Now it is time to fit together the entire advertising effort. The complete advertising effort is called a *campaign*, and you must understand campaigns if you are to understand advertising. A single advertisement usually is not effective, at least, not by itself. Just as the entire advertising effort must be coordinated in advance, so must the entire advertising effort be coordinated into the process and package that constitutes a campaign. A campaign is a long-term advertising effort that must have *unity*, *continuity* and *flexibility*.

In this section, you will come to understand the importance and use of advertising campaigns. You will also see three actual campaigns, what they tried to do, how they went about doing it, and why they were successful.

The campaigns themselves are exciting and interesting, because they were intended to attract and interest and convince the prospective customers. You'll find them interesting and exciting, too.

CHAPTERS

15 Campaign Planning—Marketing, Advertising, and Research Considerations

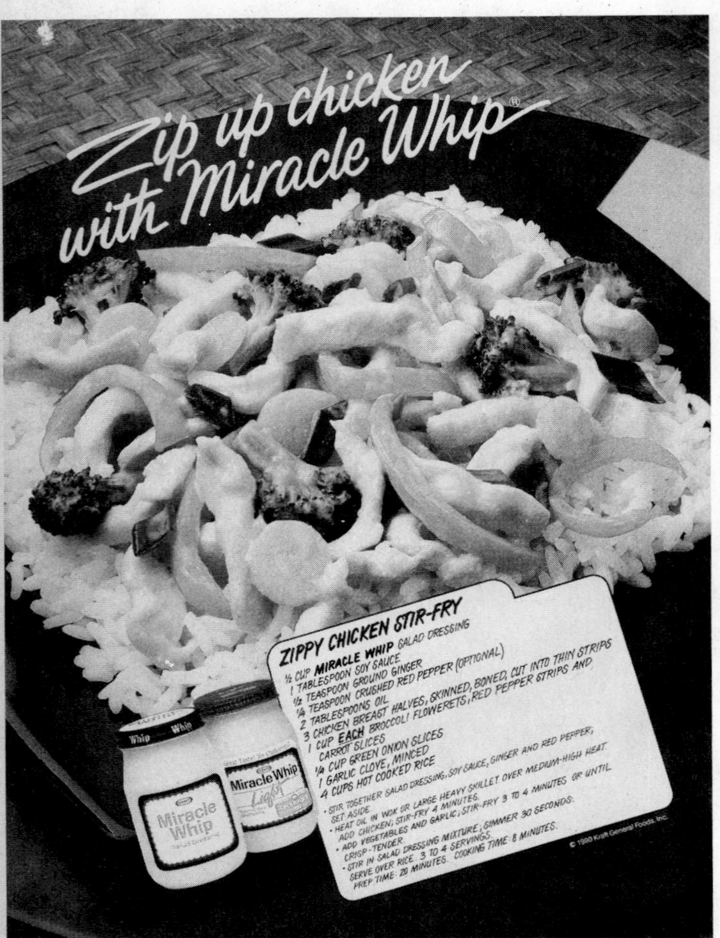

Courtesy of Kraft General Foods, Inc.

CHAPTER OUTLINE

By the time you finish this chapter, you should understand:

1. How a campaign differs from an advertisement.
2. Why the campaign principle is used in advertising.
3. What elements are involved in campaign planning.
4. The importance of the marketing mix.
5. The kinds of research needed for campaign planning.

At this point in your examination of advertising, it is well to introduce a key topic—the campaign. Perhaps you have often heard the term *advertising campaign* and thought little about it. The advertising campaign embraces all that you have studied so far—and a good bit more. In the next three chapters, you will discover why the campaign may well be the most important concept in the advertising, marketing, and selling process.

WHAT IS A CAMPAIGN?

The message you read on behalf, say, of United Airlines in *Time* this week is an advertisement—a single selling unit. The several United Airlines ads you may have noticed in *Time* since last Christmas or last September make up an advertising campaign.

An advertising campaign is *not* a single blast—no matter how explosive. A **campaign** is a series or sequence of advertising and promotion efforts, carefully planned, coordinated, and executed, over a long period of time.

campaign A series or sequence of advertising and promotion efforts.

The Campaign Uses Repetition

The advertising campaign has its roots in some of the most basic elements of human behavior. It is based on the primary rule of learning theory—repetition.

We learn by seeing and doing something over and over until we absorb its meaning. Take your own experience. You were not born knowing the alphabet. You did not sit up in the crib and start tying your shoe laces or a necktie. No, most human behavior is learned through repetition. The alphabet may be second nature to us now, but only because we were carefully and continually coached by loving parents. Many of us can instantly recite the little verse about spelling Mississippi. American mothers have been chanting it to their children for generations, and their children have been chanting it right back. Repetition! Repetition! The basic rule of human learning.

How logical then for shrewd advertisers to run their messages in a series, over time. The more we see and hear the basic message, the more easily we remember—and respond almost out of habit. Just as you were not born knowing your alphabet, you were not born knowing which soft drink is the choice of a certain generation. But you know it now. You've learned it, and that wise advertiser isn't about to let you unlearn it.

The Campaign Allows for Gaps of Coverage

Consider another, less scholarly, angle. Even though you may count yourself a regular reader of, say, *Newsweek*, you are not likely to see every issue or every single page of the issues you do read. Perhaps you are a "60 Minutes" fan and watch that program religiously. But you miss it from time to time, or you may be interrupted during part of it. So nobody sees every single advertisement for a given product in a single advertising medium. What do you do about the gaps of coverage? Certainly, a campaign—a series of messages—should help to solve the problem.

Advertising Is Only One Component

Another point (one we will shortly treat in great detail): Advertising is only part of the manufacturing-marketing process in America. It must be coordinated with all the other efforts of the total enterprise. A great ad run on the wrong day can be a waste of money. Suppose the manufacturing plant has not been able to turn out the product quickly enough to fill the channels of distribution? If people cannot find it in the stores, you may only make enemies by telling them about it. Planning and coordination are essential campaign considerations.

The Campaign Reinforces Earlier Impressions

Many people buy products on impulse—if they do not represent a great risk. (Steady, reminder ads do the job.) But some purchases are more expensive, take a lot of study, and take a long time to decide upon and complete—a car, for instance. You may see a new-car ad today and say "Wow! I'd like that!" But you may not be in a position to *buy* it for six months or a year. During that period, the advertiser is running a series of messages that repeat and reinforce your first impression.

The Campaign Involves Careful Planning

We have examined just a few of the reasons that the most effective marketers—large and small—apply the campaign principle to their advertising efforts. Planning an advertising campaign that takes advantage of all these factors—and others as well—is a little like planning a military campaign. The planner must carefully gather and study all intelligence or information; set goals or objectives; and totally marshal and deploy all resources to achieve some selling advantage over an equally enterprising competitor. The very word *campaign* implies planning, mapping out a course of action ahead of time. In actual business practice, many elements enter into campaign planning.

The Need for Information. The most crucial factor in planning is the constant need for information (what military campaign strategists call intelligence). Such background information involves thorough knowledge of the product, of the marketplace and of potential customers, as we discussed in Chapter 3.

The Need for Realistic Goals. Based on a searching analysis of this information, marketing managers must make decisions about realistic goals, about whom they want to reach, about how much money to invest in advertising, about what to say and where to say it, and about keeping advertising in step with their other marketing activities.

The Need for Precise Execution. Nothing in the plan should be left to chance or to memory. The overall strategy must be put in writing. This keeps everybody on track, even after a passage of time. And a written strategy permits replacement personnel to learn quickly about the scope of the entire operation.

In a nutshell, to plan an effective advertising campaign you have to know where you stand now, where you want to go, and what it will take to get you there in a given period of time. In fact, you will have to review the very factors that you have already studied in Chapters 2 and 3 of this book.

Then you must carry out these decisions in a very specific manner. You must set dates for messages to appear in particular publications or on particular broadcasts. You must write copy, prepare budgets, order artwork and films, and make arrangements for periodic checks to see how well the advertising is working.

In the remainder of this chapter, we'll carefully examine the many specific factors to consider in planning a campaign.

THE MARKETING MIX

Although advertising may be your chief interest, you must recall from what you read in Chapter 2 that advertising is only *part* of the total marketing mix. In many businesses, advertising is a very minor part of that mix. And overall marketing decisions heavily influence advertising decisions. No campaign of any scope can proceed without considering this mix.

What is meant by marketing mix? The many elements that go into the design, manufacturing, distribution, and sale of a product. These are generally identified as product, price, channel of distribution, packaging, personal selling, promotion, brand, service, and, of course, advertising. Sometimes the marketing mix is referred to as the "4P's": product, price, place, promotion.

Product Qualities

The nature of the product determines the importance of each other element in the marketing mix. Is it a product bought by everyday consumers? Is it a product used by business and industry? Most food and drug items—often bought on impulse—rely on heavy advertising expenditures. Many technical and industrial products require the expertise of a personal salesperson to clinch a buying decision. Some products are available for sale on nearly every block in America; some products are specially designed and built to particular specifications. You would find two quite different sets of selling problems, depending on whether you were marketing a plastic bag of cocktail nuts or a plastic bag of nuts and bolts.

Influence of Price

By and large, prices differ for various product categories. An automobile is far more expensive than a toaster. But there are ranges of prices within categories and ranges of prices within one company's line of products. Almost every major car manufacturer today offers selections in the high, intermediate, and low price classes.

Some marketers are "price" operators—all selling emphasis goes on saving the customer money. For years one clothing chain built its promotion around "low overhead." Another marketer may take a "quality" stance—offering extra in the way of special features and services—and charging more to the customer. Generally, the "low price" marketer depends more on high volume of sales than does the "high price" marketer.

Channels of Distribution

Obviously, every marketer must have channels or outlets through which the firm's products can flow to the customers. Often the chain goes from manufacturer to wholesaler to retailer. But just consider the great variety of retailers from giant supermarkets and department stores down to hole-in-the-wall operations; from large national "chains" to tiny "mama-and-papa" stores. An inexpensive, frequently purchased item—say, a snack food—can get exposure in many places from supermarkets to newsstands. But a sofa bed is available only from a furniture store or a department store.

franchise A system in which only one dealer in a community can handle a brand.

Many quality manufacturers sell through a **franchise** system in which only one dealer in a community can handle their brand of product. Some products are so specialized—certain musical instruments, for instance—that they may be blocked out of entire communities because there is not a suitable dealer present to handle and demonstrate such merchandise.

Influence of Packaging

Some packages serve only the basic practical purpose of containing the product; most packages serve a sales purpose as well. They catch the eye, show how to use or prepare the product, or suggest additional uses. In the perfume and cosmetics field, the packaging may represent a greater investment than the ingredients in the product itself; it may add style and drama to the product. In most instances, the package offers identification; we learn to recognize it. It also offers communication; it "speaks out" to the shopper from the supermarket shelves. For example, the illustration on the packaging of Lean Cuisine Dinners certainly whets the appetite of the most rigid dieter. Many times the convenience designed into a package will help to influence a sale ("packed in its own mailing tube" or "packaged in its own serving dish").

Degree of Personal Selling

The cost of a personal sales call has risen rapidly since World War II. In 1987 a personal sales call was estimated to cost $230. Yet in many business-to-business situations personal selling is far more important than advertising. Many companies use business-to-business advertising simply to pave the way for the salesperson. In some business-to-business situations the personal salesperson must be a skilled professional—a chemist, an engineer, an agriculturalist. He or she must be there to negotiate the purchase. Not so when it comes to our everyday food items. Who needs a salesperson present to explain a Pepsi, Grape Nuts, or Juicy Fruit? Chances are that the ultimate consumer knows more about the product than a sales clerk, having learned from advertising, and—more important—from experience.

Influence of Promotions

The term **sales promotion** here means all sales-building activities that fall in between personal selling and advertising. In the 1980s, management concern with immediate sales caused a boom in sales promotion, often at the expense of long-term brand image advertising. Agencies that specialized in sales promotion sprang up and prospered. A special price deal to retailers is a form of sales promotion. So, too, are cents-off coupons, contests, and premiums. A sales promotion is, generally speaking, a short-term, intensive effort to create extra excitement within the company organization, among retailers, or among consumers. Some marketers embrace promotions; others denounce promotions because they feel it is a form of price cutting.

sales promotion All sales-building activities that fall in between personal selling and advertising.

Brand

Americans are used to thinking in terms of brands. A well-respected brand can set its own price, to some extent. But not all manufacturers brand their products. It is costly to promote and protect a brand. Some manufacturers are perfectly satisfied to make products which will be sold under somebody else's label or brand. Sears Roebuck, for example, counts among its suppliers many top-notch manufacturers who build products to wear a Sears label such as Kenmore and Craftsman. The manufacturer thus operates at an assured volume level and profit level as long as Sears stays happy. But if management decides that it is going to aggressively promote a brand and build a consumer franchise, other elements in the total marketing plan are vitally influenced by that decision: packaging, promotion, advertising.

Service

service A broad term that can mean any form of help given the consumer after the purchase.

Service is a rather broad term that has different meaning in different marketing situations. It can refer to any kind of help given the consumer after purchase. Some products require special servicing arrangements and facilities. An automobile is the most obvious product in this regard. You won't buy a new car unless you know it's going to receive skilled service from a reputable dealer. But service also has to be given some consideration in the purchase of a washer-dryer, television set, or microwave oven. Service may be as basic as whether or not a dealer will deliver the product to a customer's home. A "cash-and-carry" operation will not deliver, but a "quality" operation will.

Advertising

Finally, the marketing mix contains advertising as one ingredient. As mentioned before, the importance of advertising can vary greatly. In the cosmetics and personal care field, advertising accounts for a sizable percentage of sales cost—perhaps as much as 40 to 50 percent. In the automotive field, advertising accounts for a very modest percentage—perhaps under 1 percent. Frequently purchased impulse items tend to be heavily advertised. An industrial product may be little advertised—a few pages in the trade press, an occasional mailing piece. It all depends. You can be sure only that the relative importance of advertising in the marketing mix depends on the particular marketing situation. The relative position of advertising has been decided after careful study and planning by marketing's top managers. But here's an important point to keep in mind. Most marketing managers will agree that, of all the elements in the marketing mix, advertising can be manipulated most readily to influence sales.

SPECIAL INFLUENCES ON ADVERTISING

Of the various other elements in the marketing mix, certain ones have direct and important bearing on the advertising effort—the use of it, the size of it, the content of it.

Nature of Product

The most crucial influence is the product itself. A fast-moving, self-service item needs advertising—a generous helping. As for what the advertising says—the finest, most effective advertising stems directly from the product and what it will do for people. For example, advertising of Charmin bathroom tissue is focused on softness or squeezability. Clever advertising may create a special impression about a product, but that impression is meaningless unless the product delivers what the advertising promises.

Product pricing may well control whether advertising is "class" or low-brow "schlock"; whether it has a restrained "Tiffany" touch or fire-sale bombast. Over the years, Cadillac advertising has always had a refined, quality look—as though price were no object. But some national advertisers push economy; some local advertisers never run anything but a "sale" ad.

The creation of a brand image puts a heavy burden on the advertising element of the marketing mix. A considerable and consistent investment is involved, but in this area advertising can contribute a great deal. It is very likely that the positive brand image you attribute to certain products was planted in your mind and nurtured there by the company's advertising.

Advertising and Distribution

We have already pointed out that it is hard to succeed in marketing with poor distribution. But in some cases advertising has expanded distribution by creating consumer demand. An outstanding example of this occurred with comedy genius Stan Freberg's famous "Clark Smathers, Aluminum Salesman" campaign for Kaiser Aluminum. Prospective customers saw and heard the advertising and asked their retailers to order Kaiser Aluminum from that nice young salesperson who had a family to feed. In turn, retailers asked wholesalers, and the wholesalers sought out the manufacturer. As a rule, however, poor distribution can cancel out fine advertising. It is a rare case where advertising opens up distribution.

Featuring the Package

Product packaging is featured in almost every advertisement. In much advertising, the package is the "signature." This is particularly true for perfume and liquor. Sometimes a special characteristic of the package creates advertising emphasis: a new design, for instance, or a totally new packaging idea, like the recent innovation of pump-bottle hand soap.

Featuring the Promotion

Finally, the marketing mix element of sales promotion can have a tremendous bearing on advertising. By its very nature, sales promotion is an intensive effort for a short period of time. It is a temporary stimulus or hypodermic, so to speak, such as a contest or a premium offer. To insure success, the advertising at that period almost always promotes the promotion. It would make no sense for a company to launch a big consumer sweepstakes and let its advertising ignore the event. (See Figures 15–1 and 15–2.)

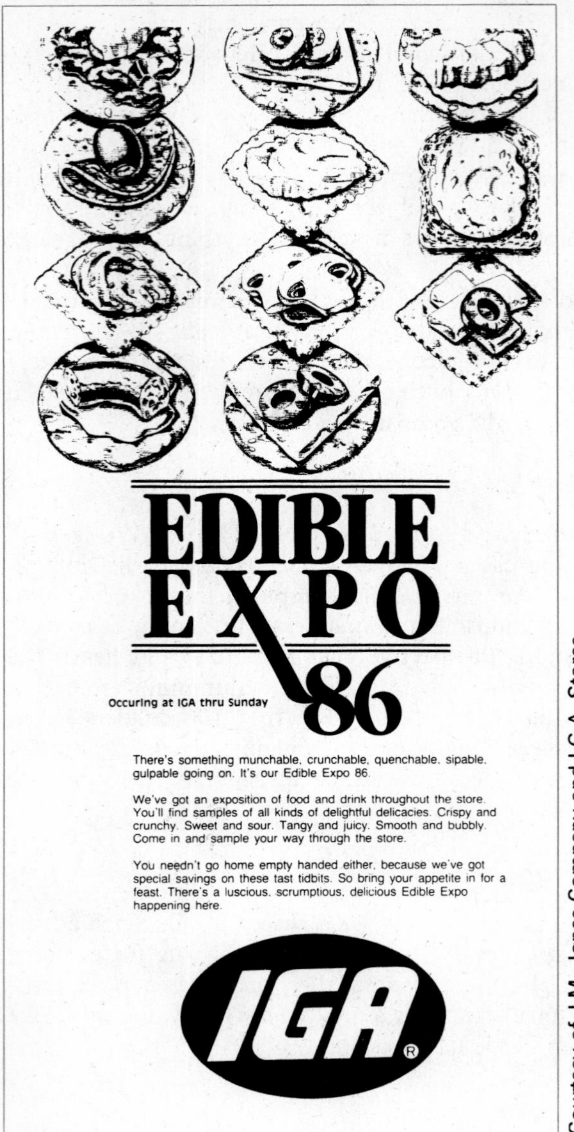

EDIBLE
EXPO
86
Occuring at IGA thru Sunday
There's something munchable, crunchable, quenchable, sipable, gulpable going on. It's our Edible Expo 86.
We've got an exposition of food and drink throughout the store. You'll find samples of all kinds of delightful delicacies. Crispy and crunchy. Sweet and sour. Tangy and juicy. Smooth and bubbly. Come in and sample your way through the store.
You needn't go home empty handed either, because we've got special savings on these tast tidbits. So bring your appetite in for a feast. There's a luscious, scrumptious, delicious Edible Expo happening here.
IGA®

Courtesy of J.M. Jones Company and I.G.A. Stores.

FIGURE 15–1
Here is a retail promotion offered by a regional chain of independent grocery stores. Notice that the time limit for the promotion is clearly stated.

KNOWING THE MARKET

For local merchants to know their market seems a relatively easy task. Their own eyes and ears and experience should keep them clued in. But national advertisers have a far more complex problem. They do not see their customers

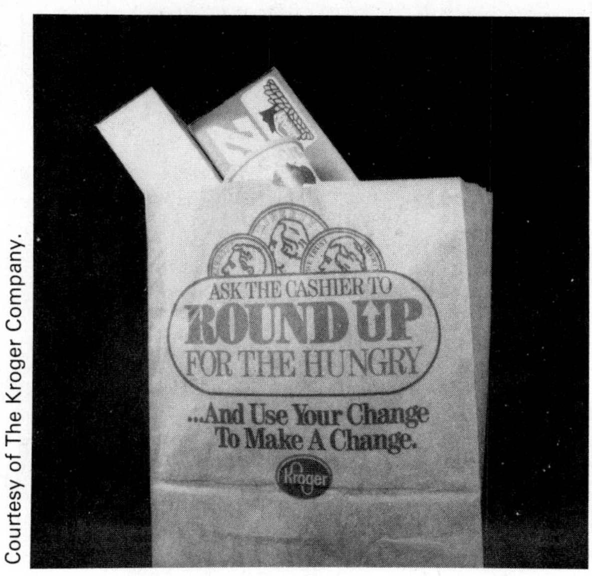

Courtesy of The Kroger Company.

FIGURE 15–2
This "Round-Up for the Hungry" promotion used by The Kroger Company reinforces the store's positive image.

face-to-face, so they must find other methods for determining who their customers are. Usually they begin with secondary research.

Secondary Research

You will remember that secondary research is research that is readily available from published sources. Sources for secondary research are all around us, simply for the seeking. They are broad in nature, not restricted to a single advertiser's problems. They are public, often available free in libraries or for a subscription fee paid to the research organization making the report. Many are continuing studies like Starch Readership Reports, Nielsen Ratings, and Simmons Market Research figures. The *U.S. Census Report* is a gold mine of information to businesspeople, yet everybody has equal access to those nuggets.

Demographics. The crudest, least sophisticated method of defining markets is through the use of demographics: age, income, education, occupation, race, position in the life cycle (and the like). Much of this information is available from the Bureau of the Census. Every year *Sales and Marketing Management* magazine organizes such information into its "Survey of Buying Power." Knowing these factors, separately and in combination, will help you evaluate your own best prospects in the marketplace. To give a crude example—if you decided that your ideal market was high-income 50-year-olds, you wouldn't try to reach them over rock music radio stations.

Although demographic information may be relatively easy to obtain, it leaves a lot unsaid about individual characteristics. A famous advertising executive made the point that while Patty Hearst and Susan Ford were almost identical demographically, it would be hard to find two women who had led more different lives than the publisher's daughter and the President's daughter.

Social Class. Some marketers make a case for structuring the market via social classes. It is generally agreed that in metropolitan areas there are six quite recognizable classes: upper upper or rich old families; lower upper or the "nouveau riche"; upper middle or well-to-do business and professional people; lower middle or white-collar workers; upper lower or wage earners; and lower lower or unskilled workers.[1]

Personality Factors. It is difficult to trace markets via character traits and personality factors such as aggressiveness, compliance, dominance, but there is a growing tendency to locate them via shared interests—boating, skiing, bridge, love of music, love of history, crafts, and the like. One noted "up front" research approach is called VALS, which classifies consumers by their Values And Life Styles.

prime prospects
The percentage of total users who consume the greatest quantity of a product per capita.

Prime Prospects. One prominent advertising agency always tries to identify the **prime prospects** for a product. These are the small percentage of total users who consume the greatest quantity of a product per capita. For example, it is pretty well agreed that 20 percent of the beer drinkers consume 80 percent of the beer. Advertising aimed at these prime prospects would really be well targeted.

Nielsen Audits. In order to know where they stand, many national advertisers subscribe to the Nielsen audits. The A.C. Nielsen Company regularly checks nearly 2,000 grocery stores and nearly 1,000 drugstores across the country serving hundreds of thousands of families. Manufacturers get an accurate bi-monthly report on the movement of goods into consumer hands (plus several other precious items of information—on special sales, use of displays, and the like).

Simmons Market Research. As you will recall from Chapter 3, another guidepost for national advertisers is Simmons Market Research Bureau, an independent research organization. Its extensive surveys of the market break the total market down into convenient product categories. Say your interest is a new cake mix. You can turn to the report on Prepared Cake

---

[1] W. L. Warner et al., *Social Class in America* (New York: Harper & Row Publishers, Inc., 1960).

Mixes and find an intensive analysis of the market before your very eyes—who uses how much how often; where users are located; family composition; income; age groups; even media usage habits.

Consumer Panel Studies. National consumer panels are operated continuously by independent research services. Such a panel would consist of a statistically correct number of consumer families from which to project national averages. The panel might keep diaries of purchases and could be asked direct questions of a marketing nature. Local consumer panel studies have been done by local media—the *Milwaukee Journal* and the *Chicago Tribune*, for example. A local or regional advertiser should always be alert to market information gathered by nearby media.

City Directories and Trade Association Reports. The local advertiser can also use city directories and various public records that are available for analysis. Trade association reports also release figures that can be helpful, particularly in revealing some activities and expenditures of competitors. One trade association, the Newspaper Advertising Bureau, has for years issued studies that have helped retailers of all kinds and sizes.

Primary Research

Unlike secondary research, primary research is planned, executed, and paid for by one sponsor at one period for one purpose. It is private. It is usually not continuing. If a local druggist sends out a questionnaire to his charge account customers, that is primary research. If Procter & Gamble does a broad-scale study of detergent uses among 5,000 families, that is primary research.

Obviously, primary research is likely to be far more costly than secondary research. The shrewd marketer may well use both.

Study of Sales Figures. Certainly no marketer would make any kind of analysis without a study of the firm's own sales figures and those of competitors (even if approximations). The research publication, *Leading National Advertisers*, can help in analyzing competition. Sales figures are an essential part of doing business—available day-by-day, year-by-year. Much can be learned through simple comparison of one period's sales figures with another, or with sales fluctuations or changes at various periods of the year. Manufacturers can see which product in their line is winning increasing acceptance, which product is performing sluggishly.

Sales Comparisons. A comparison of sales levels is the most basic kind of market survey— and it is available to everybody in business from the giant automotive manufacturer to the owner of a single hot dog stand. Department stores keep precise year-by-year sales comparisons, including the influence of weather on a particular day.

Product Analysis

For the marketer, product analysis goes far beyond just a knowledge of the product's physical properties. These are vital, but they are fixed and known quantities. The area of exploration crucial to the marketer is the misty area where the product qualities touch the consumer's interests. At the earliest planning stage, the marketer is more concerned with the want-satisfying properties of the product than the mere physical properties.

R & D Analysis. The marketer can learn more about this area first by reviewing the steps that the firm's own Research and Development people went through in creating the product. Every product has a reason for being. Nowadays that reason is to provide a satisfaction of such value that customers will seek out the product again and again. This is the goal that Research and Development people constantly had in mind as they asked and answered crucial questions—questions very like those that may occur in a consumer purchase search. R & D Analysis is available and should be reviewed before seeking further information.

Stage in Product Life Cycle. Most products go through five distinct stages in their existence—introduction, growth, maturity, saturation, and decline.[2] Various marketing factors assume different degrees of importance during each of these states. During the Introduction stage, product quality is the dominant factor; unless the new product wins respect, it will win very little in the way of sales and growth. In the Growth stage, advertising is of primary importance. In the Maturity stage, when the attributes and benefits of the product are well known and growth has slowed, price is of greatest importance. In the Saturation stage, when no new buyers are left, sales promotion or off-pricing could be most important. In the Maturity and Saturation stages, advertising would tend toward reminder messages. But in the Decline stage, advertising might have renewed importance as the manufacturer seeks new uses for the product and wishes to spread word of them widely.

Review of Past Selling Patterns. A check of past selling and buying may prove helpful. A canvass of the company's own sales personnel is an excellent source of information. A good salesperson can give a pretty accurate reading on what present customers think of the company and the product.

Retail operations call for analysis of special considerations such as store location and seasonal purchasing factors.

If such customer information is too skimpy to base plans on, then new primary research may be in order. A survey may reveal that customers do not

---

[2] Philip Kotler, *Marketing Management* (Englewood Cliffs, N.J.: Prentice-Hall, Inc., 1967).

think of the product in the same terms as does the manufacturer. Customers may not even use the product quite as the manufacturer intended. Such a survey should include present customers and prospective customers. The attitudes toward the product of the *latter* group may hold the key to the marketer's future.

Consumer Analysis

The mention of attitudes leads logically to consumer analysis, the next step in knowing where you stand before launching the marketing plan.

Consumer Behavior. Much has been written in recent years about consumer behavior. It has become a favorite study of many scholars. Chapter 2 has introduced you to it. Scientific models of consumer purchasing behavior have been mapped out. It is a fascinating subject, but many of the books on it are a bit overwhelming. If your own curiosity is aroused, you'll find a clear and compact overall look at the subject in *Consumer Behavior* by Thomas S. Robertson.[3]

Consumer Motivation. The consumer can be studied as an individual and as a member of a group. Each of us has ingrained motives for behavior. There is a sort of pattern of motives or "hierarchy" as psychologist Abraham Maslow called it. At the lowest level is self-preservation. At the highest levels are needs for esteem and self-improvement or self-fulfillment.[4] Motives in our affluent society have gone far beyond the basic necessities of preserving our skins. In some instances, our real motives are not revealed by buying behavior. Often our motives are controlled by the group to which we belong.

Opinions and Attitudes. We claim to be using our own judgment when we buy. Our "judgment" is made up of opinions, beliefs, and attitudes toward people and things. There are a number of influences on a person's attitudes. Communications is one influence (and that would surely include advertising). The sociological reference group to which a person belongs has heavy influence. A **reference group** is any collection of people that an individual respects, identifies with, or wants to join. The group influences attitudes and even the clothes a person buys or the car a person drives. Republicans have certain attitudes; accountants may think a certain way, and lawyers may think another. A person's social class makes a huge difference in a person's attitudes. (Consider a wealthy member of the country club set as opposed to a wage earner from the ghetto.) The family has a basic influence on a person's attitudes. Most of us develop our political and church affiliations through family influence.

reference group Any collection of people that an individual respects, identifies with, or wants to join.

[3] Thomas S. Robertson, *Consumer Behavior* (Glenview, Ill.: Scott, Foresman & Co., 1970).
[4] Abraham H. Maslow, *Motivation and Personality*, 2d ed. (New York: Harper, 1970).

Each individual has a network of attitudes on almost every subject. They interweave and intertwine. We resist any influence that throws our attitudes out of balance. Unfortunately we each tend to doubt whether we are making the right purchase. The more important the purchase, the greater the doubts. We conduct what we consider a rational search before making a purchase decision. But there are still risks. The wise marketer works constantly to dispel those doubts and minimize the risks.

The reason marketers are eager to measure opinions and attitudes is that they are good predictors of response in sales.

Attitude Measurement. Advertisers may find some secondary research studies on opinions and attitudes—from certain media surveys, perhaps, or trade association reports. More likely they will have to do some primary research on their own sphere of interest. The manner of questioning is crucial, and the advice of a skilled researcher should be sought.

One currently popular device for measuring attitudes is the semantic differential scale. Notice that in the sample scale shown here in Figure 15–3, a series of opposite-meaning adjectives are applied to the concept or topic under consideration. Each set of two opposite-meaning adjectives ("good" versus "bad") is separated by seven spaces of agreement. This permits some indication of intensity as well as direction of attitude. The respondent can express strong feeling in either direction, moderate feeling, or neutrality.

Discovering Wants and Needs. The shrewd marketer not only seeks consumer opinions and attitudes, but also probes for consumer wants and

FIGURE 15–3
Sample scale for measuring attitudes.

	+3	+2	+1	0	−1	−2	−3	
Logical								Illogical
Factual								Not Factual
Overstated								Understated
Emotional								Unemotional
High Credibility								Low Credibility
High in "Puffery"								Low in "Puffery"
Ambiguous								Unambiguous
Simple								Complex
Irritating								Not Irritating
Informative								Uninformative
Relevant								Irrelevant
Believable								Unbelievable
Effective								Ineffective
Necessary								Unnecessary
Deceptive								Not Deceptive
Good								Bad
Interesting								Uninteresting
Fraudulent								Not Fraudulent

needs. Locating and satisfying such wants and needs seems to be the key to successful marketing. In fact, it is the very essence of marketing. One prominent national advertising agency goes off at a slight tangent that has proved highly rewarding. This agency concentrates not on wants and needs but on problems—or, rather, on a prime prospect's problem with a particular product category. You will remember that prime prospects are the small percentage of people who consume the largest percentage of the product. That advertising agency believes that offering a solution to the prime prospect's problem is automatically an effective marketing approach. In fact, that agency defines a market as people with a common problem.

Learning What People Are Like Today. In any background study of the marketing situation involving consumer analysis, the planner must be highly alert and sensitive to public fads, interest, trends. The marketing planner must be intensely aware of changing social habits and customs. Never have the changes come faster than at present. Even such revered human institutions as marriage, home, and family are not nearly as sacred as they were only yesterday. Tastes in music, dress, and manners change even more quickly. Back in the 1930s, composer Cole Porter wrote a song lyric which says "in olden days a glimpse of stocking was looked on as something shocking." Whatever might he write today!

SUMMARY

After going through most of the steps just discussed, the advertiser has analyzed the situation and broken it down into problems and opportunities. As mentioned earlier, the advertiser wants to maximize opportunities and minimize problems, wants to put the firm's best foot forward—but where? In what direction? How big a step? We shall examine these and other essential campaign decisions in the next chapter.

TERMS TO KNOW

Now that you have finished this chapter, you should understand the following terms:

campaign	service
franchise	prime prospects
sales promotion	reference group

If you are uncertain of the meaning of any of these terms, go back through the chapter to review them.

THINGS TO THINK ABOUT

1. The Lonely Maytag Repairman is a famous figure in advertising. Can you think of one basic, simple reason he became so famous?
2. Americans like to brag that there are no class distinctions in this country. Do you agree? If not, why not?
3. Why do we rarely hear the term *mass marketing* in this day and age?
4. Most everyday products are bought in a supermarket where little personal selling is involved. Can you think of an enterprise that is highly dependent on personal selling?
5. Why do you think the advertisers of Chanel #5 perfume can simply show the bottle on a glass shelf with no words of copy whatsoever?
6. What type of packaging provides long shelf life?

THINGS TO TALK ABOUT

1. Repetition is considered desirable in advertising. Might repetition have a negative effect? Discuss.
2. Put a Yugo ad and a Cadillac ad side-by-side. As a group, analyze the two ads. List the obvious differences.
3. As a group, make a list of typical American interests and activities—school, church, shopping, reading, baseball, clothes, cars, and the like. Find out everyone's attitude toward a particular subject. Do you find some marked differences?
4. Discuss an example of what you think is outstanding product packaging.
5. Discuss how several of America's basic social customs have changed drastically in recent years.

THINGS TO DO

1. This week clip every sales promotion ad you see—contest, premium, price-off, and the like. Make a list of the expiration dates of each offer.
2. Get a bar of Dove Soap and a bar of Lava Soap. Analyze the two. Start to write an ad for each. Do you see differences developing?
3. Make a list of the names of leading perfumes. Make a list of the names of leading detergents. How many names might you interchange?
4. Everybody in the group write down the name of a "price" store in your town. Write down the name of a "quality" store. Compare lists.
5. Locate the city directory for your community. What kinds of information does it offer? Which might be useful to advertisers?

16 Essential Campaign Decisions

Advertisement Courtesy of The Dupont Company

CHAPTER OUTLINE

Campaign Essential: A Goal
- Setting Realistic Time Frames
- Difference Between Marketing and Advertising Goals
- Communications Goals
- Marketing Goals
- Positioning in the Public's Mind

Campaign Essential: A Target Market

Campaign Essential: Funds
- Determining Allocation of Money
- The Budget

Campaign Essential: Media Strategy
- The Multiple Choices in Media
- Balancing the Media Choices

Campaign Essential: Creative Strategy
- Particular Target Market
- Particular Medium
- The Budget
- Basic Nature of Product
- Pricing of Product
- Packaging of Product
- Promotion Activities
- Advertiser Image
- Basic Selling Approach

Campaign Essential: Coordination
- Sales Promotion to Consumers
- Activities with the Trade
- Public Relations Aspects

Campaign Essential: Measurement
- Sales Results Are Not Always True Tests
- Pretesting: The Internal Checklist
- Pretesting: Consumer "Jury" Tests
- Posttesting: Print, Television, Campaign Effect
- Necessity for Continuous Testing

By the time you finish this chapter, you should understand:

1. **The need for realistic advertising goals;**
2. **The importance of knowing exactly whom you are trying to reach.**
3. **How the several various campaign essentials interact with one another.**
4. **That there are several ways of deciding how much money to invest in advertising.**
5. **That there is a difference between an advertising appropriation and an advertising budget.**
6. **Who is responsible for handling the budget.**
7. **How the size of the budget influences media and creative decisions.**
8. **The importance of carefully coordinating all campaign activities.**
9. **Many of the principal advertising activities with the trade.**
10. **The function and importance of advertising measurement.**
11. **That there are several types of advertising measurement.**

As we have seen, an advertising campaign is a program of many advertising and promotion efforts that lasts a long period of time. The campaign is carefully plotted, planned, executed, and measured for results. The advertising campaign stems from the overall marketing plan and is coordinated with all other parts of the marketing mix.

The campaign planner must make a number of crucial decisions in several areas—the setting of advertising goals, the selection of a market segment, the amount of money to be invested, the creative approach, the use of media, the coordination of all elements, and the measurement of results. Fortunately, a decision in one area helps facilitate decision making in each of the other areas.

CAMPAIGN ESSENTIAL: A GOAL

After doing all the homework or spadework of market analysis, product analysis, and consumer analysis, the marketer is ready to plan the campaign. Essential to every plan is a goal. The marketer knows where the firm has been and where it stands at present; now it's time to make a carefully calculated move, but in what direction? "If you don't know where you're going, any road will take you there."

Setting Realistic Time Frames

The goal should be realistic. It should be attainable, all things being equal, and it should be attainable in some specified period of time. Goals may be short range, long range, or intermediate, but they generally have a time limit. What should the plan accomplish by such-and-such a date? For a local advertiser, the goal might be to increase traffic on Friday and Saturday during the next three months. For Procter & Gamble, the goal might be to change attitudes toward detergents in a year.

Difference between Marketing and Advertising Goals

By now, you should be aware that there are subtle differences between marketing goals and advertising goals. In Chapter 2 you learned that both are concerned with increased sales. But many factors beside advertising can influence final sales results.

Communications Goals

Since advertising's main function is to communicate, communications goals may offer a more precise way of determining advertising effectiveness. Thus, an advertising goal might be "to make 20 percent of the population familiar with the new slogan in three months." Or, as is often the case, "to make 20 percent of our target audience aware of the existence of the product." Or "to teach 20 percent of our audience new uses for an old product."

Marketing Goals

A marketing goal might concern itself with a change in share-of-market position or with the shipment of so many units in a given time.

Positioning in the Public's Mind

In recent years, one concern of advertisers has been the matter of positioning the product *in the public's mind*. For example, a car is a sports car or a family car. Certainly Maytag's famous "lonely repairman" campaign has been a masterpiece of positioning. The device of the repairman who never gets called dramatizes Maytag as *the* choice for dependability. State Farm's "like a good neighbor" campaign dramatizes its agents and their friendly, helpful service.

A small advertising agency in a medium-sized city did a fifty-call telephone survey to determine the awareness "position" with the public of all ten banks in the community. One stood out. The next few were clustered in second place. Knowing its client's position, the agency was able to make plans to lift its bank well out of the second-place cluster. It is carving out a new position of its own.

CAMPAIGN ESSENTIAL: A TARGET MARKET

In an advertising campaign—as in a military campaign—we achieve a goal by applying pressure against the most logical sector for a breakthrough. In this case, the pressure is persuasion and the sector being pressured is that consumer segment most likely to buy. The more precise the target, the more accurately we can direct the advertising campaign.

As mentioned in Chapter 3, national advertisers can use *Sales and Marketing Management*'s "Survey of Buying Power" and the Simmons Market Research Bureau reports to help zero in. They can do elaborate primary research to pinpoint the market even more closely. The local advertiser can make a modest consumer survey (like the fifty-phone-call survey for the bank), do a survey among employees, or simply ask the opinions of buyers about the ideal target market.

The term "mass market" has lost lustre in recent years. Manufacturers can rarely claim that their market is "everybody." Today markets are becoming more and more segmented—we find ourselves trying to reach teenagers, to reach sports car buffs, to reach junior executives, and to reach working mothers. Of the ideal groups of prospects, the large national marketer is likely to select a primary market and a secondary market. But, for certain, the market is not everybody; the market is groups of people of like age, like interests, or like activities. To focus on the most likely segment or segments of the market is, indeed, an art.

CAMPAIGN ESSENTIAL: FUNDS

Obviously, you cannot have an advertising campaign without the money to pay for it. That money, in some form, must be voted by corporate management. Where is it to come from? And in what proportions?

You cannot manage a campaign without a budget. You cannot set up a budget without an appropriation. You cannot arrive at a sensible appropriation without shrewd sales forecasting.

Sales managers or sales analysts generally do this job because they are thoroughly familiar with the past and present sales performance of the company and its products. They know the strengths and weaknesses of the sales force. They know the problems and opportunities in the various geographical sales areas. This allows them to estimate the amount of sales necessary to achieve the marketing goal just set. The treasurer then estimates costs of production and distribution. An earnings figure would then be added.

Once management has a realistic sales forecast, the next step is to set the appropriation. An **advertising appropriation** is the total lump sum voted for advertising expenditures; the **advertising budget** is the itemized breakdown of how that lump sum is to be invested in a given time period.

advertising appropriation The total lump sum voted for advertising expenditures.

advertising budget The itemized breakdown of how the advertising appropriation will be invested in a given time period.

Determining Allocation of Money

There is no single, ideal way to arrive at an advertising appropriation. More and more scientific procedures are being applied to marketing constantly, but arriving at the annual advertising appropriation is still an art rather than a science. It is an educated guess, but, in most instances, a very highly educated guess. Some marketers swear by one method; other marketers swear by a different method. Some use a combination of methods. Some are constantly exploring and experimenting, groping for the ultimate method of 100 percent accuracy.

Percentage of Sales. Because the allocation is based on sales estimates, many managers fall back on the traditional method of allocating advertising funds via a percentage of sales. Generally, that figure is a percentage of last year's sales. In other words, if we set an advertising allocation of 5 percent of sales and our sales last year were $100,000,000, then our advertising appropriation for the coming year would be $5,000,000. The base figure is a known quantity, thus leaving little room for argument. However, it ties this year's ad program to last year's sales results.

Many advertisers base their allocation on a percentage of future sales. This, of course, would be based on the sales forecast and would probably have to be double-checked periodically.

Unit of Sales. In some industries, such as the brewing industry and the automotive industry, a fixed amount of advertising dollars is allocated to each unit sold. A brewer, for instance, may allocate $2.00 per barrel of beer for advertising. A sales volume of 8 million barrels would make $16 million available for advertising. The success of this method obviously depends on a mighty sound advance estimate of how many units will be sold in a given period of time.

Task Method. This method is based on well-documented and well-conceived advertising goals. If the goal seems justified, management explores the specific avenues of achieving that goal—what distribution must be won, how many units must be sold, what level of profit must be maintained. Then the advertiser has to estimate how much money it will take to do the job.

Investment Spending. When a new product is introduced on the market, the advertiser knows it will be necessary to invest funds at a rate far heavier than normal. The launch or introductory period calls for greater amounts of ammunition to get attention, particularly against already successful competitors. This large introductory allocation is called **investment spending** and comes out of capital. The payout period is difficult to predict. Because of such heavy investment spending in advertising, some of America's most famous and successful brands did not show a profit for two or three years after launch date.

investment spending
A large introductory advertising allocation.

Matching Competitive Spending. Another method occasionally used seems hardly scientific. Under this somewhat primitive method, the advertiser spends at the same rate as the competition. Sometimes competitive advertising budgets are printed in trade journals. Sometimes the competitor's advertising budget must be estimated, pieced together from a study of media use.

Advertising expenditures are sometimes used as a selling influence against retailers. ("We're backing this product with a $2-million television budget. You oughta promote it with store displays.") If you match a competitor's advertising budget you may be neutralizing an advantage that the competitor had with the trade.

The Budget

Whether the allocation is scientifically determined by a mathematical formula or determined by whim, it becomes the budget that is to support the campaign plan. The budget breaks up the total allocation into particular sums for particular purposes, principally media and production costs.

Who Handles the Budget. The advertising budget generally falls into the domain of the advertising manager. A national marketer with a large advertising agency will call on his or her agency to help in making principal budgeting provisions. They are, after all, the people most closely involved with ad media and production.

Influences on Retail Budget. The advertising budget of a small retailer is a decision of the owner or manager. It is influenced by a number of local factors. A store that is old and famous does not have to advertise as much as a johnny-come-lately. A store in a large shopping mall will pick up a reasonable amount of traffic without heavy advertising. If a store faces lots of competition, it has to make its voice heard. A furniture store depends more on advertising than a dime store. And the small retailer is always governed to some degree by media situations in the community—the number of available newspapers or radio stations, and the rates they charge.

The allocation or total budget will affect the next two decision areas: what to say (creative) and where to say it (media). Certainly the budget will have a very direct effect on media strategy. Figure 16–1 is an example of a typical budget.

CAMPAIGN ESSENTIAL: MEDIA STRATEGY

The characteristics of the various media and how to buy them have been fully discussed in Chapters 11 through 14. Here we are briefly re-examining media in their function as channels of communication—the arrow carrying the message to the agreed-upon target segment in the hope of achieving the agreed-upon campaign goal. Involved in the media strategy are decisions about which

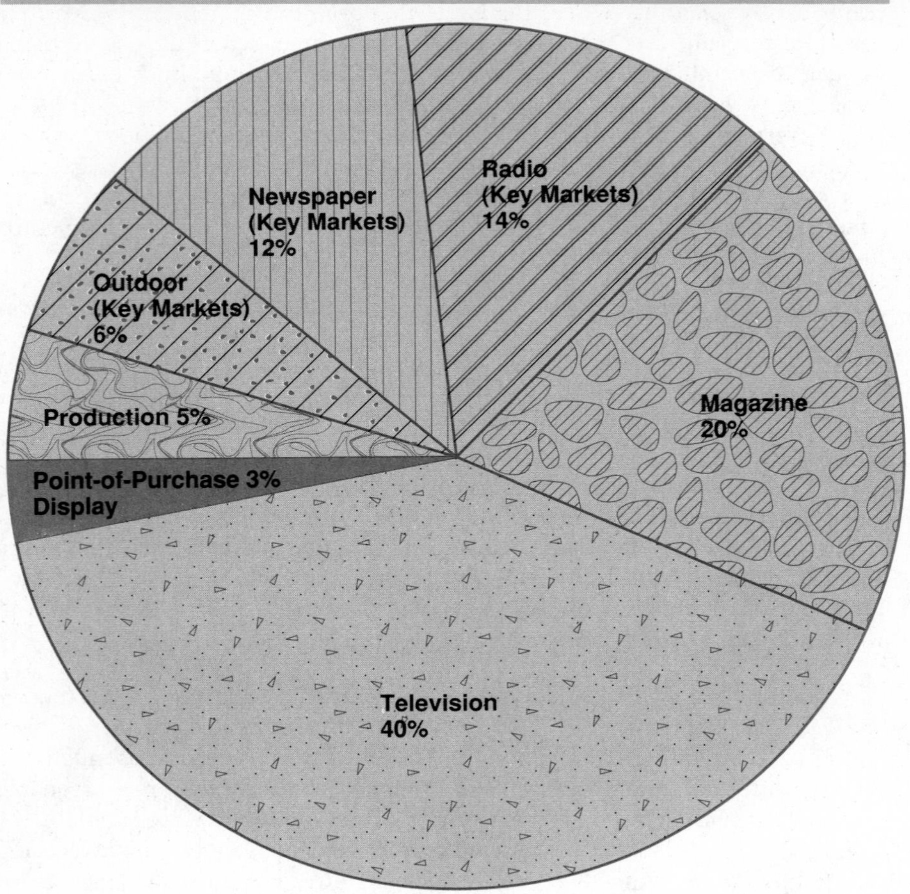

FIGURE 16–1
How the advertising allocation for a national food product might be budgeted or divided up.

basic media to use (magazines, television, newspapers, radio), which particular vehicles (*Ladies' Home Journal*, "60 Minutes," or the *Chicago Tribune*), what units to recommend (half-pages, thirty seconds), and what time of day, week, or year to use them.

The Multiple Choices in Media

The media analyst for a large national account faces literally thousands of choices—an endless series of combinations. To reach a particular target market is like putting a jigsaw puzzle together, except that in media there is no such thing as the perfect picture.

The trend in recent years has been away from the concept of the "mass market" to the concept of the segmented market. For simple proof of this fact, just stand in front of a busy magazine rack and see how many different titles are displayed there. Which magazines do you read? Several? One for news perhaps, one for sports, one for craft hobby. Who reads all those other magazines? Somebody does—and it's the media planner's job to know it.

Suppose that the product is a national quickie cake mix and that the target market is homemakers with schoolchildren. A study of Simmons has told us that. But the Simmons Market Research Bureau report also tells us that cake mix sales are heaviest to women in the Northeast and North Central sections of the country. Nagging questions run through the media buyer's mind.

Matching Product to Medium and Market. Here the media buyer has an appetizing food product that is great to demonstrate. Imagine what television could do for it! And television offers broad coverage. Yet television is so expensive. A modest television campaign would consume most of the budget.

Thinking particularly about those middle-years homemakers, the media buyer considers them to be a natural audience for women's magazines. But which magazines? What kind of coverage? How can too much duplicated coverage and too much overlap of different magazines be avoided? Which issues would seem most productive?

Putting Extra Support in Crucial Areas. What about those highly productive Northeast and North Central sections? What can be done in the way of extra effort there? Newspapers in key cities? Which newspapers? Which days? How appetizing will the product look in a black-and-white newspaper ad?

How about a supplemental radio effort in those two choice areas? Will the product lend itself to radio treatment? What length commercial? What stations? Which cities?

Outdoor posters must not be overlooked in the two key sections. They can provide an appetizing display of a food product in full color. Which cities? How large a showing?

Staying on Target. Back and forth, back and forth, question upon question confronts the media decision maker. There is something of value to be said for each medium, for each combination of media. The planner examines each in light of the one overwhelming demand—to bring maximum weight against the target market already set by the overall plan. There will be little sympathy for media suggestions, no matter how exhilarating, that do *not* point directly at that target.

Let us say that all suggestions are well targeted to sell the homemakers with small children, particularly in the Northeast and North Central states. Good. Now the next question concerns how much can be done in these various directions within the constraints of the budget.

Staying within the Budget. There is no such thing as an unlimited budget. Even those of the giant national advertisers reach a point where the whistle must be blown. The media buyer must be on target with the message and with the money.

Balancing the Media Choices

Balancing all these choices calls for more agonizing decisions. If television is chosen for broad, introductory coverage, it will consume a huge chunk of the budget at one fell swoop. Television also calls for sizable sums in production—far, far more than in the other media, as you would imagine after reading Chapter 10. It is possible that, to get the kind of television coverage we want, we may have to abandon outdoor—or outdoor and radio. The newspaper list may have to be drastically trimmed. Magazines will remain, but you might decide to use six issues instead of eight.

So it goes until the final media program is set. To do the job asked, it will be the best that the assigned sum of money will buy. No media director ever arrives at *the* perfect media plan or is ever able to make *all* the media buys that seem desirable. Hidden in every media plan is a sizable amount of compromise.

CAMPAIGN ESSENTIAL: CREATIVE STRATEGY

The same kind of campaign planning influence that bears so heavily on media strategy also bears heavily on creative strategy.

Particular Target Market

The decision to influence a certain target market (homemakers with small children) becomes the overriding consideration of the creative people. What are the problems of such women? How can our product help solve those problems? How can that help be translated into magazine advertisements and television commercials that will capture their attention and strike a responsive chord in their hearts? We cannot approach housewives with small children the way we would approach teenagers or business executives or farmers. Exactly what pictures of people and settings will have meaning for the target audience? What words, what kind of language, will trigger a response? What action, gesture, or phrase might stay in their memories?

Particular Medium

Assuming that television offers the best means of demonstrating the new quickie cake mix, *how* shall we demonstrate it? In a straightforward, news announcement way? Or with a human-interest, problem-solution handling?

Might we develop a novel musical treatment? Do we concentrate on the "how-to-do-it" or the "fun-when-it's done" angle?

In print, should we have one huge appetizing picture of the finished product or a sequence of step-by-step pictures? Should the emphasis be on taste or convenience? Should we talk differently to the readers of two different magazines? Along with all such questions goes the basic creative question of how to give our product distinction and differentiation.

The Budget

The campaign budget decision ultimately affects the creative director, too. That animated film may have to be scrapped because of cost. Those beautiful double-spread ads may have to be scaled down to bleed pages. And those striking outdoor posters may have to be tucked away for another day.

Basic Nature of Product

Other overall campaign planning decisions have a definite influence on the creative strategy. The various elements of the total marketing mix have to be considered. The very nature of the product itself points in definite directions for the creative director. Perfume copy is not written like tire-and-battery copy. And, even within categories, there are basic product qualities that almost dictate the creative treatment. General Motors would not be likely to advertise a Chevrolet Celebrity the way it advertises a Cadillac Eldorado.

Pricing of Product

The pricing of the product plays its part. A "price" operation emphasizes *savings;* a "quality" operation emphasizes *values*. There's a big difference in the way a campaign planner might illustrate and talk about the two.

Packaging of Product

The creative people must also consider the packaging of a product. Occasionally, the package itself is more important than its contents. This is especially true with seasonal packaging—as with gift decanters of liquor. Certainly the original roll-on applicator for deodorant rated equal emphasis with the deodorant itself.

Promotion Activities

If management decides that promotion will be a major feature of the campaign, creative people must respond accordingly. If, for a certain period, there is a sweepstakes or contest, then the advertising messages must give primary emphasis to that activity. Because any promotion is a short-term, high-intensity effort throughout the organization, advertising cannot be permitted to sit on the sidelines talking about something else.

Advertiser Image

Even the company or product reputation has a bearing on creative strategy. Nowhere is that more true than in retailing, where the store image holds sway over all other elements. In national brand advertising, too, there is an image that took years to build and that it may be wise to retain. It boils down to the fact that a certain kind of copy sounds right for a company or it does not.

Basic Selling Approach

The chief responsibility of creative strategy is the development of a basic selling theme or approach to which many other elements are keyed. (Unlike a slogan, a basic selling theme permits variations in message construction so long as the *focus* remains the same.) For example, a number of years ago Pepsi-Cola adopted a basic selling approach appealing to youth. Hence the varying copy lines "For those who think young," "The Pepsi Generation," and "The New Generation," plus the use of such young stars as Michael Jackson and Michael J. Fox. Although creative strategy—and the basic selling theme it develops—may be the most important single element in campaign planning, it, too, is directly affected by all the other elements in the campaign plan.

CAMPAIGN ESSENTIAL: COORDINATION

The campaign goal has been set; the target buying group has been selected; the advertising appropriation has been approved. The media plan is in shape; the creative strategy has settled on a basic selling theme. Suitable copy and layout are "in the works." What remains?

What remains to be done is a sort of mopping-up procedure: a pulling together of several loose ends—some major, some minor—that might logically fall under the heading of promotional activities. Because these take many forms, coordination to fit the overall campaign plan is essential.

Sales Promotion to Consumers

First off, there is the matter of sales promotion to consumers. You will recall that a promotion, by its very nature, is a short-term, high-intensity effort. Read the details of any promotion and you will always find an expiration date.

Coupons, Premiums, Samples, Contests. A widely used consumer promotion is the coupon redemption offer ("This coupon entitles you to 10¢ off on your next purchase of . . ."). A premium can be included in the product package ("A free Cannon Face Cloth in every box of . . ."). A premium can be self-liquidating (the cost to the consumer is a huge bargain but still covers the manufacturer's cost in buying a large quantity order.) The manufacturer may distribute free samples or offer a price deal ("This month only, two $1.00 packages for $1.50"). The advertiser may even promote a consumer contest (which involves skill) or a sweepstakes (which is a matter of pure chance).

Duplicate Incentives for Dealers. These consumer promotions often include very generous incentives for dealers in order to get their cooperation and support. The important matter is that, for the particular time involved, advertising efforts promote the promotion.

Activities with the Trade

No selling plan is likely to advance very far without the understanding and active cooperation of the dealers. The people in charge of the channels of distribution are often the manufacturer's only direct contact with consumers. It pays to have the trade on your side. Some manufacturers will sponsor annual trade conventions. Some regularly participate in trade fairs. Some have sales training programs for dealer personnel. Primarily, dealers are interested in anything that will bring them a profit. If you can convince them that your new advertising campaign will pay off in increased dollar volume and increased profits, they'll extend themselves to help your plan succeed. There are various ways to induce them.

Buying Allowances and Free Goods. Trade deals are a common persuader. Buying allowances and free goods are really price reductions. In the first instance, the dealer is given a cooperative advertising allowance of so much money for promotion and advertising on each unit the dealer buys. In the second instance, the dealer gets a certain extra amount of goods free for ordering a certain quantity. The dealer makes a higher profit per unit under terms of your deal and may buy more goods as a result.

Cooperative Advertising; Ad Allowances. Most major manufacturers of national brands offer cooperative advertising in which they reimburse the retailer for 50 percent (or whatever figure is mutually agreed upon) of the cost of local advertising that features the manufacturer's brand. Or there may be a straight advertising "allowance" of so much per case, carton, or barrel ordered. Many manufacturers will prepare ad service kits for dealer use—copy, layout, complete ads, photos, scripts, videotapes, and the like. The dealer may use as much or as little as desired. Some manufacturers may even prepare tailor-made advertising upon request from a dealer.

Listing Local Dealer with National Ad. A popular dealer promotion is the use of a dealer listing along with an important national ad. Regional editions of national publications now make this practice both practical and desirable.

Yellow Pages Listing. Yellow Pages ads are popular with dealers. They are a proven source of new sales. Often the national advertiser pays for a good part of a dealer's ad in the Yellow Pages. The national advertiser can buy space in local classified phone directories all around the country by consulting a central source.

FIGURE 16–2
Cooperative advertising extends to the outdoor medium in these eye-stopping embellished bulletins.

Courtesy of J.W. Robinson and Institute of Outdoor Advertising.

Courtesy of J.W. Robinson and Institute of Outdoor Advertising.

Directory Listings. The national advertiser can also purchase listings for important dealers in the various industrial directories. Any listings should—if at all possible—contain some reference to the campaign theme.

Point-of-Purchase Display Material. Attractive and compelling point-of-purchase display material rates a sizable investment on the part of some advertisers. Dealers are flooded with it; some is never used. But if an advertiser can furnish a point-of-purchase device that a dealer will use, increased sales will almost surely follow. Point-of-purchase displays include chiefly window displays, counter displays, floor displays, and wall displays. The display, of course, would use the basic selling theme of the campaign.

Sales Training Programs. Some national advertisers will conduct sales training programs for dealer personnel, an obvious way to familiarize them with the campaign theme.

"Push Money." It is not unknown for the manufacturer of a national brand to pay some kind of direct cash incentive to a dealer's salespeople for promoting a product. This is called **push money** or a **spiff**.

push money (spiff) Money paid directly to the dealer salespeople for promoting a manufacturer's product.

Store Demonstrator. Some advertisers will go to the expense of putting a demonstrator in a store. The selling, of course, is directed to consumers, but the dealer also benefits from the extra traffic and attention that a demonstrator may generate.

Advertising Specialties. Specialties are often sent or given to dealers and their salespeople. You will recall that an advertising specialty is an object of value that is used day in and day out, such as a calendar, a hand calculator, a ballpoint pen. In its limited space it can surely carry a constant reminder of the campaign theme.

Trade Shows and Exhibitions. Depending on the nature of the product, some advertisers invest heavily in trade shows and exhibitions. A great deal of "missionary work" and a great deal of actual selling is done at trade shows. They provide excellent contact with key customers and middlemen and are an obvious way of spreading the campaign theme. Some advertisers even have permanent traveling displays—trailer trucks they can send to exhibits everywhere.

Merchandising the Advertising. The very least a marketer can do to influence the trade is to merchandise the advertising i.e., let the dealers know ahead of time how an ad campaign is geared to influence the dealers' customers. The advertiser can send out preprints of magazine ads, photoboards of television commercials, media lists, and insertion schedules. The advertiser can explain the campaign, tell the dealer how many potential customers it will

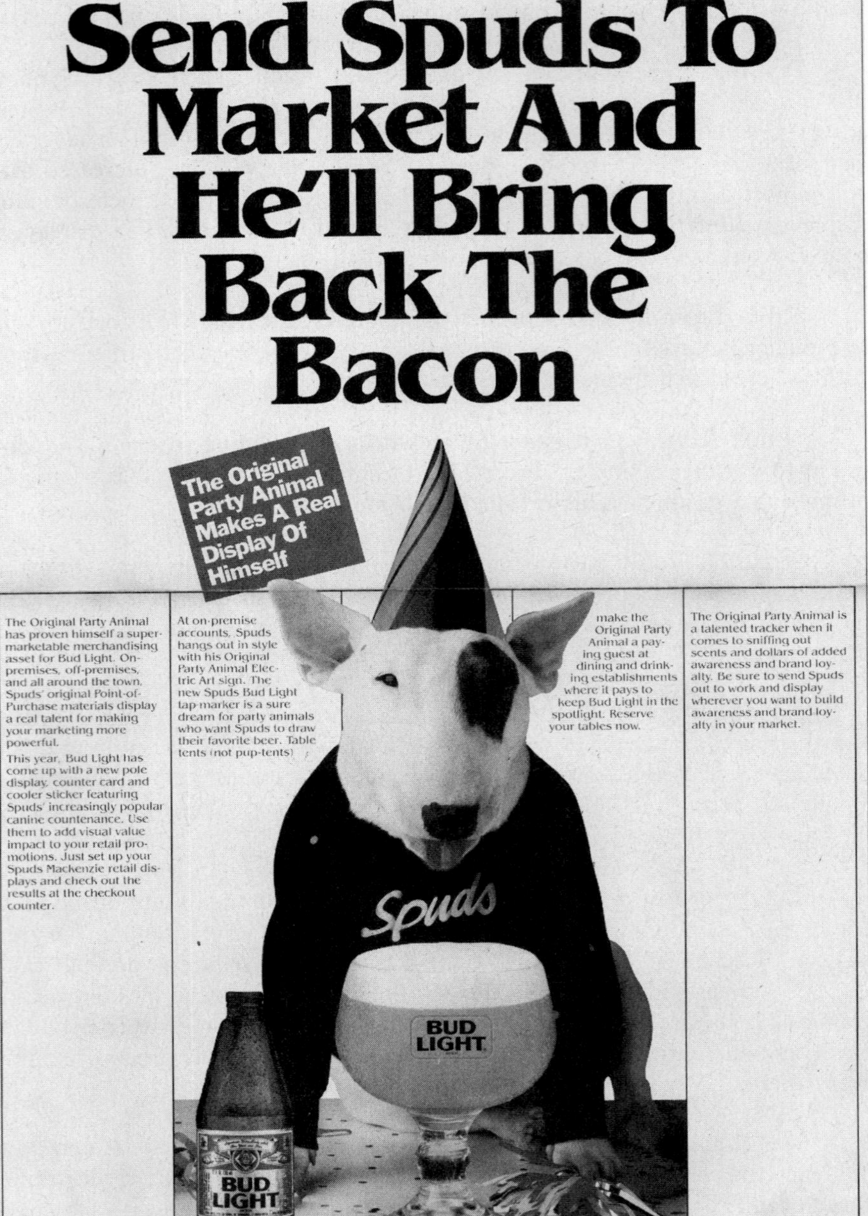

Courtesy of Anheuser-Busch, Inc.

FIGURE 16–3
A contemporary celebrity dominates this point-of-sale display piece, which reminds shoppers of fun get-togethers.

Courtesy of The Dracket Company.

FIGURE 16–4
Colorful point-of-sale display calls attention to O-Cedar products.

reach, even indicate how much money is invested in it. Most national advertisers provide company salespeople with a portfolio of advertising samples that the salesperson can explain directly to customers.

No question about it, the advertising campaign that succeeds is the campaign that insures dealer involvement.

Public Relations Aspects

public relations A program of many communications activities designed to build public good will towards an organization or product.

Public relations is a broad term that may embrace numerous activities—as indicated in Chapter 1. The most basic public relations device is the publicity release to the media. But free media coverage is not easily won. An out-and-out commercial "plug" is unacceptable. Any reference to the advertising campaign should be subtle, and it must appeal to the particular audience of a particular medium.

Speeches given by company officers to business or civic groups must be equally subtle in weaving in the campaign theme. Likewise, community projects must not be openly commercial. But even a Fourth-of-July float might carry some appropriate and inoffensive reference to the campaign theme. Films made for showing to business, civic, and school groups for educational purposes may diplomatically slip in a reference to the campaign theme.

The public relations people in almost any company are responsible for certain publications—like the annual report to stockholders; sometimes information bulletins to dealers and goodwill reminders to present customers. Each offers a golden opportunity to promote the advertising campaign theme.

Every detail about a company has certain public relations overtones and can contribute to the success of the advertising campaign—the appearance of the plant and offices; the courtesies extended to visitors; the guided tours; the mementos.

A marketing/advertising campaign is a total effort. No detail should be overlooked that may help to make the campaign a success.

CAMPAIGN ESSENTIAL: MEASUREMENT

Probably the most senseless sin an advertiser can commit is to invest a sizable sum in a campaign and then not make any organized effort to evaluate its effects.

Sales Results Are Not Always True Tests

Unfortunately sales results alone do not always give an accurate answer. Too many variables affect sales—weather, differences in performance of individual salespeople, general economic conditions, activities of competitors, public attitudes at the time, to name a few. For instance, the failure of the Edsel car was not the fault of the advertising but was largely due to a change in public tastes by the time the car was introduced. Sales may decline in the face of a competitive advertising program that has captured the public's fancy. Sales may increase despite a bland, middle-of-the-road advertising effort. Yet some kind of measurement should be applied to advertising in a consistent manner at consistent intervals. It is a wise advertiser who makes an attempt to test *before* advertising runs (pretest) and after advertising has appeared (posttest). While research is discussed fully in Chapter 3, a brief review of some aspects seems appropriate here.

Pretesting: The Internal Checklist

The most basic kind of measurement is self-applied—internal, so to speak. This method rates new advertising against a checklist of advertising requirements for your product or service. Using such a checklist is similar to the procedure an airline pilot goes through before takeoff.

Some writers may feel that a checklist discourages creativity. If nothing else, a checklist will prevent an advertiser from failing to include some essential point in the message.

Pretesting: Consumer "Jury" Tests

One way to see how the public will respond to your advertising ideas before they run nationally is to try them out on a **consumer jury**, a group of ordinary people who match the profile of potential customers. Consumer jury tests take many forms.

consumer jury A group of people who match the profile of potential customers.

Order of Merit: Paired Comparison. Print advertising tests generally use complete copy and layout, a very close representation of the finished ad. Several ideas are usually tested in one of two ways—an order-of-merit test or a paired comparison test. As you will remember from Chapter 3, in an order-of-merit test the consumer looks at several ideas and then ranks them numerically from first choice on down. In paired comparison testing, the consumer is shown only two ads at a time. She or he selects Ad *A* or Ad *B*. Then she or he is shown the next set of two and selects Ad *C* or Ad *D*. The winners are then paired and compared.

Dummy Magazines. Some advertisers test print copy in dummy magazines. Here is how it works. Preprints of the proposed advertising are bound into the regular editorial matter of an existing magazine. (A Canadian magazine might be used for test purposes in the United States.) Copies of the magazine are left in a given number of households. After a certain interval—a couple of days for a weekly magazine—interviewers go to those households and ask questions about ad readership.

Focus Group Interviews. Magazine advertising ideas are often pretested by a popular research device called the focus group interview. Members of a small group of prospects are shown the advertising and encouraged to talk about it in an informal, unstructured way. Their remarks are recorded and often give valuable insights to the ad writers.

TV Trailer Tests; Closed-Circuit Tests. Television copy is harder to pretest (it has to be partly produced in some recognizable form), but researchers find ingenious ways. Some do in-home projector tests. Some do trailer tests, with viewing facilities set up in trailers at shopping centers. Some advertisers will actually run a sample commercial over the air on some special closed-circuit arrangement or over a cable TV station.

TV Theater Tests. A popular form of television testing is the theater test. One theater method employs a brand preference pretest and posttest.

Another theater method uses a mechanical dialing device for indicating reactions for or against, thus giving the advertiser a second-by-second report on how the viewer responds to the message.

Pros and Cons of the Consumer Jury. There are things to be said for and against consumer jury tests—though the good far outweighs the bad. Consumer jury tests are relatively easy, fast, and inexpensive. Most important, they give the reactions of the very people the advertiser is trying to reach.

But the advertiser must be sure to have the right kind of consumer jury—legitimate prospects for the product. (There would be little point in asking a MADD group its opinion of a beer campaign.) Many consumer jury members may give answers that put themselves in a good light but are not necessarily honest answers. And most respondents, humanly, start commenting as advertising experts rather than as consumers. Also, the size of the consumer jury is always subject to question. Some consumer juries may involve twenty-five people; some consumer surveys may run into the thousands.

Mechanical Testing Methods. Researchers are very ingenious. They are constantly seeking newer and more scientific ways of probing consumer reactions. Some measure dilation of the eye pupil. Some measure sweating on the palms of the hands. Some measure eye-speed reaction to fast-moving slides. Some study eye movement across a page.

Posttesting: Print, Television, Campaign Effect

Once print advertising has appeared in a national magazine, the longest continuous research system in the advertising business—the Starch Readership Reports—can provide a measurement of it.

Recognition Test: Print. The Starch INRA Hooper organization interviews the public and reports a national readership percentage figure in three categories: Noted, Associated, and Read Most. The Starch test is called a recognition test because respondents have only to say, when shown, that they saw that magazine and that ad. Look back at the example in Chapter 3.

Starch is an independent research service to which advertisers and agencies subscribe. Starch notifies its subscribers six months ahead which issues of which magazines will be surveyed. Only rather short-sighted subscribers would fail to arrange their media insertion schedules to take advantage of the Starch testing.

Recall Test: Print. Another readership survey is provided by the Gallup-Robinson research organization, which insists that respondents recall or remember something they read in a particular issue of a magazine before testing their memory of the ads themselves. This is a recall test. It is more stringent than Starch. It also reports consumer comments, which Starch does not.

Recall Test: Television. A different kind of recall test is applied to television. This is a telephone recall survey done immediately after a television broadcast or the following day. The most widely used TV test currently is Burke Day-After Recall.

Coupon and Inquiry Tests. All direct marketing advertising is tested after the fact because the customer has to respond directly via a coupon or a key number or a coded address.

Many advertisers test copy appeals by seeking inquiries. Some do this by using coupons. Others use a "hidden offer"—the inducement to respond is buried in the body text of the ad. One popular inquiry test device is the split-run test in which each of two test ads appears in every other copy of a particular issue of a publication. The page remains the same, the position on the page remains the same, the surrounding editorial content remains the same, the geographical distribution remains the same—only the two ad variables being tested change. A modest amount spent in split-run testing may determine the direction of a big-budget national campaign.

Sales Tests. The ultimate test of advertising effectiveness is also the most difficult–the sales test. Two markets of approximate size and makeup are selected. In the control city, the old/current advertising is run–or no advertising. In the test city, the new advertising appears. An inventory count is made in each city before and after the advertising test period.

Researchers can test copy appeal or media mix or budget variations; though, as pointed out earlier, many factors can influence sales results no matter how scientific the research procedure.

Necessity for Continuous Testing

The important thing to remember about testing is that you must use *some* form of it. Even a modest phone survey is better than no research at all. Without some kind of playback from customers and prospective customers, the advertiser is likely to drift aimlessly.

SUMMARY

We have seen in these two chapters that an advertising campaign is a full-scale, long-term, multifaceted operation. First, a goal must be set. Second, a target market must be selected. Third, money must be allocated. Fourth, a basic theme must be evolved as focal point of the creative strategy. Fifth, a media strategy must be worked out to bring the message to the right audience at the right time at the right price. Sixth, the advertising campaign must be coordinated with all other elements of the marketing mix. And, last, measurements must be devised to check progress.

No two advertising campaigns are alike. Each has to fit its own set of circumstances. In the next chapter we will look at examples of actual campaigns—some quite large, some rather small, some national, some local, but all interesting, and all demonstrating ingenuity and thoroughness in applying campaign principles.

TERMS TO KNOW

Now that you have finished this chapter, you should understand the following terms:

- advertising appropriation
- advertising budget
- investment spending
- push money (spiff)
- public relations
- consumer jury

If you are uncertain of the meaning of any of these terms, go back through the chapter to review them.

THINGS TO THINK ABOUT

1. As an admaker, can you think of an advantage that print advertising might have over radio? An advantage that radio might have over print? An advantage that television might have over print and radio?
2. If you were advertising cigars in the newspaper, in which section of the newspaper would you want your ad to appear? Why?
3. We often hear the terms *public relations* and *advertising* used in conjuction with each other. What do the two terms mean to you?
4. There's nothing very aesthetic about an advertising budget, yet it can have a direct influence on the creative direction. How is this so?
5. If you were selling men's and women's wristwatches, at what time of year would you concentrate your advertising?

THINGS TO TALK ABOUT

1. Suppose you were commissioned to advertise your own community college on television to parents of prospective students. Considering the nature of your "product," what TV programs would you want your commercials to appear in? Are there any programs in which you would not wish them to appear?
2. If everybody in class did an ad for a local restaurant, discuss how you might decide which one of the several ads to run.
3. Many small local businesses enter into a cooperative advertising arrangement with a national brand manufacturer. Discuss the advantages and disadvantages to the retailer.
4. Discuss how you might make a quite accurate estimate of a competitor's advertising expenditures.
5. Discuss the pros and cons: If you had a million dollars to spend advertising a men's shaving cream, would you buy a one-minute spot on the Super Bowl telecast even though that minute would cost you over half what you had to spend?

THINGS TO DO

1. Each of you list the publications you see fairly regularly. Compare your list with those of everybody else in the class. How many similarities? How many differences?
2. Choose a famous make of ballpoint pen priced at a reasonable figure. Write an ad to a consumer. Write an ad to a dealer.
3. Visit the largest firm in your community. Find out all the promotional and "goodwill" activities that firm engages in other than advertising.
4. Call on the owner of the largest automobile dealership in town. Ask what principle the dealer follows in determining advertising expenditures.
5. Ask the manager of the largest local supermarket on which day (or days) of the week he or she prefers to concentrate the store's advertising and why.

17 Campaign Examples

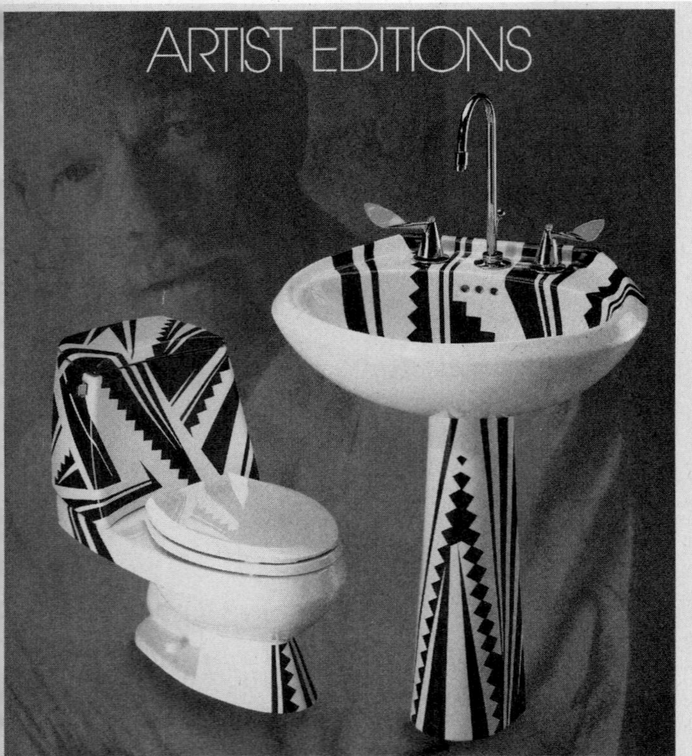
ARTIST EDITIONS
THE BOLD LOOK OF KOHLER
Cactus Cutter™ by Art Nelson. Just one triumph of Kohler's bold design freedom challenge to renowned ceramic artists. A most original series of fixtures advancing the bath as artform. Six different limited edition designs to make your own statement of taste and penchant for unique pattern, color and texture. For a complete collection portfolio of all six Artist Editions, send $3 to Kohler Co., Dept. AU9, Kohler, Wisconsin 53044.

Courtesy of Kohler Company

CHAPTER OUTLINE

By the time you finish this chapter, you should understand:

1. **That it sometimes pays to concentrate your advertising in a single medium.**
2. **That proper use of visual symbolism can speak volumes.**
3. **That great national advertising becomes even more effective when fully supported at the local level.**
4. **That people will read long, detailed copy when the subject closely concerns them.**
5. **That certain subjects lend themselves better to one medium than to another.**
6. **That you can be creative in the way you use media as well as in the way you use words and pictures.**
7. **That the best way to use advertising is to use it with consistency.**
8. **That you should apply benchmark measurements of effectiveness as your advertising progresses.**

In the last two chapters we talked about the principles of an advertising campaign—what must go before a campaign and what is essential to a campaign. In this chapter we are going to see the application of those principles to actual advertising campaigns.

You will read about three case histories here—local, national, and industrial. You'll read about the long-running campaign of a prominent national insurance and financial services company. You'll study a unique campaign for a local medical services facility. You'll learn about the creative variations in an extended business-to-business campaign.

As you read these true cases, you will see how the advertisers applied the very principles you have just studied in Chapters 15 and 16. They gathered information, selected a target market, set objectives, appropriated money, and planned a total program of activities. It will be obvious to you that the shrewd advertiser/marketer does not do things by halves.

No two of these campaigns are alike. No two marketing/advertising situations are ever precisely the same. What does remain the same is the set of principles behind every campaign plan. You can apply these principles just as the three advertisers discussed here applied them. And it does not matter whether you're performing for a huge corporation or a tiny operation. See if you don't agree.

KEMPER GROUP

There are several lessons to be learned here. First, analyze the current situation to determine where you stand competitively. Second, know your target audience. Third, find a way to reach that target audience. Fourth, create a memorable image. Fifth, when you find something that produces for you, stick with it. Sixth, make your dollars work harder than your competitor's dollars.

Before the Kemper Cavalry (Figure 17–1 at the end of this chapter) began its ride into America's living rooms, Kemper had a couple of basic communications problems to tackle. The first was that insurance competitors outspent Kemper in advertising by as much as 5, 6, or 7 to 1. This situation is still true today. Kemper is approximately the tenth largest property and casualty insurance company in the country and has to battle competitors like Allstate, State Farm, Travelers, and Hartford Insurance to get its share of the consumers' attention. Not only is Kemper being outspent, but in the early 1970s only about one-third of all U.S. heads of households were aware of the Kemper name. Kemper needed a campaign that would be uniquely identified with it and command attention from television viewers in particular. The Kemper Cavalry came riding to the rescue, as shown in Figure 17–2. (See the end of this chapter for figures.)

Why cavalry? For a number of good reasons. In the Old West, settlers turned to the cavalry in times of trouble. People call on their insurance agents in times of trouble. Insurance is largely a people-oriented business; customers deal with individual agents. So it was with the cavalry; it gained its strength from the individual troopers. Crucial to Kemper is the independent insurance agent. Crucial to the old cavalry was the independent scout who always rode in advance of the troop. The Kemper Cavalry on television glorifies the scout because the scout embodies the spirit of the independent insurance agent. So, while the introduction of the Kemper Cavalry may have been a stroke of creative genius, it was a stroke of *logical* genius.

Early on, Kemper decided to concentrate its advertising on television as the most effective medium to generate large increases in consumer awareness and favorable attitudes toward the company. Kemper's media program consists of sponsoring a wide variety of weekend sports events that are heavily viewed by adult male heads of households—Kemper's ideal target audience. The annual highlight of the company's media plan is the Kemper Open PGA Tour golf tournament, an event that celebrated its twentieth anniversary in 1987. Kemper has also made good use of **opportunistic media buys** (last-minute purchases of commercial airtime at reduced rates) and, a fairly recent development, fifteen-second television commercials to which the Cavalry imparts strong and immediate identity.

opportunistic media buys Last-minute purchases of commercial airtime at reduced rates.

The following are a number of unique elements that have been consistent parts of the Kemper Cavalry television advertising campaign:

1. The Kemper Cavalry troopers have always been dressed in bright blue with golden neckerchieves and gold stripes on the legs of their trousers. All troopers wear Kemper "logo" patches on their sleeves.
2. A scout always leads the Kemper Cavalry troop. As mentioned, the scout represents the independent insurance agent who sells Kemper insurance and therefore leads the "cavalry" to Kemper customers.

It was important to Kemper from the start that the independent insurance agents who represent Kemper have a prominent role in the advertising.

3. The Kemper Cavalry is nonviolent, a troop that carries no weapons of any kind. Although the Kemper Cavalry frequently comes to the rescue, it does so in a symbolic, nonviolent way.
4. The Cavalry troop features a bugler who has played the same Kemper bugle call for the entire length of the campaign.
5. The Cavalry troop also features a flag bearer who carries the Kemper signature banner wherever the Cavalry rides. This banner gives extra opportunities to promote the Kemper name identity throughout the Cavalry commercials.

These elements of consistency in the messages, coupled with a consistent network television media program, have paid excellent dividends for Kemper. Kemper's corporate awareness rating—the percentage of heads of households who have heard of Kemper insurance—has increased from the 1974 rating of 33 percent when the Kemper Cavalry first charged across the nation's television screens. In 1987 some 73 percent of heads of households recognized Kemper as an insurance company. In 1974 only 12 percent of survey respondents had said they could recall seeing a Kemper advertisement within the preceding six months; in 1986 the figure had increased to 45 percent who said they could recall a Kemper advertisement. Not only that, but 34 percent of those survey respondents said they would consider purchasing insurance from Kemper.

Much of the credit for the public's growing awareness of Kemper rests with the long-running Kemper Cavalry television campaign. The success of the Cavalry ads is important to Kemper sales efforts. Research shows that people are more than twice as likely to buy insurance from a company they recognize than from one they don't.

As successful as the television Cavalry has been, Kemper does not let it ride alone. Instead, the Cavalry seen on national television is supported in many ways at the local, or agent, level. Kemper offers quite a range of advertising and sales promotion programs to its agents.

First, there's a Co-op Advertising Guide that offers taped radio spots built around the adventures of independent agent *par excellence*, George Pierson, a fictional hero (see Figure 17–3). There's a scripted radio campaign with sixty-second and thirty-second Cavalry-oriented spots. In addition, there are 39 newspaper ads covering most insurance products, plus two TV spots and a guide to planning, advertising, and hosting a local Mini-Kemper Open golf tournament. Kemper pays 50 percent of all eligible local advertising expenses for its agents.

Second, Kemper offers its agents an impressive variety of beautifully prepared Sales Promotion items (see Figure 17–4). On a number of pertinent topics of public and personal interest, Kemper offers brochures, folders, envelope stuffers, posters, mailing pieces, and the like. Quantities are available to agents at a nominal cost.

Third, there is a program called the Kemper Collection, an assortment of specialty advertising and marketing aids from Cavalry hats and bugles to inscribed desk sets to golf balls and putters (see Figure 17–5). These attractive items can be used as giveaways, drop-in inducements in newspaper and radio ads, or donations to charitable and community groups. Every item is priced to the agents at or below Kemper's cost.

Fourth, Kemper is a staunch believer that listing in the Yellow Pages is a key marketing opportunity for agents. Kemper shares the cost; it even has its own Yellow Pages advertising agency that solicits the agents.

Fifth, Kemper provides agents with Custom Advertising assistance through its own Advertising Department (see Figure 17–6). The skilled personnel of the Kemper Advertising Department will develop custom materials unique to each eligible insurance agency. These materials can include newspaper, radio, TV, and Yellow Pages display ads; direct mail campaigns; agency logotypes; and agency brochures. Insurance agency partners of Kemper pay only half of Kemper's total development costs, which are far below the costs they would pay to develop the same materials themselves.

But the key efforts by Kemper, of course, are the Kemper Cavalry television commercials that are aimed at male heads of households, ages 25 or older, who have annual incomes of $30,000 or more. To reach that audience, Kemper spends approximately $5 million per year on advertising. Much of the advertising budget is spent on commercials that are aired on the telecasts of the Kemper Open and Women's Kemper Open, as well as during other sports events, especially golf. These sports telecasts give Kemper large audiences who fit the company's target market.

In commenting on the success of the long-running Kemper Cavalry campaign, a company spokesman summed up thus:

> Since 1974 the company has conducted an almost textbook example of targeting an audience, concentrating a message on that audience, and getting as much recognition as possible. It's a success story that gives Kemper an awareness among the insurance-buying public out of proportion to the size of the company and the amount of money we spend on advertising.

As an interesting side note, the photographs shown in this book of the Kemper Cavalry were taken in Monument Valley near the Arizona-Utah border. Monument Valley is the setting of the most famous John Ford/John Wayne cavalry movies including *She Wore a Yellow Ribbon*. (See Figure 17–2.)

MERCY HOSPITAL[1]

A generation ago it was a rare hospital, indeed, that advertised. Now they all seem to be doing it. The medical services business in America has be-

[1]After this text was written, Mercy Hospital, the dominant community hospital in the twin cities of Champaign-Urbana, Illinois, merged with the next largest community hospital. The two together have now adopted a new name: Covenant Medical Center.

come big business. Marketing holds sway where it had never been dreamt of before.

Some medical service practitioners equated the word "marketing" with advertising. They jumped on the marketing bandwagon with "image advertising." That was the soft-sell way to get into marketing; hawking the price of healthcare was inappropriate.

Mercy Hospital in Urbana, Illinois, fortunately had two top executives with thorough marketing training. So Mercy Hospital went about the marketing process in a scientific manner. Mercy Hospital started with a year-long research endeavor, interviewing the general public, assembling financial data on key programs, and developing a market position for Mercy Hospital based on the results.

While mutually exchanged hospital statistics indicated that Mercy was losing market share to one of its two main competitors, community image surveys showed that the general public was not aware of the many specialty programs that Mercy had initiated. As a result of the research, a slogan and a platform were developed for Mercy Hospital that would reflect several different facets of the hospital's service.

The slogan arrived at—"One of a Kind"—was firmly rooted in three bases:

1. The sixty-year-old hospital is owned and operated by the Servants of the Holy Heart of Mary, a Roman Catholic order of religious women. Their philosophy and mission are at the heart of everything Mercy Hospital does. Programs and services are offered because the community needs them, not just because they generate business. In fact, Mercy Hospital offers some programs that are money-losers.
2. Mercy Hospital offers several programs that were the first of their kind in the area. These special services include inpatient psychiatric care, inpatient rehabilitation, open heart surgery (through a joint program with two local clinics), neonatal intensive care, hemodialysis, and hospice care. These six services formed the basis for the early phases of Mercy's "One of a Kind" advertising campaign.
3. Community image surveys backed up the strong feeling of the marketing executives that the caring approach taken by Mercy Hospital's staff and physicians was truly one of a kind. So the advertising featured employees and physicians in that manner.

The medium selected was the local newspaper, which does a very thorough job of covering Mercy Hospital's market. Reach rather than frequency was Mercy Hospital's primary goal. The messages themselves called for striking visuals along with lengthy, detailed copy. The newspaper was ideal.

The appearance of the advertising had to be highly professional and dignified. Hence, the editorial layout form was chosen. It lends itself admirably to serious discussion of serious problems.

The campaign progressed through a series of phases. (See the figures at the back of this chapter.) The purpose of the first phase (Figure 17–8) was to create awareness of Mercy Hospital's programs and philosophy. The purpose of the second phase (Figure 17–9) was essentially the same, but the ads were slightly changed to feature *all* the programs at the same time. The purpose of the third phase (Figure 17–10) was to create awareness among interested parties about Mercy's special programs, giving in-depth information to those who might be interested. Phase four (Figure 17–11) was an emotional series featuring actual patients. Phase five (Figure 17–12) was a series of ads featuring employees of Mercy Hospital. Regardless of the focus of a particular ad, all ads were keyed to the main campaign theme of "One of a Kind."

response mechanism A coupon that readers can clip from an ad to send in for more information.

At one point in the third phase, Mercy Hospital started to include a direct **response mechanism**—a coupon that readers could clip out and send in for more information and a telephone number they could also call for immediate response.

With this response mechanism, Mercy Hospital's "One of a Kind" campaign generated enough call-backs and eventual patient admissions to more than offset the cost of the advertising. And during the second year of the campaign Mercy Hospital saw its market share increase by 2 percent, not a hefty amount in and of itself but quite remarkable when measured against what had been a steady decline.

From a creative point of view the Mercy Hospital ads projected a high-quality image of professionalism. The editorial layouts were clean and uncluttered. The photographs were relevant and interesting. Headlines were provocative. Body copy was serious but friendly, packed with detailed information. The campaign was highly admired locally, and nationally it won a merit award in the HealthCare Marketing Report annual marketing contest.

The budget for Mercy Hospital's "One of a Kind" campaign was approximately $60,000 spread over the course of two years. This remarkable educational campaign has done an outstanding job and will continue to do so. The phrase and the tag line "One of a Kind" will continue to identify Mercy Hospital's marketing efforts for various promotional projects. The "One of a Kind" campaign has itself proven to be one of a kind.

UNITED STATES GYPSUM

Next to its corporate signature, United States Gypsum discreetly carries the two words "Building America." How true those two words are! Because U.S. Gypsum is one of the largest producers of building materials in the world. Yet the company is comparatively little-known to the general public because its products are sold mainly to other manufacturers and builders. And the company's advertising—skilled and varied as it might be—is concentrated in the business-to-business field. From this keenly contested arena, U.S. Gypsum provides us with the story of a long-running advertising campaign that has achieved outstanding success in face-to-face competition with a strong and brilliant competitor.

Among the many different products manufactured by U.S. Gypsum is ceiling tile, a sound-control item dear to the hearts of America's architects, designers, and builders. In 1980 U.S. Gypsum was definitely in the ceiling tile business but lagged far behind the #1 name in the field, Armstrong. Far outspending U.S. Gypsum for advertising, Armstrong had for years made a practice of buying the first one to three opening two-page spreads in each relevant magazine directed to architects, decorators, and builders. Armstrong had a long-established reputation fostered in part by excellent and extensive advertising. U.S. Gypsum gave its advertising agency, Marstrat, Inc., a modest $300,000 budget and challenged it to provide a "presence" and to look important in the ceiling tile field. This was no simple task in the face of Armstrong's much larger purse.

The creative solution was in part a layout or graphics solution and in part a media solution. (See the four-color insert following page 365 for the figures referenced in text.) It consisted of buying space units starting with a 3/4-page or a page-and-a-half spread, followed immediately by two to five consecutive right-hand half pages (Figure 17–13). Can you picture that? You are reading your architectural magazine and you suddenly come across a U.S. Gypsum ceiling tile ad that is spread across both pages in front of you. Now that's a big ad. Difficult to ignore. Wonder of wonders, as you turn the right hand page, directly under your hand is *another* USG ceiling tile ad, a half page. As you start to turn *that* page, directly under your hand is *another* USG ceiling tile half-page ad. And so on, often for as many as five consecutive half pages. Each of the succeeding half pages featured a particular ceiling tile product sold on its own merits. There was no "umbrella" word theme, only a distinctive graphic look to tie everything together. This ingenious media and layout device of the double-spread followed by several consecutive right-hand half pages had tremendous impact, a cumulative effect far greater than the media costs would seem to allow.

U.S. Gypsum continued to run that "space spectacular" advertising for some three years, weaving in new product introductions as they developed. The initial "space spectacular" phase of the USG ceiling tile advertising enjoyed remarkable success measured by the yardsticks available to the advertising agency:

1. Inquiries generated by the ads numbered well over 33,000.
2. Readership was outstanding, with 22 top readership awards won.
3. Awareness research showed U.S. Gypsum moving up from an "also ran" in 1980 to a strong second in 1982.

In 1984 U.S. Gypsum decided to go to a different format for its ceiling tile advertising. First, campaign planners felt that the "space spectacular" format had matured and was no longer fresh. More important, there was need for a greater flexibility in the media schedule. The new format called for two-page spreads and single full pages. The spreads were to carry the overall USG selling story, and the individual full pages were to highlight individual products. Full pages could carry a more complete story of individual products than could the previous half-page format. And available full-page ads could be inserted in cover positions that magazines often made available to U.S. Gypsum.

Research showed that aesthetics or appearance was a prime factor in the choice of ceiling products—especially by architects, owners, and decorators. The success of USG's lower-priced line meant that practically any building job could afford the newest in aesthetics. In other words, U.S. Gypsum was not only making beautiful ceilings but was making them affordable. Hence the new theme line for advertising: "USG makes the most elegant ceilings affordable."

With the new theme line in place, two creative executions fell into line. The first used spreads featuring a large single tile. The second focused on a distinguished-looking gentleman dressed in evening clothes and placed in elegant contemporary settings. This gentleman embodied the selling idea of "class products at affordable prices." The photography in the ads gave a most distinctive interpretation to that theme (see Figures 17–14 and 17–15).

The suave gentleman in the tuxedo held sway until 1986 when U.S. Gypsum broadened the line to include truly high-styled new ceiling tiles. These products were so attractive in and of themselves that the campaign was built on single-page ads, each featuring a magnificent close-up photograph of a single tile placed in a lush contemporary setting with a full ceiling background of the featured tile (see Figures 17–16, 17–17, and 17–18). These close-up "portraits" of single tiles have rated extremely well in readership studies.

Thus the advertising for United States Gypsum ceiling tiles has evolved over several years, embracing product changes, design changes, and pricing changes. The advertising has been bold, attractive and, above all, consistent. And it has definitely had an impact on the designing and building trade. United States Gypsum has steadily risen to a position of prominent runner-up to a long-entrenched leader with a much larger budget.

NOTE: Figures 17–13–17–18 are shown following page 365.

SUMMARY

You have now read three case histories of actual advertising campaigns. You have seen how these advertisers applied the very principles you were studying earlier in this book. You saw nothing mysterious, nothing miraculous. For the most part, even the creative work displayed might be described as "sound and sensible" rather than "brilliant and inspired."

Marketing peculiarities differed. Budgets differed. But the methods of finding and solving a communications problem did not differ. You now know those methods. You can apply them, whether you're promoting a one-person shop or a mammoth corporation. Follow with confidence the basic steps pointed out in this book. You will soon discover that advertising is ever-fascinating but rarely baffling.

If there is one piece of advice that the experts here discussed would pass along to you, it is this: Plan on a six-to-twelve-month basis and stick with it. It pays to be consistent.

We hope that these three different campaign examples have opened your eyes to the real world of advertising. Here you have seen actual advertising people at work solving real and specific problems. Perhaps their true stories have inspired you to want to go forth and do likewise. How you go about doing that, how you embark on an advertising career of your own, is the subject of the next chapter.

TERMS TO KNOW

Now that you have finished this chapter, you should understand the following terms:

opportunistic media buys
response mechanism

If you are uncertain about the meaning of these terms, go back through the chapter and review them.

THINGS TO THINK ABOUT

1. Think about some of the ways a local fast-food franchise might supplement its national advertising.
2. If you had a toy shop, would you advertise to children or parents?
3. Do you think there is any danger in a bank's advertising being folksy and informal?
4. Many soft drinks do interesting and entertaining advertising. Which campaign do you think does the best job of differentiating its product?
5. In what ways do you think an audience of students would differ from the regular, permanent residents of a large university town?

THINGS TO TALK ABOUT

1. Suppose this year marked the hundredth anniversary of your largest local department store. Discuss how you might handle that fact in your advertising and promotion.
2. Discuss the various customer segments of the local hardware dealer. Which segment is most important to the business?
3. Most department store advertising sells merchandise. Discuss some possibilities for "institutional" advertising on behalf of your local department store.
4. Campaigns are long-term and consistent. Consider some circumstances that might force an advertiser to change a campaign.
5. Discuss the automotive advertising campaign—national or local—that you think does the most distinctive job.

THINGS TO DO

1. Make a list of the fast-food franchises near you. Which is the local standout? Why? Describe its advertising.
2. Talk to one of your local bankers. Ask how the bank tries to establish a "personality" through its advertising.
3. Make a list of the slogans businesses in your community use. Which do you think is most suitable? Why?
4. Talk to the ad manager of the largest local department store. Find out how often the store advertises in a year.
5. Ask your local men's or women's clothier to explain its cooperative advertising agreement with its chief national supplier.

Welcome to our new course of action.
We're continuing a great tradition in our exciting new home, the TPC at Avenel.
The Kemper Group is proud that the Kemper Open has raised more than $825,000 for local and national charities during the eight years in which the tournament has been held in this area. Your support is greatly appreciated.
On behalf of our more than 17,000 employees and the 2,800 independent agents and brokers who represent us, we are pleased to be bringing you the very best in professional golf.
And for the very best in insurance service and protection, we hope you'll ride with the Kemper Cavalry, symbol of insurance from the Kemper Group.
KEMPER GROUP
Once you compare Kemper, you'll ride with us.

National Insurance Companies.

FIGURE 17–1*a*
The biggest annual promotional event for the Kemper Group is the Kemper Open Golf Tournament. From the Tournament program, here is a Kemper advertisement and an editorial piece on Kemper's sponsorship of the event.

FIGURE 17–1*b*

BEHIND THE SCENES

Meet the Kemper Group

If you watch golf telecasts, the Kemper Cavalry may be a familiar sight as it rides across your TV screen. However, you may not be quite as familiar with the Kemper Group, sponsor of these ads and of this tournament.

The Kemper Group is composed of an array of insurance and financial services companies with worldwide facilities. Besides writing property and casualty insurance for businesses and individuals, Kemper provides consumers with life and health insurance, mutual funds and other investment services.

The company began as a single mutual insurance company, formed in the early 1900s by James Scott Kemper to help Chicago-area lumbermen provide workers compensation insurance at a reasonable cost. This company, Lumbermens Mutual Casualty Company, gradually expanded into other areas of personal and business insurance.

In 1979 "Kemper Group" was chosen as the name for the growing organization. The two major components riding under the Kemper Group banner are Lumbermens and Kemper Corporation. The latter is a non-operating holding company.

The Kemper Group believes strongly in returning something back to the community in which it operates. The company actively supports a number of charities and social service organizations. In addition, it supports higher education, medical research and other socially responsible causes through the James S. Kemper Foundation. Finally, the Kemper Group also encourages its employees to make charitable contributions by providing a matching gift program.

These and other socially responsive activities are as much a part of the Kemper Group as the services it sells.

So the next time the Kemper Cavalry rides across your TV screen, know that more than insurance and financial services are under its banner. □

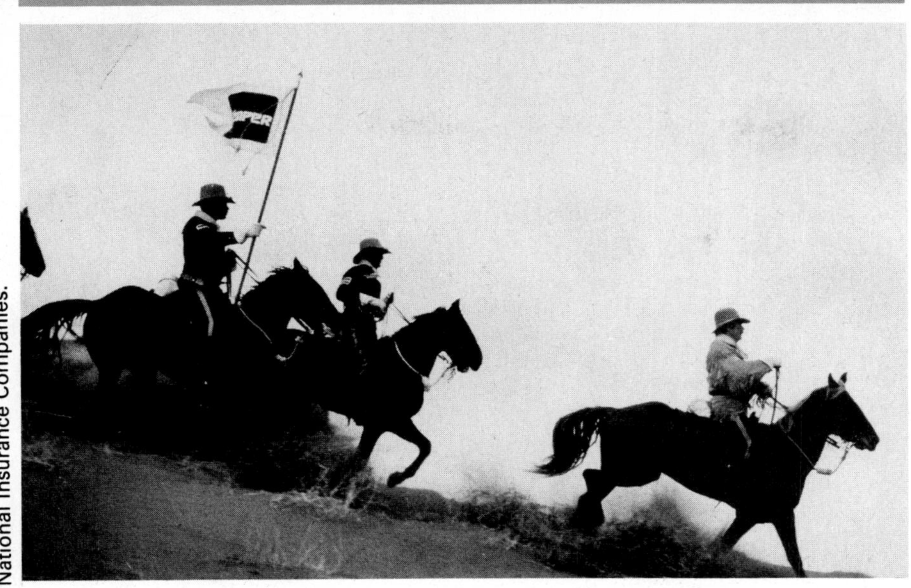

National Insurance Companies.

FIGURE 17–2
Here is the Kemper Cavalry riding to the rescue, on location in Monument Valley.

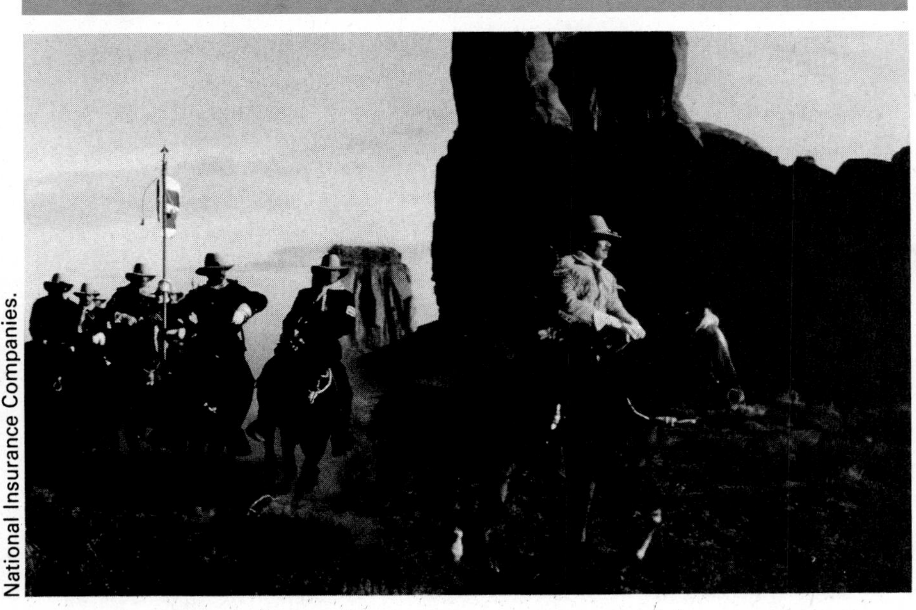

National Insurance Companies.

Homeowners—General

"Butchy" **(KGP-8706)**

Mrs. Meegle: Butchy, say "Hi" to Mr. Pierson.

Butchy: No.

Mrs. Meegle: Butchy . . .

George: Hi, Butchy. I'm your mom's independent Kemper insurance agent.

Butchy: Then where's your bugle?

George: Bugle?

Butchy: On TV the Kemper people blow bugles. Like the Cavalry.

George: Well, in real life we don't blow bugles.

Butchy: So what do you blow?

George: We don't blow anything, Butchy. We help folks find the right insurance coverage to fit their needs.

Butchy: Where's your horsie?

George: I don't have a horsie.

Butchy: How 'bout a moo-cow?

George: No. But I have a hamster.

Butchy: You ride your hamster to the rescue?

George: No. But I help people like your mom choose the right kind of Kemper homeowners coverage.

Mrs. Meegle: Like broader coverage to insure our house and everything in it for its full value, Butchy.

Butchy: We live in a condo.

George: You still need to protect your belongings. Right, Mrs. Meegle?

Mrs. Meegle: And that's why we're here, Butchy. Tell Mr. Pierson what you did.

Butchy: I roasted weenies in the living room.

George: You have a fireplace?

Butchy: Nope.

Mrs. Meegle: We don't have a couch now, or a coffee table, or a bookcase, either.

George: Don't worry, Mrs. Meegle. You're covered. *(bugle)*

Announcer: *(Agency tag)*

Auto and Homeowners—Price

"The Lovebirds" **(KGP-8707)**

She: George, we're sorry you couldn't play your Kemper bugle at our wedding.

George: Well, this Kemper bugle is just a symbol. See, I don't really play it. So, what can George Pierson, "Independent Insurance Agent," do for you two lovebirds.

Both Well, we have a new home now . . . And a new car . . . And each other.

George: So you need some Kemper Insurance.

He: Yes, Auto.

She: Yes, Homeowners.

She: Gumdrop, we need Kemper Homeowners Insurance. We'll get bargain auto insurance at "Discountland."

He: Butterfly, we need Kemper Auto Insurance. We can get cut rate homeowners insurance at "House of Insurance."

George: Well, folks, if you're trying to save a few dollars, you may be sacrificing protection for price.

He: Then we need Kemper . . .

He: Homeowners.

She: Auto.

He: Sweetlips, George just said . . .

She: I heard him, Boopsie.

He: Well, then, Knobby Knees.

She: Knobby Knees!

George: *(blows bugle)*

Both: George?!

George: You can have Kemper's low-cost Homeowners *and* Auto Insurance both.

Both: We can?

George: Sure. Kemper has quality insurance coverage at a competitive price.

She: Great! But George, I thought you couldn't play the bugle.

George: Well . . . *(bugle)*

Announcer: *(Agency tag)*

National Insurance Companies.

FIGURE 17–3*a*
Kemper's Guide Book for cooperative advertising by agents has scripts of prerecorded radio commercials and mats of available newspaper ads.

Business — General

"A Cowboy Singer" **(KGP-8708)**

George:	*(sings "Home, home on the range")*
Man:	You're awful flat.
George:	I'm not a cowboy singer, Bert.
Man:	Aren't you George Pierson, independent insurance agent and member of the Kemper Cavalry?
George:	Yes, but the Kemper Cavalry is just on TV.
Man:	And when you sold me business insurance for my new guitar boutique and frozen yogurt stand, you said two things. One, I could rely on your service and two, you know cowboy songs.
George:	But Bert, I didn't know you were looking for someone to sing at your grand opening!
Man:	Keep rehearsing.
George:	*(sings "Home")* Bert, are you pleased with the Kemper coverage . . .
Man:	I'm in ecstasy. You custom-tailored the right coverage at the right price for my new business. But sing, please sing.
George:	*(sings "Home")* Look, I'll find you a singer.
Man:	No, I sent out the flyers announcing you.
George:	*(sings "where the deer and buffalo")*
Man:	Antelope!
George:	*(sings "antelope play")*
Man:	Tuck in your tummy and smile.
George:	*(sings "Where seldom is heard")*
Man:	And you call yourself a singer?
George:	No *(chuckle)*, I don't.
Man:	Well, can you do rope tricks? *(Bugle)*
Announcer:	*(Agency tag)*

There's Time for You, Too!

All of the George Pierson taped commercials leave approximately 10 seconds for a *live announcer tag* to be read at the close. Suggested tags will be sent with your tape order. Or, you may decide to write and use your own agency tag.

Here are a few guidelines you may find helpful if writing your own tag. Note that time may permit you to include only one or two of these suggestions.

- Include your agency name and telephone number. If time permits, include your agency address.
- Include your agency's own tagline, if you have one.
- Re-emphasize the main point made in the commercial.
- Or, include Kemper's corporate tagline.

Suggested Tags

Here are some examples of effective *live announcer tags.*

- For full details on how you can save with Kemper's auto and homeowners insurance, call *(agency name, agency phone number).*
- For full details about Kemper auto insurance, call *(agency name, agency phone number, agency tagline).*
- Once you compare Kemper, you'll ride with us *(agency name, agency phone number, agency phone number).*
- Once you compare Kemper auto insurance, you'll ride with us *(agency name, agency phone number).*

National Insurance Companies.

FIGURE 17–3*b*

Independent Agent

2-column: KCN-8741
1-column: KCN-8742

Business & Personal

2-column: KCN-8743
1-column: KCN-8744

"An independent insurance agent serves you better."
Kemper
SAMPLE
We believe it . . . and so does Kemper.
Call out the Cavalry today and find out how an independent agent can help you get more insurance value for your dollar. Once you compare Kemper, you'll ride with us.
Kemper GROUP

KCN-8741

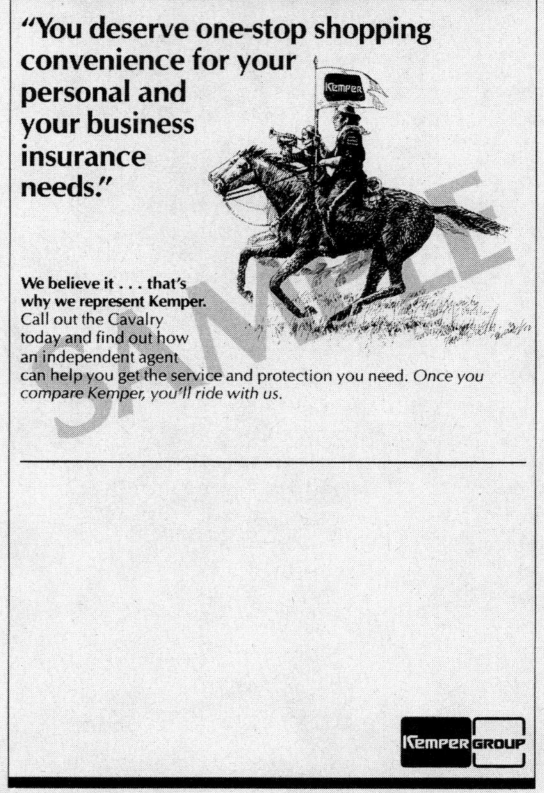

"You deserve one-stop shopping convenience for your personal and your business insurance needs."
Kemper
SAMPLE
We believe it . . . that's why we represent Kemper.
Call out the Cavalry today and find out how an independent agent can help you get the service and protection you need. Once you compare Kemper, you'll ride with us.
Kemper GROUP

KCN-8743

FIGURE 17–3*c*

National Insurance Companies.

Professionalism

2-column: KCN-8745
1-column: KCN-8746

"You deserve expert advice before you buy insurance."

We believe it . . . and so does Kemper.
Call out the Cavalry today. Find out how to choose the right protection from an independent agent whose professional service and expertise come from years of experience. *Once you compare Kemper, you'll ride with us.*

KEMPER GROUP

KCN-8745

National Insurance Companies.

FIGURE 17–3*d*

What to do in case of an accident
XD 3382
Accident reporting kit can be carried in glove compartment of insured's car. Kit costs $11 per 100; minimum of 100 required. Lists claims facilities, plus:
Driver's notes*
Provides space to record vital information about an accident.
Witness card*
Can be used to document the witnessing of an accident.
Fits a #10 envelope.
*Included in accident reporting kit

New!
Does your auto insurance leave you feeling empty?
XK 0393
Pre-approach two-piece stuffer/mailer with envelope. Includes die-cut for business card. 250 free. Additional quantities sold in lots of 50 at $5/50.

Kemper Total

Brochure
XAK 0350
Describes how *Kemper Total* new car "repair or replacement" coverage protects an insured's new car. Can be used with *Kemper Total* display stand. Fits a #10 envelope.

Stuffer
XAK 0351
Describes *Kemper Total* new car "repair or replacement" coverage. For insureds who have not yet purchased a new car. Fits a #9 envelope.

Display stand
XAK 0352
Point-of-purchase display holds 50 *Kemper Total* brochures. *Brochures must be ordered separately.* Contains capsule summary of coverages. Has space for agency stamp.
Fits an 11½" × 14½" envelope.
(Stand measures 10" × 12")

Poster
XAK 0354
Illustrates *Kemper Total* new car "repair or replacement" coverage.
Poster measures 17" × 22".

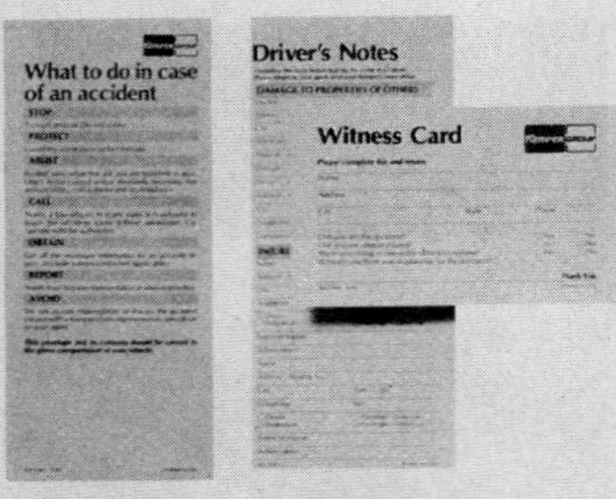

XD 3382

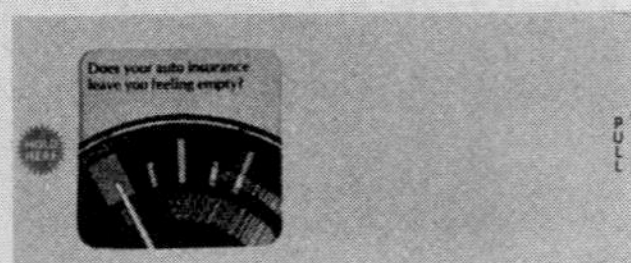

XK 0393

XAK 0350 XAK 0351

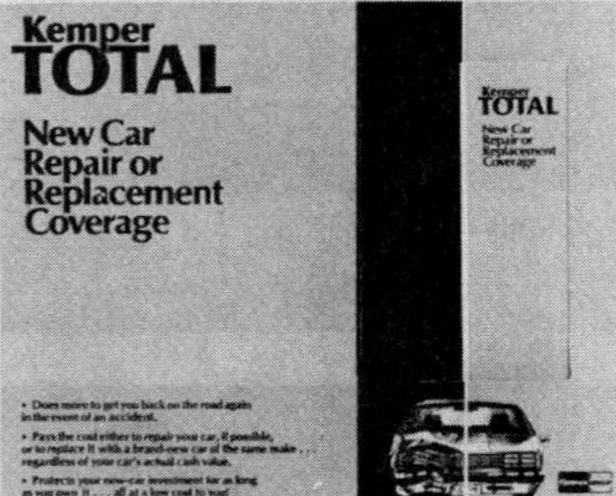

XAK 0352

XAK 0354

National Insurance Companies.

FIGURE 17–4
Kemper's Sales Promotion Catalog for agents features the many available brochures and folders covering a wide variety of insurance-related topics.

SPECIALITIES

A. ◇ NEW! **Big Cavalry Mug.** New 12 oz. capacity mug offers a substantial feel. Sure to become a classic for office use. Spirited addition for table settings at awards banquets or agency functions.
#69124 . . . . **$4.35 ea.**
Min. order with imprint: 72
#69125 . . . . **$4.95 ea.**

B. Lapel Pin. The classy way to show your Kemper spirit. Wear this distinctive cloisonne lapel pin with pride. Great identifier for agency personnel, appreciated memento of a job well-done.
#67938 . . . . **$.85 ea.**

C. Memo Cube. Classic Cavalry design marks this functional cube of 4" x 4" memo papers, padded on one side (approx. 350 sheets/cube). Kemper look remains visible throughout use of pad.
#67939 . . . . **$3.95 ea.**

A four-line imprint can be any four lines of information. Your agency name plus a special message promoting a specific product line, for instance.

D. ◇ NEW! **Leather Bag/Luggage Tag.** Keep your identity covered with this beautiful blue leather tag. Ideal for luggage, briefcase, golf bag or sport bag. A great all-purpose handout. Holds standard business card with leather cover and snap closure. Gift-boxed.
#69176 . . . . **$2.75 ea.**

E. ◇ NEW! **Leather Key Fob.** Beautiful blue cowhide sports the Kemper Flagbearer hot-stamped in gold. A perfect thank-you for auto and home insureds.
#69128 . . . . **$1.25 ea.**

F. ◇ NEW! **No-Spill Mug.** Space-age design and rubberized base keeps mug from spilling and slipping. Big handle and wide mouth makes for easy handling. Perfect desk-toppper, staff welcomer or client give-away. Packed in it's own box.
#69139 . . . . **$2.75 ea.**
Min. order with imprint: 144
#69140 . . . . **$2.85 ea.**

G. Cavalry Flag. Show your true Kemper spirit with some great flag waving. Our 4" x 6" flag is silk-like rayon, hemmed and mounted on black staff with gilt spear. Base included. It's the perfect desk accessory, place setting marker or centerpiece grouping at agency functions, community events. Available only while quantities last!
#67936 . . . . **$2.65 ea.**

4

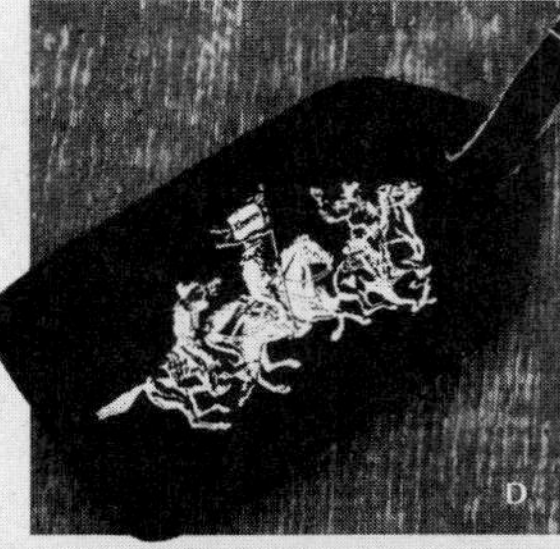

National Insurance Companies.

FIGURE 17–5
The Kemper Collection Book for agents features an assortment of attractive items that can be used as awards, handouts, inducements, and identifying symbols.

Television commercials

Telling your advertising story to a large audience can result in unbelievable impact. And television is the popular medium that can do it. As a Partner, your personal television advertising plan can go in just about any unique direction—explaining the product, creating a mood, making a blockbusting announcement or trying out a product in certain areas.

For $275, we'll write your television scripts for you, with video suggestions included for local production. Please give us 4 weeks to complete the request.

If you need assistance with commercial production, your local TV stations will be happy to help. Ask your local station rep about special packages that may be available. Remember that TV isn't always as costly as you may think.

To co-op on the media costs, fill in your Partner Co-op Application (XK 0305-3) and follow regular Co-op procedures.

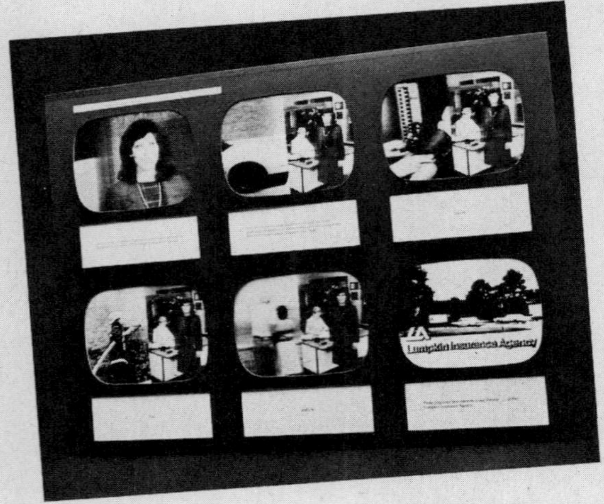

Yellow Pages listings

Listing your agency information in a familiar, well-used publication provides instant access to your business. And the *Yellow Pages* will do that. A *Yellow Pages* listing is where your name, address and phone number are listed under a Kemper heading in your local *Yellow Pages* directory. And as a Kemper Agent Partner, you get a listing in your *local* directory at half price.

Here's how:
Each year you're solicited for a local directory listing by our national *Yellow Pages* agency, Telephone Marketing Programs (TMP). When you receive the solicitation for your local directory, check to see that your name, agency name, address and phone number are all correct. Then, return it with your check for the billed amount, which is half the cost of a regular listing.

If you would also like to be listed in a *neighboring* directory, contact the National Advertising Coordinator at (312) 540-2521. He'll give you the information you need. Or send him the name(s) of the town(s) in which you want to be listed and how you want your listing to appear. His address is Kemper Group, Advertising D-5, Long Grove, IL 60049.

National Insurance Companies.

FIGURE 17–6*a*
The Kemper Custom Advertising Guide shows agents the kind of skilled ad service available at headquarters to help solve special problems.

Yellow Pages display ads

A *Yellow Pages* display ad can be an effective marketing tool that brings consistency to your *total* advertising plan. It can lend personal recognition to your insurance business as well as call special attention to your products and services at a time when the prospective customer is in the mood to buy.

To help you take advantage of this appropriate advertising medium, we'll develop a *Yellow Pages* display ad for your agency at a cost of $125. We'll provide copy and layout ideas for your approval, and then send you camera-ready artwork for printing. And, if we produce your *Yellow Pages* display ad, we'll also co-op space costs with you. When your ad *first* appears in the local directory, send us the following:

1
A tear sheet or photocopy of the page showing your new ad.

2
A copy of the breakdown sheet from the phone company showing the *exact cost of your Yellow Pages display ad.*

3
A copy of your phone bill.

Send these directly to the Co-op Desk, Advertising D-5, Kemper Group, Long Grove, IL 60049.

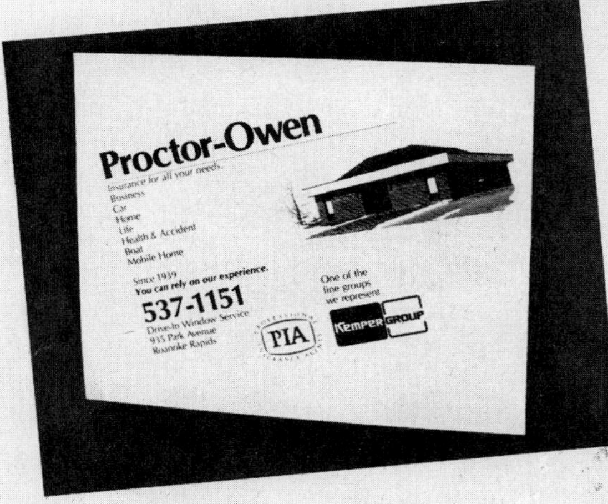

Direct mail

Using the written word with an individual touch can reach your prospects at a personal level. Direct mail allows you extreme flexibility—from sales letters and postcards to leaflets and booklets. Direct mail is just about any form of direct advertising that is sent through the mail.

By using this method, you can make the coverage as intensive as you like. And because direct mail moves quickly and selectively, you can take advantage of timely or seasonal appeals like mature driver discounts for people over 50, student discounts when the school year begins, or encouraging customers to upgrade coverage during inflationary times.

But experience has taught us that in order to make your direct mail campaign a success, you must follow up to turn your repliers into buyers. If you can't follow up on leads, DON'T start a direct mail program.

Kemper will write your direct mail letter for a cost of $25. If you would like us to create a campaign consisting of letters, a stuffer, or any combination of these items, we'll develop that for you, too, at a charge of $150. And of course, we'll send you initial copy for your approval before we proceed. Please allow us 4-8 weeks to complete the project.

If we prepare your letter, we'll also pay for 50% of your postage costs—*but* please be sure to talk to your PLMM/CLMM for full Co-op information. Upon approval, send your postage bills directly to the Co-op Desk, Advertising D-5, Kemper Group, Long Grove, IL 60049.

National Insurance Companies.

FIGURE 17–6*b*

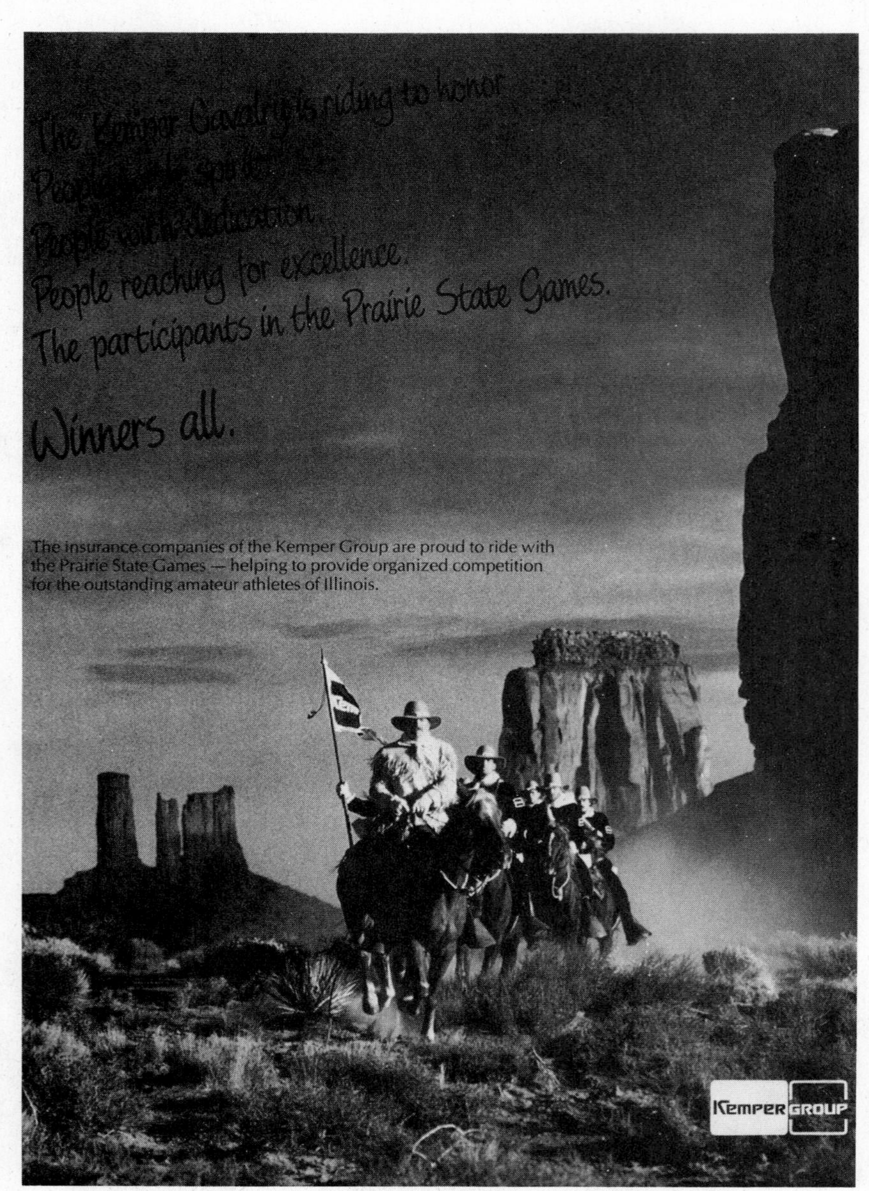

The Kemper Cavalry is riding to honor
People reaching for excellence.
The participants in the Prairie State Games.
Winners all.
The insurance companies of the Kemper Group are proud to ride with the Prairie State Games — helping to provide organized competition for the outstanding amateur athletes of Illinois.
Kemper GROUP

FIGURE 17–7
Kemper's public-spirited ad department produced the Prairie State Games souvenir program. Here is a rare Kemper Cavalry print ad from that program.

National Insurance Companies.

Mercy Hospital's "One of a Kind" campaign progressed through a series of phases as illustrated in these ads.

Neonatal Intensive Care Unit

One of a kind.

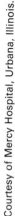

At Mercy Hospital, our approach to health care is different. It's not mass-produced . . . it's not a matter of juggling our patients like facts and figures. It's individualized . . . it's unique . . . and, most of all, it's responsive to the needs of our community.

Over the years, Mercy has been a leader in introducing new programs. From highly technical to highly human, these services have always been designed to fulfill unmet needs.

Some services have since become attractive to other hospitals and have been copied. Others have not. What remains constant is that one hospital is uniquely committed to the needs of this community.

Mercy Hospital. We're one of a kind . . . and so are many of our services.

• **The community's first Neonatal Intensive Care Unit for premature and high-risk infants.**

Mercy Hospital

1400 West Park Street
Urbana, Illinois 61801
337-2000

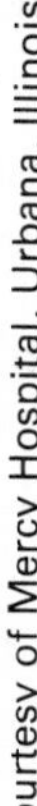

FIGURE 17–8
This is one of the newspaper ads introducing Mercy Hospital's "One of a Kind" campaign.

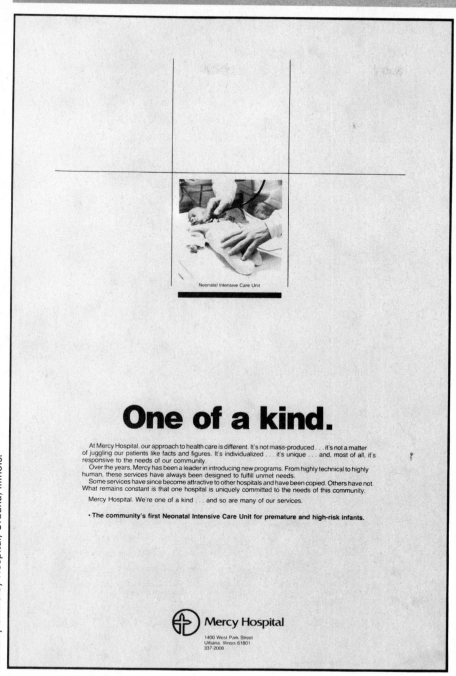

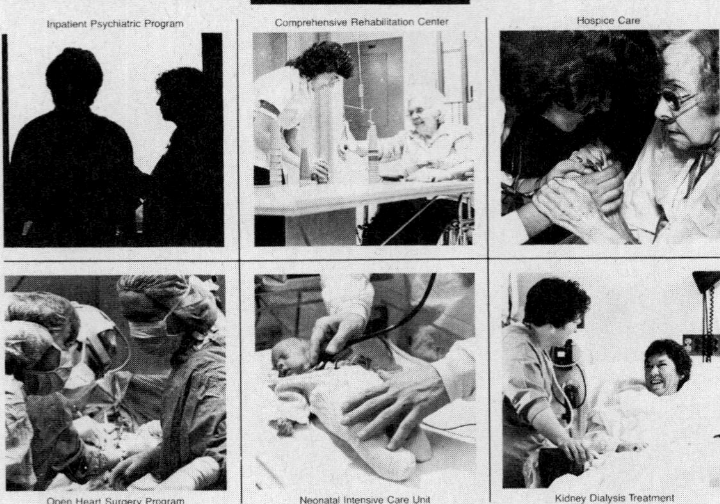

One of a kind.

At Mercy Hospital, our approach to health care is different. It's not mass-produced . . . it's not a matter of juggling our patients like facts and figures. It's individualized . . . it's unique . . . and, most of all, it's responsive to the needs of our community.

Over the years, Mercy has been a leader in introducing new programs. From highly technical to highly human, these services have always been designed to fulfill unmet needs.

Some services have since become attractive to other hospitals and have been copied. Others have not. What remains constant is that one hospital is uniquely committed to the needs of this community.

Mercy Hospital. We're one of a kind . . . and so are many of our services.

- **The community's first Neonatal Intensive Care Unit for premature and high-risk infants.**
- **The area's first and only Hospice Program, which provides care and support for terminally ill patients and their families.**
- **Site of the area's first and largest Open Heart Surgery Program — a cooperative effort offering patients access to the best health care resources in the community.**
- **The only inpatient Psychiatric Program in Champaign County, a program emphasizing short-term stays which prepare patients for return to the community.**
- **Champaign-Urbana's only Kidney Dialysis Program for patients who require ongoing, life-sustaining treatment.**
- **The only inpatient, comprehensive Rehabilitation Program in Champaign County, offering stroke victims and others an opportunity to return to independent living.**

1400 West Park Street
Urbana, Illinois 61801
337-2000

Courtesy of Mercy Hospital, Urbana, Illinois.

FIGURE 17–9
Second round of ads in the campaign featured *all* the services contributing to the "One of a Kind" theme.

When you need open heart surgery, your hospital's experience counts.

Imagine an open heart surgery procedure.

Imagine an emergency open heart surgery procedure. The order comes for surgery to begin immediately. The patient's very survival depends on the speed, experience and extensive training of the open heart surgery team.

The team assembles quickly. Two cardiovascular surgeons, an anesthesiologist, a certified nurse anesthetist, four highly trained scrub nurses, a circulating nurse and a perfusionist all move swiftly into action. A hemodynamic technician stands ready to relay blood samples to the laboratory. Even in the large modern operating room, space around the operating table is tight. The atmosphere is carefully controlled and serious.

Everyone takes his or her accustomed place. Anesthesia is administered. The team works quickly, methodically and in perfect concert. Everything is in the right place at precisely the right time. No motion is wasted. No instruction misinterpreted. And just 10 minutes later the heart is exposed. Surgical repair begins.

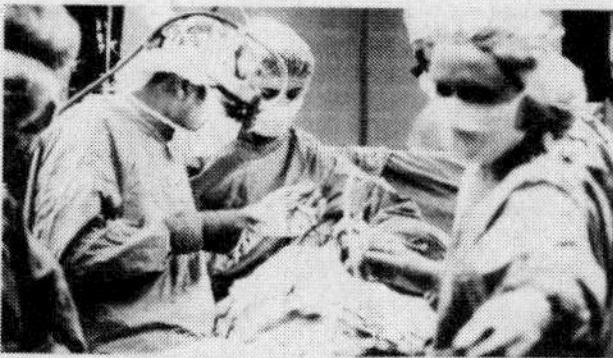

Open heart surgery team

Teamwork makes the procedure successful.

Open heart surgery is a highly technical procedure, but people make it successful. At Mercy, we not only have the finest equipment and facilities money can buy, we've also been working for 15 years to develop our team and procedures. Recruiting, training, cross-training and retraining so that today we have a team second to none. Using procedures and protocols that have been perfected and proven year after year and case after case.

We've been developing our program for 15 years.

After all, Mercy brought open heart surgery to Champaign-Urbana. And more than twice as many procedures have been performed at Mercy as anywhere else in the area. In fact, we're large enough that we exceed nationally accepted standards for quality of care. That means our team constantly gets the practice it needs to maintain its skills. And our patients get a surgical team of recognized quality.

We're proud of our skills.

Every nurse in Mercy's operating room is cross-trained to assist in open heart surgery. Only Mercy, of all local hospitals, has nurses with the prestigious qualification "Certified Operating Room Nurse." Virtually every nurse in each of Mercy's critical care units has met the exacting demands of certification for Advanced Cardiac Life Support (ACLS). Some even teach the course. Our head of Anesthesiology is also an expert in the management of life threatening situations. Our chief Perfusionist (who maintains critical life support functions during surgery) not only trained at the Texas Heart Institute, but actually has a Ph.D in his discipline.

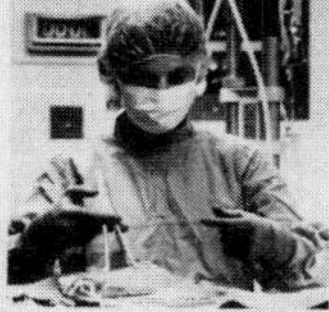

Julie Ingold, Surgical Technician

We cooperate to offer the best resources in the community.

Perhaps best of all, Open Heart Surgery at Mercy is a cooperative program. For the last 10 years, Mercy, Christie Clinic and Carle have pooled resources to offer the community *one* program of optimal quality. Christie and Carle surgeons operate together in Mercy's surgical facilities; Carle maintains the extensive catheterization facilities necessary to diagnose heart conditions. And the community benefits because each institution specializes so expensive facilities and staff are shared, not duplicated.

Mercy's commitment goes deeper than the bottom line.

Over the years, Mercy has grown to be far more than just a community hospital. In addition to offering a complete range of medical and surgical services, we have:

- led in initiating the unique programs most needed by the community
- introduced the latest medical technology to support them
- developed a nursing staff with an unusually high level of training and expertise
- retained our belief in "holistic care" — the conviction that patients' psychological, emotional and spiritual needs must be cared for, as well as their specific medical conditions

This dedication to both technology and caring goes beyond a gimmick or a slogan. It stems from the philosophy of the Sisters (Servants of the Holy Heart of Mary) who have operated Mercy for over 60 years. It is a commitment that goes deeper than the bottom line. It is our reason for being.

And, just like all the programs we've pioneered — Neonatology, Hemodialysis, Rehabilitation, Hospice and Psychiatry — it is this philosophy that makes Open Heart Surgery at Mercy . . . One of a kind.

Mercy's Open Heart Surgery Program . . . One of a kind

Courtesy of Mercy Hospital, Urbana, Illinois.

FIGURE 17–10
Third round of ads in the "One of a Kind" campaign featured in great detail Mercy Hospital's special programs.

Bret Hufford, Rossville, a former patient of Mercy's Rehabilitation Center. We thank Bret for sharing his personal experience.

Imagine being 16... and unable to tie your shoes.

He was young — just four days past his 16th birthday. And of course, he was healthy and active. Sure, Bret Hufford had played football . . . been on the track team . . . even made the starting lineup in basketball.

But ironically, it was in a physical fitness class that Bret suffered a neck fracture which left him a quadriplegic.

How do you recover when your life has been changed so drastically in just a moment's time? For Bret and his parents, Joetta and Tom, the East Central Illinois Rehabilitation Center at Mercy Hospital was the answer. And finding a fully accredited, comprehensive rehabilitation program so close to home enabled Bret to see his family and friends from Rossville often.

In downstate Illinois, *only* Mercy Hospital offers this one of a kind program. "I have nothing but praise for Mercy Hospital and the Rehabilitation Program. I never gave up. But my therapists were the reason why. They kept my spirits up and gave me specialized care. Both the occupational and physical therapists got so involved in my routine . . . I could see they cared very much," Bret said.

Mercy offers programs most needed by the community.

Like the many other programs we've pioneered — the Neonatal Intensive Care Unit, Open Heart Surgery, inpatient Psychiatric treatment, Kidney Dialysis and Hospice — the Rehabilitation Program is an expression of a commitment that goes beyond traditional hospital care . . . a one of a kind commitment to people like Bret.

Bret Hufford walked on his own just 7½ weeks after entering the Rehabilitation Program. His doctors had estimated it would take 18 to 24 months. And today — two years later — Bret is studying at Southern Illinois University to become a physical therapist.

Except for a slight limp, you'd never know how serious Bret's condition once was. And thanks to Mercy Hospital's commitment, he's looking forward to using his experience to help others.

The East Central Illinois Rehabilitation Center at Mercy Hospital . . .
One of a kind

1400 West Park Street
Urbana, Illinois 61801

Courtesy of Mercy Hospital, Urbana, Illinois.

FIGURE 17–11
Fourth round of ads in the "One of a Kind" campaign were highly emotional messages featuring patients.

"The O.R. is no place for timid people to work."

Lois "Lou" McCalpin, R.N.,
Manager, Operating Room

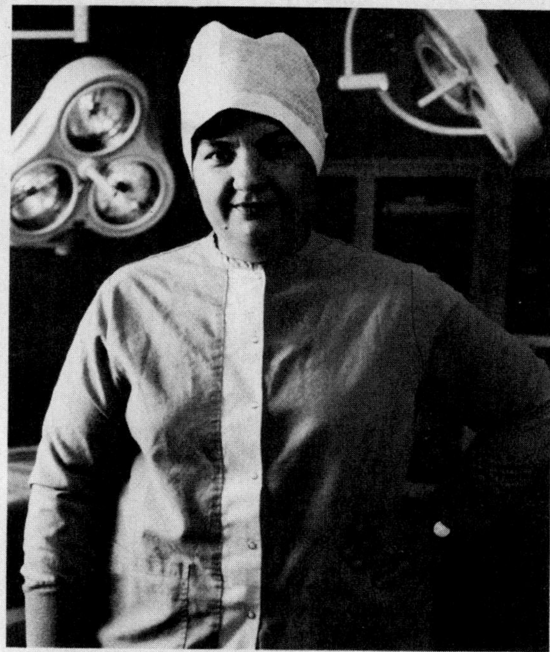

Lois McCalpin of Champaign, known to her co-workers as Lou, is manager of Mercy Hospital's 7 operating rooms. A 1969 graduate of the Mercy School of Nursing, Lou has been involved in nursing management at Mercy since 1974. She received training in open heart operating room techniques from Drs. Michael DeBakey and Denton Cooley.

They can stop a person's heart from beating, help to repair it, and get it started again . . . maybe in less time than it takes to put a new water pump on your station wagon.

The operating room can be an intense place to work. Lou McCalpin is in charge of the nurses who work there.

"As an O.R. manager," says Lou, "you're going to have some of the most energetic, assertive people in the hospital, put them into a closed, high-stress situation, and get them all to work toward one goal as a team. I think Mercy has an exceptional track record at it.

An excellent support staff

"The only way I will be successful as a manager is through those people. There is no way I am going to manage 7 operating rooms simultaneously every day unless I have excellent people on the team."

And she *does* have excellent people. Their level of professional and personal dedication helps to make Mercy's surgery service the envy of the region.

"The philosophy in our OR is that all nursing staff—RNs and surgical techs—are given the opportunity, and expected, to function in all services we offer," says Lou. "And we have never had an inability to staff this OR on any given day or night, no matter what the situation, even if everybody else on call was already in surgery."

The surgeons of Christie and Carle depend on them.

Mercy surgical personnel are vital to the joint Carle/Christie/Mercy Open Heart Surgery Program, the oldest, largest, and most versatile program of its kind in the region.

In fact, a Mercy open heart team stands by at Carle Foundation Hospital so physicians there can perform angioplasty.

What makes Mercy's team so special? Trained to the highest standards, they work with a special dedication—a personal toughness—that helps them to be prepared for any challenge. One example:

"To 'scrub' a case is one of the roles in the O.R.," Lou explains. "[You] set up the sterile field, handle instrumentation, and generally anticipate the surgeon's needs. When you learn to scrub, the standard procedure is to start with the less complex procedures.

"The philosophy [on Dr. Cooley's service, where Lou learned open heart O.R. procedures in 1970] was that you were there to learn, and that you could learn best through hands-on experience. So on my second case there, the head nurse told me 'scrub it.'

"This was the first case I ever solo-scrubbed—an aortic valve for Denton Cooley! I wouldn't recommend it for everyone, but *I* sure learned from it!"

Lou McCalpin . . .
One of a Kind

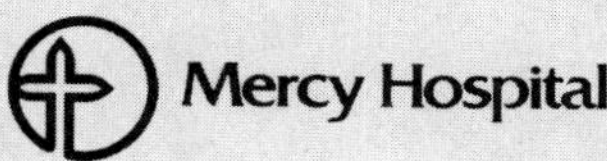

Courtesy of Mercy Hospital, Urbana, Illinois.

FIGURE 17–12 Fifth round of ads in the "One of a Kind" campaign featured individual employees of Mercy Hospital.

SECTION 5

Your Life With Advertising

All of the material in the book up to this point have been useful and instructive. But it will mean even more if you intend to put it to work.

There are two ways you can put to work what you have learned about advertising. First, and most obvious, you could go to work in the advertising industry. Second, and perhaps not so obvious, you can make good use of your understanding of advertising as a consumer who sees and hears advertising every day.

In both cases, you will make use of advertising, either from the point of view of the advertiser who sends out the advertising message, or from the point of view of the consumer who receives the advertising message.

So this section stresses your life in advertising, first in a career where you may find great satisfaction working in the exciting field of advertising. And then you will learn how to make the best use of advertising in the rest of your everyday life, as a consumer—how we can all use advertising successfully.

CHAPTERS

18 Careers in Advertising

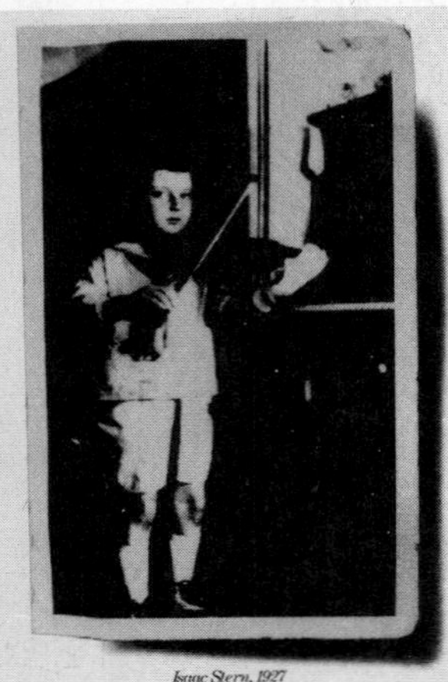

Courtesy of Bloomingdale | Fallon-McElligott

CHAPTER OUTLINE

Size of the Advertising Business
- Is Advertising Growing?

What is Needed to Work in Advertising
- Sales
- Copywriting
- Art and Layout
- Media Planning and Buying
- Agency-Advertiser Contact
- Management
- Research
- Supplier

How Advertising Jobs Relate to Other Fields

How to Prepare for an Advertising Career
- Where to Get More Information
- Get Involved

By the time you finish this chapter, you should understand:

1. **The career opportunities that are available in the advertising industry.**
2. **How to prepare for an advertising career.**
3. **Specific advertising job responsibilities.**
4. **How to look for an advertising job.**
5. **Where to get more information about advertising careers.**

By now, you may be getting interested in more than just learning about advertising. Perhaps you might be interested in working in the advertising business. But even if an advertising career is not your goal, this chapter will help you understand more about the organization of the advertising industry and the varied and special skills that are necessary in advertising.

SIZE OF THE ADVERTISING BUSINESS

Nobody is quite certain how many people work in advertising in the United States. There are several reasons for this. First, a large number of individual companies have advertising departments, which may employ anywhere from one person to more than a hundred people. Then there are all the people who work for advertising media, for advertising agencies, and for related firms involved in advertising production, photography, and similar services. To make it even more difficult, not all these people work full time in advertising, and not all of them have job titles that mention advertising.

All we know is that probably more than 100,000 people are employed in advertising in this country—and that as many as 10,000 new positions in advertising open up every year. The reasons for the new positions are many: Some people retire or leave the advertising business for other reasons; new people are needed each year to serve the ever-expanding advertising business; new businesses want to advertise to help make their operations successful.

Is Advertising Growing?

In some ways, it may seem that the advertising business is not growing. About ten or fifteen years ago, it was common for an advertising agency to employ ten people to handle each $1 million of business; now an agency may have only four or five employees for that much business—a reduction of more than half, it would seem. But remember that constant inflation means that each dollar of business fifteen years ago would be about two dollars or more of business now, just to afford the same amount of advertising. And during that same time period, the expenditures for advertising in the United States have gone from less than $25 billion to more than $100 billion. In fact, one current estimate is that we are spending more than $130 billion each year on advertising in this country![1] So surely the number of people needed to handle this growing advertising investment is growing too.

WHAT IS NEEDED TO WORK IN ADVERTISING

Suppose you are interested in working in advertising, either now or sometime in the future. What kinds of skills, traits, and abilities will you need?

Well, you are working on your first qualification right now. Taking college courses is good preparation for advertising jobs. A poll of advertising managers and agency executives showed that 80 percent of them think that college is helpful in advertising work, not just to learn about advertising, but to learn how to approach problems, think logically, and become a more well-rounded person. So you are getting the basic background for an advertising position by doing what you are already doing.

But the kinds of work available in advertising vary a great deal, and the necessary skills differ from one job to another. Let's go through some of the kinds of jobs that occur in advertising to see what skills and abilities are important and in what kinds of specific working situations each one may be found.

Sales

There are probably more opportunities for sales jobs in advertising than any other kind of work. Many of these jobs are open at the "entry level"—meaning that persons without much experience, looking for their first full-time job in advertising, may qualify. Selling involves meeting other people, helping them with their advertising and marketing problems, and serving their needs and requests.

Sales positions may also involve more than just selling. Some sales representatives for newspapers and local radio and television stations can get involved in the actual preparation of advertisements or even in entire campaigns. Besides writing and producing advertisements, salespeople may also schedule advertisements in the media as well as work on other facets of marketing and merchandising for their clients. So sales jobs in advertising are not limited to selling: They may include all sorts of other functions, too, combining some of the facets of copywriting, media planning, and general marketing and merchandising coordination. (See Figure 18–1.)

[1] Randall Rothenberg, "Advertising: Slow Growth Projected for Spending," *New York Times*, June 15, 1990, D15.

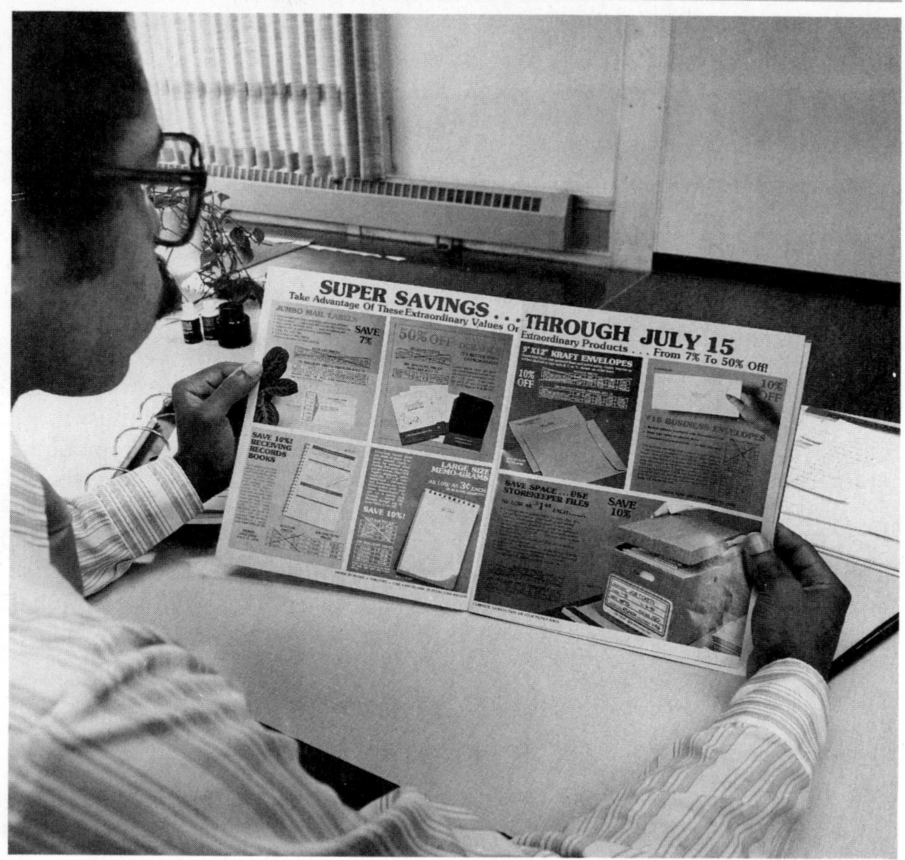

FIGURE 18–1
Circulars are part of the advertising campaign, which is planned by the newspaper advertising sales representative and the retail store.

Sales Jobs Are Plentiful. Newspapers provide more sales jobs than any other medium, primarily because there are so many daily and weekly newspapers and newspapers serve so many retail customers who need sales assistance. A newspaper **sales representative** (*rep* is the slang term) usually calls on several local stores and service establishments, reminding them of the need to advertise, taking orders for advertisements, picking up the advertisements, possibly preparing advertisements, and checking advertisements after the printer has readied them.

sales representative An advertising salesperson working for a newspaper.

The store owner may also want to know about special issues that are coming up, any new promotional ideas that the newspaper has started, contract qualifications and requirements, and anything else that may make the store's advertising more productive and efficient. After a while, the store manager and the newspaper sales representative work together as a team in many instances, both with the same general goal: using newspaper advertising to help the store.

Other Sales Positions. Local radio and television stations also offer sales positions. The work is similar to sales work with newspapers, except that the number of advertisers may be slightly smaller and the purposes of the advertising may involve support for campaigns in other media as well as total advertising campaigns on radio. Successful radio advertising sales requires an understanding of sound and music, and television advertising sales requires an understanding of motion and other visual elements.

The radio and television networks also use sales representatives to sell advertising time. Usually these positions require some selling experience, and the number of potential clients is still smaller because of the relatively few advertisers who can afford network advertising. These sales contracts are usually made with relatively high-level managers, and the selling effort must make the advertising tie in with the rest of the firm's advertising and promotional efforts. Much planning and forecasting is involved at this level of advertising.

Magazines, too, must employ salespeople to tell their advertising stories. These sales representatives must understand some of the complicated aspects of producing magazines and various printing techniques. The rate schedules of magazines may be complex as well, with regional editions, color, bleed, and special production costs all figured into the advertising rates.

Copywriting

copywriter A person who composes the written portion of an advertisement.

Copy is the written portion of an advertisement. It takes much skill and hard work to write good, effective advertising copy. A **copywriter** must have not only a flair for creativity and the ability to write well, but also the ability to continually produce and develop good original ideas. The best copywriters are flexible so they can edit and improve their own writing as well as accept the suggestions that other people may have to change the copy.

continuity A script for radio and television station announcers to follow.

As we have already mentioned, some sales representatives may also write copy, and there may be special copywriters at newspapers who take the sales representatives' written notes and create suggested advertisements from them. At radio and television stations, copywriters may also be expected to write what is called **continuity**, a script for the station's announcers to follow. It provides uniform flow for the programming, including introductions to programs, lead-ins to commercials, and conversational material that makes the entire broadcast presentation fit together. (It is not the same as the term continuity that is used in advertising media.)

Agency Copywriting. Advertising agencies have copywriters who work on advertisements for the agencies' clients. This is a very specialized job that requires a love for writing and great ability to produce new ideas that are workable and applicable to specific marketing and promotional problems. It is

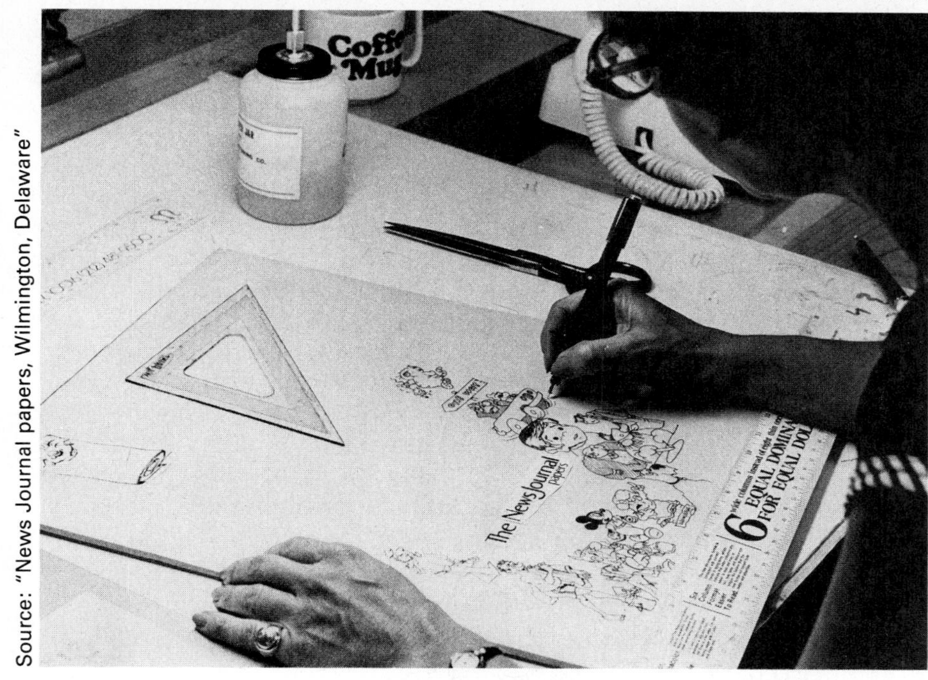

Source: "News Journal papers, Wilmington, Delaware"

FIGURE 18–2
A copywriter and artist need to work together to write advertisements.

hard for new copywriters to find jobs with large advertising agencies because these people must produce good ideas all the time, and there is little chance for on-the-job training.

Some copywriters work on advertisements for the same product or service, while others work on a variety of the agency's accounts. Usually a copywriter will work closely with an artist combining efforts to come up with new ideas that will sell (Figure 18–2). When two or more people work on the creative aspects of an advertisement or a campaign, it is often difficult to know for sure who actually suggested the initial idea that was eventually refined and turned into the finished advertisement.

Retail Copywriting. Some retail stores employ their own copywriters, either for a single store or for a chain of stores. The advertising copy is written for the newspaper and broadcast advertisements that will be used to promote the store's merchandise. Some retail copywriters write advertisements for catalogs; large retail chains such as Sears, Roebuck & Company, Spiegel, and J.C. Penney employ many copywriters to produce their catalogs. The growth of direct response marketing means that lots of catalogs are produced, both large and small. And many stores mail out a Christmas or other special sale catalog that is written by the copywriters. (See Figure 18–3.)

FIGURE 18–3
Here is a copywriting test used at one large advertising agency. You may want to try it yourself, to test your own creative abilities.

Part 1

Provide selected samples of your best writing, whether published or not. Short stories, articles, plays, poetry, humor, song lyrics, etc., are all appropriate. Term papers, unless unusually distinctive, should be omitted.

Part 2

Write a brief autobiography. You will probably want to include anything in your background which leads you to believe you may be successful in a career of writing and selling, such as any work you have done in these areas. Attempt to disclose those activities, thoughts, and philosophies that will permit us to know you better.

Part 3

Pick six advertisements for six different products and/or services from current issues of such national magazines as *Time, Reader's Digest,* or *Newsweek.* The first three should be advertisements which you feel are superb. Tell us why you think so, and do the next advertisement in the series for each. The second three should be advertisements which you think fall short of their goal. Tell us why and show us how you would improve each.

Part 4

Invent three new or improved products. At least two of the three should be in a category where major product differences may not be apparent (such as soap, beer, gasoline, airlines). Write at least two advertisements and one 60-second television commercial for *each* product.

Part 5

If everyone in the United States gave you 5¢, you would have in excess of $10,000,000 for yourself or any cause you supported. You have three minutes on television to persuade them to give this sum. Write the script. (Invent the facts you need, if necessary.)

General Instructions for Parts 3 and 4

Try to pick a variety of products and advertisements/commercials. For example, one advertisement could be on food, another on cosmetics, still another on travel. Limit the number of poster-type advertisements, as they do not show writing ability to the best advantage. Be sure to consider these fundamentals:

1. To whom is your selling message directed?
2. What are the particular advantages which would make the product uniquely satisfying to the potential consumer?
3. How can these advantages be expressed with the utmost clarity and excitement?

Art work is not required. Simply line off the area you feel should be devoted to a picture and describe in that space the illustration you visualize. If you wish, you may use your own rough drawing to depict the illustration. Roughly letter in the headline on the advertisement, and write the copy on a separate sheet.

A one-minute television commercial is composed of less than 150 words. In writing for television, you must also explain the action that takes place. This may be accomplished by drawing a vertical line down the center of the sheet of paper, heading one column "AUDIO" (for the spoken words) and the other column "VIDEO" (for a short description of the visual).

Assemble the completed application, autobiography, samples of previous writing and the copy work you have done. Attach the original advertisements from the magazines to the new advertisements you have created for Part III of this assignment. Be sure to retain copies of materials you send. We cannot assure the return of any material, although we will make every effort to do so.

FIGURE 18–3 (cont.)

Art and Layout

If you have a flair for art that has been improved and refined through formal art training, you'll find many job opportunities in advertising. Artists often work for newspapers, magazines, radio and television stations, outdoor poster companies, and other media. Many retailers employ artists to work on advertisements as well as in-store promotions. And advertising agencies need artists, too, to prepare advertising for their clients.

There are also opportunities for artists who want to do part-time freelance work in advertising or who prefer to work for large art suppliers (which will be discussed later).

Media Planning and Buying

media planners and buyers Advertising professionals who plan media approaches.

Media planners and buyers seldom work for the media channels themselves. Instead, they are employed by advertising agencies, and sometimes by advertisers, to plan the best media approaches and to contact the media for the best rates, times, and positions within the media vehicles.

Because media buyers and planners need to compare various media and their individual vehicles and calculate rates and audience sizes, they must be good at details and must like working with numbers and calculations. They must also be able to understand and interpret the volumes of research findings that provide information on target groups and markets, media audiences, cost efficiencies, advertising rates, and similar information. In some advertising agencies, working in the media department is also a good preparation for eventual careers in client services.

Agency-Advertiser Contact

Both the advertising agency and the advertiser must have people who maintain contact with one another to make certain that the advertising plans are coordinated and follow the proper procedures and approaches. This kind of liaison role requires the ability to work with other people and get along with them. (See Figure 18–4.)

client services Agency-advertiser contact assigned to specific individuals at advertising agencies.

account executive A person at an advertising agency assigned to maintain contact with an advertiser.

account supervisor A person in charge of a client's account.

At the advertisers' end, this contact position may go right along with the job of advertising manager or marketing manager. At advertising agencies, it is more common to assign specific individuals these duties in what are known as **client services**. If the major responsibilities include maintaining contact with the advertiser (client), finding out the advertiser's wishes and reactions to suggested advertising, and presenting the prepared advertising to the advertiser, then this person may be called an **account executive**. If this person is also in charge of the agency's work on that client's account—making sure that everything is done properly and getting the right people involved in the job at the appropriate times—then the person's job title may be **account supervisor**.

Management

creative director A management position for copywriters.

research director A management position for researchers.

All facets of the advertising business need good managers. Usually, though, managers start with other jobs and eventually move up within the advertising business. It is possible to be promoted to the managerial level within certain job functions: A copywriter may eventually become a **creative director**; a researcher may become a **research director**; a media planner may be promoted

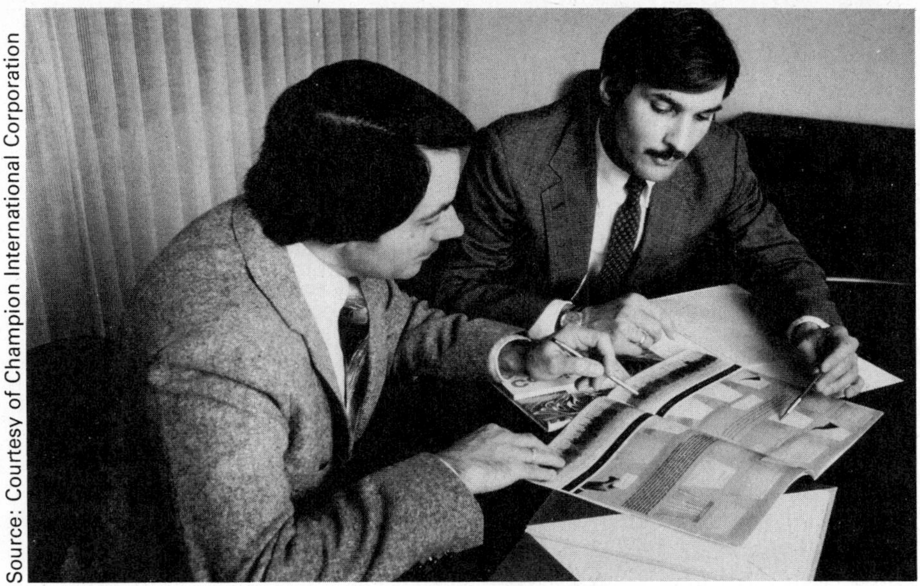

Source: Courtesy of Champion International Corporation

FIGURE 18–4
An advertising agency account executive discusses new advertising campaign ideas with his clients, representatives of the advertiser.

to **media director**; an artist may climb to **art director**. There are also general management positions, such as *advertising manager*, *vice president of marketing*, *administrative coordinator*, *executive vice president*, and many others.

An **advertising manager** must maintain contact, make decisions, handle unexpected problems, plot strategies, coordinate plans and approaches, deal with personnel situations, and take care of all the other various details that come into the operation of an advertising department, agency, or medium.

media director A management position for media planners.

art director A management position for artists.

advertising manager A general management position in the advertising industry.

Research

Researchers must pay close attention to detail. They often work behind the scenes, locating information that other professional people will eventually use to prepare the advertising campaign. Researchers can work for advertising agencies, for large advertiser companies, for large stores and store chains, for media, and for syndicated research services that sell their findings to advertisers and agencies. (See Figure 18–5.)

Supplier

Many firms operate on the fringes of advertising, providing the various services that the advertising industry occasionally needs to make an advertising campaign complete. We referred to this support function earlier as *logistics*. The people who supply this support include photographers, who take pictures of advertised products; printers and engravers, who prepare newspaper and

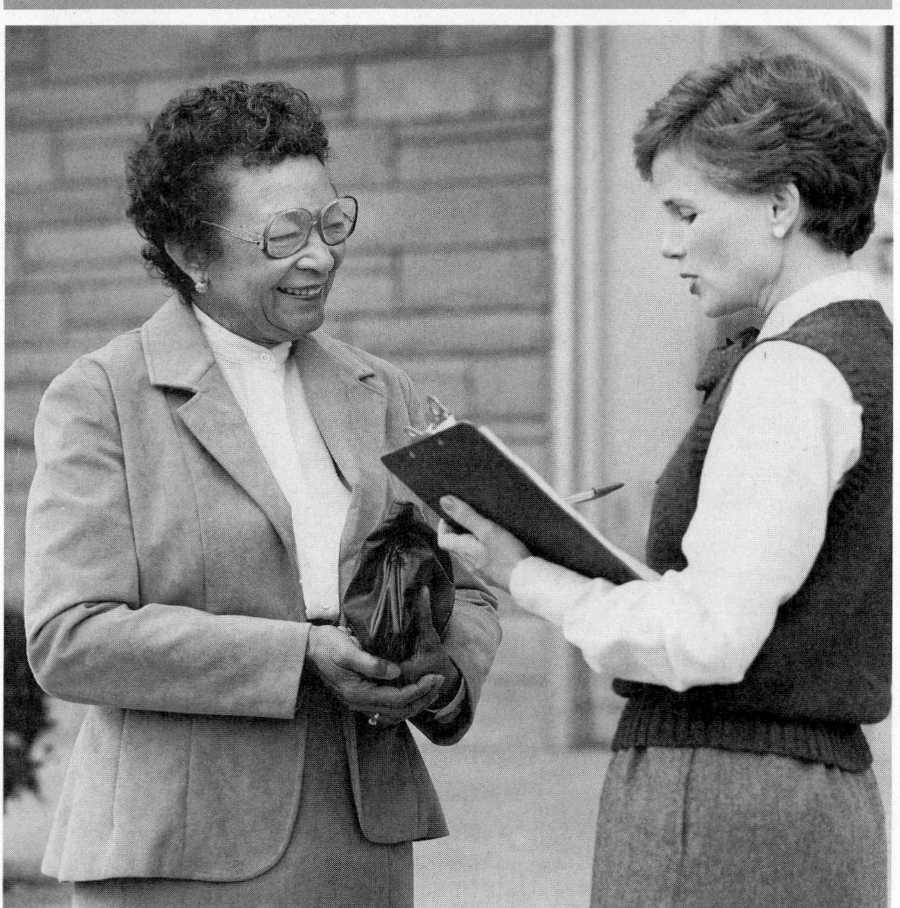

FIGURE 18–5
An advertising researcher conducts a new product survey with a consumer.

magazine advertisements for the press run; and camera operators, sound technicians, and videotape experts who produce television commercials. Some firms specialize in making **mats** (slang for "matrix" or "matrices"), which are soft impressions of printing plates that can be mailed inexpensively to print media around the country. Researchers, artists, and others can work for these external service suppliers, too.

mats Soft impressions of printing plates that can be mailed inexpensively to print media.

HOW ADVERTISING JOBS RELATE TO OTHER FIELDS

Keep in mind that people who work in advertising cannot function in isolation from the rest of business. There are aspects of public relations, promotion, merchandising, and other facets of marketing involved in the advertising industry—and advertising includes some of those functions, too. There are no definite boundaries where one stops and the next begins.

This means that we must be prepared to carry out many kinds of job functions when we work in advertising; we cannot just plan to write copy or buy media and do only that one thing. Advertising people are versatile and get involved in lots of different activities. In fact, that variety is one advantage of advertising that keeps the job interesting and ever-changing.

HOW TO PREPARE FOR AN ADVERTISING CAREER

The first thing to remember is that you are already preparing yourself by taking college courses, especially courses in advertising, marketing, promotion, writing, and related subjects. You may want to stay in school, combining a general background with the specific career preparation for sales, marketing, or advertising.

Because advertising always involves selling ideas, products, and services, you may want to gain some sales experience. Maybe you can work to help support the costs of going to school. Or you can work part-time or during school vacations in retail sales or door-to-door selling. Any kind of selling job experience should be helpful eventually.

Sometimes advertising agencies, advertising departments, or media may allow you to serve as an intern (with or without pay). Even if there are no jobs open in the firm, you may get an opportunity to observe and find out as much as you can without requiring pay or office space from the firm. (See Figure 18–6.)

You may also want to test yourself to find out where your abilities lie. Your school advisor or counseling office may be able to find aptitude tests that you can take to determine your own strengths. And the kind of test that copywriters take (such as the example in this chapter) should be helpful, too.

Try to talk to advertising practitioners whenever you get a chance. Call on them at their offices or attend local advertising or sales club meetings and get to know the professional advertising people in your community. Maybe you can go along with a sales representative who is visiting store accounts. And talk with any professional practitioners who may visit your classes as guest speakers.

Where to Get More Information

If you are really interested in an advertising career, start at the local level, find out all you can, get experience, make contacts, and be prepared to learn and grow. You may also want to write to some of the professional advertising organizations for more information about working in advertising.

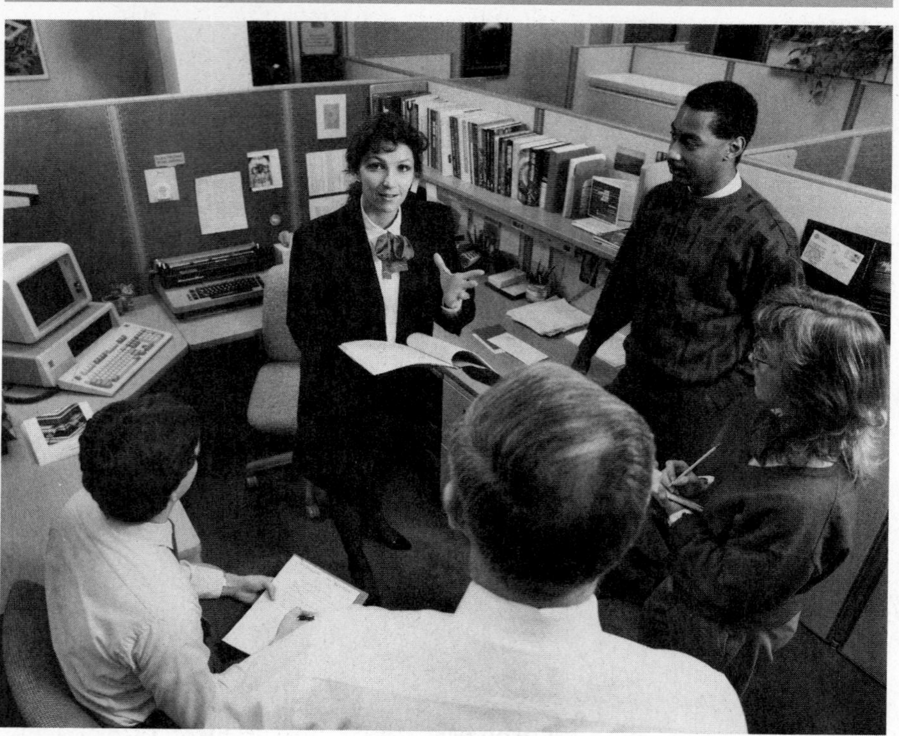

FIGURE 18–6
Some advertising agencies conduct special training programs for their new interns.

The American Advertising Federation, 1400 K Street, N.W., Washington, D.C. 20005, may be able to send you career information. So can the American Association of Advertising Agencies, 666 Third Avenue, New York, N.Y. 10017-4056. There are many other specialized advertising organizations that your instructor may be able to help you find, or you can look up the organizations and addresses in your school's library.

Advertising Age
A magazine about advertising, published every week.

Read **Advertising Age** magazine regularly; it is published every week. And you may find it interesting to read the *Journal of Advertising*, *Marketing and Media Decisions*, *Broadcasting*, *Sales and Marketing Management*, and other periodicals that will help you find out what is current in the advertising industry. Many local newspapers carry an advertising and marketing column, or at least a general business section, too. (See Figure 18–7.)

If you are interested in studying advertising in college, check with your school's counseling office. And you can send for a copy of "Where Shall I Go to College to Study Advertising?" available from Advertising Education Publications, 3429 55th Street, Lubbock, Texas 79413. It gives detailed information on courses, costs, scholarships, faculty, and other facts about many college advertising programs in the United States.

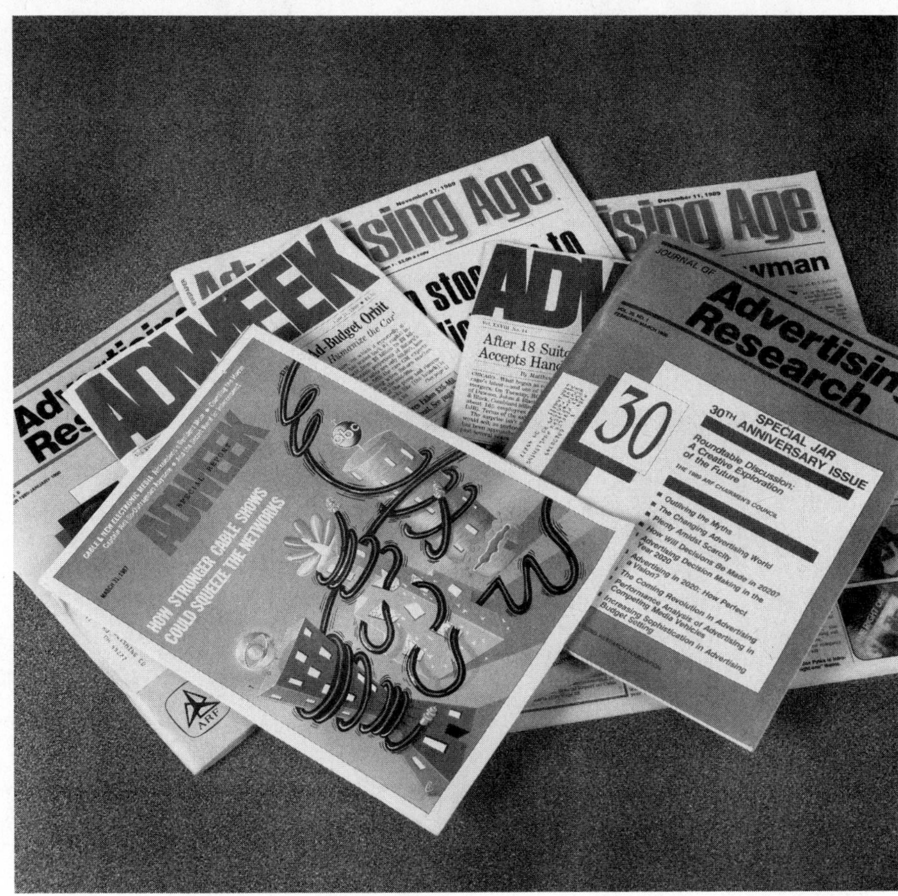

FIGURE 18–7
Some major publications in the advertising industry.

Get Involved

Attend your local Advertising Club if there is one. And think about starting a college advertising club at your school if you don't already have one. The American Advertising Federation can help you.

The organizations listed earlier may be able to give you helpful information about other aspects of advertising, too, even if you decide you do not want to work in advertising. The next chapter should give you helpful ideas on other places where you can get help in dealing with advertising.

SUMMARY

Now you can see that there are many kinds of potential careers in the advertising business. You may also begin to realize that learning about advertising may be valuable for other careers, outside of advertising.

If you are interested in an advertising career, begin now to plan your education so that you will be properly and completely prepared for the specific job you want. If you cannot make up your mind right now about the specific position that may interest you, you can still take a variety of courses and gain some practical on-the-job experience, which will both prepare you and help you make your eventual career choice.

You may also want to write to advertising industry organizations to get more information and to have valuable insights and contacts.

TERMS TO KNOW

Now that you have finished this chapter, you should understand the following terms:

sales representative	account executive	research director
copywriter	account supervisor	media director
media planners and buyers	creative director	advertising manager
continuity	art director	*Advertising Age*
	client services	mats

If you are not certain of the meaning of any of these terms, go back through the chapter and review them.

THINGS TO THINK ABOUT

1. What kinds of careers are available in advertising?
2. What is involved in sales jobs other than just selling?
3. What does an account executive do? How does an account executive's job relate to other advertising jobs?
4. How do the various supplier jobs relate to advertising?

THINGS TO TALK ABOUT

1. What is required in all advertising careers? What traits are important for each kind of advertising position?
2. Why is there a need for new people in advertising if the advertising business is not growing?
3. Why is agency-advertiser contact work so important?
4. What are the best ways to prepare for a career, including an advertising career?
5. Of what help is a college background in an advertising career?

THINGS TO DO

1. Make a list of the characteristics and traits required in an advertising job of your choice, and then rate yourself against the list.
2. Invite a recent graduate of your school who is now working in business to talk with you about finding a job.
3. Read a recent issue of *Advertising Age*. Look for the other advertising publications mentioned in this chapter, too.
4. Write to the addresses listed in the chapter for more information about careers in advertising.
5. Look through college catalogs to find out what kinds of advertising courses are available.

19 How You Can Use Advertising Every Day

Proposal
GO!
THE LESS SAID THE BETTER.
When People Count On You, Count On Post-it Notes.

Post-it
Note Pad
Self-Stick Removable Notes
3M

3M Commercial Office Supply Division

CHAPTER OUTLINE

By the time you finish this chapter, you should understand:

1. **How to use advertising to help you when you shop for and buy products and services.**
2. **How to understand what an entire advertisement means.**
3. **How to decipher individual advertising claims.**
4. **How guarantees and loan information in advertisements can help you.**
5. **Where you can get help in dealing with misleading sellers and advertisers.**

Whether or not you want to work in advertising, you can still make good use of your knowledge about it. Because advertising is an important source of information for consumers and you're a consumer, advertising can be very valuable to you. Just because advertising is paid for by a store or a manufacturer or an airline does not mean that advertising serves only the seller. In fact, that would be a waste of the huge amount of money that is spent on advertising each year.

Remember the advertising concept that we talked about in Chapter 1? The consumer is at both ends of the advertising process. So advertising centers on the consumer—on you! And you can use advertising to make your role as a consumer more productive, efficient, and satisfying.

HOW TO USE ADVERTISING AS A SHOPPING AID

Advertising can save you time, money, and energy. You can save your own muscle power—and you can save expensive gasoline and parking fees that you would spend if you went to every store yourself gathering the information that you can get from advertisements.

Sure, you'll have to go to the store sometime, to buy the merchandise you want—unless you are buying from a catalog or over the telephone. But using advertising first, before you get to the stage of actually visiting stores, can simplify the shopping you must do.

Use advertising to locate the items you may be interested in and to find out about items you didn't even know existed or were for sale. Compare product features, durability, materials, styles, colors, and even quality levels within entire lines of merchandise just by reading and listening to the advertisements to which you are exposed every day. (See Figure 19–1.)

You can tell high blood pressure by these symptoms:

____

____

____

____

____

(Very often, there are none!)

It's hard to believe that over 35 million Americans have a dangerous disease...very often without a symptom. But that's what high blood pressure (hypertension) is like. A hidden illness, yet one of the easiest to detect—and to treat. Untreated, it can affect your brain (stroke), your vision, heart (infarction), blood vessels and kidneys. Anyone can be affected, although factors such as age, sex, race or family background play a role.

Fortunately, there's plenty that can be done to treat this condition. Only your doctor can diagnose hypertension, but you can help head it off through healthier living—reducing weight, cholesterol, salt intake, stress, anxiety and stopping smoking. An improved lifestyle, and blood pressure-controlling medicines can substantially lower your risk for heart attacks and stroke. But the first step is to see your doctor.

For a poster-sized reprint of this message, write: Pfizer Pharmaceuticals, P.O. Box 3852BHH, Grand Central Station, New York, NY 10163.

A message
in the interest
of better
health from
Pfizer
PHARMACEUTICALS
A PARTNER IN HEALTHCARE

Courtesy Pfizer Pharmaceuticals.

Figure 19–1
There is a lot of helpful information in many of the advertisements you already see every day.

Comparison Shopping

Then, compare prices, payments, and financing. Compare quality of service. Compare guarantees. Compare availability of the items. Compare everything you can until you narrow down your choices. You may still need to go to the stores to make the final comparison, but by using advertising you can eliminate some of the alternatives—and you can decide just what features you want to concentrate on when you get to the store.

HOW TO READ AN ADVERTISEMENT

If you're going to use advertising as a shopping aid, then first you must know what the advertisements actually mean. For example, you may hear a radio commercial for a local shoe store that says something like

> Our big annual clearance sale is on right now. Don't miss this once-a-year opportunity to save on the shoes you want to buy. Not all styles are available in all sizes, so be sure to come in early for fullest selection.

What does that advertisement actually mean to you? First, it is a clearance sale, so the store is trying to get rid of the shoes that didn't sell. It is an annual sale; some other stores may have sale after sale and almost never sell anything at the regular price. Instead of saying that these are leftover shoes that nobody bought all year long, the copywriter has turned the idea around by suggesting that you should go to the store right away because some styles may have sold at their regular nonsale prices and not many remain.

There is nothing wrong with such advertisements; you hear them all the time. You simply must decide for yourself whether it is worthwhile for you to visit the store and search through unsold merchandise in hopes of finding something you like—and whether the savings in marked-down sale prices are attractive enough for you to invest your time in this search.

Now let's look at several other common advertisement claims to see what they really mean.

Deciphering Advertising Claims

You'll often see an advertisement that features a low price and says that the item "formerly" sold at some higher price; the phrases "sold for" and "marked down" tell you the same thing. In each case, the advertisement is telling you that the item once sold at a higher price and now the price has been reduced. If the phrase used is "originally," it should mean that the selling price has been reduced at least once before, so this is the second (or third, or more) price reduction. If the advertisement says "regularly," it indicates that was the price immediately before it was reduced; it also implies that the price may soon be returned to its former higher level—although the store would not be legally obligated to mark up the price again.

Advertisements that say "compares to" or "comparable value" indicate that this particular merchandise may never have been intended to sell at that higher comparison price, but only that you might find a similar item at that higher price if you shopped at enough stores. "Values up to" is a similar comparison that does not necessarily reflect the actual selling price of this particular advertised item. You should be aware that most of the comparable items may not be worth that much, but only that at least one sale item might compare to another nonsale item at that particular price.

Promises of Savings

"Save Up to 50 Percent" means that the regular price on some item has been cut in half—but most of the items may have been reduced in price by much less than half. The same applies for such claims as "Save $10 to $40." They indicate that some savings of $40 are available but that most of the items may be marked down by the lesser amount.

If an advertising claim says "free," then legally something must be given to you free. Some "free" additional gift when you purchase the regular item must be offered with the regular item at its normal price; it cannot be marked up to help cover the cost of the gift. So "free installation" means that you should not have to pay anything beyond the price of the item to have the merchandise installed. Reputable retailers will specify "plus installation" or "installation extra" if there will be an additional charge for this service.

"Free layaway" means that the store will put the item aside for some specified period of time until you can afford to pay for it, and that you will not be charged for this service nor will you be charged loan interest on the price of the item. Other "layaway" plans may charge interest, so know what you are agreeing to do. Some stores say "90 days same as cash" to indicate that you can pay one-fourth of the price now and another one-fourth at the end of each month for three months without any loan interest; the store may still require you to meet its credit requirements, of course.

Other Claims

If an advertisement for an automobile mentions good gas mileage, then it should give details on the authorized combined mileage estimates. In the same way, "truth-in-lending" laws require full details of loan interest and the total costs if a certain credit offer or monthly credit payment is mentioned in an advertisement. We shall discuss these lending regulations in more detail in a few pages.

Watch for advertising disclaimers such as "not exactly as shown" to indicate that the item for sale does not look quite like the one shown in the advertisement illustration. "Must be assembled" or "assembly required" means that you'll have to put together the item yourself; its parts come in a box, but they are not fully assembled. "Limited quantities" indicates that the offer might sell out before you get to the store, and the store does not intend to issue "rain checks" or other coupons that will entitle you to the same price when the item is restocked; in fact, it may never be restocked.

And the advertisement that says "special purchase" or "special buy" is really telling you that this merchandise is not normally stocked by the store, but instead was purchased specifically for this sale offer. It may or may not be of the same quality as the store's regular line of merchandise.

LEARN ABOUT PRODUCT COMPONENTS

You've probably seen an advertisement that said "Wear the look of leather" or described a pair of jeans as "denim-look." In the first case, the material is probably vinyl that appears and feels the same as leather or at least closely resembles leather—and the jeans are some material other than cotton denim, even though they look like regular denim. That doesn't mean that these goods are inferior: Leather is hard to clean and it is expensive, so vinyl may serve your needs better; jeans made from a synthetic fiber may wash better and dry without wrinkling, whereas cotton denim might not.

If you buy anything with animal fur, it must be properly labeled to tell you what kind of animal the fur came from and whether it has been dyed or otherwise altered. Be careful, though: The advertisement for such a fur item need not have this information, even though the item itself must be properly and accurately labeled.

Most clothing now must have laundering and care instructions on a permanent label sewn into the item. The label, and the advertising, may also tell you if the item is permanent press under normal laundering conditions. Clothing that is "preshrunk" merely means that the cloth was washed and allowed to shrink at least once before the item was made from that material; it may not be the same as Sanforized material, which is guaranteed not to shrink more than a very small amount. In the same way, there may be a difference between one manufacturer's "nonstick" cookware and Teflon or Silverstone nonstick coatings.

Reputable merchandisers will carefully spell out the differences between their regular items and any "extra duty" or "heavy duty" items; the large retail chains such as Sears, Roebuck & Company are very careful and clear about these differences. But remember that a disreputable retailer may say that some item is "heavy duty" and not have much reason nor evidence for doing so. Again, reputable firms will tell you why they consider some merchandise to be "first line" or "first quality," but there are still retailers around who use these terms to enhance the image of their merchandise without factual support.

WHAT DOES A GUARANTEE MEAN?

Anyone who sells merchandise provides an implied guarantee that the item will serve in the use for which it is intended. There does not need to be any separate supporting guarantee card or document. But if a manufacturer or seller provides an expressed guarantee, the firm is offering to make it up to you if the item does not meet the stated standards.

complete guarantee The promise to replace an item free or give money back if an item doesn't perform well forever.

limited guarantee Anything less than a complete guarantee.

Until a few years ago, warranties and guarantees were confusing. Legally, the difference was that a warranty was written, while a guarantee might be spoken. Now there are only two kinds of guarantees: A **complete guarantee** is a promise that the item will be replaced free or that your money will be refunded if the item does not hold up and perform well forever; anything less than that must be called a **limited guarantee**. (See Figure 19–2.)

Warranties Are Optional

Manufacturers are not required to offer warranties, but if they do, the terms and the contents of the warranty are closely regulated. You have the right to examine the warranty before you decide to buy the item, and to get a copy of the written warranty if you buy the merchandise. But be sure to get a copy in writing or printing: Any verbal agreement or promise made by a sales clerk may not be legally binding.

The most important thing to know is that an advertisement that claims "one-year warranty" does not provide you with enough information to know exactly what is guaranteed, what happens if your item doesn't hold up, what your obligation may be, and other details of the offer. Only the written or printed guarantee can tell you what you need to know.

TAKING A LOAN IS SAFER NOW

Recent federal legislation makes it safer for consumers to borrow money to buy things, because the consumers must be provided with all the necessary information before they sign the loan agreement. And if an advertisement talks about a loan payment (or car payment or any other installment loan payment) of a certain amount per month, then details of the interest rate, total cost of the item including the loan, time period of the loan, and amount of down payment must be included, too. Such information would not be needed if the advertisement only said "financing available," however. (See Figure 19–3.)

An advertising claim of "no down payment" indicates that you can take the item after signing a proper loan agreement and meeting the lender's credit requirements, but that you need not pay anything initially unless you want to; the entire cost of the item can be borrowed, if necessary. Such a no-down-payment offer may result in a higher rate of interest than a loan for the remaining balance after some initial payment is made, however, in which case that information must be included in the advertising.

Occasionally you may see a Christmas advertisement that offers "no payments until February." In that case, you might sign the loan agreement when you buy the merchandise, but monthly payments would be delayed for a couple of months to help meet all the Christmas bills. You should know, however,

©1990 Whirlpool Corp.

Why wait for appliances built like this? Whirlpool has them today.

Refrigerators that stop spills cold? Quiet dishwashers? Easy-to-clean ranges and ovens? Washers that get even big loads really clean? Maybe someday every appliance company will build a full line of appliances with this kind of thinking. But Whirlpool is doing it, today.

Refrigerators. Our DesignerStyle™ side-by-side refrigerators keep big spills from becoming a big mess. The exclusive SPILLGUARD™ glass shelves can hold up to a 12-ounce spill.

Dishwashers. Most dishwashers are too noisy to let you use the kitchen phone. But Whirlpool Quiet Wash™ dishwashers not only get dishes really clean, they run quietly. So quietly, in fact, we guarantee it.*

Laundry. Whirlpool® super capacity washers have a special washing system, so you can fill them to the limit and still get the whole load clean.

Cooktops and ovens. It's easy to make a mess when you're cooking. So we designed our whole line of contemporary cooktops, built-in ovens, and free-standing ranges to clean up fast.

Microwave ovens. We offer microwaves with and without turntables, both designed to cook food evenly. And our convection model will bake, broil, roast and even brown.

Trash compactors. Our trash compactors are made to run quietly, and open with just a touch of your toe.

Quality you can count on. Every appliance we build is made to work hard and last a long time. And you can be confident that we're always ready to help you. With our toll-free, 24-hour Cool-Line® service. Just call 800-253-1301. And our 5,000-plus factory-authorized Whirlpool service centers.

Why wait? If you're in the market for appliances, planning to build or remodel, why wait for appliances you can count on like these? Whirlpool is building them today.

Whirlpool
Home Appliances

Quality you can count on...today.

*You'll be satisfied with how quietly our Quiet Wash dishwasher runs, or we'll give you your money back within the first 30 days, finance charges not included. ®Registered trademark/TM trademark of Whirlpool Corp.

Courtesy Whirlpool Corporation.

Figure 19–2 Warranties and guarantees are now closely regulated to protect consumers.

Advertisement

1967 20th ANNIVERSARY SPECIAL! 1987

Phil Rizzuto, former Yankee great and current sportscaster.

FIXED RATE 2nd MORTGAGE LOANS

AS LOW AS TODAY'S PRIME RATE

9% A.P.R.*

"Just think - 20 years ago The Money Store started with one small store,and now they're America's Number 1 independent home equity lender with offices coast-to-coast," said Phil Rizzuto spokesman for The Money Store,on the occasion of their 20th anniversary.

"Right from the beginning," Mr. Rizzuto added, "The Money Store showed a whole generation of homeowners how to convert their built-up equity into purchasing power to buy the things they need and want."

Low Fixed Rates

"Today's homeowners", said Mr. Rizzuto, "shop around for the lowest rates possible. The Money Store now offers loans as low as today's prime rate of **9¾%**. Of course, longer term loans may require higher charges. And what's more,"he added,"at The Money Store you never have to worry about rising interest rates. Fixed-rate payments are locked in for the life of the loan. The small monthly payments never change - and there are no balloons."

Instant Approval

"As a qualified† homeowner you can receive Instant Approval right over the phone. You can borrow up to $100,000 or more. The Money Store will work out a re-

Borrow up to $100,000 or more

payment plan that fits your budget. If you want to repay the loan sooner, you can do it any time. You pay interest only on the amount you owe. There's never an application fee."

Borrow For Any Reason At All

"Want to consolidate your debts, make home improvements, or finance a wedding? No matter what your borrowing needs are,"he said, "The Money Store listens and responds in a hurry.And don't forget-according to recent tax laws, interest payments on your 2nd Mortgage Loan may be tax deductible."

A Free Money Store Master Card

"To celebrate 20 years of leadership in making 2nd mortgage loans,"Mr. Rizzuto continued,"The Money Store is now offering to all qualified borrowers a Money Store sponsored Master Card. And as a special anniversary gift to you-the first year's annual fee is FREE!"

Call Today - Don't Delay

"A loan specialist at The Money Store will answer all of your questions and you can be certain that your application will be treated in a confidential manner."

THE MONEY STORE®

FAIRLAWN....794-6803
ENGLEWOOD....569-2050
SADDLEBROOK....843-8800
HACKENSACK....488-3030
LYNDHURST....507-0001
UPPER SADDLE RIVER....825-3900
RIDGEWOOD....427-6668

Mon.-Fri. 9 to 7 • Sat. 9 to 12

Out Of Area Call Toll Free 1-800-221-9000

*ANNUAL PERCENTAGE RATE †CREDIT WORTHY

©1987 THE MONEY STORE ®

Created by Joseph Costa for The Money Store.

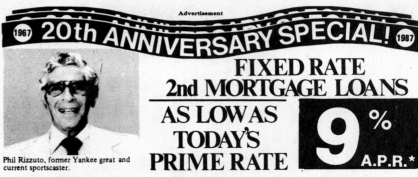

Figure 19–3
Even advertisements that feature only loans must tell the consumers some details of the loan arrangement.

that you might still be paying interest for the intervening period, even though you don't have to start paying off the loan.

WHERE TO GET HELP

If you deal with a seller or advertiser who does not keep promises or whose merchandise does not meet your standards, you first should try to settle the matter with that store or firm. If the sales clerk cannot handle the matter, you may need to ask for the manager or owner.

Sometimes, however, you may need outside help. If your town has a Better Business Bureau, call or visit it and ask for assistance. If there is no

Figure 19–4
Your local Better Business Bureau may be able to help if you have problems with advertisements or stores.

Better Business Bureau, perhaps your local chamber of commerce can help. (See Figure 19–4.)

In most states, the state attorney general can help consumers who have problems with stores or merchandise. Many states have a special consumer protection bureau within the attorney general's office that provides prompt assistance and advice.

Local Assistance

Your town or school may also have a consumer group that can help with problems about misleading advertising, as well as rental agreements, purchase and loan contracts, product or service conditions that are not satisfactory, and similar problems. If you need a lawyer but cannot afford one, a local legal aid office may be able to help.

If your problem results from interstate trade, a federal agency such as the Federal Trade Commission may be helpful. You will recall that the FTC has regulatory powers over interstate advertising. Most federal agencies have offices in major cities around the country. If there is not one near you, there may be

THE FISH ON THE RIGHT IS BETTER FOR YOUR CAT.

Purina
Ocean Fish
Flavor
Purina Cat Chow
100% nutritionally complete cat food

Both taste great—but taste is not enough. The Purina® Cat Chow® Ocean Fish Flavor on the right is better for your cat because it's 100 percent complete and balanced nutrition. A fillet from the fish on the left isn't.

The Cat Chow Ocean Fish Flavor on the right is better for your cat because it's got certain vitamins and minerals that the fish on the left doesn't deliver.

Ocean Fish Flavor, from Purina Cat Chow Brand Cat Food. It's much more than great taste… it's more nutritious than fish.

Helping pets live longer, healthier lives™

® © Ralston Purina Company, 1987 Cat Chow Brand Cat Food

BETTER THAN FISH.

Figure 19–5
Many manufacturers want to help consumers trust the products and services of their industries. This advertisement is packed with information about how the product's benefits will help one's pet, as well as how the product compares to alternative pet diets–and it even includes a coupon for a reduced-price purchase.

a toll-free telephone number listed in your local directory. Such regulatory agencies may seem slow in responding to your individual problem, however, because they are concerned with large-scale activities that take time and effort to document and settle.

Industry Monitoring

Some manufacturers have also grouped together to help consumers with problems. For example, if you buy a clothes washer that does not perform well, an industry group may be able to get you a satisfactory settlement of the situation. Some manufacturers now promise that they will replace a new purchase that is a "lemon" or work on the problem until you are satisfied. (See Figure 19–5.)

Keep in mind that advertising can serve you and that you have rights that must be honored by everyone else, including large manufacturers and local merchants. Use advertising to assist you in your own individual ways of doing things and you will come to depend on and appreciate what advertising can do for you.

SUMMARY

Learning about advertising has done more for you than simply provide credit for another college course. For one thing, you have learned about a subject that you may someday want to make into a career. But whether or not you ever work in advertising, learning about advertising still helps you to become a better, smarter and more efficient consumer.

Now you should understand specifically what the words in an advertisement mean. And you can decipher specific advertising claims. You also can use advertising to help you understand the information about a possible loan, about guarantees, and about special sales offers.

What's more, if you have difficulties with an advertiser, or you believe that you have been misled by an advertisement, you know what kinds of assistance are available and where they are.

All of this helps you understand more about advertising. It helps you put into practice all the things that you have studied in your introductory advertising course.

TERMS TO KNOW

Now that you have finished this chapter, you should understand the following terms:

implied guarantee
expressed guarantee

If you are not certain of the meaning of any of these terms, go back through the chapter and review them.

THINGS TO THINK ABOUT

1. How can advertising help you in your shopping?
2. What is the difference between an original price and a regular price?
3. Must something be "free" if an advertisement makes a "free" offer?
4. What is the difference between an implied guarantee and an expressed guarantee? What does an unlimited, or complete, guarantee mean?
5. Will a loan offer of "no down payment" or "no payments for two months" mean a higher cost for a loan?

THINGS TO TALK ABOUT

1. Why do some sellers use misleading phrases and words in their advertisements?
2. Why have truth-in-lending laws become necessary?
3. What does a guarantee mean? To what does it entitle the buyer?
4. What kinds of help are available for consumers who are dealing with misleading advertising?
5. Should your school have a consumer protection association? Why?

THINGS TO DO

1. Look through a local newspaper and circle all the helpful shopping aid information in the advertisements.
2. Find two different advertisements for the same kind of merchandise and compare them.
3. Get a loan contract from a nearby store, bank, or finance company and try to understand it.
4. Invite a representative of your local Better Business Bureau (or your chamber of commerce, if you have no Better Business Bureau) to talk with you.
5. Get a copy of a product guarantee or warranty and read it. Compare it with other warranties.
6. Contact your state attorney general or consumer protection office and find out what kinds of consumer assistance and protection are available.
7. Explore the possibility of starting or working in a consumer protection bureau, either at your school or in your community.

Glossary

A

Added Utility Additional benefits or usefulness provided by the manufacturing process or by advertising.

Added Value The additional monetary value of an item that may be provided by advertising.

Advertising Agency A firm that assists advertisers with advertising problems, and plans and executes advertising campaigns.

Advertising Concept The idea that the advertising process both begins with and ends with emphasis on consumers.

Agate Line An amount of advertising space in a publication; it is one column wide by 1/14 inch high; there are 14 agate lines to one column-inch.

Aided Recall The amount that people remember about an advertisement after receiving prompting or other assistance from an interviewer.

Appropriation Large lump sum of money set aside by a company's financial management to cover all costs of a specific corporate task—such as advertising.

Audience The number of persons who see, hear, or read an advertisement, a publication, or a broadcast.

B

Bleed A magazine advertisement that seems to be printed off the edge of the page.

Boom Movement of camera mounted on crane.

Broadside A folded mailing piece that opens up to a very large size.

Brochure A multipage printed information piece or pamphlet about a product or service, usually larger than a folder but less elaborate than a catalog.

Budget The budget is a breakdown of the large lump sum (allocation) into specific amounts of dollars for specific purposes.

C

Calligraphy Hand-lettering.

Campaign A coordinated series of advertising messages revolving around one central selling theme but appearing over an extended period of time.

Circulation The number of copies of a publication that are distributed.

Classified Advertising Advertisements that are organized according to certain classifications or topics; usually known as "want ads."

Coarse Screen Halftone Engraving suitable for newspaper (rough, porous paper).

Cognitive Dissonance Anxiety after a purchase decision, wondering if the best decision has been made.

Column-inch An amount of advertising space in a publication, one column wide by one inch high.

Commission A standard percentage of income that is earmarked for an agent; often used in the real estate, entertainment, and advertising businesses to determine what share of income should go to an agent.

Composition The "professional's" word for typography.

Concept An idea.

Consumer Behavior The study of how and why people make their purchase decisions.

Consumer Research Study of the kinds of people who may use or purchase a product or service to be marketed and advertised.

Consumer Segments Groups of people who have similar demographic characteristics.

Consumer's Gain The additional benefits that come from owning a product or service, beyond the basic function of that item, as suggested by advertising's informative messages.

Consumer's Loss A discarded usefulness of an item that is no longer wanted because the consumer has purchased a substitute, often because of advertising.

Controlled Circulation A publication's issues can be sent only to certain kinds of qualified recipients.

Cooperative Advertising Slang "co-op"; in vertical cooperative advertising, a manufacturer or wholesaler pays part of the retailer's advertising costs; in horizontal cooperative advertising, several merchants pool their advertising efforts.

Copy Platform Formal or informal written guidelines for a particular ad—involving chief benefit, chief prospect, and chief objective.

Copywriting Coming up with an advertising idea; writing the advertisement.

Corrective Advertising An advertisement that is intended to make right some misleading statement in earlier advertising, often because of government intervention.

Cost per Rating Point The cost of advertising that reaches 1 percent of an audience; usually, the advertising cost is divided by the percent rating; abbreviated as "CPR" or "CPP" (which stands for "cost per point").

Cost Per Thousand A useful way of comparing the advertising rates of two advertising vehicles or media; usually, the advertising rate is divided by the size of the circulation or audience, and then multiplied by 1,000; abbreviated as "CPM."

Creative Often overused, high-toned word to describe the business of thinking up selling ideas and writing ads.

CU Close-up

Cut For the scriptwriter—an instantaneous change of picture.

D

Demographic Characteristics Population traits, such as age, educational level, income, and the like.

Differentiation Emphasis on selling points that set one advertiser apart from another.

Direct Mail An advertising medium (similar to newspapers, magazines, radio, television).

Discount A reduced advertising rate.

Display Advertising The regular nonclassified advertisements in a publication.

Dissolve Fading out of one television picture at same time another picture is faded in.

Distribution The number and location of places where the public can buy the product.

Dolly Movement of entire camera (which is mounted on rolling carriage or "dolly").

Down Broadcast term meaning decrease the volume; make it quieter.

Drive Time The commuter rush hour, which is the highest radio audience listening time.

E

ECU Extreme close-up.

ELS Extreme long shot.

Entrepreneur One who organizes, manages, and assumes the risk of a business.

F

Film TV Production "Movies," or pictures on a celluloid reel.

Fine Screen Halftone Engraving suitable for magazine (slick paper).

Flat Rate An advertising rate at a publication when no discounts are available.

Flight A period of heavy advertising.

Franchise An exclusive arrangement whereby a local businessperson is given the right to handle a particular national corporation's merchandise or services in a limited geographical territory.

Franklin Gothic A typeface used chiefly for headlines.

Frequency The number of times an advertisement is used; the average number of times that audience members see, hear, or read an advertisement.

Frequency Discount A reduced advertising rate based on the number of times that an advertisement was run in that medium, usually on a regular scheduled basis.

G

Gravure Engraving/Printing Utilizes tiny reservoirs or inkwells sunk below the surface of the plate.

Gross Rating Points The sum of the ratings of all the television commercials for a product or service during a specific period of time, such as one week, within a market; abbreviated as "GRP."

H

Halftone Engraving of artwork that has continuous tone (all shades of gray).

Hiatus A period of an advertising campaign during which there is no advertising or a reduced level of advertising activity.

Household A unit in which several people live together, pool their resources, and share tasks; often a family unit.

Households Using Televisions The percent of all households with television sets that have at least one of those sets operating at some given time.

I

Impact An indication of the power that an advertisement has upon the audience; sometimes measured in the size of an advertisement or the length of a commercial; sometimes used to describe the power of an advertisement's creative message.

In Broadcast term meaning begin or start.

Institutional That kind of advertising that does not sell products but that promotes an idea or enhances a company's reputation.

Italic A letter with a slanted or sloped stem.

K

Key A secret code number or name on a mail order ad by which a response can be traced.

L

Leading The spacing between lines of type.

Letterpress Engraving/Printing Utilizes ink on a raised surface.

Line Cut An engraving of artwork that is solid black and white.

List Broker A business that rents the use of mailing lists.

Live TV Production Action as it takes place.

Logotype The "signature" or corporate symbol of the advertiser.

LS Long shot.

M

Mail Order A direct business transaction between advertiser and buyer, eliminating the retailer or middleman.

Marketing Concept The idea that the marketing process involves consumers on both ends of the channel.

Market Research Study of the geographic areas, or markets, where a product or service may be sold and advertised.

Marketing Research Research into any and all aspects of marketing, including advertising.

MCU Medium close-up.

Merchandising Various activities—generally at the retail level—that "push" products more prominently toward customers' attention after advertising "pulls" them in. An end-aisle display, for example.

Milline Rate A method of comparing the advertising rates of two or more newspapers; usually, the line rate of advertising is divided by the circulation and then multiplied by 1,000,000.

MLS Medium long shot.

MS Medium shot.

N

Number 100 Showing The number of outdoor advertising billboards required to reach 100 percent of the mobile population within an area, at least once within a 30-day period.

O

Offset Engraving/Printing Utilizes ink on a flat surface.

Open Rate A publication's highest advertising rate, before discounts are earned.

Out Broadcast term meaning end it; take it out.

P

Paid Circulation Copies of a publication are paid for, either at a newsstand or by subscription, as opposed to freely distributed.

Pan Horizontal movement of camera right or left from fixed pivot.

People Meter Slang term for a broadcast ratings measurement device that records individual viewing.

Perceived risk The uncertainty in a purchase decision before that decision is made.

Pica Area of measurement in typography. There are 6 picas to an inch and 12 points to a pica.

Plans Board Highest level advertising agency committee, representing the key elements in advertising (marketing, creative, research, media), which reviews major recommendations before they are presented to clients.

Point System The system by which type is sized. There are 72 points to 1 inch vertically.

Primary Audience Persons who read a publication, buy it, or subscribe to it.

Prime Time The most popular television viewing times, in the evenings when network programs are usually broadcast.

Product Differentiation Determining a unique quality or benefit for an advertised product.

Product Research (or Service Research) Background analysis of the product or service to be marketed and advertised.

Production Radio Copy Produced in recording studio. May use music, sound, multivoices. Duplicates of recording are sent to stations.

Progressive Proofs Set of engraver's proofs of the four separate plates necessary to create full-color printing.

Projective Techniques Research methods borrowed from the behavioral sciences, whereby respondents are expected to project themselves into the research results.

Proof file Permanent record of all print advertising messages produced by a company.

Promotion Unlike a campaign, an advertising promotion is a short-term, intensive effort keyed to a special offer of some kind—a contest, a premium, a cents-off deal, a coupon, and the like.

Proposition The selling offer.

Prospects Those people who are potential customers.

Puffery An unsupported, nonfactual advertising claim, usually registering the advertiser's opinion.

Push Money (Spiff) Slang terms for the practice whereby a national manufacturer directly pays somebody else's retail employee for putting special selling effort (or "push") behind that particular manufacturer's brand of merchandise.

Q

Quantity Discount A reduced advertising rate based on the amount of advertising.

R

Rating The percent of all the television households, whether or not their receiving sets are operating, that are viewing a certain television program or station.

Reach The percent of a target group that an advertisement communicates to; the number of persons who see, hear, or read an advertisement.

Rebate Money is returned from the advertising medium to the advertiser because the advertiser earned a lower discount than originally contracted for.

Recall Tests Research techniques that force a respondent to supply information about what is remembered from an advertisement.

Recognition Tests Research techniques that permit a respondent to look at advertisements to determine whether that advertisement has been seen and read before, rather than force the respondent to supply information about what is remembered from the advertisement.

Register Term used for precise overlapping of two or more color engravings.

Reprints Flat proofs of a print advertisement kept on file as a record; sometimes printed in quantities to merchandise the campaign to the trade via mailings.

Research and Development Familiarly known as R & D, this is that division of a large manufacturing corporation responsible for creating and testing new product ideas.

Reverse White type against a dark background.

Roman A letter with a straight-up-and-down stem.

S

Sans Serif A typeface without those little hairline edges.

Secondary Audience Also called "pass-along readers"; persons who read a publication but who do not buy it or subscribe to it.

Segue Broadcast term (pronounced "segway") for a transition, usually musical; like a medley, music glides from one song to another, indicating change in time, place, or mood.

Serif Hairline edges on a type figure that aid the eye in reading.

Service After-purchase consideration that is very important over and above the quality of the purchased product itself. Service is an essential factor with the delivery of furniture, for example, with the maintenance of cars, washer-driers, television sets, and the like.

Sets-in-use Another term for "households using television."

SFX Sound effects.

Share of audience The percent of the television households with their sets in use that are tuned to a certain television program or station.

Shelf Talker Small printed reminder messages that attach to a store shelf adjacent to where the product is stacked.

Short Rate An advertiser owes money to an advertising medium because the advertiser did not earn as low a discount as originally contracted for.

Split Run Two different advertisements circulated to portions of the audience, to determine which of the advertisements works better.

Storyboard Hand-drawn, visual interpretation of copywriter's TV script.

Straight-radio Copy Typewritten words only, to be read by whichever station announcer is on duty.

Super Superimposition of one image over another. In commercials the Super punches home key points: the package, the selling theme, the logotype.

Sweepstakes One of several forms of advertising promotion. A sweepstakes is a random give-away.

T

Target Audience The most likely potential customers for your selling proposition.

Target Group The kinds of people to whom a product or service will be advertised or marketed.

Target Market A specific area or territory where a product or service will be advertised or marketed.

Tilt Up or down movement of camera head from fixed pivot.

Truck Shot Movement of camera right alongside a moving object or person.

Typeface Same as Type Family.

Type Family A complete set of type with distinctive visual or "facial" characteristics.

Typography The setting of type for quantity printing.

U

Unaided Recall The amount that people remember about an advertisement without any help from an interviewer.

Under Broadcast term meaning hold sound or music in background.

Up Broadcast term meaning increase the volume; make it louder.

V

Videotape Production Electronic signals recorded on magnetic tape.

Voice Over Television term for off-screen narration; abbreviated as "VO."

W

Wave A pattern of high levels of advertising interspersed with alternate periods of low levels of advertising.

Waste Circulation Copies of a publication that are distributed to persons who are not prospective customers for the advertised item.

Wipe One image is "pushed" off screen to reveal another image.

Z

Zoom Rapid picture movement in or back by manipulating Zoomar lens.

Index

A

B

C

D

E

F

G

H

I

J

K

L

M

N

O

P

Q

R

S

T

U

V

W

Y

Z

ACTIVITIES IN ADVERTISING

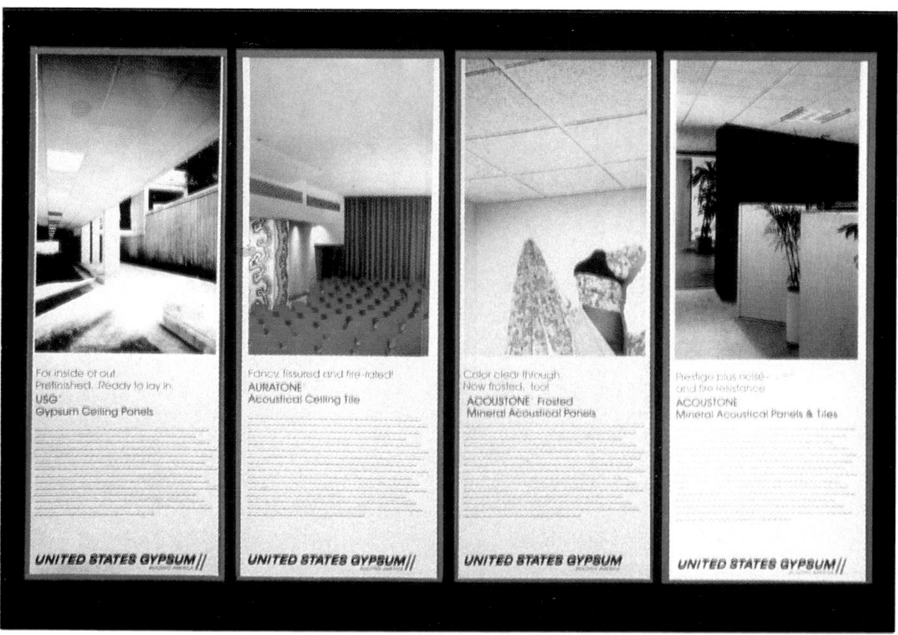

FIGURE 17-13
The "space spectacular" always featured a double-spread followed immediately by a succession of half-page ads.

Courtesy of United States Gypsum and its agency, Marstrat, Inc.

FIGURE 17-14
The theme of "affordable elegance" was promoted via interpretive photography.

FIGURE 17-15
A suave gentleman in a tuxedo became the visual symbol of the "affordable elegance" phrase.

FIGURE 17-16
When the line was broadened to include truly high-styled ceiling tiles, it rated big news.

FIGURE 17-17
After the "space spectaculars" had run their course, emphasis shifted to aesthetics.

FIGURE 17-18
The new high-styled ceiling tiles were so attractive that each design rated a page ad with a single tile placed in a lush contemporary setting.

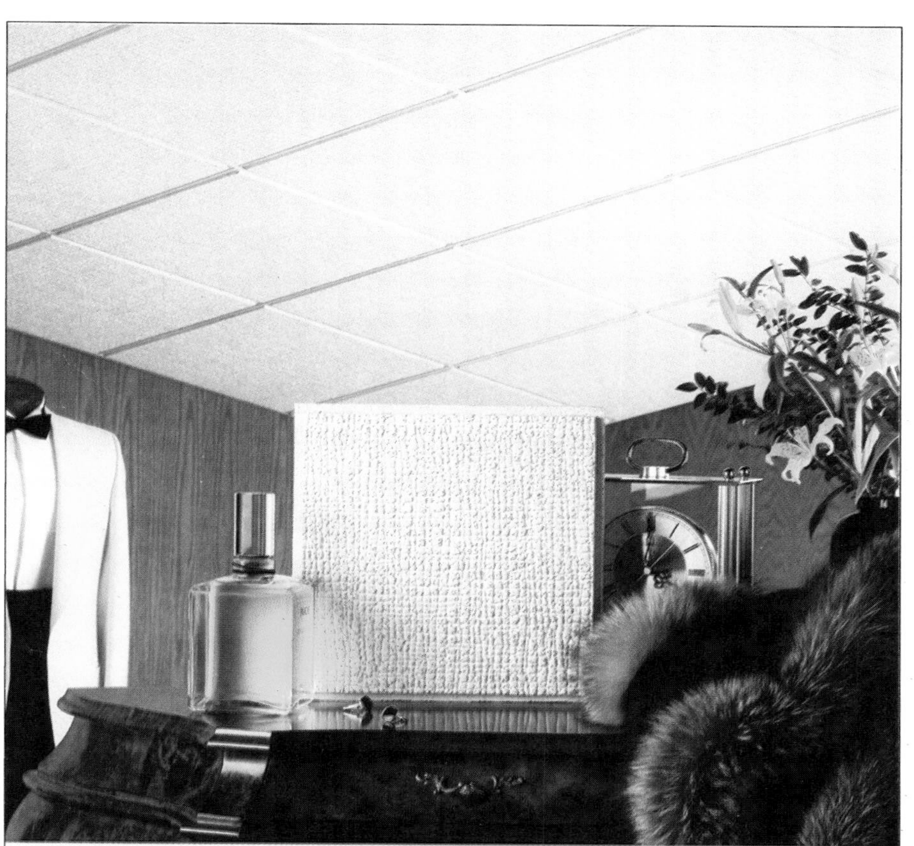

Activities in Advertising

Courtesy of Michael Belk & Company

1-1 The Size of the Advertising Business in Your Community

Look up "Advertising" in the Yellow Pages of your local telephone directory. (If you live in a small community, you may need to use the directory from a nearby larger city. In very large cities, the "Advertising" heading will have several subsections, such as "Advertising Agencies," "Advertising Research," etc.)

How many entries do you find for "Advertising?"____________

In the space provided, list the different kinds of services that are offered. (For example, are all the entries from advertising agencies? If not, what other kinds of companies are listed?)

Which kind of advertising service has the most entries? Which kind has the fewest entries? Why do you think this difference exists?

Under what other headings, besides "Advertising," would you look to find advertising services offered?

1-2 Advertising Notebook

Your **advertising notebook** is an assignment that will continue throughout the course. Your instructor may collect your notebook at stated intervals and check your work.

Your notebook should contain the following sections.

Section 1: Print Advertisements Clip out, mount, and save advertisements for both national and local advertisers. These should be advertisements that you think are exceptionally good or exceptionally poor. Each advertisement should be accompanied by a comment page on which you discuss the qualities of the advertisement that make it good or poor.

(Your criteria for these evaluations should change as you proceed through the course and learn more about advertising.)

Section 2: Broadcast Advertisement Summaries This section will be similar to Section 1, but because you cannot collect the actual broadcast commercials, you will need to summarize radio and television advertisements. Your television summaries should include what and whom you see on the screen, as well as what you hear. Radio summaries should include the content of the message and the manner in which it is delivered (types of voices, music, sound effects, etc.). Do not attempt to write a verbatim script of the commercial; try to provide an accurate representation of the message content and delivery. Each of these summaries should be accompanied by a comment page, like that described for Section 1.

(Good broadcast advertisement summaries are very difficult to achieve, but you will improve with practice.)

Section 3: Trade Publication Articles The advertising industry has many trade publications that present news, current events, and other information pertinent to advertising. Some good examples are *Advertising Age*, *Sales & Marketing Management*, and *Marketing and Media Decisions*.

Visit the library and read an advertising or related publication each week. Select one article of interest and enter a summary of the article, including its title, the publication in which it appeared, and the date of publication.

The readings will introduce you to the concerns of the advertising industry as well as the specialized language that is used by the profession.

Section 4: Advertising in the News From time to time, specific advertising practices or other advertising-related materials are part of the news. Save any newspaper or magazine article that concerns advertising. Summarize and save any television or radio news that concerns advertising. This section can help you be informed on current events within the advertising industry.

Save all these materials in a three-ring binder or similar folder, so that all the materials are together and in proper order. This also makes your notebook easier to submit for evaluation and grading.

This is a suggested format. Your instructor may alter this assignment to suit your classroom situation.

1-3 Your Thoughts about Advertising

Complete the following sentences by listing the thoughts that come to your mind when you think about advertising.

"When I think about advertising, I think . . ."

"The best things about advertising are . . ."

"The worst things about advertising are . . ."

Through class or small-group discussions, compare your lists with the section and chapter titles in your textbook. Even though the specific words may differ, do you notice similar headings? If so, list them here.

Also, list the differences that you notice.

1-4 Advertising Agency Compensation

In your textbook, various methods of compensating advertising agencies were discussed. Those methods are listed in the following table. For each compensation method, list what you consider to be its advantages and disadvantages.

Commissions

Advantages	Disadvantages

Fees

Advantages	Disadvantages

Cost-Plus (Markup)

Advantages	Disadvantages

2-1 Consumer Influences

Many factors besides advertising can influence a consumer to purchase a particular product or brand. Complete the following list by adding more influence factors.

(Use your own consumer behavior and purchasing decisions as a starting point.)

1. *Word of mouth:* A friend recommends a product or brand.
2. *Celebrity testimonial:* Someone who is well-known appears in an advertisement on behalf of the product or service.
3. *Objective endorsement:* A magazine or a product-testing service recommends a particular brand.
4.
5.
6.
7.
8.
9.
10.
11.
12.

What types of products or services require purchase decisions that are likely to be affected by each of these influence factors?

(For example, a consumer magazine endorsement may be more likely to influence higher-priced purchases such as cars or VCRs or safety products such as smoke alarms.)

2-2 Consumer Brand and Store Loyalty

List some types of products that you buy repeatedly.

(Some suggestions are provided, but you should examine your own purchase patterns and add to the list.)

Soup	Deodorant	Cigarettes
Soft drink	Beer	Laundry detergent
Milk	Soap	Toothpaste
__________	__________	__________
__________	__________	__________
__________	__________	__________

Now do the same for the kinds of stores where you shop repeatedly.

Grocery store	Bookstore	Tavern or lounge
Clothing store	Pizza parlor	Gas station
Hardware store	Department store	__________
__________	__________	__________
__________	__________	__________

For each of the products or places that you use, note the percentage of times that you repeat your purchase of the same brand or that you visit the same store.

(For example, if out of ten soap purchases you buy the same brand nine times and try another brand once, that is 90 percent loyalty to the soap brand.)

Circle in *red* the types of products and types of stores to which you are *most loyal*.

Circle in *blue* the types of products and types of stores to which you are *least loyal*.

What kinds of factors may influence you to try another brand or to visit another store? In the previous activity (Activity 2-1), you listed some factors that influence consumers; which ones relate to this situation?

2-3 Media Usage Patterns and Selectivity

Broadcast Media

In the spaces provided, identify the hours that you usually watch television (write in the letters *TV*) and listen to radio (write in the letter *R*) during a typical week.

	Morning		Afternoon		Evening	
	Early	Late	Early	Late	Early	Late
Sunday						
Monday						
Tuesday						
Wednesday						
Thursday						
Friday						
Saturday						

Now list the programs or stations to which you are most loyal (watch or listen to regularly).

Print Media

Do you read a daily newspaper?___________

If "yes," name the newspaper.______________________________

Rank the importance (how carefully you read) for each of the following newspaper sections (1 = most important, 2 = next most important, etc.)

_____ World and state news
_____ Entertainment
_____ Sports
_____ Finance
_____ Lifestyle
_____ Other (specify) _______________

Do you regularly read any other newspaper? ___________

Do you subscribe to any magazines?___________

If "yes," name them.______________________________

____

____

Do you regularly read any magazines to which you do *not* subscribe? ___________

If "yes," name them. ______________________________

How many issues a year of each magazine do you read? ___________

____

In class or small-group discussion, compare various media usage patterns and the types of products or brands that you see advertised. Note which products appear in various magazines and in various sections of the newspaper. Which are broadcast on certain days of the week or certain times of day?

From your observations, note any conclusions you have reached concerning media selectivity on the part of the consumer and on the part of the advertiser.

2-4 Demographic Profile

Using the demographic categories and descriptions supplied in the textbook, summarize your own demographic profile.

Age group	______________
Income group	______________
Educational level group	______________
Employment group	______________
Gender	______________
Race/ethnic group	______________

Now list at least 10 products or services (including brand names, if possible) for which the type of person that you have described would be a target group member.

(For example, for what types and makes of cars would auto manufacturers consider this person a part of their target market? For what kinds of clothing? Appliances? Vacation resorts? Computers? Magazines? Motion pictures?)

1. ______________
2. ______________
3. ______________
4. ______________
5. ______________
6. ______________
7. ______________
8. ______________
9. ______________
10. ______________
11. ______________
12. ______________

In class or small groups, consider various demographic profiles (anonymously, if you prefer), matched with the brands and product categories for which each profile would be considered as part of the target market or target group.

2-5 Advertising as Communication

In the following table, list two advertisements of your choice. (The advertisements may come from your notebook collection, if you have one.) For each advertisement, identify the sender and the intended receiver. Then use a demographic profile to describe each advertisement's likely audience.

	Advertisement 1	**Advertisement 2**
Sender		
Intended receiver (target market)		
Demographic profile of likely receiver		

In class or small-group discussions, present your advertisements and analyses. Evaluate the various demographic profiles.

Finally, describe the kinds of encoding decisions that an advertiser makes.

Why is it important for an advertiser to keep the intended audience in mind when making these decisions?

3-1 Secondary Advertising Research

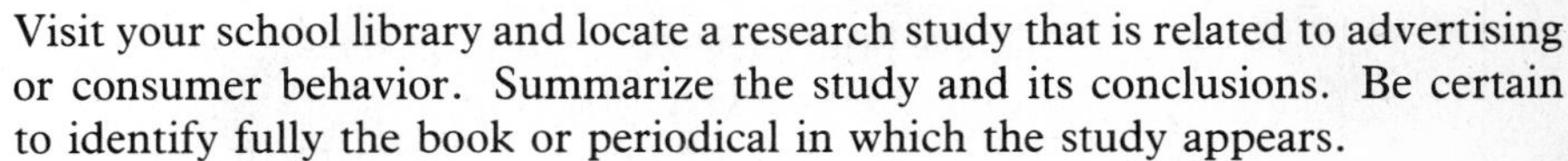

Visit your school library and locate a research study that is related to advertising or consumer behavior. Summarize the study and its conclusions. Be certain to identify fully the book or periodical in which the study appears.

What kinds of advertisers would find this information useful?

How might these advertisers use the information provided in this study?

In class or small-group discussions, compare the studies and the situations to which they might be applied.

3-2 Ranking Advertisements

List five print (newspaper or magazine) advertisements for five different brands within the same category.

(For example, find advertisements for five makes of automobiles or five brands of laundry detergent.)

Then, as a class or within small groups, analyze the advertisements:

1. Mark the five advertisements with the letters *A* through *E*.
2. Select 10 individuals as research subjects and show each of them the five advertisements.
3. Ask each person to decide how well he or she likes each advertisement and to rank the five advertisements (1 = most favorable, 2 = next most favorable, down to 5 = least favorable).
4. Enter the ranking results in the following chart.
5. On a separate sheet of paper, include a demographic profile of each of your 10 research subjects.

	Advertisements				
Persons	**A**	**B**	**C**	**D**	**E**
1.					
2.					
3.					
4.					
5.					
6.					
7.					
8.					
9.					
10.					

Calculate the average ranking for each of the five advertisements.

Which advertisement ranked most favorable (lowest average number)?

Which advertisement ranked least favorable (highest average number)?

Look again at the demographic profiles of your 10 research subjects. Did persons of similar demographic characteristics have similar preferences for the advertisements?____________

Did persons with very different kinds of demographics have more widely varying preferences?____________

How does the relatively small size of your research sample (10 subjects) affect your results and conclusions?

How might a larger sample (say, 400 persons) change your results and conclusions?

Now go back to the five advertisements. Why do you think the best-liked advertisement was ranked favorably?

(That is, what characteristics in the advertisement made it the favorite?)

Why do you think the least-liked advertisement was ranked unfavorably?

Your research method in this exercise is known as *paired comparisons.*

3-3 Association Test

As a group or as a class, make a list of 20 advertising themes. If possible, include local advertising themes in your list.

(For example, one advertising theme used by Coca-Cola is "It's the Real Thing." Wendy's has used "Old-Fashioned Hamburgers." Bayer has used "The finest aspirin the world has ever known." Be sure that your advertising themes *omit* the actual brand names.)

1.
2.
3.
4.
5.
6.
7.
8.
9.
10.
11.
12.
13.
14.
15.
16.
17.
18.
19.
20.

Now, ask 10 persons to identify the brand name for each advertising theme and list them here.

Provide a brief demographic description of each of your 10 respondents.

On a separate sheet of paper, record the demographic profiles and the answers. Which themes had the highest association scores?

Which themes had the lowest association scores?

What, if any, demographic patterns did you notice in your association results?

Record any conclusions that you reach concerning the themes that had high association scores. Also, include your conclusions concerning themes that had low association scores.

Identify some of the factors that may influence an advertising theme's association success.

4-1 Evaluating Advertising Information

Bring to class two print (newspaper or magazine) advertisements:

1. One advertisement that you think is ethical and truthful.
2. One advertisement that you think is unethical and/or untruthful.

(Selecting print advertisements is easier, because they can be brought into the classroom and discussed. If you find a particularly good broadcast advertisement example, check with your instructor to see if you can present it to the class.)

In the following space, tell why you think the first advertisement is ethical and truthful. Be specific in your analysis. Also identify any additional kind of information that you think might have been included in this advertisement.

Now tell why you think the second advertisement is unethical and/or untruthful. Be specific in your criticism. Also describe any information that should be changed or added to this advertisement to make it more ethical and truthful and to make it more helpful to a consumer.

Present your advertisements and comments in class or small-group discussions. Do members of the group agree with your analyses? What conclusions can you draw about evaluating the helpfulness of information in advertising?

4-2 Regulatory Hearing

In class, you will simulate a regulatory hearing.

As a class, select several advertisements that you believe may leave a misleading impression on the audience. From these, select one advertisement to be the focus of the hearing.

From your class members, you will need to identify several groups:

1. A five- to seven-member regulatory commission, which will preside over the hearing and make recommendations at its conclusion.
2. Two small teams of two or three members each:
   a. One team opposing the advertisement, pointing out its misleading characteristics and calling for specific corrective measures to be taken
   b. Another team representing the advertiser or the agency, defending the advertisement's claims and opposing the need for punishment or correction
3. The remainder of the class, which will act as a sample of consumers available to offer opinions before the commission

Each of the two small teams should prepare its arguments in advance of the presentation.

The hearing proceeds with each team presenting its arguments before the regulatory commission. Both teams and the commission may incorporate consumer opinions into the hearing when appropriate.

The commission will conclude the hearing with a recommendation. Recommendations against the advertiser may include

- An order to produce research data supporting the advertisement's claims
- A cease-and-desist order
- A fine
- An order for corrective advertising

Recommendations in favor of the advertiser may simply dismiss the complaint against the advertisement and conclude that the advertisement is not misleading and does not employ illegitimate techniques.

If time allows, repeat the procedure with another advertisement and with new participants in designated roles.

4-3 Competition

The following table contains two columns, one for the advantages of competition and one for the disadvantages of competition.

Fill in as many of the advantages and disadvantages of competition as you can.

Advantages of Competition	Disadvantages of Competition
1.	1.
2.	2.
3.	3.
4.	4.
5.	5.
6.	6.
7.	7.
8.	8.
9.	9.
10.	10.

Now, look through magazines and newspapers to find advertisements that illustrate or exemplify these advantages and disadvantages and list them here.

Also explain how each advertisement that you find fits the particular advantage or disadvantage that you have in mind.

You may wish to compare your lists and your examples with those of your classmates.

5-1 Advertising Appeals Based on Customer Information

Bring to class two advertisements whose main appeal is based on customer or consumer information:

1. One ad representing a nationally distributed brand
2. One ad representing a local retailer

In the space provided, describe the kind of research that the advertiser might have used to identify the appeal for each ad. Include in your description the types of questions that the advertiser might have asked customers about their attitudes or shopping behavior.

In class or group discussion, compare the appeals used in these ads and the possible customer surveys that preceded their development.

5-2 Advertising Appeals Based on Competitive Comparison

Bring to class two ads whose main appeal is based on a comparison between the advertised brand and either named or unnamed competitors:

1. One ad representing a nationally distributed brand
2. One ad representing a local retailer

In the space provided, describe the kind of research that the advertiser might have used to identify the competitive advantage as an appeal in each ad. Include in your description the types of questions that the advertiser might have asked about the product and the competitor's product.

In class or group discussion, review the comparison-oriented appeals used in these ads and the possible research that preceded their development.

5-3 Gathering Information: Your First Attempt at Ad Research

Activities 5-3, 5-4, and 5-5 are information-gathering exercises. They include suggested guidelines for

1. A client interview
2. Structured observations
3. A consumer survey

As a class or group activity, secure the cooperation of a local retailer who will act as the client for your group's research activities. The retailer should be informed that his/her cooperation will include being interviewed, allowing members of your group to make observations at the retail establishment, and permitting a brief survey of a sample of consumers.

The Client Interview

The interview should be arranged at your client's convenience. It can take place at school with all group members participating or at the retail establishment with several members representing the entire group.

As a class or group activity you should prepare a list of questions before the interview is to take place. These prepared questions will provide the structure for the interview, but be prepared to form and ask questions as they arise during the interview.

Suggested Areas to Cover during the Interview

The following is an outline of suggested categories to cover during the interview. This is a general outline and should be altered to suit the specific type of store that you are researching.

I. Product Information
   A. General description of product (store, its merchandise, and services offered)
   B. Location (strength and weaknesses)
   C. Length of time in business (at present or previous location)
   D. Sales history (approximate rate of growth or decline)
   E. Sales fluctuations and consumption patterns (busy and slow hours of day, days of week, or months of year)

II. Customer Information

A. Demographic profile of primary target market
B. Demographic profile of secondary target markets (if any are significant)

III. Competition
A. Identification of primary competitors
B. Comparison with primary competition (review of I and II)

IV. Past Advertising
A. Ad content and appeals used
B. Media used and scheduling strategy
C. Approximate size of advertising budget

Using the preceding outline as a guide, compose your interview questions in the space provided.

As a class or group activity, compose your final interview format and record your client's responses on the following page.

Client Interview

Client name: ________________________________

Store name: ________________________________

Interview date: ____________________ Time: __________

Prepared by: ________________________________

5-4 Gathering Information: Structured Observations

Following the client interview each group member should arrange to visit the retail establishment. Your visits should be scheduled so as to cover a broad range of the retailer's business hours (weekday and weekend: mornings, afternoons, and evenings). Before each visit the group member should preview the information obtained in the client interview. Your client should be informed in advance of your visiting schedule.

What to Look For

The primary purpose of these observation periods is to allow you to gain a first-hand perspective on your client's business and compare your observations with the data obtained in the client interview.

If possible, group members should also try to visit and observe each of the identified competitors. In addition, competitor advertising should be collected for study.

Again, the following outline is intended only as a suggested guide. Add to or otherwise change the outline to suit your specific situation.

I. Product Information
  - A. Store exterior (setting, location, window displays, signs, visibility)
  - B. Store interior (merchandise, displays, layout and amount of space allocated to different products, lighting, decor, general atmosphere)
  - C. Sales attitude (style and manner of salespeople)

II. Customer Information
  - A. Number of customers observed
  - B. Demographics of customers (your own conclusions)
  - C. Number and types of purchases observed

Using the previous outline as a guide, record the observations made during your visit.

On-Premises Observations

Client name: ______________________________

Store name: ______________________________

Observation date: ____________________

Observation time: from __________ to __________

Prepared by: ______________________________

5-5 Gathering Information: Consumer Survey

As a class or group activity construct the questions for your survey well in advance of the day(s) you plan to use them. If possible, test your survey with a small sample first to see if it provides the information you seek.

What to Ask

The following is an outline of suggested categories of information you might seek in your survey. As in the preceding two exercises you should add to or otherwise change this outline to suit the specific needs of your client and your classroom situation.

I. Actual Shopping Behavior
   A. Where do the people surveyed shop for the types of products offered by your client?
   B. How frequently do the people surveyed shop for these products?
   C. For whom are the people surveyed buying this type of product?
   D. When (part of day, week, or year) do the people surveyed shop for this type of product?

II. Levels of Consumer Awareness
   A. Are the consumers surveyed aware of the existence of your client's store?
      1. How many?
      2. Which ones (demographically)?
   B. Are the consumers surveyed aware of other stores that offer this product?

III. Consumer Motives
   A. What factors influence the consumers surveyed to buy this type of product at a specific place (e.g., price, service, convenience)?

IV. Media Patterns
   A. Which newspapers are read by the consumers surveyed?
   B. Which radio stations are listened to by the consumers surveyed?
   C. Which TV programs are watched by the consumers surveyed?

V. Demographic Profile

Each survey should include a brief demographic section.

How to Use

Consumer surveys come in many forms and lengths. Usually there is no single correct format. Question formats include: fill-in-the-blank, multiple choice, agree-disagree, and essay oriented.

As a class or group activity use the following pages to formulate the specific questions that will be included in your survey.

Note: The sampling-related questions of where to ask, whom to ask, and how many to ask will be left to the discretion of the class.

Consumer Survey

Location of survey: ______________________________

Date: ____________________ Time: __________

Prepared by: ______________________________

Final comments: These last three activities represent your first attempt at advertising research. They are not a test to measure what you've mastered. On the contrary, they are learning activities designed to provide you with an initial research experience. You may encounter problems and frustrations, but if you can subsequently identify some of the things you would have done differently and why, then they have served their purpose.

5-6 Identifying Advertisable Facts: Sorting and Eliminating

In class or group discussion, review the information you have collected concerning your client's product, your client's competition, and consumer behavior and attitudes. Include in your discussion a review of past advertising approaches used by your client and his competitors.

In the space provided, list *at least* 10 bits of information that you think could be developed into effective ad appeals.

In class or group discussion, compare your lists and collectively assemble a master list of advertisable facts. Place an asterisk by those facts that you feel most effectively differentiate your client from the competition.

5-7 From Advertisable Facts to Communications Goals

In the following space, we have formed the beginning of a communications goal statement.

Using the facts identified in Activity 5-6 and a separate sheet of paper, if needed, complete the goal statement for each advertisable fact that differentiates your client from the competition. Either select one of our suggested verbs or provide your own. It is important to note that a communications goal is stated not in terms of the advertiser (sender) but in terms of the target market (receiver). Why?

"In the advertising campaign we want to get our target market to (know, be aware of, remember, believe, form the attitude that). . ."

Note: One good way to practice developing communications goal statements is to use the ads in your notebook collection and formulate the communications goal that led to the development of those ads.

In class or group discussion, compare the communications goal statements that you have prepared for your client. Include in your discussion the relative effectiveness of each suggested goal.

6-1 Copywriting for Print Media: Evaluating Headlines

Bring to class four ads:

1. Two ads that have effective headlines
2. Two ads that have ineffective headlines

In the space provided discuss the characteristics of the effective headlines. Include in your discussion

1. The type of headline used in each ad
2. The attention-getting ability of each headline
3. The ability of each headline to interest the reader in the ad copy

In the space provided, discuss the characteristics of the ineffective headlines. Include in your discussion the type of headline used in each ad and the reason you think it is not successful. Rewrite each headline in a way that you think would make it more effective.

In class or group discussion, compare the headlines that you have collected and your comments on their relative effectiveness. Include in your discussion why it is important to know your target market when writing headlines.

6-2 Copywriting for Print Media: Writing Headlines

In Activity 5-7 you were asked to write communications goals based on advertisable facts that differentiated your client from the competition.

In the space provided, write at least three headlines for each communications goal listed in Activity 5-7.

In class or group discussion, compare the headlines that you have written. Include in your discussion

1. The ability of each headline to convey the content of the communications goal
2. The effectiveness of each headline in attracting the attention and interest of the target market

6-3 Copywriting for Print Media: Evaluating Body Copy

Bring to class two ads:

1. One ad whose body copy is well written in accordance with the textbook guidelines
2. One ad whose body copy is poorly written and not in accordance with the textbook guidelines

In the space provided, analyze the well-written body copy. Include in your analysis:

1. A list of the specific facts about the product stated in the copy
2. The number of times the words *we* (or *I*) versus *you* are used in the copy
3. An outline of the appeals used in the copy
4. The call to customer action mentioned in the copy

In the space provided, analyze your example of poorly written body copy. Include in your analysis:

1. Any generalities about the product that would be more effectively stated as specific facts
2. The number of times the words *we* (or *I*) versus *you* are used in the copy
3. An outline of the appeals used in the copy
4. The call to customer action that is mentioned in the copy

In class or group discussion, compare your analyses of the well-written and poorly-written body copy examples. Include in your discussion the criteria that are necessary for body copy to be well written and effective.

6-4 Copywriting for Print Media: Writing Body Copy

In Activity 6-2 you were asked to write three headlines based on previously developed communications goals.

In the space provided, write the body copy for a headline you've selected from Activity 6-2. Use the information you gathered in Activities 5-3, 5-4, and 5-5 as a source of specific facts to be included in the body copy.

Headline:

Body copy:

Before you present the headline and accompanying body copy, consider the following questions:

1. Does the headline have attention-getting value for my target audience?

2. Does the headline communicate my basic idea (primary appeal)?

3. Is there good transition from headline to body copy?

4. Does the body copy amplify and expand on the headline with specific information?

In class or group discussion, compare and analyze your headlines and body copy.

6-5 Copywriting for Print Media: The Role of the Illustration

Look again at the headline and body copy you developed in Activity 6-4. In the space provided describe the illustration or picture that you feel should be included with the headline and copy. If you feel that no illustration is necessary, use the space provided to explain your decision.

Why do you feel that the illustration you've described would work well with the headline and body copy?

In class or group discussion, evaluate the various headline-illustration-body copy proposals. Include in your discussion the working relationship of each of these elements and their contribution to the total communication effort.

6-6 Copywriting for Print Media: Experimenting with Layout

In the previous two exercises you have proposed a specific headline, illustration, and body copy based on your information-gathering activities.

In the space provided, sketch at least two different layout patterns that you feel would be effective in communicating the information you've proposed.

In class or group discussion, compare the suggested layout formats. Include in your discussion the advantages and disadvantages of each layout suggestion.

7-1 Copywriting for Broadcast Media: A 30-Second Radio Script

On the following page write a 30-second radio commercial for the same client you researched earlier.

Your radio commercial should work in coordination with the print ad you wrote for this client in Chapter 6. Your radio commercial should be presented in the proper form as demonstrated in your text.

Before you start the commercial, complete the following phrase to form the communications goal that the ad will help accomplish.

"To get our target market to (know, be aware of, remember, believe, form the attitude that). . ."

Before you present the ad, consider the following questions:

1. Does the ad help accomplish the stated communications goal?

2. Does the ad stick to one basic idea?

3. Does the ad repeat the basic idea often enough? Too often?

4. Does the ad have a conversational tone?

5. Does the ad have proper timing—neither cluttered nor sparse?

6. Does the ad coordinate with the print ad from Chapter 6?

30-Second Radio Script

Client: ______________________________

Prepared by: ______________________________

7-2 Copywriting for Broadcast Media: A 30-Second TV Script

On the following page write a 30-second television commercial for the same client you researched earlier.

Your television ad should work in coordination with the print ad and the radio ad of the previous exercises. Your television commercial should be presented in the proper format as demonstrated in your text.

Before you start the commercial, complete the following phrase to form the communications goal that the TV ad will help accomplish.

"To get our target market to (know, be aware of, remember, believe, form the attitude that). . ."

Before you present the commercial, consider the following questions:

1. Does the ad help accomplish the stated communications goal?
2. Does the commercial stick to one basic idea?
3. Does the ad repeat the basic idea often enough? Too often?
4. Is the message told primarily in pictures?
5. Do the video and audio messages reinforce each other?
6. Does the ad have proper timing—neither cluttered nor sparse?
7. Does the TV commercial coordinate with the print and radio ads prepared for this client?

30-Second Television Commercial

Client: ______________________________

Prepared by: ______________________________

Video **Audio**

8-1 Comparing Yellow Pages Ads

Bring to class two Yellow Pages ads from the same product or store category as the client that you researched in earlier exercises:

1. One that you consider attention-getting, well written, and attractively composed
2. One ad that you consider poorly done; it lacks attention-getting value or is poorly written or unattractive in appearance

In class or group discussion, compare the positively evaluated ads with the negatively evaluated ads.

8-2 Writing and Designing Yellow Pages Ads

On the following page, neatly sketch the Yellow Pages ad that you would recommend for the client that you researched in earlier exercises.

Before you start the ad, complete the following phrase to form the communications goal that the ad will help accomplish.

"To get our target market to (know, be aware of, remember, believe, form the attitude that). . ."

Before you present the ad, consider the following questions:

1. Does the ad help accomplish the stated communications goal?

2. Does the headline have attention-getting value for my target market?

3. Does the headline communicate my basic idea?

4. Does the ad include complete, accurate information regarding location and phone listing?

5. Does the ad appear organized and attractive—neither too cluttered nor too sparse?

6. Is the ad consistent with my client's other advertising efforts?

Yellow Pages Ad

Client: ______________________________

Prepared by: ______________________________

Date: __________

8-3 Copywriting for Other Media: Direct Marketing

Write a direct-marketing letter selling to an unknown prospect an actual book you have read recently. Review your text (pages 138–140) for hints on procedure. Bring the book you're writing about to class.

Remember, in direct-marketing messages you must tell the complete sales story every time. This is a rather long written assignment, and a challenging one. It will test your patience with its insistence on detail.

In the space provided, jot down notes or outline points to include in a direct marketing letter that sells an actual book you have recently read to an unknown prospect. Then submit a final draft of your letter.

8-4 Copywriting for Other Media: Direct Mail

Prepare a simple folder extolling (and selling) your favorite vacation area. Make a dummy layout. Take an ordinary sheet of typing paper and fold it in half vertically. Number the pages. Consider page 1 as the headline/illustration portion of any ad. To whom is this message directed? Adults? Senior citizens? Swingers? Families with young children? What is the biggest benefit you can offer your target audience? Get that and an appropriate illustration on page 1. You may treat pages 2 and 3 as separate pages or as a double spread (all one unit of space). Decide how you're going to handle the content. Editorial style, with long copy? Or broken up with pictures and copy? Or some combination of the two? Page 4 becomes the place for specific details: name, address, phone, directions, a map or diagram, perhaps.

Present dummy layout and typed copy for this project.

8-5 Copywriting for Other Media: Billboards

The key to being a great admaker is the ability to reduce a strong selling idea to its bare essence. That is what advertising billboards are all about—the story in a nutshell. All nonessentials are stripped away. You communicate with a strong, involving illustration (generally displaying a story-telling situation) combined with roughly five or six words of copy related to the illustration. In most instances, the product itself (package) becomes the signature, thus saving you words.

Test yourself. Rough out a billboard for Heath's English Toffee Bar. Begin by turning a sheet of typewriter paper on its side. Roughly draw a line all around about an inch in from each side. This approximates the horizontal shape of a billboard. As always, start thinking of the benefit you will feature. To whom is your billboard directed? You might try a bit of word association. What does the word "English" conjure up? What does the word "toffee" bring to mind? Keep your idea simple. The key to great posters is simplicity.

9-1 Print Advertising Production: Comparing Typefaces

From a type specimen book supplied by your instructor or by a local printer, choose two traditional (serif) type families that you like. Study them carefully, letter by letter. In the space provided list six of the distinguishing characteristics of each type family. See Figure 8-1 in the text for an example.

Typeface: ____________________ **Typeface:** ____________________

9-2 Print Advertising Production: Comparing Halftones

Clip an ad illustration that is a coarse-screen halftone. Clip an ad illustration that is a fine-screen halftone. Cut a small section from each and paste the sections side-by-side in the space provided so that we can see with the naked eye the difference in size of the halftone dots.

Coarse-Screen Halftone	**Fine-Screen Halftone**

10-1 Broadcast Advertising Production: Straight Radio Spot

For your favorite magazine (or product of your choice) write a 30-second "straight" radio commercial. Words only. When you have the words exactly the way you want them, record your message on an audiocassette. Read the copy with enthusiasm and expression. Play it back and see how it sounds to you. Was it well paced or hurried? Did you "write it short" as suggested in your text?

Present your taped commercial to the class.

In class or group discussion, analyze the various commercials presented. Did one or two stand out as being particularly effective? Why?

10-2 Broadcast Advertising Production: TV Commercial

To give you at least a little taste of television production, we are asking you to make an 8 mm home movie or videotape commercial. The subject: Elmer's Glue (or a product of your choice). This will be a silent movie for which you will probably letter homemade subtitles. If you feel very creative you might prepare an audiocassette sound track to play in synchronization with your film or tape. Unless you have editing equipment available, it is best to work out your idea on paper first and then shoot the scenes in sequence.

Perhaps your instructor would prefer to make this a group project.

Present your home movie commercial to the class.

In class or group discussion, analyze the various television commercials presented. Did one or two stand out as being particularly effective? Why so?

11-1 Print Media Content Analysis

Collect print advertisements from a single medium for a single category of advertiser (for example, newspaper advertisements for automobile dealers or women's cosmetic advertisements from consumer magazines).

[Try to have a fairly large collection, a minimum of 30 advertisements and preferably at least 50.]

As you collect the advertisements, keep track of the specific vehicle in which you found each advertisement.

Then analyze the content and approach of these advertisements according to the following characteristics.

Total number of advertisements collected: ____________
Category of product or service: ____________________________________
Medium: ________________________
Bleed
  Number of bleed advertisements collected: ____________
  Number of nonbleed advertisements collected: ____________
Color
  Number of four-color advertisements: ____________
  Number of other (one-color, two-color) advertisements: ____________
  Number of black-and-white advertisements: ____________
Size
  Number of large advertisements: ____________
  Number of small advertisements: ____________

Now, based on the information from your collection of advertisements, what can you determine about the media units used by this category of advertiser? If you were a competing advertiser in this product or service category, how would these results affect your advertising media placement?

11-2 Print Media Purchase Decisions

Select a category of advertiser, such as tire manufacturer, shoe retailer, passenger airline, dog food marketer, or automobile repair.

> [For best results, you should use the same category as your collection in the previous activity or a similar category. You will use this advertiser category for the next few activities.]

Next, look up "Newspapers" in *Ayer's Directory* if your library has it, or in your local telephone Yellow Pages.

List all the newspapers that might be considered by an advertiser in your category.

Are there any newspapers listed that would *not* be considered by that advertiser? Why would these newspapers be omitted?

Would this advertiser consider the use of any magazine to carry advertising? If so, why? If not, why not?

What percent of this advertiser's total advertising budget would you recommend be spent on newspaper advertising? ____________% Why?

If other print media would be used by this advertiser, what percent of the total budget would each of these media receive? Why?

Rank the newspapers that you would recommend for this client's advertising, according to the portion of the budget that each newspaper would receive. Discuss the reasons for your decisions.

1.

2.

3.

4.

5.

6.

In class or small groups, consider the various recommendations. In your discussion, focus on the major media planning factors.

11-3 Attention-Getting and its Implications for Print Media

Bring to class one print (newspaper or magazine) advertisement that you consider to be an effective attention-getter. (For best results, you will want to stay with the same category of advertiser used in the two preceding activities.)

How does this advertisement capture the attention of the intended audience?

Name various elements (other than the size of the advertisement) that an advertiser might use to increase the attention-getting value of a print advertisement.

What effect, if any, will the use of these attention-getting tools have on the cost of the advertisement? How might this affect the number of advertisements afforded by the budget?

How does this type of decision (that is, more attention-getting features versus increased total number of advertising insertions) relate to the media factors of reach and frequency?

Would a reach-oriented or frequency-oriented media strategy be more appropriate to this type of advertiser? Why?

In class or small groups, consider the various attention-getting techniques and their implications for media strategies.

12-1 Broadcast Media Content Analysis

This exercise will require some time to complete adequately.

Watch a single television channel for an entire morning, an entire afternoon, or an entire evening.

Pay special attention to the advertisements (commercials) that you see, and enter information about them in the space provided.

How many commercials were there? ____________

For how long did you watch television? ____________ hours

What was the average number of commercials per hour? ____________

Color

Were any commercials not in color? If so, how many? __________

Length

How many commercials were 60 seconds or longer? ____________

How many commercials were 30 seconds in length? ____________

How many commercials were 15–20 seconds in length? __________

How many commercials were less than 15 seconds? ____________

Categories

What were the most-advertised categories of products and services?

What conclusions can you draw about the most common television advertising? How would advertisers use this information? Specifically, how would competitors use this kind of information to improve their advertising media plans?

12-2 Broadcast Media Purchase Decisions

Consider that you are working on the advertising for the same advertiser you used for the Chapter 11 activities.

If your library has *Broadcasting Yearbook*, look up television stations in your area. Otherwise, use your telephone Yellow Pages for the same function.

List all the television stations that might be considered by your advertiser client.

Now, do the same for radio stations.

Are there any television or radio stations that definitely would not be considered for this advertiser? If so, which ones? Why?

What percent of this advertiser's total advertising budget would you recommend be spent on television? ____________%

On radio? ____________%

Justify your allocation.

Now, describe the times of day, days of the week, and (if possible) the names of programs that you would recommend for your client's television and radio advertising. Include the reasons for your recommendations.

Compare your broadcast recommendations with those of other members of your class.

12-3 Attention-Getting and its Implications for Broadcast Media

Watch a variety of television programs.

[Do *not* view several programs in a row; instead, select one morning program, an afternoon program, and an evening program.]

Take notes on the advertisements that you consider to be effective attention-getters. You may wish to watch for characteristics that were described in Chapters 5 and 7.

What similarities do you notice about television commercials that attract your attention?

Name various elements (other than the length of the commercial) that an advertiser might use to increase the attention-getting value of a television advertisement.

What effect, if any, will the use of these attention-getting tools have on the cost of the advertisement? How might this affect the number of advertisements afforded by the budget?

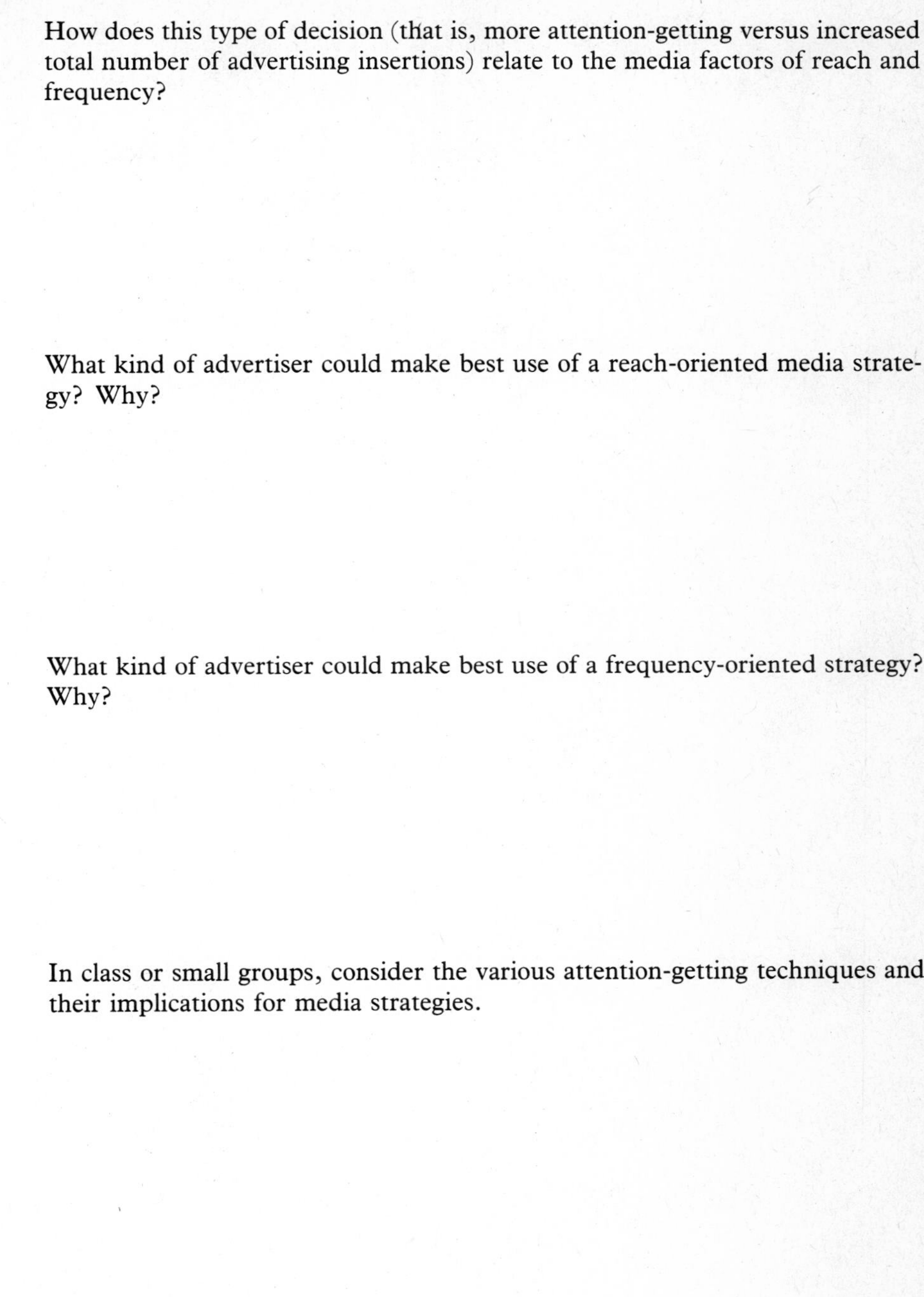

How does this type of decision (that is, more attention-getting versus increased total number of advertising insertions) relate to the media factors of reach and frequency?

What kind of advertiser could make best use of a reach-oriented media strategy? Why?

What kind of advertiser could make best use of a frequency-oriented strategy? Why?

In class or small groups, consider the various attention-getting techniques and their implications for media strategies.

13-1 Attention-Getting and its Implications for Media

Select one type of miscellaneous advertising medium (direct mail or specialty will work best).

Collect advertisements from that medium that attract your attention. Or you may wish to find a single advertisement for your kind of advertiser (used in the Chapter 11 and 12 activities) in your medium.

How is the attention of the intended audience captured in this medium? What techniques seem to work best for attention-getting?

Name various elements that an advertiser might use to increase the attention-getting value of an advertisement in this medium.

What effect, if any, will the use of these attention-getting tools have on the cost of the advertisement? How might this affect the number of advertisements afforded by the budget?

In class or small groups, compare your conclusions with those for other types of miscellaneous media.

13-2 Purchase Decisions for Miscellaneous Media

Using the same advertiser as for the Chapter 11 and 12 activities, select from the various miscellaneous media that are still available for consideration.

Indicate the percents of the total budget that you would recommend for use by your advertiser.

Other Media	Percent of Total Budget
Direct mail	________%
Specialty	________%
Outdoor	________%
Transit	________%
Point of purchase	________%
Others (specify)	________%

Justify your selections and allocations.

How will these media work together with the major media (newspaper, magazines, television, radio) in your proposed advertising campaign?

In class or small group discussions, compare your recommendations with those of your classmates.

14-1 Media Planning

Go back through the activities for Chapters 11, 12, and 13, and review the advertising media budget allocations that you have made. Now, summarize your advertising budget decisions.

Newspapers	________%
Magazines	________%
Television	________%
Radio	________%
Direct mail	________%
Specialty	________%
Outdoor	________%
Transit	________%
Point of purchase	________%
Other: ______________	________%
Contingency fund	________%
Total	100%

Newspapers: ________% Summarize your newspaper plans. Include specific recommendations as to newspapers to be used, days of week, and other scheduling preferences.

Magazines: ________% Summarize your magazine plans. (Remember, magazines may not work well for local retail advertisers, so if you are not using this or any other medium, say why.)

Television: ___________% Summarize your television plans. Include specific recommendations as to stations to be used, days of week, times of day, and other scheduling preferences.

Radio: ___________% Summarize your radio plans. Include specific recommendations as to stations to be used, days of week, times of day, and other scheduling preferences.

Direct Mail: __________% Summarize your direct mail plans.

Other Media: __________% Summarize your plans for any other media that you would use.

Contingency Fund: __________% Discuss the need for a contingency fund for your advertiser. What competitive, economic, social, marketing, or other changes might alter your advertising campaign plans?

If possible, obtain advertising rate cards from your recommended media vehicles, and compute the costs of the various media plans.

15-1 Campaign Planning: Marketing, Advertising and Research Considerations

In the next two activities (embracing Chapter 15 and Chapter 16) you are asked to produce a complete advertising campaign *plan* in written report form. This plan can be approached either as an individual project or as a group activity with teams functioning as advertising departments.

The background data for this campaign plan can be either (1) primary, a new client with original research being conducted or (2) secondary, use of data furnished via client research in the Chapter 5 activities.

Use the outline on the next page as a guide in the organization of your campaign plan. For this particular activity, complete only steps I, II, and III of the outline. The remaining steps in the outline will be completed in the next activity. The activity numbers in parentheses refer to those you may wish to review in preparation for that section of your plan.

Campaign Plan Outline

- I. Introduction
  - A. Client identification
  - B. Purpose of report
- II. Research (Activities 2–1, 2–2, 2–3, 2–4, 3–1, 3–2, 3–3, 5–1, 5–2, 5–3, 5–4, 5–5)
  - A. Product research
    - 1. Purpose
    - 2. Method
  - B. Market research
    - 1. Purpose
    - 2. Method
  - C. Consumer research
    - 1. Purpose
    - 2. Method
  - D. Research findings and conclusion
- III. Campaign Goals (Activities 5–6, 5–7)
  - A. Marketing goal(s)
  - B. Communications goal(s)
  - C. Identification of target market(s)
- IV. Advertising Appropriation and Budget
  - A. Role of advertising in marketing mix
  - B. Advertising appropriation
  - C. Advertising budget
- V. Media Strategy (Activities 2–3, 11–1, 11–2, 11–3, 12–1, 12–2, 12–3, 13–1, 13–2, 14–1)
  - A. Restatement of target market(s)
  - B. Discussion of each medium included in media plan
    - 1. Its role in the media strategy
    - 2. Budget allocation
    - 3. Specific vehicles and scheduling
- VI. Creative Strategy (Activities 5–6, 5–7)
  - A. Restatement of communications goal(s)
  - B. Discussion of campaign theme
    - 1. Positioning and differentiation
    - 2. Representative ad or script for each medium used in the campaign to demonstrate execution of the theme
- VII. Recommendations for Postmeasurement
- VIII. Appendix (Exhibits from Previous Sections)

Campaign Plan Notes

The following pages are provided as worksheets in the preparation of your campaign plan.

Campaign Plan Notes

Campaign Plan Notes

Campaign Plan Notes

16-1 Campaign Planning: Essential Campaign Decisions

In this exercise you are to complete your written campaign plan begun in the previous activity. Review your Campaign Plan Outline, starting with Section IV, Advertising Appropriation and Budget.

The following pages are provided as worksheets in the preparation of your campaign plan.

When you have completed writing your campaign plan, it should be assembled neatly into a notebook, ready for formal presentation.

Campaign Plan Notes

Campaign Plan Notes

Campaign Plan Notes

Campaign Plan Notes

17-1 Campaign Planning: Oral Report

Under normal circumstances, you would be expected to make an oral presentation of your campaign plan to client or agency management people. Instead you are to prepare an oral presentation of your campaign plan for the class. Your instructor will tell you at the outset how much time you have in which to make your presentation.

It helps if you have exhibits for the audience to see while you're talking: perhaps a flip chart on which key points of your plan are lettered; certainly a chart of your media plan and schedule; and, of course, layouts and copy of your ad ideas.

In the space provided, list the questions that you, as the client or as any critical observer, would raise to check the validity of each section of the campaign plans presented.

In class or group discussion, assess the presentations and compare the listed questions by which a campaign plan can be evaluated.

18-1 A Personal Assessment for Advertising Careers

In the space provided, list the activities in this course that you have enjoyed the *most*.

In the space provided, list the activities in this course that you have enjoyed the *least*.

What differences do you see between your two lists? What similarities, if any, are there between your two lists?

Based on the likes and dislikes that you have noted, describe the type of advertising position for which you feel best suited. In your description, include the responsibilities of this position and the characteristics and traits that you possess that you could successfully apply to these responsibilities.

18-2 Career Characteristics

Across the top of the following diagram are several types of personality characteristics.

Then, down the left side of the diagram, there are several types of advertising career opportunities.

Where each personality characteristic intersects a career opportunity, evaluate whether this personality characteristic would be a benefit, a detriment, or a neutral factor. For each evaluation, print the following notation in the square where the personality characteristics and the career opportunities meet:

benefit	+
detriment	–
neutral factor	○

	Aggressive	Thoughtful	Artistic	Competitive	Patient	Perfectionistic	Outgoing	Careful	Introspective	Compliant	Social	Hurried	Individualistic	Conformist	Domineering
Newspaper ad salesperson															
Copywriter															
Media buyer															
Research director															
Agency account executive															
Production assistant															
Radio researcher															
TV program director															
Agency art director															

What patterns do you see?

You may wish to repeat this exercise, using your own personality characteristics, to determine where you might fit best in the advertising business.

Compare your results with those of others in your class.

19-1 Advertising Use by Consumers

Collect a variety of advertisements.

[You may wish to use the advertisements that you have been collecting in your portfolio during the school term.]

Analyze these advertisements, using the following tests.

Which advertisements make the best consumer shopping aides?

Why are these advertisements helpful?

Why are other advertisements not helpful?

Which advertisements provide the best product or service information?

What kinds of information are most helpful?

What kinds of information are not very helpful?

Using the information provided in Chapter 19, analyze the copy in your advertisements. What have you learned about reading advertisements that may be helpful in reading these particular advertisements?